Cross and Cruciform in the Anglo-Saxon World

MEDIEVAL EUROPEAN STUDIES XI

Patrick W. Conner, Series Editor

OTHER TITLES IN THE SERIES:

Via Crucis: Essays on Early Medieval Sources and Ideas
Thomas N. Hall, Editor, with assistance from Thomas D. Hill and Charles D. Wright

Hêliand: Text and Commentary
Edited by James E. Cathey

Naked Before God: Uncovering the Body in Anglo-Saxon England
Edited by Benjamin C. Withers and Jonathan Wilcox

Theorizing Anglo-Saxon Stone Sculpture
Edited by Catherine E. Karkov and Fred Orton

Old English Literature in its Manuscript Context
Edited by Joyce Tally Lionarons

Ancient Privileges: Beowulf, Law, and the Making of Germanic Antiquity
Stefan Jurasinski

The Postmodern Beowulf: A Critical Casebook
Edited by Eileen A. Joy and Mary K. Ramsey

The Power of Words: Anglo-Saxon Studies Presented to Donald G. Scragg on his Seventieth Birthday
Edited by Jonathan Wilcox and Hugh Magennis

Cædmon's Hymn and Material Culture in the World of Bede
Edited by Allen J. Frantzen and John Hines

The Cross and Culture in Anglo-Saxon England
Edited by Karen Jolly, Catherine E. Karkov, and Sarah Larratt Keefer

Perspectives on the Old Saxon Heliand: Introductory and Critical Essays, with an Edition of the Leipzig Fragment
Edited by Valentine A. Pakis

Cross and Cruciform

in the Anglo-Saxon World

STUDIES TO HONOR THE MEMORY
OF TIMOTHY REUTER

Volume 3 in the *Sancta Crux/Halig Rod* series

Edited By

Sarah Larratt Keefer
Trent University, Ontario

Karen Louise Jolly
University of Hawai'i at Mānoa

Catherine E. Karkov
University of Leeds

WEST VIRGINIA UNIVERSITY PRESS
MORGANTOWN 2010

West Virginia University Press 26506
© 2010 by West Virginia University Press

All rights reserved.

First edition published 2010 by West Virginia University Press

18 17 16 15 14 13 12 11 10   9 8 7 6 5 4 3 2 1

ISBN-10: 1-933202-50-5
ISBN-13: 978-1-933202-50-1
(alk. paper)

Library of Congress Cataloguing-in-Publication Data

Cross and cruciform in the Anglo-Saxon world : studies to honor the memory of Timothy Reuter / [edited by] Sarah Larratt Keefer, Karen Louise Jolly, Catherine E. Karkov. -- 1st ed. p. cm. -- (Sancta Crux/Halig Rod series; v. 3)
  Includes bibliographical references and index.
  ISBN-13: 978-1-933202-50-1 (pbk. : alk. paper)
  ISBN-10: 1-933202-50-5 (pbk. : alk. paper)
  1.   Crosses--England--History--To 1500--Congresses. 2. Anglo-Saxons--Religion--Congresses. I. Reuter, Timothy. II. Keefer, Sarah Larratt. III. Jolly, Karen Louise. IV. Karkov, Catherine E., 1956-

BV160.C75 2010
246'.558094209021--dc22

Library of Congress Control Number: 2009027723

Contents

Abbreviations vii

In Memoriam Timothy Reuter xi

Introduction 1
   Sarah Larratt Keefer, Trent University, Ontario
   Karen Louise Jolly, University of Hawai'i at Mānoa
   Catherine E. Karkov, University of Leeds

I. The Cross: Image and Emblem

The Cross and the Book: the Cross-Carpet
Pages of the Lindisfarne Gospels as
Sacred Figurae 17
   Michelle P. Brown

A Cross and an Acrostic: Boniface's Prefatory
Poem to his *Ars grammatica* 53
   David A. E. Pelteret

Abbot Ælfwine and the Sign of the Cross 103
   Catherine E. Karkov

II. The Cross: Meaning and Word

Sources or Analogues? Using Liturgical
Evidence to Date *The Dream of the Rood* 135
  Éamonn Ó Carragáin

Writing/Sounding the Cross: *The Dream
of the Rood* as Figured Poetry 166
  Helen Damico

Old English "Cross" Words 204
  Rolf H. Bremmer Jr.

Signifying Christ in Anglo-Saxon England:
Old English Terms for the Sign of the Cross 233
  Ursula Lenker

III. The Cross: Gesture and Structure

The Staff of Life: Cross and Blessings in
Anglo-Saxon Cereal Production 279
  Debby Banham

The Anglo-Saxon Chapel at Bradford-on-Avon, Wiltshire 319
  David A. Hinton

New Media and the Nunburnholme Cross 340
  Martin K. Foys

The *Enkolpion* of Edward the Confessor: Byzantium and Anglo-
Saxon Concepts of Rulership 369
  Lynn Jones

Abbreviations

ANQ	*American Notes and Queries*
ANS	*Anglo-Norman Studies*
ASE	*Anglo-Saxon England*
ASMMF	Anglo-Saxon Manuscripts in Microfiche Facsimile, ed. Philip Pulsiano, A. N. Doane, et al. 14 vols. Tempe, AZ: ACMRS: 1994–
ASPR	Anglo-Saxon Poetic Records: A Collective Edition, ed. George P. Krapp and Elliott van Kirk Dobbie. 6 vols. New York: Columbia University Press 1931–53. ASPR 1 = George P. Krapp, ed., *The Junius Manuscript* (1931); ASPR 2 = George P. Krapp, ed., *The Vercelli Book* (1932); ASPR 6 = Elliott van Kirk Dobbie, ed., *Anglo-Saxon Minor Poems* (1942)
BAR	British Archaeological Reports
BL	British Library
BMC	British Museum Catalogue
BNF	Bibliothèque Nationale de France
BNJ	*British Numismatic Journal*
Bodl. Lib.	Bodleian Library
BT(S)	Joseph Bosworth and T. Northcote Toller, *An Anglo-Saxon Dictionary* (Oxford: Clarendon Press, 1898); T. N. Toller, *Supplement* (Oxford: Clarendon Press, 1912)
CASSS	Corpus of Anglo-Saxon Stone Sculpture
CCCC	Cambridge, Corpus Christi College

Abbreviations

CCCM	Corpus Christianorum, Continuatio Medievalis
CCSL	Corpus Christianorum, Series Latina
Clemoes	Ælfric's Catholic Homilies: the First Series, ed. Peter Clemoes. EETS s. s. 17. Oxford: Oxford University Press, 1997
CLLA	Codices Liturgici Latini Antiquiores, ed. Klaus Gamber. 3 vols. Spicilegii Friburgensis Subsidia. 2nd ed. (Freiburg: Universitätsverlag Freiburg Schweiz 1968–88)
CSASE	Cambridge Studies in Anglo-Saxon England
CSEL	Corpus Scriptorum Ecclesiasticorum Latinorum
CUL	Cambridge University Library
DOE	Dictionary of Old English in Electronic Form A-F, ed. Angus Cameron, Ashley Crandell Amos and Antonette di Paolo Healey. Toronto: Pontifical Institute Press, 2003
DOEC	Dictionary of Old English Corpus online (*http://www.umdl.umich.edu/cgi/oec*) [requires subscription]
EEMF	Early English Manuscripts in Facsimile
EETS	Early English Text Society
Godden I	Ælfric, Catholic Homilies: Introduction, Commentary, and Glossary, ed. Malcolm Godden. EETS s.s. 18. London: Oxford University Press, 2000
Godden II	Ælfric, Catholic Homilies: the Second Series. Text, ed. Malcolm Godden. EETS s.s. 5. London: Oxford University Press, 1979
Gneuss	Helmut Gneuss, Handlist of Anglo-Saxon Manuscripts: A List of Manuscripts and Manuscript Fragments Written or Owned in England up to 1100. Tempe, AZ: ACMRS, 2001
HBS	Henry Bradshaw Society

Abbreviations

HE	*Bede's Ecclesiastical History of the English People*, ed. Bertram Colgrave and R. A. B. Mynors. Oxford: Clarendon Press, 1991 (rev. ed.)
JEGP	*Journal of English and Germanic Philology*
Ker	N. R. Ker, *Catalogue of Manuscripts Containing Anglo-Saxon*. Oxford: Clarendon Press, 1957
MA	*Medieval Archaeology*
MED	*Middle English Dictionary* online (*http://ets.umdl.umich.edu/m/med/*)
MGH	Monumenta Germaniae Historica
n.s.	new series
OED	*Oxford English Dictionary*
OLD	*Oxford Latin Dictionary*, ed. Peter G.W. Glare. Oxford: Clarendon Press, 1982
o.s.	original series
PG	Patrologiae cursus completus, Series Graeca, ed. J-P. Migne. Paris, 1857–66
PL	Patrologiae cursus completus, Series Latina, ed. J-P. Migne. Paris, 1844–82
PMLA	Publications of the Modern Language Association
RSB	*Regula Sancti Benedicti*
Skeat	*Ælfric's Lives of Saints*, ed. Walter Skeat. 2 vols. EETS 94, 114. London: Oxford University Press, 1881–1900
s.s.	supplementary series
Thorpe	*The Homilies of the Anglo-Saxon Church, The First Part containing the "Sermones Catholicae" or "Homilies of Ælfric" in the Original Anglo-Saxon, with an English Version*, ed. and trans. Benjamin Thorpe. 2 vols. London, 1844–1846. Repr. Hildesheim: Olms, 1983

In Memoriam Timothy Reuter

1947–2002

EULOGY, DELIVERED JULY 6, 2003
Patrick Wormald, Oxford University

As this symposium's last chairman (but one), I should first like to say something about Tim, in whose memory and honor it has been held—especially as I could not be present at his funeral nine months ago. A case like this is no place for mealy mouths or minced words. Tim's death was absolutely and utterly a tragedy: most of all of course for Georgi and their family; but also for many, many friends in and out of academia—Tim had a rather special gift of friendship, especially for those in any way down or out and, not least, for the study of history on the continent and in England, and in English and continental languages, over the centuries on either side of the first millennium. Tragedy like this, the wanton and inexplicable extinction of a cherished life, makes one want to be angry, even if one cannot quite think who to be angry with. And then, as I was wondering quite what else to say this afternoon, my memory alighted on a famous passage of *poeta noster*: "Better (*selre*) it is for us all," says Beowulf, "to avenge his friend than to mourn him much"—that close observer of a human's life well knew what it was to feel anger at its loss. "We must all," he goes on, however, "expect an end to the world's life; let he who can earn fame before death; for a lifeless warrior, that epitaph is best (*selest*)" (lines 1384–9). It is Tim's well-earned fame that we have, in our own way, been celebrating this weekend.

In Memoriam
Barbara Yorke, University College, Winchester

It is very appropriate that this volume should be dedicated to Timothy Reuter who died on October 17, 2002, at the tragically young age of 55. The third Cross Conference was held at University College, Winchester (formerly King Alfred College) in July 2003 under the aegis of the Wessex Medieval Center, a group Tim had set up to act as a forum for all those in the region who were researching into aspects of the Middle Ages. The international nature of the conference and the wide range of its papers reflected his own broad interests and the great respect in which he was held throughout the academic world. The good fellowship of the conference was something that he would very much have enjoyed, and the absence of his contributions to the discussion, which one can envisage would have been both trenchant and witty, was much regretted. A moving tribute to Tim was delivered at the conference by Patrick Wormald who was sadly also to die prematurely in September 2004, and his presentation notes for that eulogy stand before my own contribution here in this volume.

Tim was an undergraduate at Cambridge (1965–68) and moved to Oxford for postgraduate research with Karl Leyser. His doctorate thesis on "The Papal Schism: the Empire and the West 1159–69" was submitted in 1975. Karl was an important intellectual influence on Tim, but typically Karl and his wife Henrietta also became close friends, and, after Karl's death in 1992, Tim published two volumes of Karl's collected essays, *Communications and Power in Medieval Europe: the Carolingian and Ottonian Centuries* (London, 1994) and *Communications and Power in Medieval Europe: the Gregorian Revolution and Beyond* (London, 1994).

In 1971 Tim was appointed lecturer in medieval history at the University of Exeter. As an undergraduate student in my third year when Tim arrived, I found his lectures on early medieval European history inspiring, particularly his decoding of the sources and

In Memoriam

appreciation of medieval *realpolitik*. While at Exeter, Tim contributed to and edited a volume of essays on St. Boniface—*The Greatest Englishman: Essays on St Boniface and the Church at Crediton* (Exeter, 1980)—which remains one of the best introductions in English to Boniface and his mission. In the year following its publication, Tim was to follow Boniface's example in moving from Devon to Germany, when he took up a position at the Monumenta Germaniae Historica in Munich. It was a return to his paternal roots for both his father and grandfather had been born in Germany, and in the post-war period his grandfather Ernst was a much respected mayor of Berlin. Tim himself had great affection for the German language and culture, especially its music.

At the Monumenta, Tim was responsible for pioneering work on the computerization of texts which came to fruition in 1990 with the publication (with Dr. Gabriel Silagi) of an electronic concordance to Gratian's *Decretum*, and with the groundwork for the eventual computerization of the whole corpus of Monumenta texts. It is to be hoped that Tim's own edition for the Monumenta of the letter-book of Wibald of Stavelot, which had still to be completed at the time of his death, will be published in due course. Tim's period in Munich was very productive in other ways and saw the publication of several important papers, including "Plunder and Tribute in the Carolingian Empire" (*Transactions of the Royal Historical Society* 5th series 35 [1985]: 75–94) and his *Germany in the Early Middle Ages, c. 800–1056* (London, 1991). He wrote many reviews of German books in English and of English books in German, thus performing an invaluable role for academic speakers of both languages.

Tim returned to England to take up the chair in medieval history at the University of Southampton in 1994 and enjoyed a highly productive final decade. He provided leadership both in his department, where he ushered in major administrative and curriculum changes, and to the broader History community. He was chairman of the Southampton Record Series, was on the council of the Royal

Historical Society and was a general editor for Oxford Medieval Texts. In addition to the publication of many papers in English and German on an impressively wide range of topics, Tim edited the third volume of the *New Cambridge Medieval History* (1999) and, with the Wessex Medieval Center, organized a major conference to commemorate the 1100th centenary of the death of King Alfred. Although nominally organized by a committee, it was Tim who did the bulk of the work and raised an international cast of speakers; this was typical of the energy and attention to detail that he brought to all that he did. He completed most of the editorial work on the conference proceedings before his death, and the volume, *Alfred the Great* (Aldershot, 2003), was seen through the press by his colleague David Hinton. Shortly before his death Tim heard that he had been awarded a prestigious research professorship by the British Academy to carry out a long cherished project on medieval bishops and their dioceses.

Tim was one of the most influential historians of his generation, with a European-wide range that few could match on the study of medieval texts, politics, and historiography. He was also a good and generous friend, a humane and fair colleague, and one of the most amusing people that one could hope to spend time with. He was a lifelong socialist and practiced what he preached in trying to bring about a more just and equitable society. Family, friends, and colleagues have all felt bereft by his death, and it is evident that some of his most important work was still to be completed when he died. However, he leaves an impressive legacy and one which all medievalists living and future can celebrate. I can do no better than to follow Patrick Wormald by honoring him with the celebrated closing lines from *Beowulf*:

> He was the man most gracious and fair-minded,
> kindest to his people, and keenest to win fame.

Introduction

SARAH LARRATT KEEFER, *Trent University, Ontario*
KAREN LOUISE JOLLY, *University of Hawai'i at Mānoa*
CATHERINE E. KARKOV, *University of Leeds*

THE CROSS IN EARLY MEDIEVAL ENGLAND was ubiquitous to such a degree that it has become virtually invisible to the modern eye, and yet it played an innovative role in Anglo-Saxon culture, evident in art, architecture, material culture, literature, ritual, medicine, and popular practice. The cross functioned as both individual artifact and base design on which other physical art forms or buildings were modeled. Associated with the paradox of shameful death and glorious resurrection, it was used as a spatial gesture in rituals wherever "making the sign of the cross" was prescribed, and served as inspiration for literary meditation and ritual invocation alike. The cross therefore represented one of the most powerful relics, emblems, and images in medieval culture because its simple construction could be presented in many forms, and thus was accessible to every layer of society. Consequently the cross had a substantial symbolic value in pre-Conquest England, since its association with protection and strength as well as with torture and punishment invoked the central intriguing tension in Christian thought between suffering and salvation. The variety of forms and meanings of the cross may be one reason why no synthetic transdisciplinary treatment of its role in Anglo-Saxon life has yet emerged, despite numerous studies of particular aspects within genres. This volume is the last of three produced by *Sancta Crux/Halig Rod*, an interdisciplinary project that sponsored seminars and conference sessions on both sides of the Atlantic between 2001 and 2003, seeking to fill the lacuna just noted by bringing together applications of diverse scholarship and setting them in dialogue with one another.

The volume, and the series as a whole, speaks to critical issues of cultural investigation and their resulting interpretations, pertinent for Anglo-Saxonists and early medievalists of all disciplines, as well as for those interested in the study of cultures and their development. Our approach takes one image, the cross, and shows how its shape and implications are seen to cut across both the culture of a society and the boundaries of academic disciplines—history, archaeology, art history, literature, philosophy, and religion. Moreover, the different disciplinary methodologies used are instructive because they provide insights into how symbols function within society. The flexibility, portability, and adaptability of the Anglo-Saxon understanding of the cross suggest that a shared typology linked word, image, and performance, joining the physical and spiritual, the temporal and eternal, earth and heaven in the Anglo-Saxon imaginative landscape. When gathered and analyzed together, the fragments of this culture of the cross informing our various scholarly interests allow us to bridge the temporal gap between ourselves and those whom we study.

The multifaceted nature and benefit of collaborative research that hallmarked the early *Sancta Crux/Halig Rod* discussions generated specific questions about the role of the cross in early medieval England. Questions addressed in the seminars and studies that make up the series have included:

1. How, within our discrete disciplines, do we see ways in which the Anglo-Saxon mind equated the specific shape of the cross with a larger, aesthetic meaning, and are there places of cultural intersection?

Introduction

2. In what ways do popular belief and prescribed ritual meet or become contiguous through the various aspects of the cross as it was understood in Anglo-Saxon England?

3. What are the implications, both for Anglo-Saxon society and for our own modern study of it, of the tension represented by the dual aspects of the cross as public symbol of salvation and the cross as personal emblem of devotion?

4. How did various Anglo-Saxons identify with the cross: through ritual performance, in private meditative practice, in corporate worship, and with specific or directed intent?

5. How did devotion to the cross affect the Anglo-Saxon apprehension of the acts of seeing and reading?

These questions illustrate the connections made between ritual, art, and belief that inspired the project initially, and sustained it as it expanded to include a wider range of scholars and disciplines. A brief history of the project's growth will help to contextualize the issues addressed in the essays of this volume.

History of the *Sancta Crux/Halig Rod* Project

This inherently interdisciplinary project began with questions about Anglo-Saxon liturgy, which has remained the baseline to which virtually all contributing scholars have returned for grounding throughout the project. In 1999, the three initial collaborators began a fruitful dialogue on the visual and liturgical connections of the cross in manuscript illuminations, the cultural significance of cross marks in medicinal remedies, and the rituals of the cross in church service books. Once the ramifications of studying the cross from multiple perspectives came into focus, we recognized that the possibilities were bigger than an art historian, a cultural historian, and a liturgical scholar could manage, because the arms of the cross indeed reach deep into multiple areas of study.[1] Over the three years of the project (2001–2003), we invited many experts into the discussion and the conversation expanded to include political historians, literature specialists, art historians, numismatists, archeologists, paleographers, and experts on religion, as well as scholars outside the field of Anglo-Saxon studies.

The three sponsored seminars—Durham in 2001, Manchester in 2002, and Winchester in 2003—formed the core of the project, which carried its interlocking themes through to our project report at the 2001 ISAS meeting in Helsinki and our sponsored sessions at Leeds and Kalamazoo in 2002 and 2003. The project seminars in England grew in size and diversity, starting with twenty-six participants and eight speakers at Durham in 2001 and expanding to forty participants and sixteen speakers in Manchester 2002; the final 2003 seminar in Winchester attracted forty-three participants and sixteen speakers and included papers comparing continental and Byzantine practices to those of Anglo-Saxon England. Yet the project preserved its consistent focus across the three years, primarily because certain key themes remained at the center of study, particularly the role of liturgy in relation to material and literary artifacts of Anglo-Saxon culture.

The 2001 "Cross and Culture in Anglo-Saxon England" seminar in Durham, whose proceedings formed the core of the first volume of the series, was held in honor of George Hardin Brown, professor emeritus of English at Stanford University.[2] The sessions focused on

---

1 We presented initial results in a July 2000 conference *Ritual and Belief: Rites of the Anglo-Saxon Church* in Oxford that attracted the interest of many scholars. Those papers were published as part of the conference proceedings in Helen Gittos and M. Bradford Bedingfield, ed., *The Liturgy of the Late Anglo-Saxon Church*, HBS Subsidia 5 (Woodbridge: The Boydell Press, 2005), pp. 143–184, 213–243 and 245–269.

2 Publication of essays based on this seminar are to be found in Karen Louise Jolly, Catherine E. Karkov, and Sarah Larratt Keefer, ed., *Cross and Culture in*

Introduction

the social, religious, literary, and artistic significance of the cross as an artifact, gesture, and concept in Anglo-Saxon culture. Several threads emerged from the discussions and continued in later seminars: the cross as the key to Anglo-Saxon understandings of the relationship between temporal life and death; public versus private aspects of the cross in both individual devotional practice and corporate worship; the relationship between ritual and didactic functions of the cross, and practical uses that were made of it for power and protection; the diverse nature of the cross as *gesture* in performative rituals, as *text* in verbal or written invocations, and as *object* or *image* in art and archeology; and lastly, the wide spectrum of performers and audiences responding to it in monastic, clerical, or secular contexts. Perhaps the most cogent concept was introduced at the outset of the Durham seminar by its honored guest, George Brown, who highlighted the "image-shifting" nature of the cross; this concept re-emerged in the closing session at Durham when the discussion focused on the power of the cross to shape and direct aesthetic and cultural beliefs. One large question left lingering at the seminar's close was the issue of change and context raised by several participants: when, how, and why did the cross and its role in early medieval Britain change from the sixth to the eleventh centuries? These questions drove some of the directions taken in the next two seminars.

The 2002 Manchester seminar "The Place of the Cross in Anglo-Saxon England," co-sponsored by the Manchester Centre for Anglo-Saxon Studies, went further in exploring the inter-relationship between the cross and its locations.[3] Amongst other issues, papers dealt with the ways in which the cross serves as a marker in manuscripts and literary texts, and as a sign of individual reading; its presence or participation in the rituals behind the making of a manuscript or monument; the range of words for the cross found in place-names, and

---

Anglo-Saxon England (Morgantown: West Virginia University Press, 2007).
3   Catherine E. Karkov, Sarah Larratt Keefer, and Karen Louise Jolly, ed., *The Place of the Cross in Anglo-Saxon England* (Woodbridge: Boydell Press, 2006).

what they tell us about the Anglo-Saxon landscape; and how legends of the cross (such as Constantine's CHI-RHO) function as both historical fiction and model. Two lessons emerged from the Manchester papers. First, the words for, references to, and descriptions/depictions of the cross are not as simple and straightforward as one might think. The cross takes on a range of functions and meanings, some of which we can identify, classify and explain, while others remain in need of further investigation. Second, in a phenomenon already noted across recent scholarship, liturgy seems to be far more important to all aspects of Anglo-Saxon culture than we might originally have thought. Opening up these issues fulfilled part of the purpose of the project and moved us forward to its final stage.

In Winchester, the 2003 seminar on "Cross and Crucifix in Anglo-Saxon England and the Continent" was held to honor the memory of Timothy Reuter, professor of history at the University of Southampton; prior to his death in October 2002, he had encouraged the development of the Winchester seminar and inspired us to add a continental perspective. This last seminar, the basis for the volume in hand, tied together many of the earlier themes while broadening our outlook to include other cultural influences from outside Anglo-Saxon England, so that the English perspective might be contextualized within its own socio-political geography. For example, the seminar entertained papers on Byzantine artistic influences, the Carolingian cult of the cross, and Anglo-Scandinavian cross imagery. In addition to analyses of Anglo-Saxon crosses from the perspective of archeology, paleography, art history, liturgy, politics, literature, and even agrarian skills and culinary arts, considerable attention was directed on various ways of understanding *The Dream of the Rood*, now re-evaluated through the work of the previous three years.

All three seminars included visits to local cross monuments as foci of discussion: Ruthwell and Bewcastle in 2001, St. John's Chester and Sandbach in 2002, Romsey, Headbourne Worthy, and Breamore in 2003; in addition, the 2002 visit to the Manchester Museum to view the recently painted cast of the Ruthwell monument provided

Introduction

continuity with Durham. Again, at these monuments the role of liturgy was a key element of discussion, from meditations on the Ruthwell cross at the 2001 Durham seminar to multiple discussions of *The Dream of the Rood* at the 2003 Winchester seminar. These enduring monuments also demonstrated just how vital the Anglo-Saxon cross remains to contemporary culture. Although the three published volumes include many of the illustrations accompanying the seminar papers, one of the experiences that the print versions cannot recapture is that of standing in the presence of these ancient sculptures with leading and thoughtful scholars commenting on what crosses may have meant to the Anglo-Saxons. Such an experience highlights how important the immediacy of place can be to our understanding and interpretation of such a symbol.

These seminars and conference sessions together have built a multidisciplinary collection of materials around a single cultural phenomenon, the cross in Anglo-Saxon England. The project has drawn on the expertise of scholars from a wide range of fields in order to consider different forms and uses of the cross in England circa 800–1100, with the result being a greater understanding of the cross's symbolic and aesthetic importance to Anglo-Saxon clerical, monastic, and lay society. The three *Sancta Crux/Halig Rod* volumes present the fruit of this collaborative enterprise by developing a rich and diverse portrait of a religious culture and its wide-ranging use of one of the most enduring of its symbols in the early medieval period.

Cross and Cruciform in the Anglo-Saxon World: Themes and Issues

The original Winchester seminar included studies that moved beyond the borders of Anglo-Saxon England and out into the larger cultural geography that the English shared with their Frankish and Germanic contemporaries on the continent and beyond—the "Anglo-Saxon world" of the volume's title. In this expansion, we were encouraged by Timothy Reuter, professor of history at the University of Southampton, whose tragically unexpected death cut short his great enthusiasm for what could be seen from considering the larger picture of insular and continental insights taken together. It has been our wish to honor his memory with this volume which bears not one but two memorial dedications. The first, still in note form, was delivered by Patrick Wormald, chair of the seminar's concluding session and a close contemporary of Timothy. However, scarcely more than a year after the Winchester seminar was held in 2003, many of Patrick's words about untimely endings returned to haunt those of us who had heard him utter them: Patrick himself died in 2004, like Timothy, at far too young an age. The second, more complete memorial for Timothy has therefore been prepared by Barbara Yorke, professor of history at University College (formerly King Alfred's College), Winchester; she served as our on- site faculty hostess, and our gratitude to her for this piece, and for all of her dedication and help with the seminar, is enormous.

The studies included in this final volume of the series have sought to continue the exploration of those places of intersection where differing disciplines shed new light on one another by considering the cross in Anglo-Saxon England. They were also intended to bring the project to its natural conclusion. The third phase of the *Sancta Crux/Halig Rod* series therefore expanded its boundaries of investigation from cross to cruciform, inquiring as to the significance of a cross-shaped design, and the ways in which the complex cultural semantics of the cross worked to inform artifacts, illustrations, or architecture that consciously incorporated the cruciform into their constructions. To this end, the contributions to this book have been divided into three different apprehensions of that which is shaped as a cross is: planar design upon the page ("Image and Emblem"); oral or textual understanding of the cross's lexical or allegorical implications ("Meaning and Word"); and the physical incorporation into buildings, monuments, gestures or *objets d'art* of the cruciform in its wider applications ("Gesture and Structure").

Introduction

Michelle Brown explores the implications of the influences underlying early Northumbrian design in "The Cross and the Book: the Cross-Carpet Pages of the Lindisfarne Gospel as Sacred Figurae" in the essay which opens both the volume and its first section, "The Cross: Image and Emblem." She sets out a very detailed technical and aesthetic context for the construction and conceptualization of the Lindisfarne Gospels' carpet pages in a survey of monuments, artifacts, metal work, and ornament from insular and even continental cultures that were contemporary with the creation of the Lindisfarne Gospels. Her cultural survey aptly sets the scene for a consideration of Anglo-Saxon aesthetics in the early medieval, larger world picture to which they belong. The second essay, entitled "A Cross and an Acrostic" by David Pelteret, examines Boniface's poem "Versibus en iuvenis," the preface to his *Ars grammatica* and cruciform in layout, enclosing the words *Iesus Xristus* spelled out horizontally and vertically within its lines. Pelteret considers the art and learning to be found in Boniface's complicated construct, describing the innovations and intentional difficulties within the poem, together with the evidence available to us for the ways in which it was to be read; he provides a comprehensive edition of this remarkable piece at the essay's close. The final study of the first section focuses on the visual presentation and devotional function of the cross in the two eleventh-century books for which Ælfwine has traditionally been considered responsible. In her "Abbot Ælfwine and the Sign of the Cross," Catherine Karkov discusses his "prayerbook" (London, British Library MSS Cotton Titus D. xxvii and D. xxvi) and the Liber Vitae of the New Minster (London, British Library MS Stowe 944) for what they tell us about Ælfwine's understanding of the cross for himself and his community at Winchester.

"The Cross: Meaning and Word" is the second section of the volume and contains four essays that function as pairs, each set considering a common text or common lexical issues that focus on the cross or the cruciform. Éamonn Ó Carragáin and Helen Damico have contributed essays that consider *The Dream of the Rood*, though from

Introduction

two very different viewpoints. Ó Carragáin's study, entitled "Sources or Analogues? Using Liturgical Evidence to Date *The Dream of the Rood*," draws on his decades of work with the liturgical sources and connections lying behind both the Vercelli poem and the Ruthwell Cross runic verse, to rehearse the evidence for an extremely early avatar of *The Dream of the Rood*. Damico's essay, "Writing/Sounding the Cross: *The Dream of the Rood* as Figured Poetry," explores the implications of its unusual scansion and metrical structure, providing both a history and a cultural context for traditional *carmina figurata* against which to consider *The Dream of the Rood* as a "figured poem." While the authors of these two studies differ in their approaches to the Old English poem that they each discuss, the second pair of essays, by Rolf H. Bremmer, Jr. and Ursula Lenker, were undertaken with the aid of mutual consultation in order to present a comprehensive picture of the lexical range of words used to refer to "cross," "cruciform," and "signing the cross" in Anglo-Saxon England. Bremmer concentrates his efforts on words which actually refer to a "cross," including *rod*, *galga* and *cruc*, and on the Anglo-Saxons' use of such words and their derivatives; Lenker focuses on words which indicate the signing of the cross—*rodetacen* and *cristes mæl* and their derivates—and like Bremmer, she painstakingly constructs a clear lexical picture of word use and its circumstances in Anglo-Saxon England.

The final section of the volume moves the reader further out into the issues of everyday practice and patronage, where its four studies examine different applications of the cross and the cruciform within Anglo-Saxon society. Its subtitle, "Gesture and Structure," encompasses both cross as construct and cross as appropriated ritual. "The Staff of Life: Cross and Blessings in Anglo-Saxon Cereal Production" by Debby Banham is a practical and intriguing exploration to ascertain the degree to which the production of bread in Anglo-Saxon England can be seen to employ the cross as gesture, invocation, or sign. Banham traces the complete process of cereal growing, from plowing, through seeding, crop care, and harvest, to the grinding of flour and making

Introduction

of bread, for evidence of the cross as emblem of Christian dedication and apotropaic symbol used within lay society. David Hinton's study of "The Anglo-Saxon Chapel at Bradford-on-Avon, Wiltshire" compiles the findings from the 2000 archaeological investigation of the remains of this chapel dedicated to St. Laurence. His comparison of its cruciform design to that found in other pre-Conquest church structures serves as a starting point from which to discuss how the chapel at Bradford-on-Avon may have been used in the Anglo-Saxon period, and he considers the other implications to be made from the archaeological evidence as it pertains to the original design and intent of the chapel. Martin Foys presents the Anglo-Scandinavian Nunburnholme Cross as the focus of his study of innovative ways in which scholarship may consider a sculpture in "New Media and the Nunburnholme Cross." Since the current condition of this monument creates perceptual difficulties for those who study it, Foys argues for the digitization of images of it which can then be used in a program of technology "to accommodate the temporal and spatial eccentricities or disjunctions so emblematic of the Nunburnholme Cross in particular and many Anglo-Scandinavian and Anglo-Saxon crosses in general" (p. 344). "The *Enkolpion* of Edward the Confessor: Byzantium and Anglo-Saxon Concepts of Rulership" by Lynn Jones is the last essay in our volume. It focuses on the now-lost "golden crucifix richly adorned and enameled," (p. 371) that was taken from Edward the Confessor's tomb in 1685 and given to James II. Jones argues persuasively that this was an *enkolpion*, a Byzantine cross reliquary; the balance of her essay discusses what we know of such crosses from Byzantium, the likeliest routes by which Edward's *enkolpion* might have come to the English court, and the political implications that his possession of such an artifact might suggest about his attitude towards being a king in late Anglo-Saxon England.

Overall, then, *Cross and Cruciform in the Anglo-Saxon World* suggests new ways to connect multidisciplinary data by identifying common threads that reach past the insular to the continental cultures of the

Introduction

time, and approach a truly interdisciplinary understanding of the cross within the Anglo-Saxon imagination. Like its predecessors, this third volume challenges existing assumptions and categories about early medieval religiosity, while introducing to a wider audience both textual and visual primary sources related to the cross in secular and religious contexts. The issues the volume addresses extend beyond the cross itself to tackle larger problems such as the relations between pagan and Christian, public and private, lay and clerical, Anglo-Saxon innovation and continental borrowing, and popular culture and reform movements. The authors and editors hope that the thematic consistency of the volume will help Anglo-Saxonists and medievalists in all fields, as well as scholars and students of culture and religion, to understand the particular texts and artifacts discussed, while simultaneously taking away with them a larger, more complex picture of Anglo-Saxon culture.

Acknowledgments

From such a collection of studies, we may see that the cross is a dynamic concept, affording scholars insight into many layers of Anglo-Saxon culture and benefiting from the interdisciplinary cooperation achieved in this project. Consequently, the project organizers would like to thank all those who encouraged, contributed to, and supported this project—it became so much more than we originally imagined it might be, because of the efforts and generosity of so many, and we hope the fruits of this project will benefit many more.

The editors would once again like to thank those who made the 2001 "Cross and Culture in Anglo-Saxon England" seminar possible: St. John's College, Durham and the University of Hawai'i Conference Center for the facilities and registration; David Rollason and Rosemary Cramp of the University of Durham for hosting us so ably; Joyce Hill and David Rollason for supplemental transportation on our excursion. We remain very grateful to all those who made

Introduction

the Manchester seminar possible: the University of Manchester, MANCASS, and most especially Don Scragg, Kathryn Powell, and Mary Syner; and the Manchester Museum, especially John Prag, for arranging for us to see the Ruthwell and Bewcastle casts before they were on public display. We are also very grateful to Lori Johnston of the Trent University Conference Centre whose cheerful professionalism and competent interaction with the staff of the Conference Centre at University College (formerly King Alfred's College), Winchester, allowed the long-distance organization of the 2003 Winchester seminar to be effected without any complications. To George Hillard III a special mention of thanks; a committed participant in these seminars, he worked out our 2003 excursion route, made arrangements with all of the churches involved (especially his own parish of St. Mary's, Breamore), and acted as tour guide on the bus. Finally, our enduring gratitude to all of our distinguished speakers and participants in all of the *Sancta Crux/Halig Rod* seminars, including those at the Leeds and Kalamazoo sessions, many of whom willingly contributed their essays to our volumes, and have shown exemplary patience in waiting for them to appear.

We express our thanks to the Social Science and Humanities Research Council of Canada for three Internal SSHRC Grants awarded to the *Sancta Crux/Halig Rod* project to facilitate the Winchester seminar and the publication of the three volumes resulting from the project. We also thank Trent University's Office of Research and Graduate Studies for the support and encouragement that these grants represent. We are grateful to Catherine Karkov's former institution, Miami University of Ohio, and its School of Fine Art and Department of Art, as well as to the Philip and Elaina Hampton Fund for their generous support of travel to England and Helsinki at various stages of this project. We thank the Memorial University of Newfoundland for providing William Schipper with a subvention grant, allowing for his participation in the first seminar at Durham and its proceedings volume. At the University of Hawai'i, *mahalo*

Introduction

to the University Research Council, the UH Endowment for the Humanities, the Hung Wo and Elizabeth Lau Ching Foundation, and to Dean Judith Hughes of the College of Arts and Humanities for supporting research travel halfway across the globe.

We would also extend our appreciation to those who have contributed to the project throughout its duration. We gratefully acknowledge the support of the International Society of Anglo-Saxonists (ISAS), both of its leaders and its members, for promoting and encouraging the project. To the authors of the essays appearing in this volume, the editors would like to acknowledge with gratitude their willingness to start and stay with the project as it has evolved from the Durham seminar in 2001 to the final meeting at Winchester whose proceedings are represented herein.

Finally, we honor the memory of Timothy Reuter to whom we dedicate this volume: it was a great sorrow to us all that he could not be present for a meeting about which he was so enthusiastic and encouraging.

I

The Cross: Image and Emblem

The Cross and the Book: the Cross-Carpet Pages of the Lindisfarne Gospels as Sacred Figurae

Michelle P. Brown

THE ART OF THE LINDISFARNE GOSPELS is the epitome of the "Insular" style produced in the British Isles and Ireland during the sixth to ninth centuries.[1] This reflected the cultural and ethnic diversity of these islands, blending influences from Celtic, Pictish, Germanic, Anglo-Saxon, and Mediterranean art (including the Roman, Italo-Byzantine, Byzantine, Syriac, Armenian, and Coptic traditions).[2] This process of synthesis was long-lived and can

---

1 This paper is based in part upon research presented in a monographic study of the volume and its context: Michelle P. Brown, *The Lindisfarne Gospels: Society, Spirituality and the Scribe* (London and Toronto: British Library and University of Toronto, 2003); see particularly pp. 312–45.
2 For overviews of Insular illumination, see generally Carl Nordenfalk, *Celtic and Anglo-Saxon Painting* (London: Chatto and Windus, 1977); Françoise Henry, *L'Art Irlandaise* (Yonne: Zodiaque, 1964); J. J. G. Alexander, *Insular Manuscripts, 6th to the 9th Century* (London: Harvey Miller, 1978); George Henderson, *From Durrow to Kells: the Insular Gospelbooks* (London: Thames and Hudson, 1987); Michelle P. Brown, *Manuscripts from the Anglo-Saxon Age* (London: British Library, 2008). For discussion of contacts and parallels between the Christian cultures of the eastern Mediterranean and the Insular world, see Michelle P. Brown, "The Eastwardness of Things: Relationships between the Christian Cultures

be observed occurring from the seventh century in the finds associated with the manufacturing processes of metalwork at the fort of Dunadd, the ceremonial focus of kingship rituals in the expatriate Irish kingdom of Dalriada in western Scotland.[3] Likewise, the Mote of Mark, a fortress near Dumfries in the British kingdom of Rheged which seems to have passed into English hands, has yielded archaeological evidence of metalworking in which British, Celtic, and Anglo-Saxon styles co-exist.[4] Yet nowhere are these elements blended in as masterly a fashion as in the Lindisfarne Gospels. As such, this remarkable volume forms an aesthetic encyclopedia of the post-Roman world at a time when people signaled their cultural, ethnic, religious, and political affiliations by visual display through style, sign, and symbol—one of the most significant of which was the Cross.

Those planning the Lindisfarne Gospels were evidently taking pains to devise a layout in which lections from several sources were synthesized into a new decorative program designed to articulate the text and to enshrine not only an authoritative version of Jerome's Vulgate edition of the gospels but also the liturgy, including some of the most up-to-date papal thought on the subject.[5] The inclusion of

---

of the Middle East and the Insular World," in *The Genesis of Books: Studies in the Interactions of Words, Text, and Print in Honor of A.N. Doane*, ed. Matthew Hussey and John D. Niles (Turnhout: Brepols, forthcoming).

3   E. Campbell and A. Lane, "Celtic and Germanic Interaction in Dalriada: the 7th-Century Metalworking site at Dunadd," *The Age of Migrating Ideas*, ed. R. Michael Spearman and John Higgitt (Edinburgh: National Museums of Scotland, 1993), pp. 52–63; see also Susan Youngs, *"The Work of Angels:" Masterpieces of Celtic Metalwork, 6th–9th Centuries AD* (London: British Museum, 1989).

4   Lloyd Laing, "The Angles in Scotland and the Mote of Mark," *Transactions of the Dumfriesshire and Galloway Natural History and Antiquarian Soc.*, 3rd ser., 50 (1973): 39–52, and "The Mote of Mark and the origins of Celtic interlace," *Antiquity* 49 (1975): 98–108; see also D. Longley, "The Mote of Mark: the Archaeological Context of the Decorated Metalwork," *Pattern and Purpose in Insular Art*, ed. Mark Redknap et al. (Oxford: Oxbow, 2001), pp. 75–89.

5   See Brown, *Lindisfarne Gospels*, pp. 182–99. For an introduction to the place

lections introduced into the liturgy of Rome in 715, coupled with a study of the artifactual and historical context of this remarkable book point to its production at the Columban foundation of Lindisfarne on Holy Island in the Anglo-Saxon kingdom of Northumbria around 715–20, by a single artist-scribe who was probably also its key planner and who was probably Bishop Eadfrith of Lindisfarne (698–721).[6] Unity and the avoidance of schism seem to have been a major consideration, not only textually but in the careful balancing within the decoration of iconic and non-figural decorative features—an impressive feat of tightrope walking at a time when iconoclasm and the whole question of idolatry (whether it is acceptable to depict the divine in human form) was a highly controversial issue in both East and West.[7]

When the opening words of the gospels explode across the decorated incipit pages of the Lindisfarne Gospels, they become an icon in their own right, the manifestation of the Word which is God, for "In the beginning was the Word, and the Word was with God and the Word was God" (John 1:1). Their maker has devised a similar solution to the dilemma to that which would be explored by Islamic scribes several centuries later—sacred calligraphy, in which the manifestation of Logos, the creating force, is the written word which is glorified by the beautiful manner in which it is written and by the opulent materials used.

A similar solution is embodied in the five great cross-carpet pages (see Figures 1.1–5) that introduce St. Jerome's *Novum Opus* preface and the four gospels. Together, these cross-carpet pages and the facing incipit pages form magnificent devotional diptychs at the point

---

of Jerome's Vulgate in the process of biblical transmission, see *"In the Beginning": Bibles Before the Year 1000*, ed. Michelle P. Brown (Washington DC: Smithsonian Institute, 2006).

6 For a full discussion of the attribution to Lindisfarne and a date later than the previously favored 698, the date of the translation of St. Cuthbert's relics, see Brown, *Lindisfarne Gospels*, pp. 13–57.

7 See discussion by Brown and Kessler in Brown, *Bibles Before the Year 1000*, pp. 54–55, 69, 71, 80, 83, 92.

of entry into the book as a whole and into each of the gospels. They are joined in this introductory role by the Canon Tables and four evangelist miniatures and, with them, form a series of sacred *figurae*, or symbolic diagrams embodying Christian exegetical thinking.

Until recently, discussion of the cross-carpet pages tended to focus on their layout and on their stylistic relationship to other artifacts, notably the metalwork finds excavated at Sutton Hoo or on Bettystown Beach (the "Tara" brooch). And yet the jewel-like designs of the cross-carpet pages are not merely influenced by the style of contemporary metalwork but go to some technical lengths to reinforce the stylistic analogy. For example, the central roundel of the St. Mark cross (folio 94v) is carefully laid out on a geometric grid and drawn in such a way that the perspectival effect of a raised boss is achieved. Such glass or enamelwork bosses feature in deluxe items of eighth-century liturgical Irish metalwork, such as the Ardagh chalice and the Derrynaflan paten, and were also sometimes set into the heads of sculptured stone crosses to cover relics.[8] Such stylistic recollections of metalwork, so overtly expressed within the Lindisfarne cross-carpet pages, are likely to have represented intentional visual and semiotic allusions to the *crux gemmata*, the jeweled cross which for early Christians was a symbol of the Second Coming—a symbolism also invoked by the metalwork processional crosses which were carried before the gospel-book during liturgical procession. The humble rough-hewn cross, unwitting instrument of torture, thus becomes ennobled by Christ's triumphal sacrifice and is honored by a cladding of jewels and precious metals, a theme eloquently expressed in the later Anglo-Saxon age in the poem *The Dream of the Rood*. Like the bodies of the letters on the facing decorated *incipit* pages, the forms of the crosses are inhabited by a writhing mass of living creatures which are sustained by the life-giving cross and by the Word. The Lindisfarne Gospels' crosses are thus every bit as alive as the foliate crosses of living green wood in later Anglo–Saxon manuscript art,

---

8 See note 61, below.

and become flesh, just as the living Word is made word on the text pages opposite.[9]

The use of a page of ornament, often with a cross design embedded within it, to introduce major texts was of ultimately Coptic derivation and has traditionally been termed a "carpet page" by art historians because it bears a superficial resemblance to an oriental rug. However, as we shall see, references in books from Monkwearmouth/Jarrow to an *ordo* for the celebration of Good Friday indicate that prayer mats were used in Europe at this time. If you were venerating the cross on Holy Island on Good Friday around the year 720, you might have spent part of the day praying in an easterly direction on a prayer mat: an indication of the dissemination of the shared rituals and cultures of the eastern Mediterranean and its various faith groups during the early Middle Ages.

Yet why should such non-figural expressions of divine mystery be favored? The fear of idolatry, enshrined in the second Commandment, was bequeathed by Judaism to the other monotheistic religions of the word. From its inception Islam fostered the use of sacred calligraphy in a religious context to avoid such dangers. In the early Christian Church, images had already assumed an iconic status as *foci* of veneration, which might be misinterpreted as the objects of worship. Yet even during the state-sponsored iconoclasm that flourished in eighth-century Byzantium under Leo the Isaurian, certain symbols could be used as an alternative to figural representation. Thus it was that the cross and the book became the acceptable symbols of orthodox Christianity at a time when other iconic images, such as the crucifixion and the Virgin and Child, carried implications of theological controversy and the schismatic debates surrounding the vexed issue of how in Christ the divine and the human wills were reconciled.

The Council of Nicaea of 787, however, supported attempts by the Empress Irene to restore images and stated that "We therefore

---

[9] Michelle P. Brown, "'In the Beginning was the Word:' Books and Faith in the Age of Bede," (Newcastle-upon-Tyne: Jarrow Lectures, 2000), p. 2.

follow the pious customs of Antiquity and pay these icons the honor of incense and lights just as we do the holy gospels and the venerable and life-giving cross."[10] Thus the practice of portraying the Godhead by means of abstract or symbolic images was reinforced within the Christian tradition from an early date. In the magnificent diptychs of cross-carpet page and decorated incipit in the Lindisfarne Gospels, the crosses and adorned words embody the Godhead, and we are presented with the physical embodiment of the face (figura) of the divine in the form of schematic figurae (diagrams).

The accompanying evangelist portraits, in which the gospel writers are depicted as scribes with their identifying symbols—the man (Matthew), the lion (Mark), the calf (Luke), and the eagle (John)—feature the bearded figures of Byzantine art for Matthew and Luke and the "Roman" youthful unbearded figures of Mark and of John, the disciple whom Christ loved, who fixes the viewer with a challenging, unwavering gaze. These monumental figures remind us of the frescoes, panel paintings, and mosaics of early Christian art and are imbued with an iconic quality. Their iconography, especially that of the St. Matthew miniature with its mysterious figure peeping from behind the curtain, offers a compelling insight into the theology of the period and the exegetical world of scholars such as Bede.[11]

10 Translated in David Ayerst and A. S. T. Fisher, trans. and ed., *Records of Christianity* (Oxford: Blackwell, 1971), p. 103.
11 Michelle P. Brown, *The Book of Cerne: Prayer, Patronage and Power in Ninth-Century England* (London and Toronto: British Library and University of Toronto, 1996), pp. 73–114; "Embodying Exegesis: Depictions of the Evangelists in Insular Manuscripts," *Le Isole Britanniche e Roma in Età Romanobarbarica*, ed. Anna Maria Luiselli Fadda and Éamonn Ó Carragáin (Rome: Herder, 1998), pp. 109–28; and "'In the beginning was the Word': books and faith in the age of Bede;" see also Jennifer O'Reilly, "Patristic and Insular Traditions of the Evangelists: Exegesis and Iconography," *Le Isole Britanniche e Roma*, ed. Luiselli Fadda and Ó Carragáin, pp. 49–94, and "The Library of Scripture: Views from the Vivarium and Wearmouth-Jarrow," *New Offerings, Ancient Treasures. Essays in Medieval Art for George Henderson*, ed. Paul Binski and William G. Noel (Stroud:

The Cross and the Book

Just as complex in their invocation of the mysteries of faith are the five carpet pages with their embedded cross motifs.[12] These colorful pages are paired with the facing incipit pages, with their magnificent decorated initials and panels of display script which commence each gospel and with the prefatory letter addressed by St. Jerome to Pope Damasus. These incipits are adorned with a vibrant menagerie of birds and beasts, who are distant relatives of the fauna of eastern hunting scenes in ivory and silk, and still closer cousins of the more naturalistic inhabitants of the vine-scroll motif (symbol of Christ's Eucharistic sacrifice), lately imported from Mediterranean climes to the moorlands of Northumbria. In the Lindisfarne Gospels, the forms of the letters of sacred text and the crosses of the carpet pages become themselves the vine, inhabited by a throng of living creatures partaking of their sustenance. These creatures' forms are interwoven in rhythmic interlacing patterns interspersed with curvilinear trumpet spirals and pelta motifs derived from Celtic La Tène art, which had originated in the Iron Age and still enjoyed currency in Celtic Christian art. Parallels for such features are to be found in masterpieces of metalwork, such as the Irish "Tara" (or Bettystown) brooch and Ardagh chalice and the treasures of the Anglo-Saxon Sutton Hoo ship burial. They also adorn the carvings of the early Irish high crosses (notably those at Ahenny near Cashel and the St. John's Cross on Iona) and the Tullylease slab, as well as Pictish sculptures and metalwork (some of the Meigle stones, especially no. 5, the Aberlemno Churchyard slab, and the silver bowls from the St Ninian's Isle Treasure). They also feature in other Insular manuscripts, such

---

Sutton, 2001), pp. 3–39.
12   When a page of ornament serving as a spacer between texts, known as a "carpet page," contains cross motifs within its decoration it is accordingly termed a "cross-carpet page." On carpet pages in general, see Robert Calkins, *Illuminated Books of the Middle Ages* (Ithaca and London: Cornell and Thames and Hudson, 1983), p. 42. On Islamic and Hebrew carpet pages see Leila Avrin, *Scribes, Script and Books* (London: British Library, 1991), pp. 132–33, 242–43

as the Durham and Echternach Gospels, the Lichfield Gospels, the Book of Durrow, and the Book of Kells.[13] This wealth of decoration enriches the underlying structure of the decorated letter-forms, with their Roman, Greek, and Germanic runic features, which convey the major openings of sacred text. The letters have exploded across the page in a riot of ornament, themselves assuming the status of icons and invoking the presence of Christ within the mystery of scripture. Such pages are indicative of the changes in thought that transformed the world of late antiquity into that of the Middle Ages.[14]

The program of decoration extends to the architectural arcades, again replete with a wealth of abstract and zoomorphic detail, which call to mind the entrance to the chancel, the holy of holies, and which frame the Canon Tables,[15] themselves an embodiment of Christ's mission conveyed in symbolic numeric guise.[16] The same ornamental

---

13 For images and discussion of these and related Insular artworks, see in general Henry, *L'Art Irlandaise*; David M. Wilson, *Anglo-Saxon Art* (London: Thames and Hudson, 1984); Ryan, *Treasures of Ireland* (Dublin: Royal Irish Academy, 1983); Henderson, *Insular Gospelbooks*; Youngs, "*Work of Angels*;" Peter Fox, ed., *The Book of Kells, MS 58, Trinity College Library Dublin*, 2 vols., facsimile and commentary (Luzern: Faksimile Verlag, 1990); Bernard Meehan, *The Book of Kells* (London: Thames and Hudson, 1994) and *The Book of Durrow* (Dublin: Town House, 1996); Brown, *Manuscripts from the Anglo-Saxon Age*.

14 J-C. Bonne, "De l'Ornemental dans l'Art Médiéval (VIIe-XIIe s.). Le Modèle Insulaire," *L'Image, Fonction et Usage, Cahiers du Léopard d'Or* 5, ed. Michel Pastoureau (Paris: Leopard d'Or, 1995): 185–219; see also E. Pirotte, "Le Signe de la Croix dans les Manuscrits Insulaires: Camouflages et Apparitions," *Annales de l'histoire de l'art et d'archéologie* 16 (1994): 23–45; R. B. K. Stevenson, "Aspects of Ambiguity in Crosses and Interlace," *Ulster Journal of Archaeology* 44/45 (1981-2): 1–27; Leslie Webster and Michelle P. Brown, ed., *The Transformation of the Roman World*, (London: British Museum, 1997), pp. 211–12, 234–35; Brown, *Lindisfarne Gospels*, pp. 331–45.

15 For background on the development of decorated canon tables and their significance, see C. Nordenfalk, *Die Spatantiken Kanontafeln*, 2 vols, (Goteborg: O. Isacsons Boktryckeri, 1938), passim.

16 This aspect of numeric symbolism provides an interesting link with the geometric principles underlying much of the design, as discussed below, pp. 25–30.

repertoire enlivens the major and minor initials which mark important sections in the text. This program of employing decoration to articulate text divisions is extended to even the smallest initials and *litterae notabiliores* (enlarged letters) which mark chapters, the Eusebian sections listed in the Canon Tables and the readings (lections or *pericopes*) used in the liturgy, partly as practiced in the center in which the Lindisfarne Gospels was made, seen, and occasionally used, and partly as an expression of the harmony of the various liturgical traditions. Lections of Roman, Columban, Aquileian, and Neapolitan use are all distinguished by minor initials.

Compasses, rulers, and dividers were used to lay out the carpet pages and Lindisfarne's complex animal interlace was designed on a grid in the practical manner of the sculptor, but the details of the ornament were then worked up freehand, allowing for the playful challenges to symmetry to be observed throughout; these are nonetheless governed by the geometric principles of design by which creation might be understood.[17] A similar approach to layout, assisted by compass-work, may be seen on the metalwork objects from the Donore hoard,[18] upon which La Tène spiralwork and zoomorphic interlace are engraved, having been compass-constructed and finished freehand. As Michael Ryan observes, "together with the 'Tara' brooch and the Lagore buckle, the objects provide strong evidence for the adoption of the style seen in the Lindisfarne Gospels in the East Midlands of Ireland around the beginning of the eighth century."[19] The same might also be said of sculptures in southern

---

17 Robert Stevick, *The Earliest Irish and English Bookarts: Visual and Poetic Forms Before AD 1000* (Philadelphia: University of Pennsylvania, 1994), p. 13; see also the discussion below, pp. 28–30.

18 Youngs, "*Work of Angels*," nos. 63–66, and discussion by Michael Ryan, *Treasures of Ireland*, p. 127.

19 Youngs, "*Work of Angels*," p. 67. On a similar connection with Irish filigree metalwork, see Niamh Whitfield, "Motifs and Techniques of Celtic Filigree. Are They Original?," *Ireland and Insular Art*, ed. Ryan, pp. 75–84. On the cultural background, see, for example, Rosemary Cramp, "Northumbria and Ireland," *Sources of Anglo-Saxon Culture*, ed. Paul Szarmach and Virginia D. Oggins,

Ireland, notably the Ahenny crosses and the Tullylease slab, which resembles Lindisfarne's Matthew carpet page and which also carries an inscription in half-uncials of the type found in Lindisfarne.[20] This shared tradition should perhaps be seen as something approaching an Insular version of the Romanesque trans-Manche "Channel School" in terms of the regional diffusion of a style either side of a sea-channel, in accordance with the socio-historical context. This area also embraced the northern British kingdoms, as well as Anglo-Saxon Northumbria and Pictland. The same principles of design and of layout techniques are again encountered on the Hunterston brooch (Nat. Mus. Scotland, FC8) and on a slate motif-piece for a pseudo-penannular brooch from Dunadd (Nat. Mus. Scotland, GP 218), both executed in "Irish" style in Scotland sometime during the late seventh to ninth centuries.[21] These exhibit the same underlying layout technique as parts of the design of the Lindisfarne Gospels.[22] The design for areas of spiralwork is based upon a square quartered by two ruled diagonal lines forming an X. A compass mark is made at the point at which these lines cross in the center of the square, and a circle is drawn; more diagonal lines radiate from the central

---

(Kalamazoo: University of Western Michigan, 1986), pp. 185–201.

20 Youngs, "*Work of Angels*," p. 127, fig. 3; Isabel Henderson and Elizabeth Okasha, "The Early Christian Inscribed and Carved Stones of Tullylease, Co. Cork," *Cambridge Medieval Celtic Studies* 24 (Winter 1992): 2–36.

21 Youngs, "*Work of Angels*," nos. 69 and 155; for the layout of the "Tara" brooch, see Robert Stevick, "The Form of the Tara Brooch," *Journal of the Royal Society of Antiquaries of Ireland* 128 (1998): 5–16; for a full discussion of the layout technique, and a comparison with those of the Lindisfarne Gospels, see Niamh Whitfield, "Design and Units of Measure on the Hunterston Brooch," *Northumbria's Golden Age*, ed. Jane Hawkes and Susan Mills (Stroud: Sutton, 1999), pp. 296–314, where she also discusses the use of a 9mm unit of measurement which may have been influenced by Roman systems of measurement.

22 This was fully discussed by Rupert Bruce-Mitford in *Evangeliorum Quattuor Codex Lindisfarnensis*, ed. T. D. Kendrick, 2 vols (Olten and Lausanne: Urs Graf Verlag, 1956–1960), II: 226–31 and is summarized in the introduction to Alexander, *Insular Manuscripts*, fig. 3.

compass mark and are further subdivided to pinpoint the location of other compass points from which spring further arcs integral to the design. The remaining details were apparently hung, freehand, upon this underlying geometric skeleton.

    Elizabeth Coatsworth has shown that the layout underlying the design of St. Cuthbert's pectoral cross, with its precise geometry based upon grids and compass-drawn circles (the grid of 16 units square and the circle with a radius of 8 units), was also used for the central motif of one of the Lindisfarne Gospels' cross-carpet pages (folio 94v, see Figure 1.3). She has traced the tradition of such cross layouts to items of early Anglo-Saxon metalwork, such as the Ixworth and Wilton crosses, observing that "it is possible to see a very direct transfer of design technique between goldsmith and illuminator."[23] Given that there are references to Insular monks being skilled metalworkers, this is not perhaps surprising. The close stylistic relationship of the Lindisfarne Gospels to Insular metalwork, along with the technical design links, would suggest that the book's artist-scribe might himself have been an accomplished metalworker. Other aspects of the geometry underlying the design of the Lindisfarne Gospels have been discussed in detail by Bruce-Mitford, Guilmain, and Stevick.[24] Rosemary Cramp has also drawn attention to the fact that, in other media, the use of geometric aids in layout, such as are encountered in the Lindisfarne Gospels, the pectoral cross, and the Lindisfarne sculptures, form part of an ancient

---

23 Elizabeth Coatsworth, "The Pectoral Cross and Portable Altar from the Tomb of St Cuthbert," in *St Cuthbert, His Cult and His Community*, ed. Gerald Bonner et al., (Woodbridge: Boydell and Brewer, 1989), pp. 287–302 at 293–94; for the broader metalworking context, see Elizabeth Coatsworth and Michael Pinder, *The Art of the Anglo-Saxon Goldsmiths, Fine Metalwork in England, its Practice and Practitioners* (Woodbridge: Boydell and Brewer, 2002), passim.

24 Bruce-Mitford in *Codex Lindisfarnensis*, II: 226–30; Jacques Guilmain, "The Geometry of the Cross-Carpet Pages in the Lindisfarne Gospels," *Speculum* 62 (1987): 21–52; see also Robert Stevick, "The Design of Lindisfarne Gospels Folio 138v," *Gesta* 22 (1983): 3–12; "The 4 × 3 Crosses in the Lindisfarne and Lichfield Gospels," *Gesta* 25 (1986): 171–84.

British and Celtic tradition.[25] So too does the practice of using panels of ornament, which she suggests may have been connected to the use of motif-pieces (trials of designs on pieces of bone, slate, wood, and the like) in the design and transmission of sections of ornament.[26] The design context for much of the Lindisfarne Gospels' ornament therefore lies firmly within a British, Pictish, and Celtic tradition which stretched back to the Iron Age and was actively practiced in those areas around and after the time that the volume was made.

Robert Stevick has compared the interdisciplinary currency of aesthetic, mathematical, and technical principles apparent within the arts in various media of the Insular and Anglo–Saxon worlds, including the structure of Anglo-Saxon poetry, with the universality of application to "all who use measure" favored by Dürer and others in the late Middle Ages and the Renaissance.[27] He has pointed out that details of layout which have tended to be dismissed as incidental or not observed at all, are in fact influenced by complex mathematical principles of measurement, such as the Golden Rule (or Golden Mean) governing its page proportions and layout—although later trimming by binders often makes this difficult to prove. This would account for the intentional disparities in length of what seem at first glance to be truly equal-armed crosses in the carpet pages on folios 94v and 138v of the Lindisfarne Gospels, or its Jerome and Matthew 4 × 3 cross-pages (folios 2v and 26v, see Figures 1.3, 1.4, 1.1 and 1.2) which are laid out on the basis of two golden section rectangles (with sides in the ratio $2:\varphi$ or its equivalent $(\sqrt{5}-1):1$), their frames being conceived as part of the design ratios, rather than as framing devices.[28]

---

25 See Cramp in Bonner et al., *St Cuthbert*, pp. 220–21.

26 Cramp in Bonner et al., *St Cuthbert*, pp. 220–21; for the corpus of early medieval motif-pieces, see Uaininn O'Meadhra, *Early Christian, Viking and Romanesque Art: Motif-pieces from Ireland*, Northern European Archaeology 7 (Stockholm: Alqvist, 1979), passim.

27 Stevick, *The Earliest Irish and English Bookarts*, p. 4.

28 Stevick, *The Earliest Irish and English Bookarts*, pp. 90–91 and 102–7.

Such principles of design are also likely to have been imbued with their own meaning. Cast on the scales—to balance the plethora of received stylistic, formal, and iconographic influences and the aesthetic and technical invention of the Insular artist—were not only theological, exegetical, and symbolic meaning, but also the desire to explore and recreate anew, in each creation, the divine principles of harmony, measurement, and geometry which were believed to order God's creation. The creator was sometimes depicted in early medieval art wielding dividers.[29] Geometry and arithmetic, along with music and astronomy, formed the "quadrivium," a mainstay of classical and early medieval education, which Boethius characterized as providing "paths through the creation to its source in the incorporeal world wherein lies true wisdom."[30] Spiritual truths and aesthetic perfection might therefore be sought through numeric and proportional principles; the decorated pages of the Lindisfarne Gospels—especially those involving particularly complex geometric layout such as the cross-carpet pages (but also the words of the incipit pages and the evangelist miniatures and their placing in relation to their frames)—can thereby be seen at an even more fundamental level to represent a quest for the understanding, emulation, and transmission of the divine rule of time, space, and substance.

Asymmetrical components in the natural order are reflected by the Lindisfarne artist, not only in his frequent reversal of elements within the zoomorphic interlace designs or his occasional pairing of like with unlike (with subtle variations upsetting the game of "spot

---

29   As in the mid eleventh-century English Tiberius Psalter, London, British Library MS Cotton Tiberius C. vi, fol. 7v; see Francis Wormald, "An English Eleventh-Century Psalter with Pictures," *Walpole Society* 38 (1962): 1–13; and Elżbieta Temple, *Anglo-Saxon Manuscripts, 900–1066* (Harvey Miller: London, 1976), no. 98, pp. 115–17.
30   Based upon Boethius, *Proemium* to the first book of *De Institutione Arithmetica,* trans. Michael Masi, *Boethian Number Theory: a translation of the De Institutione Arithmetica,* (Amsterdam: Brepols, 1983), p. 73; see also Stevick, *The Earliest Irish and English Bookarts,* p. 13.

the difference," but nonetheless appearing at first glance balanced within the overall design), but also in his intentional proportional inconsistencies of measurement. Thus, although the "Latin" crosses of the Jerome and Matthew cross-carpet pages (folios 2v and 26v, see Figures 1.1 and 1.2) appear to observe the ratio of 4 × 3, composed of identical units of the design grid, their lowest vertical members do not measure the same as the others (the two lowest squares on folio 2v having their centers placed 46.5 mm apart and the rest 52 mm, and the two lower medallions on folio 26v being centered apart at 64 mm rather than the 59 mm of the rest).[31] Only the cross-carpet page of St. John (folio 210v, see Figure 1.5) is entirely regular in its layout and symmetry, reinforcing its exegetical interpretation as the Word transmitted directly from God, and the symbolic equation of its evangelist miniature with Christ in Majesty, indicating the fulfillment and perfection of the divine order. Thus the geometric layout of Lindisfarne's designs might have been seen as physically embodying and celebrating the Godhead, much as I have suggested the Canon Tables might do in their numeric encapsulation of Christ's incarnation, sacrifice, and resurrection.[32] To quote Stevick:

> On the St. John cross page alone he composed a small cross at the center of the frame, but too far from it to interact with it perceptually. To say it shortly, Eadfrith knew better than the others the relations between what is conceived by the mind and what is perceived by the senses.[33]

In this aspect, as in so many others, the artist-scribe of the Lindisfarne Gospels emerges as an individual well-versed in the traditions of craftsmanship and of literate Christian philosophy, theology, and

---

31 For a detailed discussion of the underlying mathematical principles and of the details of layout in the Lindisfarne Gospels, see Stevick, *The Earliest Irish and English Bookarts*, pp. 102–15, 140–50, 197–200. See also Stevick, "The Design of Lindisfarne Gospels Folio 138v," *Gesta* 22 (1983): 3–12.
32 Brown, Lindisfarne Gospels, pp. 300–12.
33 Stevick, *The Earliest Irish and English Bookarts*, p. 200.

exegesis, and able to employ them in innovative, well-planned, and supremely well-conducted ways throughout his *opus dei*. He is likely to have been one of the most accomplished, experienced, learned, and senior members of his community—perhaps even its abbot/bishop.

As already noted above, carpet pages take their name from their resemblance to eastern rugs. There may be a previously unperceived significance to this analogy. Coptic and other eastern manuscripts sometimes feature such pages of decoration, including crosses formed of or set against interlace, as in New York, Pierpont Morgan Library MS Glazier Codex 67, folio 215r, and a later Persian copy of an early Diatessaron (Florence, Biblioteca Medicea–Laurentiana MS Orient 81, folio 127v).[34] They are quite widely represented in Coptic and Christian Arabic manuscripts of the ninth century onwards, and may also have played a role in the development of the great decorated pages of Islamic Qur'ans. Early Coptic bindings also often feature tooled or raised designs resembling cross-carpet pages and may have served as a direct influence, as attested by the binding of the St. Cuthbert Gospel.[35] Another interesting later occurrence of carpet pages is to be found within medieval Hebrew biblical manuscripts (especially those of Iberia which exhibit Islamic influence) where the threefold division into the Law, the Prophets, and the Psalms is marked by groups of carpet pages with geometric, abstract, and foliate designs

---

34   Illustrated in Alexander, *Insular Manuscripts*, figs. 12–13.
35   For the former, and for the general context for such patterned bindings in the eastern Mediterranean, see for example, Maria Cramer, *Koptische Buchmalerei* (Recklinghausen: Beitrage zur Kunst des christlichen Ostens, 1964), passim, and for the latter, Avrin, *Scribes, Script and Books*, pp. 132–33, who also points to a resemblance between the "tabula ansata" projections from the sides of such designs with the zoomorphic "escutcheons" of the Lindisfarne Gospels carpet pages, pp. 266–67. For a comparison of a Coptic binding of the seventh-eighth century (New York, Pierpont Morgan Library MS 569) with the St. Cuthbert Gospel, see Avrin, *Scribes, Scripts and Books*, p. 310. On eastern and Insular contacts in general, see Brown, "The Eastwardness of Things: Relationships between the Christian Cultures of the Middle East and the Insular World," passim.

resembling textiles, like the curtains which were lifted in the Judaic Temple to reveal sacred text.[36] The earlier existence of such features has, given the survival rate of manuscripts, often to be deduced from their occurrence in later copies, but one particularly early example of a cross with interlace fill serving as a major text divider is to be seen in Oxford, Bodleian Library MS Bruce 96, a Gnostic papyrus of the fifth-sixth century.[37] Similar sources are likely to have inspired the phenomenon in early Insular manuscripts. The Book of Durrow features six carpet pages, at the beginning and end of the book and before each gospel, most with crosses embedded within their ornament, as well as a four-symbols page in which the evangelist symbols are arranged in the quadrants of a central cross (a feature again paralleled in the Persian Diatessaron).[38] The Durrow carpet pages are accompanied by full-page miniatures of the individual evangelist symbols, the four-symbols page facing the first carpet, and decorated incipits with enlarged initials and display script (occupying only part of the page, unlike the Lindisfarne Gospels' full pages). Durrow provides the closest analogy and probable precursor for much of the Lindisfarne program (even if its evangelist miniatures do not employ the same symbolic ordering). An earlier occurrence of a carpet page is to be found as the frontispiece to the Milan Orosius (Milan, Biblioteca Ambrosiana MS D. 23. supra, folio 1v), a copy of his *Chronicon* made in the Irish foundation of Bobbio in northern Italy, part of the *parochia* of St. Columbanus, probably during the early seventh century.[39] This features a rosette or marigold, an antique symbol of life and rebirth, flanked by four smaller rosettes.

---

36 See, for example, Christopher de Hamel, *The Book. A History of the Bible* (London: Phaidon, 2001), pp. 44–45, pl. 27 for London, British Library MS Oriental MS 2628, a Hebrew bible from Lisbon, 1483.

37 Cramer, *Koptische Buchmalerei*, pl. 31.

38 Illustrated in Alexander, *Insular Manuscripts*, fig. 14 and no. 6, pls. 11, 12, 13, 20, 21, 22. A seventh, preceding Matthew's gospel, may have been lost.

39 Alexander, *Insular Manuscripts*, no. 3, pl. 6 and, for a discussion of the origins of carpet pages, see p. 11.

The Cross and the Book

Transmission of the concept of carpet pages to an Insular milieu may therefore have occurred via Italy and Ireland, or from more direct importation of manuscripts from the eastern and southern Mediterranean. They enjoy a limited currency within subsequent Insular book art and it may be useful to rehearse here the context for Lindisfarne's remarkable set. The Lichfield Gospels retain one example (as well as a four-symbols page akin to Durrow's) featuring a Latin cross which is closely related stylistically to the St. Matthew carpet page of the Lindisfarne Gospels (see Figure 1.2), although it replaces the chalice-shaped terminals of the latter with the square-shaped terminals of Lindisfarne's St. Jerome carpet page (see Figure 1.1). Codicology suggests that the Lichfield Gospels may have contained others, but if so it is surprising that Lindisfarne's St. Matthew carpet page should have served as the model for that introducing St. Luke's gospel in Lichfield, since the artist of the latter seems to have copied directly the designs of each of Lindisfarne's decorated incipit pages.[40] Perhaps, therefore, there were only ever intended to be one carpet page and one four-symbols page in the Lichfield Gospels' scheme; these introduce St. Luke's gospel, which would be appropriate as this was the one that, for exegetes such as Bede, signified Christ as the immolatory victim of the crucifixion.[41] The Latin form of the cross would have been accorded primacy as representative of the western tradition and of Roman orthodoxy, whereas the artist-scribe of the Lindisfarne Gospels was more concerned to emphasize ecumenical relationships and their ultimate harmonization through the variant forms of his carpet pages. For the crosses embedded within them adopt the following forms: the prefatory matter introducing Jerome's Latin Vulgate edition of the Gospels opens appropriately with a Latin cross (see Figure 1.1); Matthew's Gospel commences with a Latin cross with chalice-shaped terminals (see Figure 1.2);[42] Mark's Gospel

---

40   Alexander, *Insular Manuscripts*, no. 21, pl. 77.
41   Michelle P. Brown, "Embodying Exegesis," pp. 109–28.
42   See Catherine E. Karkov, "The Chalice and the Cross in Insular Art," *The*

features a ring-headed or solar cross of an ancient type which was gaining popularity in Celtic Ireland (see Figure 1.3); Luke's cross is of equal-armed Greek form with TAU-shaped attached terminals (see Figure 1.4);[43] a smaller Greek cross also features at the center of the John cross-carpet page, where it is flanked by several TAU crosses in a more fragmented or exploded design (see Figure 1.5). The TAU form, also known as the Egyptian cross or the cross of St. Anthony, was particularly favored in Coptic Egypt, Nubia, and Ethiopia. Perhaps their occurrences here, both attached to Luke's Greek cross and separated from but still in association with John's Greek cross, may have been intended to betoken the fragmentation of the churches of the Christian Orient as a result of the monothelete controversy, whilst signaling the underlying harmony and continued association of the two forms.[44]

The Maihingen Gospels from early eighth-century Echternach also retains only one carpet page which precedes St. John's gospel,[45] the Irish St. Gall Gospels has a cross-carpet page preceding the genealogy of Christ,[46] and the same position in the text is occupied by the only carpet page in the Book of Kells (in which a double-armed cross like that of Durrow is again embedded). The decoration of the Kells page is indebted to the style and zoomorphic ornament of the Lindisfarne Gospels, which it carries to further heights of complexity in its interlace, and exhibits a particular stylistic debt in its inclusion of animal-headed escutcheons on the side of the frame and in its stepped corner-pieces.[47] Other late examples of the genre

---

Age of Migrating Ideas, pp. 237–244.
43   The Greek cross was, from early Christian times, associated with the four cardinal directions, whereas the Latin form, with elongated foot, recalled the form of the cross upon which Christ was crucified.
44   Brown, *The Lindisfarne Gospels*, pp. 323–24.
45   Alexander, *Insular Manuscripts*, no. 24, pl. 119.
46   Alexander, *Insular Manuscripts*, no. 44, pl. 200.
47   Alexander, *Insular Manuscripts*, no. 52, pl. 245. Kells also features several four-symbols pages.

occur as the frontispiece to the late eighth- or early ninth-century Breton St. Gatien Gospels,[48] on a single leaf from an Irish gospel-book of similar date from St. Gall,[49] and two cross-carpet pages from an Insular book belonging to Bobbio and now known as the Turin Gospels (the volume was largely destroyed by fire, rendering interpretation of its codicological complexities difficult, but it appears that it may have been a seventh-century volume which was significantly repainted during the ninth century).[50] In Freiburg-im-Breisgau, Universitätsbibliothek, Codex 702, a gospel-book probably made at Echternach in the early eighth century, and the Kentish Stockholm *Codex Aureus,* the crosses are liberated from their own self-contained pages and are superimposed upon the text itself throughout the book, to resemble the *carmina figurata* (poems with pictorial overlays that served to isolate part of the text to form a poem within a poem).[51]

Thus, to judge from the limited surviving evidence, carpet pages could be used by Insular artists as frontispieces to books (usually gospel-books) or to mark a particular point in the text—with the interesting phenomenon of introducing the genealogy and incarnation of Christ in St. Matthew's Gospel with a cross-carpet page as well as a CHI-RHO initial, and of a cross-carpet page and four-symbols page to introduce the other gospel that treats of Christ's humanity through his crucifixion: St. Luke. In a very few of the earlier gospel-books, including Lindisfarne, they might also feature as part of a more ambitious program to introduce the work and the individual gospels. It is as if each has its own dedication cross, with the work on each major text being dedicated to the Lord.

---

48 Alexander, *Insular Manuscripts,* no. 56, pl. 273.
49 Alexander, *Insular Manuscripts,* no. 58, pl. 282.
50 Alexander, *Insular Manuscripts,* no. 61, pls. 277–78.
51 Alexander, *Insular Manuscripts,* nos. 25, pls. 117–18 and no. 30, pls. 138–39. For *carmina figurata,* see Helen Damico, "Writing/Sounding the Cross: 'The Dream of the Rood' as Figured Poetry," in this volume, pp. 166–203.

The practice of physically marking the fabric with a cross during the liturgical dedication of church buildings and altars may therefore also be relevant in interpreting the meanings of the cross-carpet pages.[52] Columban monks even extended the practice of signing with a cross to artifacts associated with their daily labors, such as the quern-stone inscribed with a cross from Dunadd (Argyll) and now in the National Museums of Scotland. Manuscripts penned in the Monkwearmouth/Jarrow scriptorium, or those exhibiting its influence like London, British Library MS Royal 1. B. vii, likewise have a small cross written in their top left-hand corner of their pages, perhaps inscribed to dedicate and invoke a blessing upon each page of the work for God.[53] I suggest that in the Lindisfarne Gospels the cross-carpet pages, along with the golden rubrics on the facing incipit pages which invoke the name of Christ and of the evangelists, serve a similar dedicatory function.

There was also, of course, a long-lived tradition relating to the talismanic function of the cross as a device to ward off evil which may have contributed to its funerary popularity and to its appearance on jewelry found in furnished Anglo-Saxon graves.[54] Such a function may also have been an aspect of its role within Insular books for, as Cassiodorus informed his readers, each word written was "a wound on Satan's body,"[55] and, to quote an inscription on a ninth-century

---

52 Carol Farr, "Lection and Interpretation: the Liturgical and Exegetical Background of the Illustrations in the Book of Kells," unpubl. PhD dissertation, University of Texas at Austin, 1989; and *The Book of Kells and its Audience* (London and Toronto: British Library and University of Toronto, 1997), pp. 44–50, 152–55.

53 This feature was adopted from earlier Italian manuscript production; see discussion in Brown, *Lindisfarne Gospels*, p. 316.

54 John Mitchell, "Script about the Cross: the Tombstones of San Vicenzo al Volturno," *Roman, Runes and Ogham*, ed. John Higgitt et al., (Oxford: Shaun Tyas, 2001), pp. 158–174; see also Stevenson, "Aspects of Ambiguity in Crosses and Interlace," pp. 1–27, and Brown, "In the Beginning" (Jarrow), pp. 11–12.

55 Cassiodorus, *Institutiones*, see PL LXX, 1144–1145; see also Michelle P. Brown and Carol Farr, ed., *Mercia: An Anglo-Saxon Kingdom in Europe* (Leicester:

funerary cross from the Carolingian monastery of San Vincenzo Al Volturno in Italy, "Crux Xpi: Confusio Diaboli Est" (the Cross of Christ confounds the devil).[56]

The metalwork analogies with the ornament of the carpet pages in both the Book of Durrow and the Lindisfarne Gospels are striking. The palette of Durrow is restricted to green, orange, and yellow, the traditional colors of Coptic and Merovingian manuscript painting, which are also used for Lindisfarne's introductory Jerome carpet page—probably as a consciously archaizing visual reference. In Lindisfarne the palette then expands into a sophisticated range of colors and tones. In the cross-carpet pages the polychromy of Insular and Germanic metalwork is summoned up, with details such as the boss at the center of the Mark carpet (folio 94v, see Figure 1.3) incorporating a *trompe-l'oeil* three-dimensionality in emulation of a raised metalwork glass boss or stud, of the sort which adorn the Ardagh chalice and the Derrynaflan paten.[57] The suggested inclusion of gilded details within Lindisfarne's carpet designs, as in the Matthew incipit page, would have further heightened this metalwork effect. A more specific analogy is probably being drawn with metalwork processional crosses which are known to have been used in an Insular milieu, as attested by the fragments of gilt copper foil and the bosses which formed one such cross found in Dumfriesshire (in the southern zone administered by Lindisfarne, and now in the National Museum of Scotland).[58] The Rupertus Cross, made on the continent under Insular influence, even features such polychrome glass paste studs set into it as bosses against inhabited vine-scroll ornament on the body of the cross.[59]

Leicester University, 2001), p. 14.
56 Mitchell, "Script about the Cross," pp. 164–65.
57 Molds for such glass bosses have also been excavated on Iona: Susan Youngs, personal communication.
58 See Richard N. Bailey, "Ambiguous Birds and Beasts: Three Sculptural Puzzles in South-West Scotland," *Fourth Whithorn Lecture*, 1995 (Whithorn: Whithorn Lecture, 1996), fig. 12.
59 See Leslie Webster and Janet M. Backhouse, *The Making of England: Anglo-Saxon Art and Culture AD 600–900* (London: British Library, 1991), no. 135, and

The free-standing stone crosses of Britain and Ireland are thought to have imported elements from the plan of such metalwork processional crosses into their designs.[60] The cross erected on Lindisfarne to commemorate Bishop Æthilwald (d. 740) and commissioned by him prior to his death, is the earliest documented example of a free-standing stone cross, although there are some earlier undated examples with cross-shapes tentatively and somewhat crudely emerging from the slabs upon which they are carved at Fahan and the St. Patrick's Cross at Carndonagh. These sculptured slabs date perhaps from the seventh or early eighth century; both are to be found on Inishowen, Co. Donegal, adjacent to Lough Foyle whence Columba sailed on his *peregrinatio* to Iona, a region therefore enshrined within the Columban federation's collective memory. When painted, as many of them undoubtedly were, the comparison would have appeared even more striking, and it is increasingly apparent that some of them carried inset metalwork bosses (some possibly holding relics), such as that which is recorded as being pried out of a cross by thieves at St. Cedd of Holy Island's foundation of Lastingham in E. Yorkshire.[61]

Sculptured crosses upon slabs may also be related to the cross-carpet pages. They occur, for example, on the aforementioned cross-slabs in Co. Donegal, in a funerary memorial context on the name-stones of Lindisfarne and Hartlepool (perhaps modeled upon Lombardic stones which also influenced the ninth-century name-stones of San Vicenzo al Volturno), on the Berechtuine slab at Tullylease in Co. Cork, and on the recumbent Irish slabs, such as those at Clonmacnoise. They

---

also no. 133. Polychrome studs also occur on the "Tara" brooch and the Moylough belt shrine and a mold for them has been excavated at Tarbat.

60 See, for example, Douglas Mac Lean, "Technique and Contact: Carpentry-constructed Insular Stone Crosses," in *From the Isles of the North*, ed. Cormac Bourke (Belfast: Her Majesty's Stationery Office, 1995), pp. 167–75.

61 Bailey, *Whithorn Lecture*, pp. 10–11. For Lastingham, see James T. Lang, *Corpus of Anglo-Saxon Stone Sculpture, III, York and Eastern Yorkshire* (Oxford: Oxford University, 1991), III, pls. 582–83.

occur prior to this on Coptic slabs, similar in size and shape to the Northumbrian name-stones, such as those preserved in the Coptic Museum in Cairo, and, in a later eastern Mediterranean context (perhaps preserving older traditions) on the memorial stones of Armenia, such as the Khatchk'ar of Aputayli, from Sewan, Noraduz Cemetery, and dating to 1225 (British Museum, MLA 1977, 5–5,1).[62]

The processional crosses that preceded the gospel-book during liturgical procession have already been mentioned. The *ambo* (pulpit) from which the Word was preached could also be adorned with a cross embedded within panels of ornament, such as that at Romainmoutiers, an Irish foundation in Switzerland, which strongly resembles a cross-carpet page with its cross embedded in interlace. Altars might also carry not only dedication crosses but more ornamental crosses, such as the eighth-century altar frontal from Flotta, Orkney, with its central panel containing a cross (now in the National Museum of Scotland).[63] There are therefore compelling analogies with other liturgical focal points—the processional cross, the altar, and the pulpit—for the design of Lindisfarne's cross-carpet pages. The gospel-book thus completes the suite of artifacts that supported the liturgy of the Word and the liturgy of the sacrament, all of them sanctified by the symbol of the cross, which is itself the sign of benediction.

A further such analogy, which has previously escaped notice, is that of carpets themselves, for the prayer mat (*oratorio*) featured in the liturgico-devotional practices of Rome, as well as of the East, as a brief examination of the development of the liturgical Veneration of the Cross in Rome will demonstrate.[64] During the first quarter

---

62 Vrej Nersessian, *Treasures from the Ark, 1700 Years of Armenian Christian Art* (London: British Library, 2001), no. 14.
63 It was the practice to dedicate altars with a cross, as, for example, those inscribed on the wooden core of the portable altar which is one of St. Cuthbert's relics.
64 For a full discussion of this subject, see Éamonn Ó Carragáin, *Ritual and the Rood: Liturgical Images and the Old English Poems of the Dream of the Rood*

of the seventh century, the tradition of the Veneration of the Cross on Good Friday was introduced to Rome, under eastern influence from Constantinople. The earliest liturgical text from Rome for the Veneration of the Cross in St. Peter's, Rome, is the *Ad crucem salutandum in sancto petro*:

> Deus qui unigeniti tui domini nostri iesu christi praetioso sanguine humanum genus redemere dignatus es, concede propitius ut qui ad adorandam uiuificam crucem adueniunt a peccatorum suorum nexibus liberentur. Per dominum.

> [God, who has deigned to allow the human race to be redeemed by the precious blood of your only-begotten son our Lord Jesus Christ, grant we beseech you that those who come to adore the life-giving cross may be freed from the bonds of their sins. Through our Lord.][65]

This occurs in the Sacramentary of Padua-Paduense,[66] and was celebrated on September 14 (as the finding of the True Cross was celebrated at Jerusalem on that date). In 614 the Persians captured Jerusalem and the relic of the True Cross. Emperor Heraclius recovered it and returned it to Jerusalem in 629, but it was still at risk and so was transferred to Constantinople in 635. Its triumphant entry—the imperial *aduentus*—was the focus of its exaltation there.[67] This developed into the formal Veneration of the Cross on Good Friday.

Tradition (London and Toronto: British Library and Toronto University, 2005), pp. 180–279.

65 English translation taken from Ó Carragáin, *Ritual and the Rood*, pp. 190–91, fig. 35.

66 *Die älteste erreichbare Gestalt des Liber Sacramentorum anni circuli der römischen Kirche*, ed. P. K. Mohlberg, (Münster: Liturgiegeschichtliche Quellen, 1927), p. 54, no. 665; text from Jean Deshusses, *Le Sacramentaire Grégorien* (Fribourg: Éditions Universitaires, 1979), I. 271 (Introit, *Hadrianum* no. 690).

67 Louis van Tongeren, "Vom Kreuzritus zur Kreuzestheologie: die Entstehungsgeschichte des Festes der Kreuzerhöhung und seine erste Ausbreitung im Westen," *Ephemerides Liturgicae* 112 (1998): 215–45 at 243–5.

The Cross and the Book

By the mid-seventh century, when the earliest Anglo-Saxon clerical pilgrims reached Rome, a mass for the Exaltation of the Cross had been composed and was used in many of the churches there. Roman liturgy emphasized the life-giving cross as an image of Christ (focusing upon John 3:14, the raising up of Christ on the cross, which also symbolizes resurrection, for "when you have raised up the Son of Man then you will realize that I am he," John 8:28). It seems to have escaped notice that the prayer mat (*oratorio*) was used to allow everyone to kneel and kiss the cross, as shown by a late eighth-century *ordo* adapted from Roman use for use north of the Alps.[68] I suggest that carpet pages may indeed be meant to recall such prayer mats, which still feature in the observances of the churches of the Christian Orient and within Islam. The adoration of the cross was followed by the Eucharist. Thus the zoomorphic decoration on the processional crosses and on the Lindisfarne cross-carpet pages summoned up the Tree of Life, celebrating the eucharistic communion of creation.

In the Burchard Gospels, at the beginning of the Passion (John 18:1), is an annotation by a Monkwearmouth/Jarrow scribe: "in ebd. maiore feria vi ad Hierusalem legitur passio dni" (in Holy Week on Friday at Jerusalem the Passion of the Lord is read), noting the Good Friday station as part of a list of the stations kept at Monkwearmouth/Jarrow. They were evidently familiar with this liturgical practice in early eighth-century Northumbria. There is also archeological evidence for stational crosses within the monastic enclosure on Lindisfarne, and references within the anonymous and Bedan lives of St. Cuthbert to pilgrims undertaking the *turas* or pilgrimage round of the "holy places" there, in accordance with both existing Irish tradition and more recent liturgical observances introduced from Rome.[69]

---

68 See Ordo XXIV, paragraphs 29–31 in Michel Andrieu, *Les Ordines Romani du haut Moyen Age*, 5 vols (Louvain: Spicilegium Sacrum Lovaniense, 1948), III. 293.

69 See Éamonn Ó Carragáin, "A Liturgical Interpretation of the Bewcastle Cross," *Medieval Literature and Antiquities: Studies in Honour of Basil Cottle*, ed. Myra Stokes and T. L. Burton (Cambridge: Cambridge University, 1987), pp.

Pope Symmachus (498–514) provided a reliquary for a chapel of the Holy Cross at the Vatican; this was adorned with gems containing a fragment of the cross, and Emperor Justin II presented another reliquary cross to the Vatican. Lindisfarne's carpet pages with their metalwork resonances might also therefore be intended to symbolize such cross reliquaries. This might account for the varied forms of cross displayed in its various cross-carpet designs. Those preceding the *Novum Opus* and St. Matthew's Gospel (see Figures 1.1 and 1.2) are of Latin form, with either square or chalice-shaped terminals; as such, they are effectively equal-armed crosses set upon shafts, as the extra terminal midway down the lower leg emphasizes, a feature also encountered on the Rupertus Cross and on several of the Lindisfarne name-stones (some of which also fill the cross with interlace), and on the Irish Tullylease slab. The cross upon a shaft or column may be of Byzantine derivation. On the churchyard slab at Carndonagh, the theme is elaborated further with a "crucifixion" set upon a column which in turn rests upon a lower cross.[70] The Lindisfarne Gospels' Mark cross (see Figure 1.3) is a Greek, equal-armed cross with a ring-head of Irish fashion.[71] Luke's is also of Greek near equal-armed form, with TAU-headed terminals (see Figure 1.4). That which precedes St. John's Gospel is of "exploded" form with a precisely symmetrical central equal-armed cross flanked by four TAU crosses. Bonne has pointed to the influence of a specific relic of the *tabula ansata* inscribed with Christ's title, which was nailed to

---

15–42; and "The City of Rome and the World of Bede," (Newcastle-upon-Tyne: Jarrow Lectures, 1994), pp. 26–27; and *Ritual and the Rood*, pp. 190–95. On early Irish pilgrimage rounds see Michael Herity, "Early Irish Hermitages in the Light of the Lives of Cuthbert," in Bonner et al., *St Cuthbert*, pp. 45–63. On the archeological and textual evidence, see the discussion in Brown, *Lindisfarne Gospels*, pp. 24–26.

70   This is thought to date from the seventh century and belongs to a region in Co. Donegal with strong Patrician and Columban traditions.

71   With some intentional disparities in measurement, as noted by Stevick, "The Design of Lindisfarne Gospels Folio 138v," pp. 3–12.

the head of the cross as an explanation for the double-armed cross (as seen in the Book of Durrow and the Book of Kells), although the "cross and crucifixion" conjunction of the Carndonagh slab may also be relevant in this respect.[72] Werner has also highlighted the possibility of a connection between the design of a cross-carpet page in the Book of Durrow and the cult of the True Cross as known at Iona.[73] Perhaps the artist of the Lindisfarne Gospels was paying visual homage to known reliquaries and buildings and/or to the different Christian traditions of East and West, as represented by their various cross types. Such visual devices would have served to reinforce the Gregorian ideal of diversity within unity, which Bede records was so important to Benedict Biscop and his community.[74] The cross would therefore stand as a potent symbol of the all-embracing *œcumen*, which transcends all human divisive structures.[75]

Above all, as we have seen, the Lindisfarne Gospels' cross-carpet pages are the embodiment of the *crux gemmata* (jeweled cross), the symbolic representation of the Godhead by means of abstract, symbolic substitution which had been favored in the Early Christian tradition. Such substitution had proven especially valuable in the face of the continuing debate concerning iconoclasm and the veneration of images. The *crux gemmata* and the gospel-book serve as the embodiment of Christ in the fifth-century mosaics of the baptistry in Ravenna, where they occupy the throne and the altar as symbols of orthodoxy.[76] In the 720s the iconoclast party in Constantinople

---

72 Bonne, "De l'Ornemental dans l'Art Médiéval," pp. 185–219.
73 Martin Werner, "The Cross-Carpet Page in the Book of Durrow: The Cult of the True Cross, Adomnan and Iona," *Art Bulletin* 72 (1990): 174–223. On a similar theme in relation to the Book of Kells, see Martin Werner, "Crucifixi, Sepulti, Suscitati: Remarks on the Decoration of the Book of Kells," *The Book of Kells*, ed. Felicity O'Mahony (Aldershot: Scolar Press, 1994), pp. 450–88.
74 Ó Carragáin, "City of Rome," pp. 26–27.
75 On the principle, see Arnold Angenendt, *Der Memorial-und Liturgiecodex von San Salvatore / Santa Giulia in Brescia*, (Hanover: Hahn, 2000), pp. 295–303.
76 Brown, *Lindisfarne Gospels*, pp. 74, 324.

tore down the effigy of Christ on the palace gate and replaced it with a cross.[77] These were very much live issues, and even though a greater tolerance towards images prevailed in the West, it did not go unquestioned, the debate continuing into the Carolingian age. The West took its cue from the letter of Gregory the Great to the iconoclast Bishop Serenus of Marseilles, around 600, in which he urged restraint on the grounds that

> it is one thing to adore a picture, another to learn what is to be adored through the history told by the picture. What scripture presents to readers, a picture presents to the gaze of the unlearned. For in it even the ignorant see what they ought to follow, in it the illiterate read. [78]

Nonetheless, a residual unease may be detected in the Insular preference for oblique, symbolic meaning rather than direct iconic representation of the Godhead. In 692 the Council in Trullo, held in Constantinople, passed a canon (no. 11) rejecting the established symbolic iconography of John the Baptist, the "Precursor," pointing to the image of Christ as the lamb for a more literal representation of the crucifixion as an image of redemption; this was a move that would contribute to an iconoclastic unease which erupted into the mob that removed the crucifix from the imperial palace gates in 726.[79] The Pope refused to subscribe to

---

77   Brown, "In the Beginning" (Jarrow), p. 2.
78   Translated in Ayerst and Fisher, *Records of Christianity*, pp. 101–2; see also Celia Chazelle, "Pictures, Books and the Illiterate: Pope Gregory I's Letters to Serenus of Marseilles," *Word and Image* 6, no. 2 (1990): 138–153; and Brown, "In the Beginning" (Jarrow), p. 4.
79   F. Cabrol and H. Leclercq, *Dictionnaire d'Archéologie Chrétienne et de Liturgie* III (Paris: Letouzey, 1914), 3083; see also the general discussion herein on the cross. The iconoclast party replaced the crucifix with a cross accompanied by a plaque which read:
"The Emperor Leo and his son Constantine/ Thought it dishonour to the Christ divine/

the Council, perhaps accounting for the prominent retention of the John the Baptist imagery on the Ruthwell and Bewcastle Crosses, but there appears to have been an initial western move in favor of depicting the crucifixion as it was advocated (seen in the Durham Gospels' crucifixion miniature) in the sculptures at Carndonagh, Co. Donegal, and in the eighth-century Athlone crucifixion plaque. This trend seems to have been subsequently toned down as tension escalated in the East, resulting in the subtler imagery of the Lindisfarne Gospels.[80] The symbolic resonance and labyrinthine complexity of the carpet pages, which must have served something of the function of prayer labyrinths (akin to those of the later Gothic cathedrals, such as Chartres) for their maker when he lost himself in meditation during their painting, make them a sophisticated example of such trends.[81] In accordance with a traditional art-historical tendency to attribute a primacy to figurative naturalism, discussions of the relationship between the Lindisfarne Gospels and the Durham Gospels have assumed that the figural image of the crucifixion in the latter represents a later development than the cross-carpet pages in the former. Principles of abstraction would tend, however, to support the opposite conclusion, that the complex abstraction and symbolism of the Lindisfarne carpet pages could be the more sophisticated and later.

That on the very palace gate he stood/ A lifeless, speechless effigy of wood./ Thus what the Book forbids they did replace/ With the believer's blessed sign of grace." Translation from Ayerst and Fisher, *Records of Christianity*, p. 102; see also Brown, "In the Beginning" (Jarrow), p. 2.

80 F. Cabrol and H. Leclercq, *Dictionnaire d'Archéologie Chrétienne et de Liturgie* III. 3083, nos. 4–5; G. Millet, 'Les Iconoclastes et la Croix', *Bulletin de Correspondence Hellénique 34* (1910), pp. 96–109; see also Éamonn Ó Carragáin, Jane Hawkes, and Ross Trench-Jellicoe, "John the Baptist and the *Agnus Dei*: Ruthwell and Bewcastle Revisited," *Antiquaries Journal* 81 (2001): 131–53.

81 Pirotte, "Le Signe de la Croix," pp. 23–45; Bonne, "De l'Ornemental dans l'Art Médiéval," pp. 185–219.

Thus an icon from the Mediterranean area, or a manuscript miniature such as that in the sixth-century Syrian Rabbula Gospels,[82] may have inspired the artist of the Durham Gospels (and the makers of other aforementioned early Insular crucifixion scenes), while the designer of the Lindisfarne Gospels took as his ultimate inspiration a more symbolic, decorative cross motif originating in the Christian Orient or Coptic Egypt and represented within the Columban tradition in the Book of Durrow.

I have already touched upon the importance of the symbolism of the cross in Northumbria. It is celebrated above all in the words of that great Anglo-Saxon poem, *The Dream of the Rood*, which is echoed upon the Ruthwell Cross.[83] Here the cross is seen as a living tree, clad in gold and set on its cross-beam with five jewels symbolizing the wounds of Christ—the cross itself becomes identified with Christ, the "angel of the Lord" (*The Dream of the Rood*, 9b–10).[84] On the early eleventh-century Anglo-Saxon Brussels reliquary cross (Treasury, Cathedral of St Michel, Brussels), the relationship is made even more explicit: this is a jeweled metalwork cross, inscribed with a distych based upon *The Dream of the Rood*'s text, which contained a relic of the cross.[85] On the processional and reliquary crosses, the sculptured crosses, and the cross-carpet pages of the Insular world, the cross appears in this guise, proudly displaying its wounds as bosses and covered with the vine-scroll, the *vitis vera* of John 15:1, symbolizing the living tree of the crucifixion and Christ as the true vine nourishing his Church. The birds and beasts inhabiting it signify not only this Church, but also all creation dwelling in a

---

82 Nersessian, *Treasures from the Ark*, no. 108.
83 Ó Carragáin, *Ritual and the Rood*, pp. 325–27.
84 Ó Carragáin, *Ritual and the Rood*, pp. 325–27; for the full text of the poem, with discussion, see Michael Swanton, ed., *The Dream of the Rood* (Manchester: Manchester University Press, 1970).
85 See the full discussion in Ó Carragáin, *Ritual and the Rood*, pp. 339–54; see also D. H. Turner and Leslie Webster, *The Golden Age of Anglo-Saxon Art* (London: British Museum, 1984), no. 75.

new paradise (Psalm 104:16).[86]

In a number of thought-provoking ways, the diptychs of cross-carpet pages and decorated incipit pages in the Lindisfarne Gospels therefore weave together a plethora of stylistic, cultural, liturgical, and exegetical allusions to create one of the most beautiful and prayerful evocations of creation sustained by the cross and the Word, to have appeared in Christian thought and art.

These are no mere pages of decoration, they are complex sacred figurae which, like prayer mats, hallow the entrance to the holy ground of sacred text, which serve to dedicate the work entailed in its transmission, and which herald the Second Coming of the Logos. The divine geometry which underpins their design echoes that of creation itself, while the creatures that inhabit their cosmos are interwoven together in a sublime rhythmic harmony. These pages do indeed symbolize the very image, or figurae, of the divine.

---

86 Karl Hauck, "Das Einhardkreuz: mit einem Anhang zu den Problemen des Rupertus-Kreuzes," *Frühmittelalterliche Studien* 8 (1974): 105–15.

Fig. 1.1: The Lindisfarne Gospels, Prefatory carpet page (London, BL Cotton Nero D.iv, folio 2v). Courtesy of the British Library Board.

Fig. 1.2: The Lindisfarne Gospels, Matthew carpet page (London, BL Cotton Nero D.iv, folio 26v). Courtesy of the British Library Board.

Fig 1.3: The Lindisfarne Gospels, Mark carpet page (London, BL Cotton Nero D.iv, folio 94v). Courtesy of the British Library Board.

The Cross and the Book

Fig. 1.4: The Lindisfarne Gospels, Luke carpet page and incipit page (London, BL Cotton Nero D.iv, folio 138v). Courtesy of the British Library Board.

Fig. 1.5: The Lindisfarne Gospels, John carpet page (London, BL Cotton Nero D.iv, folio 210v). Courtesy of the British Library Board

A Cross and an Acrostic: Boniface's Prefatory Poem to his *Ars grammatica*

David A. E. Pelteret

IN ONE OF HIS MANY SERVICES to scholarship, Timothy Reuter compiled in 1980 a little book of essays by himself and his then-colleagues at Exeter, entitled *The Greatest Englishman: Essays on St. Boniface and the Church at Crediton*.[1] At the conference on the holy cross dedicated to the memory of Timothy Reuter where this paper was first delivered, it seemed fitting to me to devote some attention to considering an acrostic poem by St. Boniface that contains the shape of the cross in its center enclosing the words *Iesus Xristus* written vertically and horizontally (see Figure 2.1).[2] Composed in the

---

1 *The Greatest Englishman: Essays on St. Boniface and the Church at Crediton*, ed. Timothy Reuter (Exeter: Paternoster Press, 1980).
2 Born ca. 675, possibly in Crediton in Devon, Boniface was martyred at Dokkum in the present-day Netherlands in 754. There is an early Life written by Willibald of Mainz: "Vita Bonifatii auctore Willibaldo," in *Vitae sancti Bonifatii archiepiscopi Moguntini*, ed. Wilhelm Levison, MGH Scriptores rerum Germanicarum in usum scholarum ex Monumentis Germaniae historicis separatim editi 57 (Hannover and Leipzig: Hahn, 1905), 1–58 (text); *The Anglo-Saxon Missionaries in Germany*, ed. and trans. Charles H. Talbot (London: Sheed and Ward, 1954), pp. 25–62 (translation). For a modern scholarly biography, see Theodor Schieffer, *Winfrid-Bonifatius und die christliche Grundlegung Europas: mit*

early eighth century, this cross poem, "Versibus, en iuuenis,"—part of Boniface's small extant poetic *oeuvre* that includes three rhythmical octosyllabic poems and twenty hexameter *enigmata* on the virtues and the vices (themselves acrostic poems)—is arguably the most complex and difficult of his verse compositions.[3]

Acrostic poetry is a little-studied genre of literature and so it might be appropriate to provide some background information.[4] Though its origins lie in Greek literature and beyond, for the present purposes we need only focus on a few Latin poets of late antiquity. Latin acrostic poems can have various forms. A purely acrostic poem consists of the

---

e. Nachw. z. Neudr., Unveränd. reprograf. Nachdr. (Darmstadt: Wissenschaftliche Buchgesellschaft, 1972), a reprint of the 1954 edition (Freiburg im Breisgau: Herder) with a bibliographical update for the period 1954–1971.

3 The three rhythmical poems are "Vale Christo ueraciter," ed. and trans. Vivien Law, "An Early Medieval Grammarian on Grammar: Wynfreth-Boniface and the *Praefatio ad Sigibertum*," Law, *Grammar and Grammarians in the Early Middle Ages*, Longman Linguistics Library (London and New York: Longman, 1997), pp. 169–87 at 172–73 (text) and 175 (translation); a verse acrostic, reading (as reconstructed by M. R. James) "NITHARDUS VIVE FELIX," in James, "Boniface's Poem to Nithardus," *English Historical Review* 29 (1914): 94; and a fragment appended to a letter addressed to Abbess Eadburg of Thanet, in *Die Briefe des heiligen Bonifatius und Lullus*, ed. Michael Tangl, MGH Epistolae Selectae 1 (Berlin: Weidmannsche Buchhandlung, 1916), pp. 8–15 (no. 10), at 15. The latest edition of the *Enigmata* is "Aenigmata Bonifatii," in *Variae collectiones aenigmatum Merovingicae ætatis*, ed. François Glorie, CCSL 133 (Turnhout: Brepols, 1968), 278–343 (with a German translation by K. I. Minst). These works are briefly discussed in Andy Orchard, *The Poetic Art of Aldhelm*, CSASE 8 (Cambridge: Cambridge University Press, 1994), pp. 61–63 and 248–53. For *enigmata* see Orchard, "Enigmata," *The Blackwell Encyclopaedia of Anglo-Saxon England*, ed. Michael Lapidge et al. (Oxford: Blackwell Publishers, 1999), pp. 171–72.

4 Ulrich Ernst provides a splendidly comprehensive introduction to the genre in *Carmen figuratum: Geschichte des Figurengedichts von den antiken Ursprüngen bis zum Ausgang des Mittelalters*, Pictura et Poesis, Bd. 1 (Cologne, Weimar and Vienna: Böhlau Verlag, 1991). For his earlier thoughts in a briefer compass, see also Ernst, "The Figured Poem: Towards a Definition of Genre," *Visible Language* 20 (1986): 8–27.

A Cross and an Acrostic

initial letters of each line being selected in such a way as to create a separate passage of text that may or may not itself form a poetic verse, which can be called a *versus intextus*. A development of this was for lines of a consistent length to be composed so that the final letters created a *versus intextus*. Technically this is called a telestich. Another development was the devising of lines so that the middle letters resulted in a *versus intextus*, forming a so-called mesostich. And a yet further development was to create patterns *within* the body of the text of a poem. The supreme example of a poet who employed all these techniques—and more—was one Publilius Optatianus Porphyrius.[5] Exiled under Constantine the Great in the early fourth century, he had the bright idea of currying favor with the emperor by creating a couple of dozen or so poems containing visible patterns of letters. Porphyrius seemingly was not a Christian—one of his poems contains the form of a pagan altar—but he did acknowledge Constantine's new-found religion by creating several poems with the emperor's special CHI-RHO symbol.[6] Porphyrius's ingenuity evidently was successful because he was permitted to return from exile. His kind of poetry may be distinguished from the simpler acrostic/mesostich/telestich form by being termed a *carmen figuratum*.[7]

---

5   *Publilii Optatiani Porfyrii Carmina*, ed. Iohannes Polara, Corpus Scriptorum Latinorum Paravianum, 2 vols (Turin: In Aedibus Io. Bapt. Paraviae et Sociorum, 1973). For an analysis of his metrics see N. Wilbur Helm, "The *Carmen Figuratum* as Shown in the Works of Publilius Optatianus Porphyrius," *Transactions and Proceedings of the American Philological Association* 33 (1902): xliii–xlix. For what is known of his life, see R. Helm, "Publilius Optatianus Porfyrius," in *Paulys Realencyclopädie der classischen Altertumswissenschaft*, Neue Bearbeitung begonnen von Georg Wissowa, fortgefürht von Wilhelm Kroll und Karl Mittelhaus, 23.2 (Sechsundvierzigster Halbband): *Psamathe bis Pyramiden* (Stuttgart: Alfred Druckenmüller Verlag, 1959), cols. 1928–36.
6   See no. xxvi, in *Carmina*, ed. Polara, 1:103–105, for the altar poem, and nos. viii, xiv, xix, and xxiv, in *Carmina*, 1:32–36, 1:57–60, 1:72–75, and 1:93–96, for the CHI-RHO poems.
7   See Helen Damico, "Writing/Sounding the Cross: *The Dream of the Rood* as Figured Poetry," in this volume, pp. 166–203, below. The Carolingian poet, Hrabanus Maurus, may be seen as his lineal descendant. See William Schipper,

The *carmen figuratum* was turned to specifically Christian purposes by Venantius Fortunatus, the late sixth-century poet who spent much of his adult life in Gaul. Four *carmina figurata* can be found amongst his extant collection of poems. Three of these appear in a collection of poems by him on the cross, a compilation that also includes his famous non-figurative poems *Vexilla regis* and *Pange lingua*.[8] One of the figurative poems contains the outline of an elaborate cross, but the one that is especially relevant in the context of Boniface's composition is "Carmen 2.5," an incomplete poem containing an acrostic, a telestich, a single cross, and a rhomboidal shape.[9]

This late-Roman figurative poetry is characterized by three distinguishing features, shaped in large measure by the manner in which Roman writing was copied in formal manuscripts. Texts of Vergil and the like were not copied in late antiquity in the way they are represented in modern editions, for originally there was no formal word division. This *scriptura continua* enabled writers, therefore, to create blocks of text that could permit the creation of a mesostich or a telestich.[10] However, the physiological demands made on readers by continuous texts required almost everyone to read them aloud

---

"Reading the Cross in Anglo-Saxon England," in *Cross and Culture in Anglo-Saxon England: Studies in Honor of George Hardin Brown*, ed. Karen Louise Jolly, Catherine E. Karkov, and Sarah Larratt Keefer, Medieval European Studies 9 (Morgantown: West Virginia University Press, 2007), pp. 321–42. I am grateful to William Schipper for sending me a copy of his paper in advance of publication.

8 "Carmina" 2.4, 2.5, 5.6 (acrostic poems), 2.2 (*Pange lingua*), 2.6 (*Vexilla regis*), in *Venanti Honori Clementiani Fortunati presbyteri Italici Opera poetica*, ed. Friedrich Leo, MGH, Auctores Antiquissimi 4.1 (Berlin: Weidmann, 1881), pp. 30–31, 32–33, 116–17, 27–28, and 34–35.

9 *Opera poetica*, ed. Leo, pp. 32–33.

10 On *scriptura continua* see Paul Saenger, *Space Between Words: The Origins of Silent Reading*, Figurae: Reading Medieval Culture (Stanford, CA: Stanford University Press, 1997), pp. 9–13. My thanks to David Ganz for bringing this book to my attention: it has been invaluable in helping me formulate my ideas about Boniface's acrostic poem.

in order to make them intelligible. Ambrose of Milan so amazed Augustine in his ability to read silently that the latter found it worthy of special comment.[11]

The second characteristic of this poetry was an immediate consequence of *scriptura continua*: it placed a heavy emphasis on the number of letters in a line and the number of lines in a poem. In "Carmen 5.6," a figurative poem on the cross sent with an accompanying letter to Bishop Syagrius of Autun, Fortunatus displayed his cleverness by creating a poem of thirty-three lines in length with the letter *M* at its center, thirty-three signifying Christ's life-span, and *M* the median letter in the Latin alphabet.[12] Each hexameter line contains thirty-three letters, a tour de force since the natural length of a Latin hexameter is more usually about thirty-seven letters.[13]

Since reading was an oral rather than a solely visual activity as it tends to be today, the poet needed to emphasize the visual dimension by drawing attention to the letters forming the *versus intexti* of the acrostic or figure. Thus came about the third characteristic of late-Roman figurative poems. In the extant collections of Porphyrius's poetry the letters forming the figures are rubricated and different colored inks are used in Venantius Fortunatus's cross poems.[14] This

---

11 Augustine, *Confessions* 6.3, in *Sancti Augustini Confessionum libri XIII, quos post Martinum Skutella iterum*, ed. Lucas Verheijen, CCSL 27 (Turnhout: Brepols, 1981), pp. 75–76.
12 Margaret Graver, "*Quaelibet Audendi*: Fortunatus and the Acrostic," *Transactions of the American Philological Association* 123 (1993): 219–45 at 230–31. She provides an edition of the poem on 244, and a convenient translation of Fortunatus's letter to Syagrius on 238–41. In his edition of Fortunatus's works (above, n. 8), Leo edits the letter on pp. 112–15.
13 Graver, "*Quaelibet Audendi*," 230.
14 Most notably in the St. Gallen, Stiftsbibliothek, Codex Sangallensis MS 196, p. 39, version of his incomplete "Carmen 2.5," where the cross itself and the rhomboid are in green letters, the letters round the edge are in brown and the rest are in red (available in an online facsimile at *www.e-codices.unifr.ch/en/csg/0196/39*). This association of the cross with red and green was not fortuitous and can be found as late as the stained glass in the west window at Chartres

kind of poetry thus was *not* cryptographic. It was the very opposite in fact: the use of color helped draw attention to the *versus intextus* that formed the acrostic or figure that might otherwise not be noticed by the person who was concentrating on reading the work aloud.

In the present state of knowledge, it is not possible to indicate with certainty how acrostic and figurative poetry reached Anglo-Saxon England and which poems were known there. The most likely channel was through the school of Archbishop Theodore and Abbot Hadrian at Canterbury in the last thirty years or so of the seventh century.[15] One of their pupils was the learned Aldhelm, later to be abbot of Malmesbury and subsequently bishop of Sherborne, who studied at Canterbury for some years, probably sometime between 670 and 675.[16] Certainly he was familiar with acrostic poetry because the prefaces to both his *Enigmata* and his *Carmen de uirginitate* are in this form.[17] The sources of his inspiration have still fully to be determined. In this connection it is relevant to mention the Latin poem

---

Cathedral, where Christ is depicted on a cross whose margin is red but whose inner coloration is green. As Martin Miller, the renowned English-speaking guide to Chartres Cathedral, pointed out to me many years ago, the red signifies the blood of Christ that was shed for the sins of humanity (cf. the black at the periphery of "Carmen 2.5") and the green prefigures Christ's resurrection that was to come, thereby offering new life to humankind.

15 *Archbishop Theodore: Commemorative Studies on his Life and Influence*, ed. Michael Lapidge, CSASE 11 (Cambridge: Cambridge University Press, 1995) provides an introduction to Theodore and his background; and *Biblical Commentaries from the Canterbury School of Theodore and Hadrian*, ed. Bernhard Bischoff and Michael Lapidge, CSASE 10 (Cambridge: Cambridge University Press, 1994), a more detailed analysis of the scholarly products of this school.

16 Orchard, *Poetic Art of Aldhelm*, pp. 3–4, and references there cited.

17 *Aldhelmi Opera*, ed. Rudolf Ehwald, MGH, Auctores Antiquissimi 15 (Berlin: Weidmann, 1919), pp. 97–99 and 350–52. See further, Rudolf Ehwald, "De aenigmatibus Aldhelmi et acrostichis," in *Festschrift Albert von Bamberg zum 1. Oktober 1905 gewidmet vom Lehrerkollegium des Gymnasium Ernestinum zu Gotha* (Gotha: Friedrich Andreas Perthes Aktiengesellschaft, 1905), pp. 1–26. For Commodianus's writings see *Commodiani Carmina*, ed. Joseph Martin, CCSL 128 (Turnhout: Brepols, 1960), pp. 1–113.

known as *Versus Sibyllae de die iudicii*. This work translates from the Greek thirty-four hexameter verses forming an acrostic found in the eighth book of the *Oracula Sibyllina*, and the translation succeeds in retaining the acrostic form.[18] Bulst has associated the translation with the circle of Theodore and Hadrian at Canterbury.[19] The sole extant manuscript preserves it with a text of Aldhelm's *Enigmata*. Michael Lapidge has ventured the suggestion that it might have provided the model for Aldhelm's prefaces, though Andy Orchard is more doubtful. Lapidge has suggested that Aldhelm was familiar with Fortunatus's eleven-book collection of occasional verse, in which case he may well have encountered the latter's acrostic poems.[20] Orchard has also noted

---

18 The *Oracula Sibyllina* is a substantial collection of oracles written in Greek that draws on a variety of religious traditions, Jewish, Hellenistic, and Christian. Assembled in its current form in the sixth century, the oracles range in date from the mid-second century B.C.E. to the fourth century C.E. There is a convenient English translation by J. J. Collins in *The Old Testament Pseudepigrapha*, vol. 1: *Apocalyptic Literature and Testaments*, ed. James H. Charlesworth (London: Darton, Longman and Todd, 1983), pp. 317–472.

19 Walther Bulst, "Eine anglo-lateinische Übersetzung aus dem Griechischen um 700," *Zeitschrift für deutsches Altertum und deutsche Literatur* 75 (1938): 105–11 at 109–11; reprinted in his *Lateinisches Mittelalter: Gesammelte Beiträge*, ed. Walter Berschin, Supplemente zu den Sitzungsberichten der Heidelberger Akademie der Wissenschaften, Philosophisch-historische Klasse, Band 3, Jahrgang 1983 (Heidelberg: Carl Winter Universitätsverlag, 1984), pp. 57–63 at 61–63. Bernhard Bischoff, *Mittelalterliche Studien: Ausgewählte Aufsätze zur Schriftkunde und Literaturgeschichte*, 3 vols (Stuttgart: Anton Hiersemann, 1966–81), 1:154–55, cites Bulst without taking a specific position on the matter. This version of the poem is placed in its literary historical setting by Patrizia Lendinara, "The *Versus Sibyllae de die iudicii* in Anglo-Saxon England," in *Apocryphal Texts and Traditions in Anglo-Saxon England*, ed. Kathryn Powell and Donald Scragg, Publications of the Manchester Centre for Anglo-Saxon Studies 2 (Cambridge: D. S. Brewer, 2003), pp. 85–101 at 95–96 (a reference that I owe to Michael Lapidge).

20 Richard W. Hunt, "Manuscript Evidence for Knowledge of the Poems of Venantius Fortunatus in Late Anglo-Saxon England," *ASE* 8 (1979): 279–95, Appendix by Michael Lapidge, "Knowledge of the Poems in the Earlier Period," at 289. Orchard provides further evidence of Aldhelm's knowledge of Fortunatus's work in *Poetic Art of Aldhelm*, pp. 191–95.

that two acrostic-telestich poems whose first and last letters read "SEDULIUS ANTISTES" circulated with Sedulius manuscripts in late Anglo-Saxon England. The preface to Aldhelm's *Enigmata* had the same acrostic-telestich form and Sedulius was a major influence on him, though unfortunately the two poems offer no convincing verbal parallels.[21] One must not, however, exclude the possibility that the form came to Aldhelm from Welsh or Irish sources,[22] and that he essayed this form in order to prove that he was the equal of his Celtic-speaking contemporaries.

Boniface was so intimately familiar with Aldhelm's writings that he naturally absorbed phrases and verbal patterns from him.[23] This led the formidably learned Paul Lehmann astray, when in 1931 he published in full for the first time the text of a letter addressed to Sigeberht that forms part of the prefatory material to Boniface's *Ars grammatica*—and ascribed it to Aldhelm,[24] only to be corrected

---

21 Orchard, *Poetic Art of Aldhelm*, pp. 165–66.
22 I owe the suggestion to David R. Howlett.
23 A cursory examination of Aldhelm's *Carmen de uirginitate* and his *Enigmata* (*Aldhelmi Opera*, ed. Ehwald, 350–471 and 97–149 respectively) has revealed the following exact parallels: *Dapsilis* in line 20 as the initial word in a line (see *De uirg.* 2517) and *regnator Olimpi* in line 24 (see *De uirg.* 108 and 1197), as well as the following close metrical/verbal parallels: *stipabunt pace tribunal* in line 9 (cf. *De uirg.* 2882: *stipant sublime tribunal*), *sub Tartara trusi* in line 15 (cf. *De uirg.* 2552: *sub tristia Tartara trusit*), *Omnipotens genitor* in line 22 (cf. *Enig.* 91.1: *Omnipotens auctor*) and *Grammate doctor* in line 36 (cf. *De uirg.* 1382: *grammate biblis*). Cf. also n. 55 below. No doubt more borrowings and parallels could be found.
24 Paul Lehmann, "Ein neuentdecktes Werk eines angelsächsischen Grammatikers vorkarolingischer Zeit," *Historische Vierteljahrschrift* 26 (1931): 738–56 at 752, reprinted in Lehmann, *Erforschung des Mittelalters: Ausgewählte Abhandlungen und Aufsätze*, 5 vols (Stuttgart: Anton Hiersemann, 1959–62), 4:148–71 at 158. To be fair to Lehmann, he did allow the possibility that the poem might be from Aldhelm's circle. In response to Fickermann (see n. 25 below), he published a further paper, "Die Grammatik aus Aldhelms Kreise," *Historische Vierteljahrschrift* 27 (1932): 758–71, which he appended to the reprint of his 1931 article at 162–71.

A Cross and an Acrostic

in print some months later by Norbert Fickermann.[25] Fickermann made the connection between Boniface's *carmen figuratum* addressed to Dud(d), the letter to Sigeberht, and the *Ars grammatica*. Since that time, Boniface's authorship of the three works and their close association have been accepted, not least because there is on the verso of the Würzburg manuscript of the poem an invaluable gloss on it drawn from Boniface's introductory letter addressed to Sigeberht.[26] The extract from Boniface's letter explains the form of the poem:

> Nam prior pars circuli huius usque ad medium crucis quibusdam pentametris intersertis decurrens pinguitur uersibus, qui licet <non> pedestri remigio tranent, non tamen heroici nec omnino perfecti decurs[i] esse noscuntur. P[ost] crucem autem supradictam in circulo heroici uersus et perfecti decursant.

> [For the first part of this circle, down to the middle of the cross, is embellished with some pentameter verses interspersed, which although they do <not> splash around in prose, none the less are acknowledged not to be flowing down in heroic form [i.e. hexameter] nor in any sense perfect. After the aforementioned cross in the circle, however, the verses flow down in perfect heroic form.][27]

---

25   Norbert Fickermann, "Nachrichten 408," *Neues Archiv der Gesellschaft für ältere deutsche Geschichtskunde* 49 (1930–32): 762–64 at 763–64.

26   See Figure 2.2. The letter itself is edited in *Bonifatii (Vynfreth) Ars grammatica*, ed. George John Gebauer and Bengt Löfstedt, CCSL 133B (Turnhout: Brepols, 1980), pp. 9–12. The portions of the text cited on folio 44v are on p. 11, lines 87–91 and 93–94. The extract in the Würzburg manuscript is not textually flawless but it does preserve a better reading in *decursant* than the *decurrant* of the three manuscripts of Sigeberht's letter. For a diplomatic transcript see the *apparatus criticus* of the edition of Boniface's poem, below in Appendix 1, p. 90.

27   Like the three complete manuscript texts of Sigeberht's letter, the Würzburg manuscript omits *non* and has *decursa* for *decursi*; unlike them it incorrectly reads *praeter* instead of *post*, but is the only manuscript to preserve the reading *decursant*. My translation has been influenced by the translation of the relevant

All three texts thus rightly appear in Löfstedt's Corpus Christianorum edition of the *Ars grammatica*.

Boniface's *Ars grammatica* did not seek to be an original work. As Vivien Law has explained: "Boniface sees his role as that of the florilegist: to select the best and unite it in a single work."[28] He drew on at least a dozen sources, sometimes recasting to make the text clearer and occasionally selecting his own examples. Because he uses his original name Wynfreth in the poem addressed to Dudd, it is assumed that he compiled his grammar early in his career when he was still at the monastery of Nursling, certainly before C.E. 719 when he received the name Boniface, and quite probably before C.E. 716 when his missionary work began.[29]

Unusually for a writer, Boniface explains his working methods in the letter to Sigeberht mentioned above. It appears with his *Ars grammatica* in only a single manuscript, Paris, Bibliothèque Nationale de France MS lat. 17959, and otherwise seems to have had a separate transmission history. Lehmann's misattribution is perfectly understandable, since one of the manuscripts, Trier, Stadtbibliothek MS 1104 (1321) ascribes the text to Aldhelm.[30] Unfortunately nothing has been unearthed so far that could enable one to identify Sigeberht, the recipient of this introductory letter.

The difficulty scholars had in associating the poem with the prefatory letter and the *Ars grammatica* suggests that it would be wise to examine the poem's manuscript context first before we consider the contents of the poem itself. It survives in but one manuscript of ninth-century date, copied, according to Bischoff and Hofmann, by Mainz scribes, whence it passed to the Cathedral Library at Würzburg and is now in the University Library there on folio 44r of MS M.p.th.f.

---

portions of Boniface's letter in Law, "Early Medieval Grammarian," p. 175.
28 Law, "Early Medieval Grammarian," pp. 179–80.
29 Law, "Early Medieval Grammarian," p. 169. On Boniface's names see further below, p. 64 and n. 37.
30 For more information on the transmission history of the letter see Law, "Early Medieval Grammarian," pp. 169–70.

29.[31] The extant text can hardly be described as elegantly copied, as the facsimile shows. One should forbear, however, from engaging in that favorite sport of scholars, scribe-bashing. Paul Meyvaert, who has recently reconstructed Bede's computistical calendar attached to *De temporum ratione* in a brilliant piece of literary detective work, has emphasized how important it is to note what a medieval scribe actually conveys to us.[32] If the text appears slovenly, we should ask ourselves why this is so, rather than decry it. It is a question that will be asked shortly.

It is clear that Boniface's poem has had a checkered history. It is dedicated to one Dud(d) or possibly Dudda. A letter of Boniface of 735, which rather unusually identifies him by both his Anglo-Saxon name, Wynfreth, and his Christian name, Boniface, is addressed to a "Duddo abbati."[33] A charter of 739 mentioning Forthhere, bishop of Sherborne (Aldhelm's old see), includes in its short witness list the "signum manus Duddi abbatis."[34] And "Dud abba" also finds mention in another charter from 744 or 745, relating to Glastonbury.[35] Dud(d) and its variants are quite

---

31 Bernard Bischoff and Josef Hofmann, *Libri Sancti Kyliani: Die Würzburger Schreibschule und die Dombibliothek im VIII. und IX. Jahrhundert* (Würzburg: Kommissionsverlag Ferdinand Schöningh, 1952), p. 46 and see also pp. 135–36. The manuscript is catalogued in *Die Handschriften der Universitätsbibliothek Würzburg, 3.1: Die Pergamenthandschriften der ehemaligen Dombibliothek*, ed. Hans Thurn (Wiesbaden: Otto Harrassowitz, 1984), pp. 21–22.
32 Paul Meyvaert, "Discovering the Calendar (*Annalis libellus*) attached to Bede's Own Copy of *De temporum ratione*," *Analecta Bollandiana* 120 (2002): 5–64.
33 Tangl, *Die Briefe des heiligen Bonifatius und Lullus*, no. 34, pp. 58–59 at 58, line 20 (text); *The Letters of Saint Boniface*, no. XXV [34], trans. with an introduction, Ephraim Emerton, Records of Civilization, Sources and Studies 31 (New York: Columbia University Press, 1940), pp. 63–64 (translation).
34 *Cartularium Saxonicum: A Collection of Charters relating to Anglo-Saxon History*, ed. W. de Gray Birch, 3 vols and index (London, Whiting and Co., Charles J. Clark and Phillimore and Co., 1885–99), 3:668 (no. 1331 [1598]); see also Peter H. Sawyer, *Anglo-Saxon Charters: An Annotated List and Bibliography*, Royal Historical Society Guides and Handbooks, no. 8 (London: Royal Historical Society, 1968), no. 255.
35 Birch, *Cartularium Saxonicum*, 1:243 (no. 168); see also Sawyer, *Anglo-Saxon*

common names in Anglo-Saxon sources, but the date and associations of these latter texts are appropriate to the addressee of this poem.[36]

Wynfreth himself received his Christian name of Boniface on 15 May 719 on his first visit to Rome, being named by Pope Gregory II after a martyr venerated in Rome on 14 May.[37] As already mentioned, thereafter Boniface did not usually employ his birth name except in a few letters to English recipients such as Dud(d).[38] The poem presumably dates from before he received his new name and perhaps even before 716, when he first went to Frisia.[39] According to the acrostic in Boniface's poem, Dud(d) was a master (*magister*); if he was the same as the Dudd mentioned in the charters, he evidently had yet to attain the high-status rank of abbot.

There is strong presumptive evidence that when Boniface moved to the continent he took with him—or arranged subsequently to have sent—a copy or copies of his *Ars grammatica*. The evidence, though indirect, is two-fold. First, there is an eighth-century booklist from St. Kilian's, Würzburg, that includes a volume described as "grammatica sancti augustini et sancti bonifati [*sic*]."[40] It would have been natural

---

Charters, no. 257.

36 For other examples of Dudd and its variants, see *The Prosopography of Anglo-Saxon England* database: *http://www.pase.ac.uk/* (27 May 2005), and see also Mats Redin, *Studies on Uncompounded Personal Names in Old English: Inaugural Dissertation* (Uppsala: Edv. Berlings Boktryckeri, 1919), pp. 16, 62–63, 115, 126, 140, 145, 149, 152–53, 154, 158, 169–70.

37 See Wilhelm Levison, "Willibrordiana," *Neues Archiv der Gesellschaft für ältere deutsche Geschichtskunde* 33 (1907–8): 517–30 at 525–30, reprinted in *Aus rheinischer und fränkischer Frühzeit: Ausgewählte Aufsätze von Wilhelm Levison* (Düsseldorf: Verlag L. Schwann, 1948), pp. 330–41 at 337–41.

38 Levison, "Willibrordiana," 526 (*Aus rheinischer und fränkischer Frühzeit*, p. 338).

39 Law, "Early Medieval Grammarian," p. 169.

40 E. A. Lowe, "An Eighth-Century List of Books in a Bodleian Manuscript from Würzburg and its Probable Relation to the Laudian *Acts*," *Speculum* 3 (1928): 3–15 at 6, item 31, and pl. I, opposite 6, reprinted in his *Palaeographical Papers 1907–1965*, ed. Ludwig Bieler, 2 vols (Oxford: Clarendon Press, 1972), 1: 239–50 at 242, item 31, and pl. 27.

for a text by Boniface to have been present at Würzburg since he had assigned the see to his compatriot, Burghard. In the second place, Mainz was important in Boniface's mission to the continent: it was his personal see.[41] We are unlikely ever to recover the circumstances as to why Boniface's *carmen figuratum* was copied by a Mainz scribe in the ninth century but we need hardly be surprised that it was copied there or that it ended up at St. Kilian's.

Nor should we be taken aback that the text has manifest flaws in it. Wilhelm Levison noted on the basis of the mistakes in the manuscripts identified by Tangl that scribes seemed to have had difficulties with copying the letters of Boniface and Lull.[42] If Malcolm Parkes has correctly identified Boniface's hand,[43] we can understand how his insular cursive minuscule could have led continental-born scribes astray.

Scribal mistakes can, however, be very informative. Let us put aside the easy confusion of *flumina* ("rivers") in line 2 instead of

---

41 Wilhelm Levison, *England and the Continent in the Eighth Century: The Ford Lectures delivered in the University of Oxford in the Hilary Term, 1943* (Oxford: Clarendon Press, 1946), p. 87.

42 Levison, *England and the Continent*, p. 286; see also Michael Tangl, "Studien zur Neuausgabe der Bonifatius-Briefe. (I. Teil)," *Neues Archiv der Gesellschaft für ältere deutsche Geschichtskunde* 40 (1916): 639–790 at 652–62.

43 M. B. Parkes, "The Handwriting of St Boniface: A Reassessment of the Problems," *Beiträge zur Geschichte der deutschen Sprache und Literatur* 98 (Tübingen edition) (1976): 161–79; reprinted with additional notes in Parkes, *Scribes, Scripts and Readers: Studies in the Communication, Presentation and Dissemination of Medieval Texts* (London and Rio Grande, OH: Hambledon Press, 1991), pp. 121–42. However, Michael Lapidge regards the identification of Boniface's hand still to be an open question; see Lapidge, "Autographs of Insular Latin Authors of the Early Middle Ages," *Gli autografi medievali: Problemi palaeografici e filologici. Atti del convegno di studio della Fondazione Ezio Franceschini, Erice, 25 settembre–2 ottobre 1990*, ed. Paolo Chiesa and Lucia Pinelli, Quaderni di cultura mediolatina 5 (Spoleto: Centro Italiano di Studi sull'Alto Medioevo, 1994), pp. 103–36 + 8 plates at 115. Hartmut Hoffmann, "Autographa des früheren Mittelalters," *Deutsches Archiv für Erforschung des Mittelalters* 57 (2001): 1–62, concludes (p. 17) "wird man sie höchstens als Hypothese akzeptieren können," ("it could be accepted at most as an hypothesis").

fulmina ("thunderings")⁴⁴ and consider instead the appearance of *tentibus* in line 26 for what the acrostic shows must have originally been *gentibus*. How could such a mistake have come about? The presence of a rustic capital *T* suggests an answer. With the exception of one other rustic capital *T* at the beginning of the ante-penultimate line, the scribe has employed a mixture of uncial script (best represented in a modern font by the letters *a, G, R,* and *S,* all employed consistently in the extant text, and *B*, which is used once) and semi-uncial (*b* once and *e* consistently) to record the *versus intexti*. Now the *G* of insular semi-uncial is not unlike a semi-uncial *T*, except that it has a tail.⁴⁵ If that tail had become rubbed or, perhaps, had merged with a lower letter, a copyist might easily have mistaken it for a *T*, which was then written with a rustic capital, either through a lapse in concentration or because rustic script came more naturally to him or her.

What this suggests is that the scribe has correctly reported that an earlier copy of the text used a display script (and most likely an insular semi-uncial because of the shape of the *G*). The concept of a hierarchy of scripts seems to have been an insular invention.⁴⁶ If the scribes of the Wearmouth-Jarrow scriptorium employed a hierarchy in their manuscripts, there seems no reason to doubt that southern scribes were familiar with the practice, not least because of Aldhelm's period of study under Theodore, who in turn was in contact with Northumbria. I would suggest that the display script for the *versus intexti* in this poem goes back to Boniface himself. The literary significance of this

---

44 All the textual emendations are reported in the edition printed in Appendix 1, below.

45 See Figure 2.1, lines 14 (*G*, twice) and 7 (*T*), and cf. the *t* in *ut* in line 13.

46 T. Julian Brown, "The Irish Element in the Insular System of Scripts to circa A.D. 850," in *Iren und Europa in früheren Mittelalter*, ed. Heinz Löwe, Veröffentlichungen des Europa Zentrums Tübingen, Kulturwissenschaftliche Reihe, 2 vols (Stuttgart: Klett-Cotta, 1982), 1:101–19 at 101–2; reprinted in *A Palaeographer's View: The Selected Writings of Julian Brown*, ed. Janet Bately, Michelle P. Brown, and Jane Roberts (London: Harvey Miller Publishers, 1993), pp. 201–20 at 201–2.

A Cross and an Acrostic

is something we shall have to return to. Here it is sufficient to note that it appears to mark an innovation in the scribal representation of figurative verse, where previously color would have been used.

Before we leave the matter of display scripts, however, it is necessary to discuss a further editorial emendation, this time one made by Löfstedt.[47] The facsimile shows that the vertical presentation of the words *Iesus Xristus* is in majuscules; the horizontal equivalent is in minuscules, except for the initial letter *I*. The horizontal representation, *Iesus cristus*, ignores the Greek CHI of the vertical and thus inserts a superfluous *c*. Löfstedt has proceeded in his edition to eliminate both the CHI and the minuscule *c* and replace it with *Ch*. Thus the editor of this poem on the cross, which contains a representation of the cross at the mid-point in the poem (the horizontal arms of the cross are on line 19 of the thirty-eight line poem), has proceeded to eliminate the cruciform letter CHI from the interstices of the arms of the cross, which from a visual point of view at least is the very center of the poem. A stunning literary representation of *Iesus Xristus* on the cross has thus been destroyed.[48]

I strongly suspect, from the presence of the majuscule *I* in line 19, that Boniface originally employed the same display script for the horizontal representation of *Iesus Xristus* as he did the vertical, with the two of them sharing the letter CHI in common. Visually this would make sense with a majuscule script then filling both the horizontal *and* the vertical arms of the cross.

Two further features, the choice of vocabulary and the tortuous syntax, are probably best addressed by translating the *versus intexti* and the opening lines of the poem before moving on to examine its overall structure and contents. We shall have a considerable advantage in undertaking this task of interpretation now that Boniface's prefatory letter

---

47 *Bonifatii (Vynfreth) Ars grammatica*, ed. Gebauer and Löfstedt, p. 5, line 19.
48 Regrettably this is not the only defect of this edition. See the lengthy and detailed review of the volume by Vivien Law in *Studi Medievali*, 3rd ser., 22 (1981): 752–64.

to his *Ars grammatica* addressed to Sigeberht is to hand, because in it Boniface tells us what he had in mind when he composed the work.[49]

Let us start with the hexameter couplet that forms the acrostic and telestich (read from top to bottom, with line 1 being the acrostic on the left and line 2 the telestich on the right). The couplet is also found in what Boniface in his letter calls the "circuitum quadrangulum," the four-angled or diamond-shaped circle (also read from top to bottom, but line 1 is on the right and line 2 on the left; the initial letter of both lines, *V*, forms the apex of the rhomboid and the final letter of the two lines, *M*, forms its base). The *versus intexti* declare:

VYNFRETH PRISCORUM DVDDO CONGESSERAT ARTEM
VIRIBUS ILLE IVGIS IVVAVIT IN ARTE MAGISTRVM.

Before discussing the difficulties of the Latin text, we might essay the following translation:

> Wynfreth had assembled for Dud(d) the art [of grammar] of the ancients. With his mental ability (literally "mental strength") he continuing without intermission helped the master (i.e., Boniface) in the *Art [of Grammar]* (i.e., Boniface's textbook).

Georg Laubmann, who produced the *editio princeps* with a commendably thorough commentary, fails to translate this passage;[50] Ehwald

---

49 *Bonifatii (Vynfreth) Ars grammatica*, ed. Gebauer and Löfstedt, pp. 9–12. For the text and a valuable translation see Law, "Early Medieval Grammarian," pp. 170–73 (text) and 173–75 (translation). Her translation of this text will be cited hereinafter.

50 "Mittheilungen aus Würzburger Handschriften. I: Ein acrostisches Gedicht von Winfried Bonifatius," *Sitzungsberichte der philosophisch-philologischen und historischen Classe der k[öniglich] b[ayerische] Akademie der Wissenschaften zu München*, Jahrgang 1878, Erster Band (Munich: Akademische Buchdruckerei F. Straub, 1878), pp. 1–20. Laubmann evidently consulted Ernst Dümmler before publication as he reports several conjectural readings and interpretations made by the latter (pp. 13–17).

A Cross and an Acrostic

thought that Dudd was the author; Fickermann paraphrases the acrostic; Ruppel comments that the content of the poem is very difficult to understand and cunningly then proceeds to quote the Latin; and even Ernst, who presents a German translation of the main text, quotes Lehmann rather than supply his own translation.[51] Fickermann at least offers some help: he recognizes that one of the ambiguous words was the Latin *ars*—and that in this context it must mean *ars grammatica*.[52] In his letter to Sigeberht, Boniface makes a virtue of plundering the works of earlier grammarians by saying that if "anyone . . . should feel inclined to lacerate these modest rules of the art of grammar . . . [i]t is not some living rustic whom he harasses with his hostile darts, but the dust and ashes of defunct rhetors."[53] I would interpret his first line to mean, therefore, that Boniface had taught Dud(d) the art of grammar based on late antique sources. In return Dud(d) had assisted through his mental ability (*uiribus*) his master, Boniface, in the latter's compiling of his textbook, *The Art of Grammar*.

---

51 Ehwald, "De aenigmatibus Aldhelmi et acrostichis," 22–23; Norbert Fickermann, "Der Widmungsbrief des hl. Bonifatius," *Neues Archiv der Gesellschaft für ältere deutsche Gechichtskunde* 50 (1933–35): 210–21 at 217; Aloys Ruppel, "Der heilige Bonifatius als Dichter," in *Universitas: Dienst an Wahrheit und Leben. Festschrift für Bischof Dr. Albert Stohr im Auftrag der Katholisch-Theologischen Fakultät der Johannes Gutenberg-Universität Mainz*, ed. Ludwig Lenhart, 2 vols (Mainz: Matthias-Grünewald-Verlag, 1960), 2:28–41 at 35; Ernst, *Carmen figuratum*, p. 165 n. 59, citing Lehmann, "Ein neuentdecktes Werk," in *Erforschung des Mittelalters*, 4:168.
52 Fickermann, "Der Widmungsbrief des hl. Bonifatius," 217, points out that the two lines of the acrostic refer to each other "mit einem hübschen Wortspiel zwischen *artem* und *arte*: 'Vynfreth hatte einst Dudd in der Grammatik unterrichtet, Dudd half nun seinem Lehrer bei dieser Grammatik'" ("with a charming play on words between *artem* and *arte*: 'Wynfreth had at one time taught Dudd grammar, Dudd has now helped his teacher in this grammar'").
53 "si quis . . . has grammaticae artis normulas . . . lacerare uoluerit, sciat se . . . non uiuentem rusticum infestis iaculis insequi, sed puluerem mortuorum rethorum et cinerem sagittare:" Law, "Early Medieval Grammarian," pp. 171, lines 57–64 (text) and 174 (translation).

The most difficult word in these two lines is *iugis*. Having seen the ablative plural *uiribus*, some readers might assume that *iugis* represents the ablative plural of the word *iugum* (meaning "yoke") and in consequence would get themselves into a real pickle. In fact, the word *iugis* here is a masculine third-declension adjective in the nominative case meaning (to quote the *Dictionary of Medieval Latin from British Sources*) "continuing without intermission, constant, continual,"[54] a sense that here is perfectly apposite.

The first three lines of the poem itself present some further pitfalls for the beginner in Latin: "Versibus, en iuuenis, durant et carmina cantu, / ymnos namque Dei, ymnica dicta uiri / nisibus eximiis renouantis carmina lector." In contrast to a single form like *iugis* that could have two different meanings, other quite different words such as *uersus*, *carmen*, and *cantus* could be identical in meaning. Then, something that was a discrete word could appear in *scripta continua* simply to be a syllable, as in the case of the two letters *en*, which happen in line 1 to represent an interjection but more usually form the second syllable of the common word *nomen*. Added to this cunning selection of words is the convoluted syntax. I would interpret these three lines to mean: "Lo, young reader, through verse and poetry the songs of a man [who is] renewing with exceptional pains [his] poetry enable the hymns of God, the hymnal words, to endure."

Thus the first and last words of the initial line are linked by *et*; the word *carmina* in line 1 is to be associated with *uiri* at the end of line 2; the latter word in turn is qualified by a genitive participle *renouantis* in line 3 that has *carmina* of line 3 as its object.

Rather than a line-by-line translation and *explication de texte* of all the remaining thirty-five verses of the poem it is perhaps more useful to draw attention to some other aspects of the text. First

---

54 *Dictionary of Medieval Latin from British Sources*, Fascicule V: *I–J–K–L*, ed. David R. Howlett et al. (Oxford: Published for The British Academy by Oxford University Press, 1997), p. 1510, s.v. *jugis* 1.

let us consider the words *ruricolae* in line 31 and *rurigenae* in line 35. These are not neologisms but good Ovidian words.[55] They are amongst the few substantives in Latin that, like the noun *nauta*, "a sailor," are first-declension nouns with a masculine gender. Here Boniface has been very clever. In lines 30 and 31 he says: "Egregium regem, gnatum, praeconia faustum / ruricolae iugiter dicant cum carmine clara" (the clear commendations of the country-dweller[56] perpetually declare in poetry that [you] are the distinguished King, the Son, the auspicious one), and in lines 32 to 36 he goes on to request: "quod feruens . . . signabat Abisag / totum . . . / architenens altor, qui sidera clara gubernas, / rurigenæ præsta" (O foster-father holding the arch [of heaven], who governs the shining stars, manifest to [this] country bumpkin all that the fiery Abisag signified).

God, of course, is a foster-father because Boniface had a natural father. The first of the two words, *ruricolae*, might at first sight seem to be in the nominative plural as the subject of *dicant* but is, in fact, in the genitive singular, dependent on *praeconia . . . clara*, which, as a neuter plural (with an ending like a first declension noun in the nominative), is the real subject of the verb. The second, *rurigenæ*, refers

---

55   *Ruricola* is a word used by several classical Latin authors such as Ovid and also by Aldhelm (*Carmen de uirg.* 2495) but *rurigena* is a much rarer word, most notably being used in Ovid's *Metamorphoses* 7.765. There is always the possibility that words such as this could have been preserved as an extract in a *florilegium* but the use of both words perhaps indicates that Ovid was included amongst the classical authors in whom Boniface was schooled. A poem devoted to changes might be particularly appealing in an England where conversion was a relatively recent phenomenon and where miracles were transformations that holy persons could perform through God's grace. It should be noted, however, that Michael Lapidge (personal communication) would place less emphasis on the Ovidian association: he considers the word elements to be banal and that anyone could thus have created the word without having read Ovid.

56   As Laubmann rightly points out ("Mittheilungen," p. 17, vv. 34–36), *ruricolae* refers to Boniface himself.

like the first word to Boniface but is in the dative case. Boniface's description of his grammar in his letter to Sigeberht applies equally to his poem:

> Tibi igitur non uideatur fortuitu factum, quod in quinque declinationibus nominum tam multa ad exemplum uniuscuiusque generis uel declinationis diuersis litteris uel syllabis terminata ad exemplum posita repperies. Sed hac de re me coaceruatim talia conposuisse scies, quia singulae terminationes nominum paene singulis quibusque generibus congruere uidentur—sicut sunt quaedam specie masculina sensu feminina, quaedam e contrario specie feminina uirtute masculina.

> [Do not think that it is by chance that in the discussion of the five declensions of nouns you will find so many examples of nouns ending in different letters and syllables in each gender and declension. You will realize that I have piled up all this material because the individual terminations of nouns very nearly correspond to the individual genders; thus, there are some nouns which are masculine in form and feminine in meaning, while others are the other way around: feminine in form and masculine in force.][57]

The word *ruricolae* itself contains a wealth of meaning. Its most obvious function is to express a modesty topos. Venantius Fortunatus, in the covering letter to his *carmen figuratum* on the holy cross addressed to Syagrius, had declared that he was but a rustic—and Boniface does much the same in his letter to Sigeberht when he claims that "me paene de extremis Germaniae gentibus ignobili stirpe procreatum" (I was born of ignoble stock amongst virtually the remotest tribes of Germany).[58] Like Fortunatus, Boniface is thus ostensibly claiming to be of a humble and untutored origin

---

57 Law, "Early Medieval Grammarian," pp. 171–72, lines 67–74 (text) and 174 (translation).
58 Law, "Early Medieval Grammarian," pp. 171, lines 49–50 (text) and 174 (translation).

while proving with this poem what a learned person he was. Yet, as has just been shown, *ruricolae* also serves the mundane function of alerting the student to the fact that a Latin noun could be "feminine in form and masculine in force" and, what is more, could have a termination that could easily trap the novice reader into construing it incorrectly. Poetry, by packing many meanings into single words, is the most concise of literary forms and this passage reveals Boniface to be an adept at it.

Boniface's letter to Sigeberht goes on to provide the very *raison d'être* for his poem: "peritia grammaticae artis in sacrosancto scrutinio laborantibus ad subtiliorem intellectum, qui frequenter in sacris scripturis inseritur, ualde utilis esse," ([A] knowledge of the art of grammar is extremely useful to those who are toiling over their sacred studies to find the subtler meaning which is often concealed in the Holy Scriptures).[59] *Ruricolae* has already displayed in its use of irony one kind of "subtler meaning;" other kinds can easily be found. Someone who reads this poem for the first time is surely going to be brought up short by the two names "Magog" and "Abisag." Magog is reported without comment in Genesis 10: 3 to have been one of the seven sons of Japheth, who in turn was one of the three sons of Noah. "The land of Magog" is mentioned in one of Ezekiel's visions described in Ezekiel 38 and 39, where, however, the object of the prophet's ire is Gog, a general of two other sons of Japheth. As we shall see later, these Old Testament references have their relevance to the poem but are not the primary allusion being made here by Boniface. Instead, he is clearly referring to a dramatic part of the Revelation of St. John that drew on Ezekiel. After a millennium of peace, Satan, it is prophesied, will be loosed from his prison, ". . . et [Satanas] exibit et seducet gentes quae sunt super quattuor angulos terrae Gog et Magog et congregabit eos in proelium quorum est sicut harena maris." In the Douay-Rheims Version this text in Revelation 20: 7 is translated as: ". . . and [Satan] shall go forth, and seduce the

---

59 Law, "Early Medieval Grammarian," pp. 172, lines 77–79 (text) and 174 (translation).

nations, which are over the four quarters of the earth, Gog and Magog, and shall gather them together to battle, the number of whom is as the sand of the sea," with the outcome (verses 9–10) that "the devil, who seduced them, was cast into the pool of fire and brimstone, where both the beast and the false prophet shall be tormented day and night for ever and ever." The reference to Magog in Revelation 20 seems to be quite straightforward, but one must remember that in many works of literature an allusion can take on further resonances as one proceeds through the text, demanding that the reader explore the text anew with the insights gained from the initial perusal. A return to Magog later will prove to be desirable.

As for Abisag, anyone versed in the scriptures will know that she was the Shunamite woman who warmed David in her bosom in his dying days but did not know him carnally (3 Kings 1:1–4). What might have provoked her appearance in this poem? Ruppel (drawing on Laubmann before him) provides a functional explanation, which is good as far as it goes. By choosing a telestich that contains two *g*'s, Boniface had placed a severe constraint upon himself, for Latin words do not usually end in *g*.[60] "Magog" in line 14 thus has a functional purpose as well as being appropriate in the context of references to the last judgment. This still does not fully explain, however, why Boniface chose "Abisag" in line 32. The first editor of Boniface's poem, Laubmann, in explaining that Abisag "according to allegorical exegesis should mean the heavenly wisdom," was surely correct in pointing to Jerome's lengthy "Letter 52" in support of this interpretation.[61] In this letter Jerome explains the presence of Abisag in two ways:

> Amplexetur me modo sapientia, et Abisag nostra, quæ nunquam senescit, in meo requiescat sinu. Impolluta enim est, virginitatisque

---

60 Ruppel, "Der heilige Bonifatius als Dichter," 2:36; see also Laubmann, "Mittheilungen," p. 13.
61 "Abisag nach allegorischer Auslegung die himmlische Weisheit bedeuten soll," Laubmann, "Mittheilungen," p. 17.

perpetuæ, et quæ in similitudinem Mariæ, cum quotidie generet, semperque parturiat, incorrupta est.

[Let Wisdom alone embrace me; let her nestle in my bosom, my Abisag who grows not old. Undefiled truly is she, and a virgin forever; for although she daily conceives and unceasingly brings to the birth, like Mary she remains undeflowered.][62]

Laubmann was quite right to emphasize wisdom. Boniface, after all, states in his poem,

Almo quod feruens gremio signabat Abisag / totum, quae radiens constat sapientia iusti, / architenens altor, qui sidera clara gubernas, / rurigenæ præsta, ut certus solamina possit / tradere per sacras scripturas.

[O foster-father holding the arch [of heaven], who governs the shining stars, manifest to [this] country bumpkin all that the fiery Abisag signified with her nourishing bosom, who as the radiant wisdom of that which is just remains unchanging,[63] so that he can with assurance give consolation through the sacred scriptures.][64]

The concept of the holy wisdom was very important in Christian thought from the fifth until at least the end of the eighth century.[65]

---

62   Jerome, *Epistola* 52. 4, PL 22, col. 530 (text); "Letter LII: To Nepotian," §4, in *St. Jerome: Letters and Select Works*, [trans. W. H. Fremantle et al.], A Select Library of Nicene and Post-Nicene Fathers of the Christian Church, 2nd ser., vol. 6 (Oxford: James Parker and Co., and New York: The Christian Literature Company, 1893), p. 91 (translation, with "Abishag" amended to "Abisag"). On Jerome's exegesis of this passage see J. N. D. Kelly, *Jerome: His Life, Writings, and Controversies* (New York: Harper & Row, 1975), p. 191.

63   Fickermann, "Der Widmungsbrief des hl. Bonifatius," 219, n. 1, points out that this clause in line 33 is the elucidation of Abisag as the allegorical representation of *sapientia*. He interprets *constat* as equivalent to *est*; I have tried to retain the sense of Boniface's choice of verb.

64   Lines 32–36.

65   Wisdom received its supreme embodiment in architectural form in the world

But one can perhaps add a coda to what Laubmann said by considering Abisag and David whom she nestled in her bosom, as types of Mary and Christ. In the final rhyming poem that concludes his letter to Sigeberht, Boniface writes: "Vale Christo ueraciter, / ut et uiuas perenniter / sanctae matris in sinibus, / sacris nitens uirtutibus," (Hail to Christ in truth. May you live eternally in the bosom [*in sinibus*] of our holy mother, glowing with saintly virtues).[66] I would suggest that Mary appears in the rhyming poem and is alluded to in the acrostic poem because she, like the holy cross, had acquired a new significance in western Christendom at the time when Boniface was a young adult—and as a teacher it was his duty to apprise his pupils of these religious developments.[67]

---

of late Antiquity with the building in Constantinople of Hagia Sophia in the reign of Justinian. The concept of *sophia* remained important over two centuries later; Archbishop Ælberht dedicated the eighth-century church at York to Wisdom: Alcuin, *The Bishops, Kings, and Saints of York*, ed. Peter Godman, Oxford Medieval Texts (Oxford: Clarendon Press, 1982), p. 121, line 1520: "Sophiae sacraverat almae." Alcuin several times mentions Ælberht's love of *sophia* in this same poem (lines 1414, 1455, 1533) and writes of his own dedication to the pursuit of *sophia* from Ælberht's mouth in his epitaph to him: see *Poetae Latini aevi Carolini*, ed. Ernst Duemmler, MGH, Poetae Latini medii aevi 1.1 (Berlin: Weidmann, 1880), pp. 206–7 (no. II). On the York dedication see Richard Morris, "Alcuin, York, and the *alma sophia*," *The Anglo-Saxon Church: Papers on History, Architecture, and Archaeology in Honour of Dr H. M. Taylor*, ed. Lawrence A. S. Butler and Richard K. Morris, CBA Research Report 60 (London: Council for British Archaeology, 1986), pp. 80–89. I am grateful to Michael Lapidge for reminding me of this paper.

66 Law, "Early Medieval Grammarian," pp. 172–73, lines 111–14 (text) and 175 (translation).

67 The relationship between the cross and Mary has been explored by Éamonn Ó Carragáin in a number of works. See, for instance, his "Crucifixion as Annunciation: The Relation of 'The Dream of the Rood' to the Liturgy Reconsidered," *English Studies* 63 (1982): 487–505; "Rome, Ruthwell, Vercelli: 'The Dream of the Rood' and the Italian Connection," in *Vercelli tra Oriente ed Occidente tra tarda Antichità e Medioevo: Atti delle Giornate di studio, Vercelli 10–11 aprile 1997, 24 novembre 1997*, ed. Vittoria Dolcetti Corazza, Bibliotheca Germanica, Studi e testi 6 (Alessandria: Edizioni dell'Orso, 1998), pp. 59–100; and "Between Annunciation and Visitation: Spiritual Birth and the Cycles of the

An outline of some seventh- and eighth-century ecclesiastical developments will help to explain this. In 687 Sergius I became pope.[68] Born in Sicily of Syrian parentage, he had every reason to be interested in England since someone who shared his background, Theodore of Tarsus, was the archbishop of Canterbury.[69] The author of the *Liber Pontificalis* felt the link with England was sufficiently significant to mention that Theodore's successor, Beorhtwald, had gone to Rome to be ordained as archbishop by Sergius.[70] The writer also describes how Sergius had found a relic of the True Cross in the shrine of St. Peter: "Qui etiam ex die illo pro salute humani generis ab omni populo christiano, die Exaltationis sanctae Crucis, in basilicam Salvatoris quae appellatur Constantiniana osculatur ac adoratur" (From that day, for the salvation of the human race, this is kissed and worshipped by all Christian people on the day of the Exaltation of the Holy Cross in the basilica of the Saviour called Constantinian).[71] Furthermore, we are told that

> [c]onstituit autem ut diebus Adnuntiationis Domini, Dormitionis et Nativitatis sanctae Dei genetricis semperque virginis Mariae ac sancti Symeonis, quod Ypapanti Greci appellant, letania exeat a sancto Hadriano et ad sanctam Mariam populus occurrat.

Sun on the Ruthwell Cross: A Response to Fred Orton," in *Theorizing Anglo-Saxon Stone Sculpture*, ed. Catherine E. Karkov and Fred Orton, Medieval European Studies 4 (Morgantown: West Virginia University Press, 2003), pp. 131–87.
68 On Sergius see *Le Liber Pontificalis: Texte, introduction et commentaire*, ed. Louis Duchesne, 2 vols (Paris, 1892); re-issued with a third volume, ed. Cyrille Vogel, (Paris: E. de Boccard, Éditeur, 1955–57), 1:371–76 (text); *The Book of Pontiffs (Liber Pontificalis)*, trans. Raymond Davis, Translated Texts for Historians, Latin Series 5 (Liverpool: Liverpool University Press, 1989), pp. 82–87 (translation).
69 See *Biblical Commentaries*, ed. Bischoff and Lapidge, pp. 65–66 and n. 289. Thomas F. X. Noble, "Rome in the Seventh Century," in *Archbishop Theodore*, ed. Lapidge, pp. 68–87 at 79, swims against the scholarly current by downplaying Sergius's eastern links.
70 *Liber Pontificalis*, ed. Duchesne, 1:376, lines 15–16 (text); Davis, *Book of Pontiffs*, p. 87 (translation).
71 *Liber Pontificalis*, ed. Duchesne, 1:374, lines 15–18 (text); Davis, *Book of Pontiffs*, p. 85 (translation).

[[Sergius] decreed that on the days of the Lord's Annunciation, of the Falling-asleep and Nativity of St Mary the ever-virgin mother of God, and of St Simeon (which the Greeks call *Hypapante*), a litany should go out from St Hadrian's and the people should meet up at St Mary's.][72]

These liturgical innovations, I suggest, help to explain both the indirect reference to Mary and the central image of the cross.[73]

Boniface might have learned of these innovations through Archbishop Beorhtwald or possibly through Aldhelm, who had a rather confused awareness of a mid-August Marian feast.[74] Aldhelm had been to Rome and it is generally assumed that he went during the pontificate of Sergius, though unfortunately the evidence is shaky.[75] His support of the cult of Mary cannot be doubted as churches dedicated to her are the subject of two of his *Carmina ecclesiastica*[76] and he dedicated one of the churches at his monastery in Malmesbury to her.[77]

---

72   *Liber Pontificalis*, ed. Duchesne, 1:376, lines 4–6 (text); Davis, *Book of Pontiffs*, p. 87 (translation).
73   As Éamonn Ó Carragáin points out, "The *Liber Pontificalis* does not say that Sergius himself instituted these feasts; only that he gave them a new solemnity," "Liturgical Innovations associated with Pope Sergius and the Iconography of the Ruthwell and Bewcastle Crosses," in *Bede and Anglo-Saxon England: Papers in Honour of the 1300th Anniversary of the Birth of Bede, given at Cornell University in 1973 and 1974*, ed. Robert T. Farrell, British Archaeological Reports, [British Series] 46 (Oxford: British Archaeological Reports, 1978), pp. 131–47 at 133, where Ó Carragáin provides further details on the background to these feasts.
74   "Carmina ecclesiastica III: <In ecclesia Mariae a Bugge exstructa>," lines 59–65, *Aldhelmi Opera*, ed. Ehwald, p. 17. This passage is discussed in detail by Mary Clayton, *The Cult of the Virgin Mary in Anglo-Saxon England*, CSASE 2 (Cambridge: Cambridge University Press, 1990), pp. 30–35.
75   Orchard, *Poetic Art of Aldhelm*, p. 211, discusses the evidence for Aldhelm's trip to Rome.
76   "Carmina ecclesiastica II and III," in *Aldhelmi Opera*, ed. Ehwald, pp. 12–13 and 14–18.
77   William of Malmesbury, *Gesta pontificum Anglorum* 5. 216. 1–2, in *William of*

A Cross and an Acrostic

It is necessary to turn to Boniface's letter to Sigeberht one last time in order fully to understand the structure of the poem. Boniface explains:

> Interea circulum quadrangulum in fronte huius laboris apposui, in medio figuram sanctae crucis continentem, "Iesus Christus" exprimentem, qui ludiuaga sermonum serie duobus ambitus uersibus, aliis in transuersum currentibus, socialis adiutorii utrimque sonantes in obuiam offert litteras. Hunc autem circulum in scemate noui ac ueteris instrumenti figurari non nescias . . . Post crucem autem supradictam in circulo heroici uersus et perfecti decursant. Ita et per gratiam Christi accepta remissione peccatorum ad integrum omnia renouata et perfecta sunt.

> [I have placed a diamond-shaped circle at the front of this work with the image of the holy cross in the middle, forming the words "Jesus Christ." Formed by two verses in a wandering trail of words with other verses running across it, it presents an inscription which announces the help of my friend. You should not be unaware that this circle represents an image of the Old and the New Testament . . . After meeting the cross in the circle the verses flow along in perfect heroic form. Similarly, all things are made new and perfect through the grace of Christ once the complete remission of sins has been received.][78]

Malmesbury: Gesta pontificum Anglorum. *The History of the English Bishops*, ed. and trans. Michael Winterbottom and Rodney M. Thomson, Oxford Medieval Texts, 2 vols (Oxford: Clarendon Press, 2007), 1:544 (text) and 1:545 (translation). Another of his Malmesbury churches was dedicated to St. Michael. Could Aldhelm have been influenced by Wilfrid, who on the return from his final trip to Rome in 703x704 had a vision in which St. Michael instructed him to build a church in honor of Mary? See ch. 56 of the *Vita Wilfridi*, in *The Life of Bishop Wilfrid by Eddius Stephanus*, ed. Bertram Colgrave (Cambridge: Cambridge University Press, 1927), pp. 122 (text) and 123 (translation). For further discussion of the Malmesbury churches with references see *William of Malmesbury: Gesta pontificum Anglorum*, ed. Winterbottom and Thomson, 2: 270–71.
78 Law, "Early Medieval Grammarian," p. 172, lines 82–87 and 93–96 (text),

This passage explains several features of the poem. Its metrical structure consists of elegiac couplets (i.e., alternating hexameters and pentameters) in the first half and hexameters in the second. The elegiacs express the incomplete divine revelation of the Old Testament, which symbolically changes in the poem with the appearance of Jesus Christ, the incarnation of God. Thereafter the verse is heroic and perfect: "heroic" because the hexameter was the poetic form employed in Vergil's epic verse, and "perfect" because in the geometrical thinking of the Greeks, six formed a perfect triangle and also because the sum of the prime numbers 1, 2, and 3 equals six as does the product of $1 \times 2 \times 3$.[79]

One of the most able scholars in the field of Anglo-Latin studies has described some Anglo-Saxon acrostic poems as *jeux d'esprit*.[80] He could not have had this poem in mind. Certainly Boniface plays around with the meaning of words but it is a profoundly serious poem. Its form is not something exterior to its meaning: rather, its form *is* the meaning. Let us return to the hierarchy of scripts mentioned earlier in this essay. Our eye—remember this is visual poetry—is drawn to the cross on which Jesus Christ is literally placed, his sacrifice symbolized

---

and pp. 174–75 (translation).

79 In the *Ars metrica* attributed to Boniface, in *Bonifatii (Vynfreth) Ars grammatica*, ed. Gebauer and Löfstedt, p. 111, lines 64–65, the heroic meter is associated with Homer. See further Law, "Early Medieval Grammarian," pp. 185–86, n. 9. On the number six see Christopher Butler, "Numerological Thought," in *Silent Poetry: Essays in Numerological Analysis*, ed. Alastair Fowler (London: Routledge and Kegan Paul, 1970), pp. 1–31 at 2–3. Butler points out: "In default of the system of notation for numbers that we have inherited from the Arabs, the Greeks thought of particular numbers in geometrical fashion, for example as pebbles laid out in patterns on the ground . . . Thus they could construct progressions of number that appeared to be 'triangular' in nature." Following such an approach, one could form an equilateral triangle from six pebbles, each side of which would consist of three pebbles.

80 Orchard, *Poetic Art of Aldhelm*, p. 248, where he is specifically referring to Aldhelm's role in disseminating *enigmata* with "solutions" in acrostic and telestich form.

by the CHI placed at the interstices of the arms of the cross. Christ's sacrifice reaches out to all humankind represented by Wynfreth and Dud(d), from the beginning of time to the end—acrostic and telestich. Its arms also reach out to embrace through its diamond-shaped circle north, south, east, and west, what today would be called the four corners of the world and in the Vulgate the four *anguli*.[81] A modern reader might have expected a circular O, but if one consults the Lindisfarne Gospels, a volume that is probably contemporary with Boniface's youth, one can see that the highest of the display scripts is angular in form. The "quadrangular circle" is thus a most apposite form to represent the world (Latin *orbis*) as God's creation.[82]

The references to the four corners of the world bring us back to Revelation 20:7, which mentions Magog as one of the peoples "quae sunt super quattuor angulos terrae." Identification of the verse reinforces the symbolic significance of the "diamond-shaped circle" with its potentially redemptive message for all who might read the poem. Read at another level, mention of Magog also reinforces the instructional purpose of the poem, though this meaning is less transparent. Boniface's reference to Magog appears in the first, "Old Testament," portion of the poem, perfectly appropriately when one

---

81   Revelation 20:7: "gentes quae sunt super quattuor angulos terrae Gog et Magog." Cf. also Revelation 7:1: "post haec vidi quattuor angelos stantes super quattuor angulos terrae" (After these things, I saw four angels standing on the four corners of the earth).

82   On this kind of display script see John Higgitt, "The Display Script of the Book of Kells and the Tradition of Insular Decorative Capitals," in *The Book of Kells: Proceedings of a Conference at Trinity College, Dublin, 6–9 September 1992*, ed. Felicity O'Mahony (Dublin: Published for Trinity College Library Dublin by Scolar Press, 1994), pp. 209–33; and Gifford Charles-Edwards, "The Springmount Bog Tablets: Their Implications for Insular Epigraphy and Palaeography," *Studia Celtica* 36 (2002): 27–45, especially the form of the *O* in the word "HONOR‹EM›" that appears on St Cuthbert's altar, reproduced therein on p. 40, fig. 9. See also the *O* in Michelle P. Brown, *The Lindisfarne Gospels: Society, Spirituality and the Scribe* (London: British Library, 2003), pl. 11 (London, British Library MS Cotton Nero D. iv, folio 27r).

considers that students of the scriptures could have no concept of who Magog of Revelation 20 was unless they had recourse to Genesis 10 and Ezekiel 38 and 39. Abisag, on the other hand, appears in the "New Testament" second half of the poem, an Old Testament figure whose full significance is not apparent without consideration of the relationship of Jesus and Mary as described in the New Testament. These references to Magog and Abisag thus encapsulate the typological method of reading the scriptures.

This is deliberately difficult poetry. We are really only starting to develop an aesthetic of difficulty.[83] Literature written in this mode demands a very different cast of mind on the part of the reader from a poem composed according to Romantic principles: in its allusiveness and complexity it is more akin to reading "Hugh Selwyn Mauberley" than "The Daffodils." A moment's reflection would show that much literature, art, and music of the past century would have to be discarded if "difficult" creative works were to be condemned as barren and worthless. To appreciate such imaginative endeavors requires a receptive and contemplative mind, frequently a willingness to seek knowledge beyond the work itself, patience in unraveling its complexities and finally a sense of joy and wonderment at what is revealed. All these activities were what the medieval scholar sought to engage in when reading the Bible,[84] and I think we can fairly deduce that Boniface's poem was seeking to induct the tyro into these mysteries.

As a teacher Boniface must also have been concerned that students should be able to understand not just the senses of the words that they read in their manuscripts but also their form. In fact, before they tried to understand the meaning(s) of a word, they might well have to interpret what the word was from an abbreviated form that appeared in the manuscript. When Laubmann produced his *editio princeps*, he

---

83 George Steiner provides an introduction in *On Difficulty and Other Essays* (New York and Oxford: Oxford University Press, 1978), pp. 18–47.

84 For an introduction to these ideas (which will already be familiar to most medievalists), see Northrop Frye, *The Great Code: The Bible and Literature* (New York: Harcourt Brace Jovanovich, 1982), especially pp. 78–80.

A Cross and an Acrostic

reported the abbreviations that appear in the extant manuscript.[85] Contemporary extant manuscripts employ quite a few abbreviations, some such as ÷ for *est* being insular innovations; several of these manuscripts are southern English in origin. London, British Library MS Cotton Augustus II. 2, a Kentish charter of C.E. 679, which is certainly contemporaneous and "probably original," contains a number of abbreviations such as *nuncusq(ue)*, even though it employs uncial script, which one might have imagined was more formal than minuscule.[86] Another Canterbury charter of C.E. 732, this one written in Anglo-Saxon minuscule, contemporaneous and "very probably original," also contains quite a few abbreviations.[87] Perhaps even more interesting is London, British Library MS Cotton Tiberius A. xv, folios 175–80,[88] an early eighth-century manuscript of possibly south-western origin that might have been seen by Aldhelm:[89] it contains several abbreviations

---

85 Laubmann, "Mittheilungen," p. 5. Note, however, his omission of *tuu(m)* in line 25.

86 *Chartae Latinae Antiquiores: Facsimile-Edition of the Latin Charters Prior to the Ninth Century*. Part III: *British Museum London*, ed. Albert Bruckner and Robert Marichal (Olten and Lausanne: Urs Graf-Verlag, 1963), pp. 20 (no. 182) (facsimile) and 21 (commentary, catalogue, and text).

87 *Chartae Latinae Antiquiores*, pp. 43 (no. 190) (facsimile) and 42 (commentary, catalogue and text). To this might be added Wealdhere's letter of C.E. 704x705, which Pierre Chaplais has argued is an original: see Chaplais, "The Letter from Bishop Wealdhere of London to Archbishop Brihtwold of Canterbury: The Earliest Original 'Letter Close' Extant in the West," *Medieval Scribes, Manuscripts & Libraries: Essays presented to N. R. Ker*, ed. M. B. Parkes and Andrew G. Watson (London: Scolar Press, 1978), pp. 3–23; reprinted in Chaplais, *Essays in Medieval Diplomacy and Administration* (London: Hambledon Press, 1981), no. XIV, with "p[rae]sentis" in his 1978 edition of the text silently corrected to "p[rae]teriti" in 1981, as Susan Kelly has kindly pointed out to me.

88 *Codices Latini Antiquiores: A Palaeographical Guide to Latin Manuscripts Prior to the Ninth Century*, Part II: *Great Britain and Ireland*, ed. E. A. Lowe, 2nd ed. (Oxford: Clarendon Press, 1972), p. 20, no. 189 + pl. opposite 20.

89 For the argument, see Rodney M. Thomson, "Identifiable Books from the Pre-Conquest Library of Malmesbury Abbey," *ASE* 10 (1982): 1–19 at 8–10. Bischoff and Lapidge do not demur: see *Biblical Commentaries*, p. 249.

employed in the Boniface acrostic. Clearly any Anglo-Saxon wishing to read an insular manuscript in the early eighth century would have had to have been able to interpret abbreviations.[90]

Laubmann's edition is rather quixotic, as he sometimes expands abbreviations and sometimes retains them. His typographer was thus driven to using a smaller font for *namque tuum mon(strant)* in line 25 where Laubmann expanded the text, because the words could not otherwise be fitted in without destroying the shape of the acrostic. Though this appears to be a modern technological problem, the difficulty does, in fact, provide strong evidence for the presence of abbreviations in Boniface's original version. One may even posit that there were more abbreviations in his original text than the extant manuscript preserves: in line 29 the scribe had to place an insertion mark between the *i* and *e* and insert *n* above the line in *hominem*; an original abbreviation to "ho*min*em"[91] would

---

90 W. M. Lindsay, *Early Irish Minuscule Script* (Oxford: James Parker & Co., 1910), pp. 4–12 and pl. III, accepted the early tradition that Fulda, Hessisches Landesbibliothek, Codex Bonifatianus 3, was associated with Boniface. A gospel-book in Irish cursive script, it contains a number of the abbreviations found in our extant text, notably in the words *om(n)ia* (line 18) and *namq(ue)* (line 25). Current thinking, however, now dates it to the second half of the eighth century (and so after Boniface's death) or even s. viii/ix: see Gneuss, p. 125, no. 827.7. Its source might well, of course, have employed the same abbreviations. A less ambiguous example is Marburg, Hessisches Staatsarchiv, Fragment 319 Pfarrarchiv Spangenberg (Depositum) Hr Nr. 1 (Gneuss, p. 130, no. 849.6), an early eighth-century fragment from south-west England containing excerpts from Servius's *Commentarii* on Vergil's *Aeneid* with several Old English glosses, which Lowe considers "may actually have been brought to Germany by St. Boniface or by his English pupils or companions:" *Codices Latini Antiquiores: A Palaeographical Guide to Latin Manuscripts Prior to the Ninth Century: Supplement*, ed. E. A. Lowe (Oxford: Clarendon Press, 1971), p. 39, no. 1806. This manuscript contains a number of abbreviations, which are listed on p. 194 of a paper containing an edition and facsimile by Peter K. Marshall, "The Spangenberg Bifolium of Servius: the Manuscript and the Text," *Rivista di filologia e di istruzione classica* 128 (2000): 192–209 + pls. I–II.

91 This form happens to be found in the ablative of the word in the Fulda

A Cross and an Acrostic

have resulted in a less crowded opening to the line but might have confused a subsequent copyist who was unconsciously expanding the abbreviation. We can see that Boniface thus turned a set of scribal conventions to two different ends: he both instructed the reader and enabled himself to retain the visual acrostic form of a densely worded poem.

There was a reason for my delaying the discussion of the written form of the individual words of the poem until after a discussion of the meaning of the words and the overall acrostic patterns created by them. For the shape of the words themselves in this remarkable text reveal Boniface's innovative contribution to the acrostic form.

Irish scribes had broken with the Roman practice of *scriptura continua*, perhaps because they did not have some form of Latin as their native tongue. Instead they separated most Latin words from others by means of spaces. Anglo-Saxon scribes followed their example with Latin texts. It was a change of huge significance because it permitted the eye physiologically to process the information that it was receiving in such a way as to make silent reading possible. Continental scribes (and, for that matter, Anglo-Saxon scribes copying vernacular texts) were not to engage in this practice for several more centuries; instead they copied blocks of words with spaces in between, a practice called by Paul Saenger "aerated script."[92] One need look no further than the facsimile of the poem in Figure 2.1 to see the continental practice in action. This is why the scribe produced such a messy-looking text. Boniface was now not forced to count the number of letters in a line, as he could leave spaces of variable size to preserve the shape of the acrostics. Having a clear concept of the word as a discrete written unit, he thus was able, as has been mentioned, to select both elegiac and heroic verse to convey meaning, with the pentameter within the elegiacs representing the Old Testament that only imperfectly revealed the divine, and the hexameters the New Testament with its perfect revelation of Christ,

---

manuscript mentioned in n. 90 above.
92 Saenger, *Space between Words*, pp. 32–44.

who offered redemption for sinful humankind such as Boniface and Dud(d) through his crucifixion.

And the very use of separated words contributes to the overall meaning of the poem. For in Boniface's view the function of *Ars grammatica* was to enable one to better understand the scriptures. Mistakes could be made in the reading of those scriptures, hence his careful choice of difficult words to which teachers should draw their pupils' attention. So too the scriptures could conceal meanings: with appropriate instruction pupils could learn to understand that Old Testament figures such as Abisag might be a type of others such as Mary who had a part to play in God's final revelation in the New Testament.

We must not forget, however, that Boniface was also the writer of *enigmata*[93] and that Hrabanus Maurus tells us that he introduced cryptography to the continent.[94] A proper understanding of his personality would require us to explain his interest in both the verbally visible—this figurative poem—and his interest in hidden meanings. Here I will only observe that his literary creation displays paradoxically both kinds of use of language. By contemplating his poem, one can hardly avoid also thinking of those miraculously composed introductory verses of John's Gospel.[95] For Boniface's poem draws us inexorably on from the use of words with their wealth of meaning and the patterns they form, to the very Word, *ho logos*: "In the beginning was the Word, and the Word was with God, and the Word was God."

---

93 Andy Orchard argues in *Poetic Art of Aldhelm*, pp. 248–53, that Boniface was here strongly influenced by Aldhelm. For the text of the *enigmata* see "Aenigmata Bonifatii," ed. Glorie (above, n. 3).

94 See Wilhelm Levison's excursus, "St. Boniface and Cryptography," in his *England and the Continent*, pp. 290–94.

95 Conveniently set out *per cola et per commata* in David R. Howlett, *British Books in Biblical Style* (Dublin and Portland, OR: Four Courts Press, 1997), pp. 79–80.

Appendix 1

Text and Translation

The text that follows does not offer any dramatic new emendations other than the deletion of *c* in *Xcristus* in line 19. Line 17, however, demands further discussion, containing as it does several problems. After the word *absoluens*, the manuscript contains a dot above an angled tick-mark with a second dot appearing some distance below the latter. This has been interpreted as the insular abbreviation ÷, signifying *est*. The manuscript itself reveals, however, that the lower dot is in another, lighter ink. This may be an addition by a later corrector, knowledgeable in insular abbreviations, because the word *est* appears as an addition in the right-hand margin two lines below, between lines 19 and 20. Alternatively, it could have been added as a mark of punctuation equivalent to a modern full-stop or period. I would interpret the dot and angled tick-mark as signifying an omitted word, which the scribe has rather carelessly added in the margin. This marginal addition appears to my eyes to be in the same-colored ink as the main body of the text.

The word *est* should, therefore, be retained as part of Boniface's text. It avoids what would otherwise require an ugly hiatus between the first and second words of the line instead of a more metrically natural elision. The reading does, however, pose a problem as to how to punctuate the line. I suggest that *est* should be interpreted as the final word of a sentence. The final emphatic position of this word asserts the eternal existence of God.

The word *uitima* in the manuscript is clearly wrong but there is no alternative reading that is likely to command universal assent.

Laubmann rejected the emendation to *uictima* on metrical grounds. He pondered *uentura* (with a suspension over the *e* to represent *n*). He also canvassed *uitricia* (or, better still, *uictricia*) or *uitalia* as these would better accord with the number of graphic strokes in the manuscript. In favor of *uitalia*, he cited Lucretius 1.202: "multaque uiuendo uitalia uincere sæcla," conjecturing that Boniface might have known the line from a metrical compendium.[96] This last reading evidently appealed to Dümmler and Löfstedt, who adopted it.[97] Their emendation requires interpreting *mirifico absoluens* as an elision, which is acceptable as there are ten other examples in the poem.

Fickermann, on the other hand, preferred *uictima* (or possibly *en uictima*).[98] His second reading must assume that there were two scribal errors, with "en" presumably being lost through haplography because of *absoluens*, which seems unnecessarily complex. Like Laubmann's *uitalia*, his *en uictima* assumes an elision in *mirifico absoluens*.

I favor the reading *uictima*, explaining the dropping of *c* either because of eye-skip or because the scribe read the word as *uittima* and simplified the letters. The sense "a sacrificial beast" would be entirely appropriate in the context of the word *amni*, which I would interpret as referring to Christ's blood shed on the cross, and would provide Boniface's readers with yet another grammatical surprise, since *uictima*, with its allusion to Jesus as the sacrificial lamb in this context, is a feminine noun referring to the Son of God.

The text differs from other editions by carefully recording in italics all expansions of the abbreviations found in the single extant text. Credit to earlier editors for emendations that have been adopted is duly given in the *apparatus criticus*, which is derived from the edition by Löfstedt and Gebauer with some amendments.

---

96 Laubmann, "Mittheilungen," p. 15.
97 *Poetae Latini aevi Carolini*, ed. Duemmler, p. 16 (edition; the semi-diplomatic transcription on p. 17 retains "uitima"); *Bonifatii (Vynfreth) Ars grammatica*, ed. Gebauer and Löfstedt, p. 5.
98 Fickermann, "Der Widmungsbrief des hl. Bonifatius," 218, n. 2.

A Cross and an Acrostic

The translation aims at being a literal one that seeks to account for *all* the words of the emended text of the manuscript. It makes no pretence to literary elegance.

TEXT

Manuscript
W: *Würzburg, Universitätsbibliothek MS M.p.th.f. 29, folio 44r.*

Other Abbreviations used in the *Apparatus Criticus*:
Duemmler: *Poetae Latini aevi Carolini*, ed. Duemmler, 16 (see above, note 65).
Ernst: Ernst, *Carmen figuratum* (see above, note 4).
Fickerman: Fickermann, "Der Widmungsbrief des hl. Bonifatius" (see above, note 51).
Laubmann: Laubmann, "Mittheilungen" (see above, note 50), pp. 18–19.
Lebek: conjectural readings of Wolfgang Lebek reported in the *apparatus criticus* of the edition in *Bonifatii (Vynfreth) Ars grammatica*, ed. Gebauer and Löfstedt (see above, note 26), pp. 5–6 (cf. their preface, p. VII).

VYNFRETH PRISCORUM DVDDO CONGESSERAT ARTEM
VIRIBUS ILLE IVGIS IVVAVIT IN ARTE MAGISTRVM

  Versibus, en iuuenis, durant *et* carmina cantu, 44r

  ymnos namq*ue* Dei, ymnica dicta uiri

 nisibus eximiis renouantis carmina lector.

  Fulmina na*m*que Pius frangere iudicii

5 regmina temporibus torquebit torribus, *et* sub

excelsi fatu om*n*ia saecla diu
Tuta tenent iusti. Parit*er* tum taenia sanctis
hic dabit*ur* regni aurea; hacque pii
per caeli ca*m*pos stipab*unt* pace tribunal,
10   regnantes laudant limpida regna simul.
In pia perp*etu*æ ut dominent*ur* gaudia uitae,
sordida in terris spernere gesta uiri.
Cautu*m* e*st*, ut nu*m*qua*m* defleant supplicia cassu
omnes gentiles, impia origo Magog,
15   regmina ut p*er*dant pariter sub Tartara trusi.
Vnus ne*m*pe Deus sæcula cuncta suis
mirifico absoluens est. Victima tradidit amni
diues in arte sua om*n*ia s*a*nc*t*a gradu.
Victor na*m* Iesus Xristus sicq*ue* ordinat actu.
20   Dapsilis in pastis uernis, tua fata dicanda
deuotis concede tibi cum laudibus. Id tu,
Omnipotens genitor, fac nostro in pectore poni,
casta suum resonans rectorem ut lingua cantet,
O Deus in solio iudex, regnator Olimpi.
25   Numina namq*ue* tuu*m* monstrant p*er* sæc*u*la nomen
gentib*us* in uastis celebrant *et* gaudia mira.
Edite in terris, saluasti sæcla redemptor.
Spiritus aethrale*m* tibi laude*m* splendidus aptet,
subiciens hominem *et* p*er*lustrans limina terrae.

30 Egregium regem, gnatu*m*, praeconia faustum

ruricolae iugit*er* dicant cum carmine clara.

Almo q*uod* feruens gremio signabat Abisag

totu*m*, quae radiens constat sapientia iusti,

architenens altor, qui sidera clara gubernas,

35 rurigenæ præsta, ut certus solamina possit

tradere p*er* sacras scripturas. Grammate doctor

excerptus prisco puero*rum* indaginis usu

"Magna patri *et* p*ro*li cum flamine gratia," dicam.

1 carmine *dubitanter Duemmler* **4** Fulmina] *Duemmler*, flumina *W* **5** regmina] *Laubmann*, remina *W* **7** iusti] *Laubmann*, iuste *W* taenia sanctis] *Laubmann*, tania scanctis *W* **8** regni] *Duemmler*, regi *W* **11** In pia] *Duemmler*, impia *W* dominentur] *Duemmler*, damnentur *W* **13** defleant] *Laubmann*, defleat *W* **15** ut] *s.l. W* **17** absoluens est] absoluens *edd.* absoluens ÷ *W* uictima] uitalia *(dubitanter* uictricia) *Laubmann*, uitima *W*, uitali et *Lebek*, uictima *uel* en uictima *Fickermann (Neues Archiv 50, 218 adn. 2)* **17/19** amni: *etc., interpunxit Duemmler, an* amni. Diues ... gradu ... que ... actu? *Inter uu.* **19** *et* **20** *adscr.* est *in marg. W; signum sup.* s *alt. uocis* absoluens *(u. 17) positum ad hoc est referendum censet Fickermann (Neues Archiv 50, 218 adn. 2)* **19** Xristus] Xcristus *W*, Christus *edd.* **20** pastis, uernis *edd.*, pastis bernis *W* **26** gentibus] *Laubmann*, tentibus *W* celebrant] cælebrant *W* **27** sæcla] *cf. supra, u.* 6, secula *W* **29** limina] *dubitanter Laubmann*, lumina *W edd.* **30** gnatum, praeconia,] *Löfstedt*, gnatum praeconia *edd.* **32** Almo quod] *Fickermann (Neues Archiv 50, 219 adn. 1)* almoq; *W*, almoque *edd.*, almo quem *Lebek* **33** quae radiens] *Fickermann (l.c.)*, quadradiens *W*, quod *(dubitanter* quo) radiens *Laubmann* iusti,] *Löfstedt*, iusti. *edd.* **37** prisco] *in* prisci *corr. W In folio 44v haec adduntur in W: Nam prior pars circuli huius usque ad medium crucis quibusdam pentametris intersertis decurrens pinguitur uersibus, qui licet pedestri remigio tranent, non tamen* heroici nec omnino perfecti decursa esse noscuntur. Præter crucem autem supradictam in circulo heroici uersus et perfecti decursant.

TRANSLATION

> Wynfreth had assembled for Dud(d) the art [of grammar] of the ancients. With his mental ability (literally "mental strength") he continuing without intermission helped the master (i.e., Boniface) in the *Art [of Grammar]* (i.e., Boniface's textbook).[99]

> Lo, young reader, through verse and poetry the songs of a man [who is] renewing with exceptional pains [his] poetry enables the hymns of God, the hymnal words, to endure.[100] For the pious one will hurl the thunderbolts at the time of judgment to break with brands of fire the kingdoms[101] and through the utterance of the eminent one the just[102] will long hold all generations safe. Equally this will then give to the holy ones the golden fillets of the kingdom; and in this peace the pious ones will throng round the throne in the fields of heaven; at the same time the ruling ones praise the

---

99 As mentioned above, these lines represent the acrostic and telestich, and also the rhomboidal mesostich (Boniface's *circuitum quadrangulum*). The translation by Lehmann in "Ein neuentdecktes Werk," *Erforschung des Mittelalters*, 4:168, fails to translate fully *in arte*: "Vynfreth hatte für Dudd die Lehren der Alten zusammengetragen, dieser half dem Lehrer mit nie nachlassender Mühe" (Wynfreth had collected the teachings of the Ancients for Dudde; the latter helped the teacher with unremitting dedication).
100 Ernst's translation (p. 164) keeps closer to Boniface's word order but fails to account for the word *dicta* in line 2: "Durch Verse und Gesang dauern die Gedichte des Jünglings, der nämlich, lieber Leser, die Hymnen Gottes und hymnischen Lieder des Menschen mit außerordentlichen Anstrengungen erneuert" (Through verse and song the poems of the young man endure; the self-same renews, dear reader, the hymns of God and the hymnal songs of men with extraordinary effort).
101 Ernst follows Laubmann (p. 13): "dem irdischen Reiche" (the earthly kingdom).
102 Ernst: "nur die Gerechten" (only the just).

shining kingdoms.[103] In order that they might rule in the pious rejoicings of life eternal, they have spurned the sordid deeds of man[104] on earth. Beware that all the heathens, the impious race of Magog, will never pour forth pleas in their fall as they together, thrust down to Tartarus,[105] lose their kingdoms. Truly there is one God, wonderfully acquitting all generations of men of their [deeds]. As a sacrifice with his stream [of blood], rich in his conduct,[106] He has bequeathed all things holy in rank. For Jesus Christ the victor ordains it so through his deed.[107] Generous one in [your] vernal pastures, grant that your decisions be declared by those devoted in their praises to you. You, the omnipotent begetter, cause it to

---

103 Laubmann (p. 13), followed by Ernst, gives a different force to *simul*: "und sie loben zugleich die Herrschenden und die lichten Himmelsreiche" (and they praise both those ruling and the shining heavenly kingdoms).
104 Omitted by Ernst.
105 Laubmann (p. 15), followed by Ernst: "in die Hölle hinabgestossen werden" (will be thrown down into Hell).
106 Boniface here uses *ars* to denote Christ's conduct during his life. He is thus using the word in a different sense from the *ars* that he himself taught, which is twice referred to in the acrostic: the latter concerns the art of grammar whose goal is the understanding of words and, ultimately, the Word of God. The word *tradidit* is used in a legal sense. I would interpret lines 17 and 18 as meaning that the goodness of Christ's life has been left as a rich legacy following his sacrifice on the cross. For the allusion contained within the word *amnis*, see John 19:34: "But one of the soldiers with a spear opened his side, and immediately there came out blood and water."
107 Ernst (who largely follows Laubmann, pp. 15–16) evidently punctuates differently; in part he provides a paraphrase rather than a translation; and he fails to translate the vital word *actu*: "Denn der einige Gott hat alle Weltalter den Seinigen durch die Taufe übergeben: Dem Christentum gehört die Zukunft der Welt. Reich in seiner Kunst ordnet Jesus Christus, der Sieger ist, alles Heilige nach seinem Rang" (For the only God has bequeathed to his people all ages through baptism: the future of the world belongs to Christianity. Powerful in his art Jesus Christ, who is the victor, ordains everything holy according to its rank). *Actu*, the "deed" referred to, is, of course, Christ's dying on the cross, theologically the central message of Christianity, here placed in the central line of the poem.

be placed in our heart that the chaste tongue should sing, echoing his ruler, O God, judge on the throne, ruler of Olympus.[108] For [your] divine authority displays your name through the ages and wondrous praises amongst vast peoples honor [you]. Born on earth, O redeemer, you have saved the generations. Let the shining spirit prepare heavenly praise to you, subjecting man and purifying the portals of the earth. The clear commendations of the country-dweller[109] perpetually declare in poetry that [you] are the distinguished King, the Son, the auspicious one. O foster-father holding the arch [of heaven], who governs the shining stars, manifest to [this] country bumpkin all that the fiery Abisag signified with her nourishing bosom, who as the radiant wisdom of that which is just remains unchanging, so that he can with assurance give consolation through the sacred scriptures.[110] As a teacher of letters, chosen for the venerable task of the educating boys, I will say, "Let there be great thanks to the Father and the Son with the Holy Spirit."

---

108 Ernst: "Herrscher des Himmels" (lord of Heaven).
109 As Laubmann rightly points out (p. 17, vv. 34–36), this refers to Boniface himself.
110 My punctuation of lines 32–36 of the original text and interpretation of this passage in essence follow Fickermann, "Der Widmungsbrief des hl. Bonifatius," 219, n. 1.

Appendix 2

The Metrics of Boniface's Poem

Boniface inadvertently introduced an unintended level of difficulty for a modern reader trained in the principles of classical scansion. In at least three places, the quantities in the words he uses are at variance with classical practice: in line 13, *defleant* has to be scanned with a short initial syllable and the following word *supplicia* has to be read with a long second syllable. In line 23, *lingua* must be scanned as a trisyllabic rather than a disyllabic word.

One could dismiss these instances as metrical infelicities, blunders that were the result of ignorance.[111] It is worth remembering, however, the fact that Latin was a language in active spoken use in the eighth century. Those learning the language usually could accommodate themselves to discrepancies between the conventional written language and its spoken equivalent if they were required to copy manuscripts[112]—

---

111 Note Michael Lapidge's comment in "Autographs of Insular Latin Authors," pp. 113–14: "His [sc. Boniface's] use of elision and enjambement goes far beyond that of Aldhelm, as also does (unfortunately) the number of his faults in scansion." David R. Howlett does not know of any other examples of these three words being scanned in this way, though he has reminded me (personal communication) that there is much still to be learned about early medieval Latin verse composed in Britain.

112 This proviso is made because it is evident that in non-manuscript contexts such as personal graffiti, the Anglo-Saxons felt less constrained by conventional spelling and instead used something closer to the current pronunciation. Diornoth, who described himself on the walls of catacomb of Commodilla as a *serbus d(e)i*, "slave/servant of God," and another person called Petrus, who in the

writers of Modern English do this all the time—but in an educational system focused on the Bible, the requirement to maintain the classical conventions of vowel length was less pressing. Indeed Aldhelm had already shed the conventions in several of his rhythmical poems. Rather than condemn Boniface for ignorance, I would prefer to suggest that in his dialect, the vowel-length of certain words had changed from that of classical times, and so view them as valuable insights into the pronunciation of eighth-century Anglo-Latin.[113]

These three words aside, Boniface seems to have been very careful with metrical length and some other seeming exceptions are better interpreted as scribal errors. As Laubmann pointed out, the meter demands *celebrant* for MS *cælebrant* in line 26. In line 27 *secla* probably is a double error for *sæcla*: the *e* should be an *ę* (e-caudata) and the *l* should not have a cross stroke (perhaps influenced by its use in the same word two lines above, where the form *sæcula* is necessary on metrical grounds).

What is perhaps less acceptable is Boniface's use of hiatus. It is to be found at least three times:[114] in line 12: *sordida* || *in*; line 15: *regmina* || *ut*; and line 27: *Edite* || *in*. These examples of hiatus cannot be justified on the grounds of sense and bespeak a writer of Latin more

---

same catacomb enjoined, *biba in d(omino) d(e)o*, "Live in the Lord God," evidently pronounced words containing the classical Latin *v* with a voiced bilabial fricative represented by a *b* in the spelling (a change by no means limited to Anglo-Latin): see *Inscriptiones Christianae urbis Romae septimo saeculo antiquiores*, Nova series, vol. 2: *Coemeteria in Viis Cornelia Aurelia Portuensi et Ostiensi*, ed. Angelo Silvagni (Rome: Pont. Institutum Archaeologiae Christianae, 1935), 2:369, no. 6449. 13 and 29. There are even occasional examples in high-status sources such as the *Codex Amiatinus*, as David R. Howlett has pointed out to me.

113 There is only one clear example of a current pronunciation spilling over into spelling: *bernis* in line 20, where *uernis* might be expected if classical Latin spelling conventions were being observed. Whether it represents Boniface's written language or a copyist's cannot, however, be determined. I have emended it to *uernis* as a kindness to the modern reader.

114 Line 2: *Dei* || *ymnica*, line 6: *fatu* || *omnia*, and line 18: *sua* || *omnia* are required by meter since they are at the caesura, as Michael Lapidge has pointed out to me.

A Cross and an Acrostic

comfortable with the written than the spoken word. He is also rather too inclined to employ elision. There are ten clear examples in this poem: in line 11: *perpetuæ^ut*; line 13: *Cautum^est*; line 14: *impia^origo*; line 19: *sicque^ordinat*; line 22: *nostro^in*; line 23: *rectorem^ut*; line 29: *hominem^et*; line 35: *præsta^ut*; line 37: *puerorum^indaginis*; and line 38: *patri^et*. To these examples must be added *mirifico absoluens* in line 17, which may be interpreted as an example of elision if one accepts *est* as part of the line, which the scribe apparently intended. Viewed from the perspective of classical Latin metrics, this may be viewed as verse composed cerebrally according to technical principles rather than singing in the ear.

But this is not classical Latin poetry. It is written when the Irish and Aldhelm had already essayed poetry, composed not according to the rules of classical scansion but more in accordance with the stress rhythms of the spoken language.[115] Furthermore, Boniface's poem was written against a background of an oral Germanic tradition of poetry that emphasized alliteration and the repetitive use of words. His teacher, Aldhelm, was allegedly noted for his skill in vernacular poetry, though unfortunately none of it survives.[116] He, too, used alliteration and repetition.

When one examines Boniface's acrostic poem against the background of the vernacular tradition, one can hardly accuse him of possessing a cloth ear. He was acutely sensitive to the sounds of the Latin language. Here is his poem with the alliterative sounds marked in italics:

VYNFRETH PRISCORUM DVDDO CONGESSERAT ARTEM
VIRIBUS ILLE IVGIS IVVAVIT IN ARTE MAGISTRVM

    Versibus, en iuuenis, durant et *c*armina *c*antu,   44r

    *y*mnos namque *D*ei, *y*mnica *d*icta uiri

    nisibus eximiis renouantis carmina lector.

---

115 Orchard, *Poetic Art of Aldhelm*, especially pp. 29–37.
116 Michael Lapidge, "Aldhelm's Latin Poetry and Old English Verse," *Comparative Literature* 31 (1979): 209–31; reprinted in *Anglo-Latin Literature 600–899* (London: Hambledon Press, 1996), pp. 247–69 and 505–6, at 266–67.

Fulmina namque Pius *f*rangere iudicii
regmina *t*emporibus *t*orquebit *t*orribus, et sub
    *e*xcelsi fatu *o*mnia saecla diu
*T*uta *t*enent iusti. Pariter *t*um *t*aenia sanctis
    *h*ic dabitur regni aurea; *h*acque pii
per *c*aeli *c*ampos stipabunt pace tribunal,
    *r*egnantes *l*audant *l*impida *r*egna simul.
In *p*ia *p*erpetuæ ut dominentur gaudia uitae,
    *s*ordida in terris *s*pernere gesta uiri.
*C*autum est, ut numquam defleant supplicia *c*assu
    *o*mnes gentiles, *i*mpia *o*rigo Magog,
regmina ut *p*erdant *p*ariter sub *T*artara *t*rusi.
    *V*nus nempe Deus sæcula cuncta *s*uis
mirifico *a*bsoluens *e*st. Victima tradidit *a*mni
    diues in arte *s*ua omnia *s*ancta gradu.
Victor nam Iesus Xristus sicque *o*rdinat *a*ctu.
*D*apsilis in pastis uernis, tua fata *d*icanda
deuotis concede *t*ibi cum laudibus. Id *t*u,
Omnipotens genitor, fac nostro in *p*ectore *p*oni,
*c*asta suum *r*esonans *r*ectorem ut lingua *c*antet,
O Deus in solio iudex, regnator *O*limpi.
*N*umina *n*amque tuum monstrant per sæcula *n*omen
*g*entibus in uastis celebrant et *g*audia mira.
Edite in terris, *s*aluasti sæcla redemptor.

*Spiritus a*ethralem tibi laudem *s*plendidus *a*ptet,

subiciens hominem et perlustrans limina terrae.

30 Egregium regem, gnatum, praeconia faustum

ruricolae iugiter dicant *c*um *c*armine *c*lara.

*A*lmo quod feruens gremio signabat *A*bisag

totum, quae radiens constat sapientia iusti,

*a*rchitenens *a*ltor, qui sidera clara gubernas,

35 rurigenæ *p*ræsta, ut certus solamina *p*ossit

tradere per *s*acras *s*cripturas. Grammate doctor

*e*xcerptus *p*risco *p*uerorum *i*ndaginis *u*su

"Magna *p*atri et *p*roli cum flamine gratia," dicam.

If one puts aside the acrostic, all but four of the lines of the poem itself contain at least two alliterative words per line; in several instances there are three or more (lines 5, 7, 14, 17, 25, 31); and in some instances (lines 2, 15, 23, 28, 37) there are two different sounds that alliterate. When one examines the four lines without apparent alliteration, one will see that there are repeated consonants and in line 29 also a repeated syllable:

3: *n*isibus exi*m*iis re*n*ouantis car*m*i*n*a lector.

29: subiciens ho*min*em et per*l*ustrans *l*i*min*a terrae.

30: E*g*re*g*iu*m* re*g*em, *g*natu*m*, praeconia faus*tum*

33: *to*t*um*, quae radiens cons*t*a*t* sapien*t*ia ius*t*i,

These four lines prompt one to look for other examples in the poem. There are quite a few lines or half-lines where repeated consonants are to be found (e.g. line 9: *stipabunt pace tribunal*). Line 7 is especially striking since the letter *t* is to be found in every word in the line: "*Tuta tenent iusti. Pariter tum taenia sanctis.*" Many examples of repeated words or repeated word-stems are to be found (lines 1, 3, 31: *carmina . . . carmina . . . carmine*; line 2: *ymnos . . . ymnica*; lines 2, 16, 24: *Dei . . . Deus . . . Deus*; lines 4, 11, 14: *Pius . . . pia . . . impia*; lines 5, 15: *regmina*; lines 6, 25, 27: *saecla . . . sæcula . . . sæcla*; lines 7, 18: *sanctis . . . sancta*; lines 8, 10, 24: *regni . . . regnantes . . . regna . . . regnator*; and lines 31, 35: *ruricolae . . . rurigenæ*).[117]

Boniface has retained the principles of classical Latin scansion but, like Aldhelm before him, has incorporated elements of the Anglo-Saxon vernacular tradition into this Latin poem.[118] It thus demands a different aesthetic response from that elicited by a work of the classical Latin golden age.[119]

---

117   There are also several examples of internal rhyme (line 2: *Dei . . . uiri*; line 6: *fatu . . . diu*; line 11: *perpetuae . . . uitae*; line 30: *gnatum . . . faustum*) but only a single example of end-rhyme (lines 18–19: *gradu./ . . . actu.*). Aldhelm had shown a similar restraint in the use of end-rhyme. The internal rhyme might owe a debt ultimately to vernacular Irish poetry mediated through Aldhelm to Boniface. See further Orchard, *Poetic Art of Aldhelm*, pp. 41–42.

118   Neither Boniface nor Aldhelm adopted the double alliteration between verses, imitative of the practice in Old English poetry. Andy Orchard has identified Æthilwald, Aldhelm's pupil, as the originator of this in Anglo-Latin verse: see *Poetic Art of Aldhelm*, pp. 47–52.

119   My thanks to Hans-Günter Schmidt of the University of Würzburg for permitting me to examine Würzburg, Universitätsbibliothek, MS M.p.th.f. 29, and to Hans Sauer of the University of Munich for facilitating my access to the manuscript. Michael Lapidge kindly read an earlier draft of this essay and made a number of helpful comments. David R. Howlett and Theodore Christchev also cast their eyes over a draft of my edition, translation, and metrical excursus, and Luise Beyerlein vetted my German translations, for all of which I am grateful. The views expressed, however, are my own (unless otherwise attributed) and they should not be held responsible for any infelicities, errors, or misjudgments.

A Cross and an Acrostic

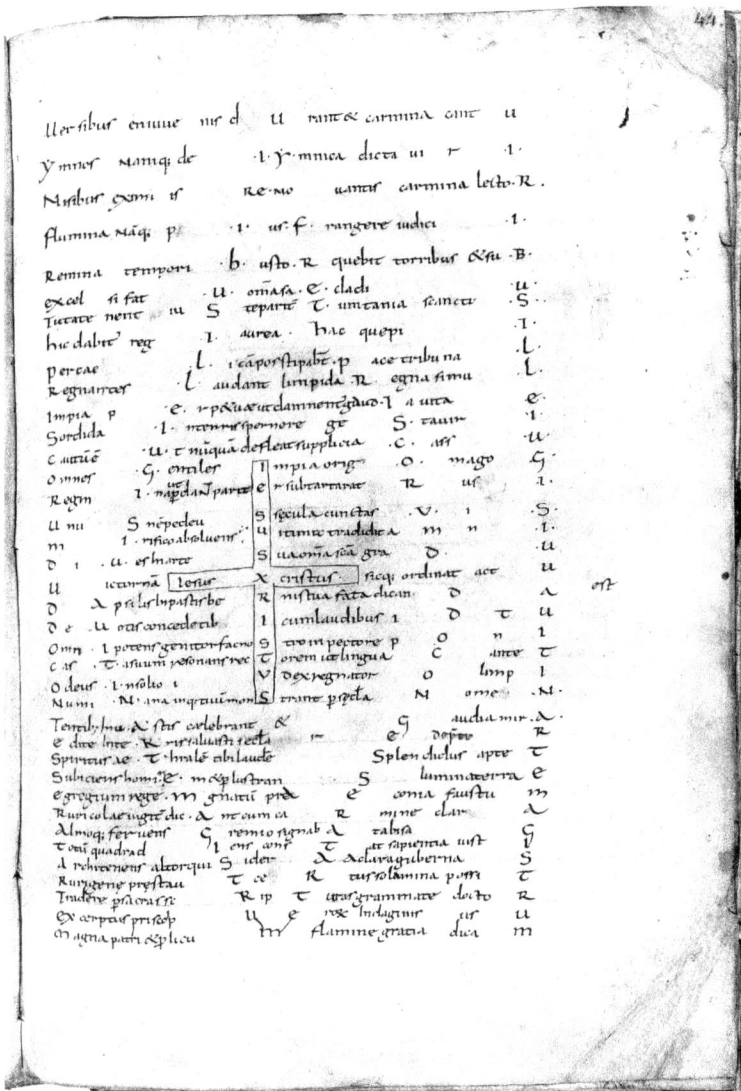

Fig. 2.1: Würzburg, Universitätsbibliothek (M.p.th.f.29, folio 44r). By permission of the Zentralbibliothek, Bayerische Julius-Maximilians-Universität Würzburg.

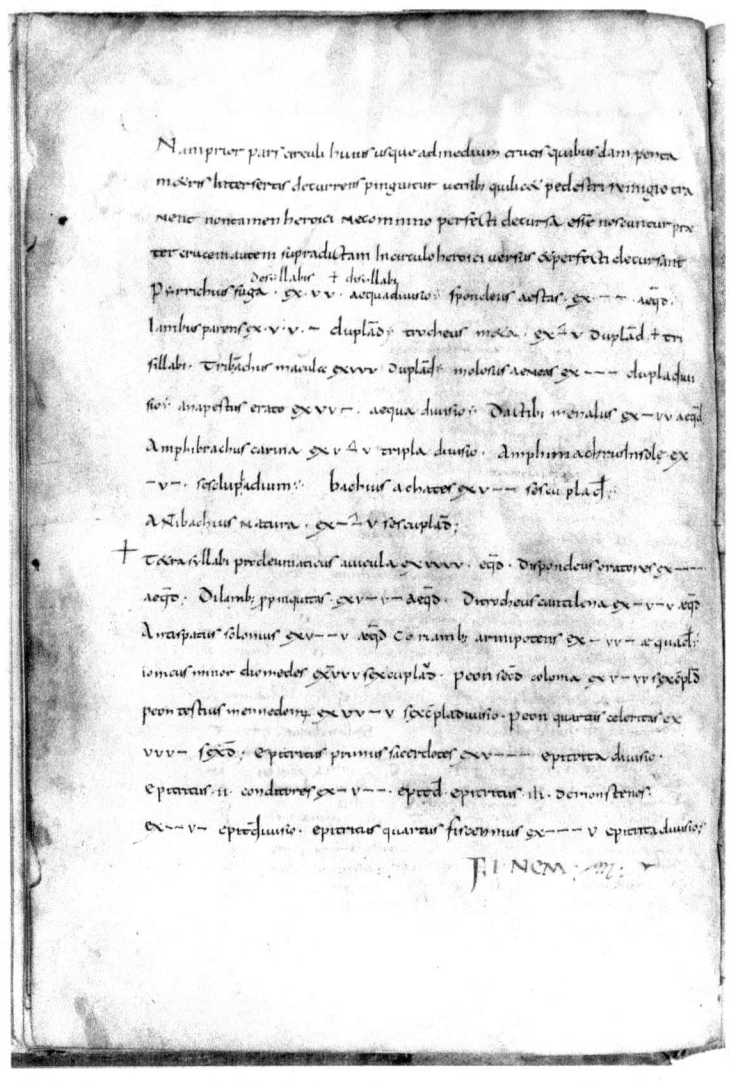

Fig. 2.2: Würzburg, Universitätsbibliothek (M.p.th.f.29, folio 44v). By permission of the Zentralbibliothek, Bayerische Julius-Maximilians-Universität Würzburg.

Abbot Ælfwine and the Sign of the Cross
Catherine E. Karkov

ÆLFWINE, ABBOT OF THE NEW MINSTER at Winchester from 1031 to 1057, is responsible for two of the most innovative and unusual manuscripts to survive from Anglo-Saxon England: the manuscript known as Ælfwine's Prayerbook (London, British Library MS Cotton Titus D. xxvii and xxvi) produced at some time between 1023 and 1031[1] while he was still dean, and the Liber Vitae of New Minster and Hyde Abbey (London, British Library MS Stowe 944) begun in 1031 shortly after he became abbot. Both manuscripts are unusual in their combination of texts, in the complexity of their illustrations, and in the way in which they relate to each other. The focus of this study will be on the ways in which both manuscripts provide evidence of the abbot's deeply personal devotion to the cross, and the way in which both manuscripts use the cross and related images and symbols to create visual programs

---

1 The manuscript was almost certainly a single volume until it was separated in Sir Robert Cotton's library. When shelf marks were assigned, the latter section of the book was incorrectly identified as coming first and received the designation "Titus D. xxvi," while the first part, containing material only ever found at the beginning of such a service book, was assigned the shelf mark "Titus D. xxvii." See Beate Günzel, ed., *Ælfwine's Prayerbook*, HBS 108 (London: Boydell Press, 1993), pp. 4–5.

of illustrations. These illustrations help to unite the different parts of the individual books, and also help in the later manuscript to draw out and make public some of the themes present in the personal and earlier Prayerbook.

ÆLFWINE'S PRAYERBOOK

The Prayerbook contains: (1) a collection of computistical and prognostic material; (2) a calendar and necrology; (3) prayers to the Holy Cross; (4) Offices of the Trinity, the Holy Cross and the Virgin; (5) a collectar; (6) a litany of the saints; (7) a series of private prayers; (8) Old English texts, including Ælfric's *De temporibus anni*; (9) a cryptographic note naming Ælfsige (one of the scribes) and Ælfwine; (10) miscellaneous texts listing the names of the Seven Sleepers, the Six Ages of the World, the length of Christ's body and the wood of the cross, weather signs, and a charm for finding a thief; (11) the three drawings (Figures. 3.1–3).[2] The manuscript is primarily the work of two scribes: Ælfsige (Scribe A) who was also the main scribe of the Liber Vitae, and Scribe B who some scholars believe might have been Ælfwine himself.[3] In support of the identification of Scribe B as Ælfwine is the fact that amongst the texts for which Scribe B was responsible are the most personal, and in many ways the most unusual parts of the book: the prayers to the Holy Cross, the Special Offices (Trinity, Holy Cross and Virgin), the private prayers on quires 13–15, and the collectar.[4] One of the private prayers names the supplicant as *famulum/am tuum/am .Ælfwine* ("your servant Ælfwine"),[5] but

---

2   For a complete list of the contents of the manuscript see Appendix 1.
3   For a summary of the different arguments see Simon Keynes, ed., *The Liber Vitae of the New Minster and Hyde Abbey Winchester*, EEMF 26 (Copenhagen: Rosenkilde and Bagger, 1996), pp. 111, 112–13; Günzel, *Ælfwine's Prayerbook*, p. 3.
4   The twenty-one prayers to the cross are evidence of a deep veneration for the cross. The Office of the Virgin is the earliest text of a Marian office, and may have been instituted by Æthelwold (Günzel, *Prayerbook*, p. 53); the litany also contains six invocations to the Virgin, an unusually high number (p. 58).
5   Günzel, *Prayerbook*, no. 76.28, p. 187.

clearly this cannot be taken as firm evidence that it was written by Ælfwine's own hand.[6] It has also been suggested that Ælfwine was the artist of the drawings in the Prayerbook (as well as of those in the Liber Vitae),[7] although there is virtually no evidence to support such a hypothesis.

The drawings in the Prayerbook are small, intimate, and express a very personal devotion that is also characteristic of the manuscript's prayers, especially those to the cross. They exhibit a concern with the fate of the soul at the moment of death that is also a feature of the devotions to the cross, as well as of other texts included in the manuscript. The drawings introduce the three major sections of devotional texts: the Crucifixion (Cotton Titus D. xxvii, folio 65v) prefaces a series of twenty-one prayers to the Holy Cross; the Trinity with Mary (Cotton Titus D. xxvii, folio 75v) prefaces the Offices of the Trinity, the Holy Cross, and the Virgin; and the drawing of St. Peter (Cotton Titus D. xxvi, folio 19v) prefaces the collectar, which begins with the Common of an Apostle. The drawings act as "pictorial markers,"[8] but they are also icons, the visual *foci* for the prayers they accompany, and together they form a diagram of devotion and salvation. The first of the drawings, the Crucifixion, depicts an event from the biblical past in which the figures are lively, interacting with each other and, in the case of the Virgin, gesturing as if reaching out towards the reader. The drawing of the Trinity with Mary represents the kingdom of heaven, past and future, and the triumph of the eternal word—as the inclusion of the figure of Arius in the mouth of hell makes clear. However, it also suggests temporal

---

6 Some of the prayers have had feminine inflections added above the lines while others seem to have been copied from an original that already contained feminine endings. See Günzel, *Prayerbook*, pp. 3–4.

7 Robert Deshman, for example, believed that the drawings in both manuscripts were by the same hand, but gave no supporting evidence for his beliefs (*The Benedictional of Æthelwold* [Princeton: Princeton University Press, 1995], p. 106). See also Keynes, *Liber Vitae*, p. 113.

8 Keynes, *Liber Vitae*, p. 113.

continuity with the crucifixion through the inclusion of the bound Satan beneath the feet of the risen Christ, a visual reference to the Harrowing of Hell.[9] In this drawing the figures interact only with each other, although the books held by the figures representing Christ incarnate and God the Father are open towards us, visually uniting the open book of the supplicant (this book) with the as yet unopened book held by the divine or risen nature of Christ.[10] In the drawing depicting Ælfwine before St. Peter, the abbot and his book are brought into the presence of Peter, who is intercessor, judge, and gatekeeper of heaven.[11] In this drawing Ælfwine would have been able to glimpse a hoped-for future in which he stood at the gates of heaven about to enter the kingdom represented in the drawing of the Trinity with Mary, the kingdom made attainable for humanity through the sacrifice of the Crucifixion. As Barbara Raw notes, the drawing relates directly to the text of the prayer to St. Peter on folio 88v which ends with the hope that Peter, *ianitor et pastor*, "doorkeeper and shepherd," "will intercede for the speaker so that after the end of his life he may be found worthy of eternal happiness."[12] These

---

9   The composition of the drawing as a whole can also be understood as a reference to the opening words of Psalm 109: "Dixit Dominus Domino meo sede a dextris meis donec ponam inimicos tuos scabillum pedum tuorum." (The Lord said to my lord: sit thou at my right hand: until I make thy enemies thy footstool). All biblical quotations are from the Vulgate Bible, and all translations from the Douay-Rheims Bible. Psalm 109 is the psalm in the Utrecht Psalter illustrated by the drawing that provided one of the sources for the drawing in the Prayerbook. See Ernst H. Kantorowicz, "The Quinity of Winchester," in his *Selected Studies* (Locust Valley, NY: Augustin, 1965), pp. 100–20.

10 The closed book perhaps symbolizes the mystery of the Resurrection as indicated by John's words, "No one has gone up to heaven except the one who came down from heaven" (John 3:13). In her *Trinity and Incarnation in Anglo-Saxon Art and Thought* (Cambridge: Cambridge University Press, 1997), pp. 158–59 and 183, Barbara Raw has an excellent discussion of this drawing, although I disagree with her description of the figures in the drawing as "remote."

11 Raw, *Trinity*, p. 183.

12 Raw, *Trinity*, p. 181.

words appear immediately before the prayer to the cross in which the supplicant requests that his name be entered in the Book of Life (*et adscribas nomen meum in libro uite*),[13] the book held by God the Father in the drawing of the Trinity with Mary.

The Crucifixion (Figure 3.1)
Possibly the most eye-catching feature of the Crucifixion miniature is the amount of text included on the page. On a purely visual level the words help to unite the drawing with the strictly textual pages that precede and follow it, a reminder of the inseparable nature of image and text in this particular manuscript. The metrical inscription at the top of the drawing of the Crucifixion serves to unite the living Ælfwine with the idea of redemption to come, symbolized by Christ's sacrifice on the cross. It reads: "Hec crux consignet Ælfwine corpore mente. In qua suspendens tra(xit) d(eu)s omnia secum" (This cross signs Ælfwine in body and in mind, on which the hanging God drew all things to him). Text and image further serve to unite Ælfwine in body and in mind with the memory of his own baptism in which he was marked by the sign of the cross, which, according to Revelation, believed by many in the early Middle Ages to have been written by John the Evangelist,[14] will sign the foreheads of the saved at the Last Judgment.[15] Ælfwine is thus here *named* and drawn to both the cross

---

13   *Salvatio Crucis Devota*, folio 89r (Günzel, *Prayerbook*, item 52.9, pp. 138–39).
14   See further Jennifer O'Reilly, "The Wounded and Exalted Christ," *Peritia* 6–7 (1987–88): 72–118, at 84–93; Jennifer O'Reilly, "St John as a Figure of the Contemplative Life: Text and Image in the Art of the Anglo-Saxon Benedictine Reform," *St Dunstan: His Life, Times and Cult*, ed. Nigel Ramsay, Margaret Sparks and Tim Tatton-Brown (Woodbridge: Boydell and Brewer, 1992), pp. 165–85 at 166; Jeffrey Hamburger, *St. John the Divine: The Deified Evangelist in Medieval Art and Thought* (Berkeley, CA: University of California Press, 2002), passim.
15   Raw, *Trinity*, pp. 185–6. Rev. 7:2–3: "And I saw another angel ascending from the rising of the sun, having the sign of the living God; and he cried with a loud voice to the four angels, to whom it was given to hurt the earth and the

Catherine Karkov

and Godhead (pictured in its different aspects in the drawing of the Trinity), and united in contemplation with the figures of Mary and John depicted and *named* on the page.[16] The evangelist writing in his book, opened towards the reader, would have served a similar function, suggesting the symbolic relationship between John's book and Ælfwine's book, in which a copy of the Passion according to St. John (John 18–19, folios 57r–64v) immediately precedes a prayer to the cross (folio 64v) and the drawing of the Crucifixion (folio 65v).[17] If Ælfwine was Scribe B (or indeed, the artist of the drawing), the association of himself with John as author and witness might have been closer still.[18]

The prayers to the cross that follow further develop the interaction of the reading figure of Ælfwine with Christ suggested by the Crucifixion in which he is drawn to the body on the cross. They begin with seven prayers to be said in front of a crucifix, and to be addressed to seven parts of Christ's body: the right foot, left foot, right hand, left hand, mouth, breast and ears. Raw believes that the opening words of the prayers addressed to the cross, Christ the King and son of David, Redeemer, Master, Eternal Word of the Father, benevolent Jesus, and living cross, "are not related in any way to Christ's wounds;"[19] but they are in fact directed to the seven points of entry into Christ's body: the five wounds, plus the mouth and ears.[20]

---

sea, saying: hurt not the earth, nor the sea, nor the trees, till we sign the servants of our God in their foreheads."

16 On the figure of John see O'Reilly, "St. John," passim.

17 Folio 65r is blank.

18 The gospel extract is in the hand of scribe A, but the prayer to the cross was written by scribe B.

19 Barbara Raw, *Anglo-Saxon Crucifixion Iconography and the Art of the Monastic Revival* (Cambridge: Cambridge University Press, 1990), p. 167. The incipits to the prayers are as follows: "O crux splendidior cvnctis astris," "Ave rex noster, fili David redemptor," "Tu es redemptor mevs," "Domine Iesv Christe, magister bone, svscipe," "O Iesv benigne, verbvm patris et eternum," "Cvm qve pervenero, iesv benigne," and "O crux viride ligno, qvia svper te."

20 See also George H. Brown, "Bede and the Cross," *Cross and Culture in Anglo-*

Abbot Ælfwine and the Sign of the Cross

We should also note that in reciting the prayers before a crucifix (or perhaps the drawing of the Crucifixion), the supplicant would have traced the body of the Lord with his (or her) mind, following its wounds and openings, all of which are clearly depicted in the drawing and named in the rubrics. The witnessing of the wounds is also a feature of John's account of the Passion (John 19:34–35), part of the text that precedes the drawing and the devotional prayers, and again offering us the tantalizing specter of the scribe associating himself with the evangelist who is simultaneously witness and author in the text. The devotional prayers alternate with seven psalms—Psalms 3, 53, 66, 69, 85, 140, 3:5[21]—which, while not mentioning all seven parts of the body, do emphasize the interaction between the supplicant's words and the body, or at least the ear of the Lord, as for example in the following passages:

> Ps 3:5: "Verba mea auribus percipe Domine intellege clamorem meum" (I have cried to the Lord with my voice: and he has heard me from his hill)[22]

> Ps 53:4: "Deux exaudi orationem meam auribus percipe verba oris mei" (O God, hear my prayer: give ear to the words of my mouth)

Or

> Ps 140:1–3: "Domine clamavi ad te exaudi me intende voci meae cum clamavero ad te dirigatur oratio mea sicut incensum in conspectu tuo elevatio manuum mearum sacrificium vespertinum pone Domine custodiam ori meo et ostium circumstantiae labiis meis"

Saxon England, ed. Karen Louise Jolly, Catherine E. Karkov and Sarah Larratt Keefer (Morgantown: West Virginia University Press, 2008), pp. 19–35.

21 Günzel (*Prayerbook*, p. 52) notes that these are not the usual penitential psalms.

22 Psalm 3 is the first psalm included, and Psalm 3 verse 5 the last.

[I have heard thee, O Lord, hear me: hearken to my voice, when I cry to thee. Let my prayer be directed as incense into thy sight; the lifting up of my hands as evening sacrifice. Set a watch, O Lord, before my mouth and a door round about my lips.]

This series of prayers and psalms is followed by a prayer that is a version of the *Kyrie* from which the inscription at the top of the Crucifixion drawing is taken,[23] reinforcing both its message and the spiritual union of Christ's body on the cross with the body of Ælfwine, the reader, in the act of devotion.

Although not directed specifically to Christ's body, his body (and its seven parts) would also have been brought to mind by the repetition of the *Pater Noster* seven times in the prayer *Ecce lignum crucis* (Günzel, item 46.9), which follows the *Kyrie*, and which was to be recited lying before the cross; in the prayer containing the seven petitions to the cross (Günzel, item 46.13); and in the repeated use of the number seven in the first verse of a prayer giving four reasons for adoring the cross (Günzel, item 46.12). The verse reads "Prima causa est, qui in una die septem cruces adit, aut septies unam crucem adorat, septem porte inferni clauduntur illi, et septem porte paradisi aperiuntur ei" (The first reason is that if a man addresses seven prayers to the cross in one day, or venerates the cross seven times, the seven gates of hell will be closed to him, and the seven gates of paradise will be opened to him).[24] The last of the prayers to the cross, which begins "Obsecro te, Domine Iesu Christe filii Dei," shifts the focus from Christ's body by redirecting the saving power of the cross back upon the supplicant's own body, imploring the cross to protect his head, eyes, mouth, hands, arms, legs, bowels, feet, "et omnia membra mea ab insidiis diaboli" (and all my parts against the snares of demons).[25] The protection of Ælfwine's body

---

23 Raw, *Trinity*, p. 178.
24 Günzel, *Prayerbook*, item 46.12, p. 126.
25 For the full prayer see Günzel, *Prayerbook*, item 46.21, pp. 127–28.

Abbot Ælfwine and the Sign of the Cross

by the cross in the prayer brings us back once again to the drawing of the Crucifixion with its inscription in which Ælfwine is signed by the cross in body and in mind. At both the beginning and end of this set of devotions, through both image and word, he is protected by the sign of the cross.

The Trinity (Figure 3.2)
While the cross itself may not be a prominent feature of the iconography of this miniature, it is nonetheless present in the cruciform haloes of Christ in both his natures, God the Father, and the dove of the Holy Spirit, and the drawing does preface the Office of the Holy Cross (in addition to those of the Trinity and the Virgin), whose texts recall the sacrifice and triumph of Christ at the crucifixion. Such verbal echoes of the visual imagery can be found throughout the manuscript. One of the private prayers to Christ and the Trinity in this section of the manuscript, for example, reads in part: "Inuoco patrem et filium et Spritium sanctum, ut sit super me signum crucis Christi, defendat me a malis operibus. Signaculum sancte crucis sit super me diebus ac noctibus. Amen" (I call upon the Father, Son, and Holy Ghost, that the seal of the Cross of Christ be upon me, defend me from evil works, that the sign of the holy cross be upon me night and day).[26] The cross of the crucifixion is further linked to the drawing by such texts as the hymn *Vexilla Regis* with its antiphon addressing the role of the cross in Christ's triumph over death (*in qua Christus triumphauit et mors mortem*), and the final prayer in which the sacrifice of Christ on the cross brings peace to both men and the kingdom of heaven, here represented by the heavenly angels (*celestium collegium angelorum*). The theological and chronological connections between the drawing of the Trinity and the drawing and inscription of the Crucifixion are evoked in one of the final prayers to the cross on folios 71v and 72r:

> Deus, qui uoliuisti pro redemptione mundi a Iudeis reprobari, a Iuda osculo tradi, uinculis alligari et agnus innocens ad uictimam

---

26 Günzel, *Prayerbook*, item 52.10, p. 139.

duci, atque conspectibus Pilati offerri, a falsis quoque testibus accusari, flagellis et obprobriis uexari et conspui, spinis coronari, colaphis cedi, cruce eleuari, atque inter latrones deputari, clauorum quoque aculeis perforari, lancea uulnerari, felle et aceto potari, tu per sanctissimas has poenas tuas ab inferni poenis me libera, et per sanctam crucem tuam salua et custodi, et illuc perduc me miserum/am peccatorem/tricem, quo perduxisti tecum crucifixus latronem; tibi cum Deo patre et Spiritu sancto honor, uirtus et gloria, nunc et in omnia secula. Amen.

[Oh God who wished for the redemption of the world, to be rejected by the Jews, betrayed by the kiss of Judas, bound in chains, led to slaughter like an innocent lamb, brought before the sight of Pilate, accused also by false witnesses, injured by scourges and insults, spat on, crowned with thorns, struck, raised on the cross, assigned a place between thieves, pierced by the points of the nails, wounded by the spear, given gall and vinegar to drink; free me from the punishments of hell through your most holy sufferings, and save and keep me though your holy cross, and lead me, a wretched sinner, where you led with you the crucified thief; to you, with God the Father and the Holy Spirit, be honour, power and glory, now and for ever. Amen.][27]

As the second of the three drawings in the Prayerbook, the image looks forward as well as back. Christ's calling Peter on the sea is mentioned in one of the first antiphons of the Office of the Holy Cross,[28] perhaps looking forward to his reappearance in the last of the manuscript's miniatures. Admittedly, the echo, if intended, is subtle, but the private prayers in the Office of the Virgin Mary that follow include a prayer to Peter, keeper of the keys to heaven.[29] The

---

27 Translation from Raw, *Trinity*, p. 179 n. 57.
28 "Salua nos, Christe saluator, per uirtutem cruces, qui saluasti Petrum in mari, miserere nobis" (folio 80r, Günzel, *Prayerbook*, p. 132): "Save us, Christ savior, by virtue of the cross, who saved Peter on the sea, have mercy on us."
29 "O Beate Petre . . . custos clauium regni celorum" (Günzel, *Prayerbook*,

texts that now separate these prayers from the miniature of Peter and the collectar were added to the manuscript at some time in the first half of the eleventh century by a new scribe.[30] Moreover, as one of the patron saints of the New Minster, Peter would surely have had a special place in Ælfwine's prayers and heart.

Ælfwine and St. Peter (Figure 3.3)

The drawing of Ælfwine and St. Peter highlights Peter's role as judge and gatekeeper through the prominent image of his double cross-key, through the similarity of the book that he holds to the book of judgment held by God the Father in the drawing of the Trinity, and through the similarity of the rainbow-arc on which Peter sits to that on which the Father and Son are enthroned in the previous drawing.[31] The globe on which Peter sits is usually also an attribute of God or Christ in Majesty, and helps visually to establish the spiritual connection between Peter and Christ. The power of locking and unlocking symbolized by the key had been delegated to Peter by Christ, and like Christ, Peter had been crucified, an event to which the cruciform patterns of the key may refer. As Robert Deshman points out in his discussion of the Benedictional of Æthelwold (London, British Library MS Additional 49598), Peter's cross-key was for this very reason an allusion to the apostle's own resurrection, which was itself made possible by Christ's victory over death.[32] The presence of the key in the drawing of Peter in the Prayerbook is thus an allusion back to the first two drawings, to the inscription of the Crucifixion page, and to the eventual salvation of Ælfwine through the sign of the cross. The key and the cross were cognate symbols of victory and the opening of the gates of paradise.[33] The first prayer of the Collectar (for the

---

item 52.8, p. 138): "O blessed Peter . . . guardian of the keys to the kingdom of heaven."
30 Ker, no. 202; Günzel, pp. 6–7.
31 See also Raw, *Trinity*, pp. 146 and 181–82.
32 Deshman, *Benedictional*, p. 76.
33 Deshman, *Benedictional*, p. 76.

vigil of an apostle) on the facing page picks up on this aspect of the drawing's symbolism in its reference to being shown the kingdom of God: "Iustum deduxit Dominus per uias rectas et ostendit illi regnum Dei et dedit illi scientiam sanctorum, honestauit illum in laboribus et compleuit labores illius" (The Lord conducted the just through the right ways and showed him the kingdom of God, and gave him the knowledge of holy things, made him honorable in his labors, and accomplished his labors).[34]

Just as the drawing is connected theologically and iconographically with the first two drawings, it is also a visualization of a theme that echoes throughout the Prayerbook: the fate of the soul at the hour of death, the moment at which Peter would admit the saved into heaven and into the presence of the Trinity and Mary.[35] This is a theme that occurs repeatedly in the devotions to the cross—Raw notes especially the prayer *O Iesu clementissime* with its refrain "Dum superuenerit mihi mortis hora horibilis"[36]—as well as in a series of private prayers requesting the intercession of Mary, Michael, and Peter, both individually and as a trio.[37] The longest of the three prayers to Mary, Michael, and Peter, one which may be unique to this manuscript,[38] calls for the intercession of Mary, for Michael's protection of the soul on Judgment Day,[39] and for the hope that Peter will open the gates of heaven and lock the gates of hell.[40] Peter is described in the prayer as a senator of the heavenly hall (*celestis aule*

---

34 Günzel, *Prayerbook*, item 73.1, p. 158: the prayer derives from Wisdom 10:10.
35 Günzel, *Prayerbook*, pp. 52–53; Raw, *Crucifixion*, p. 62.
36 Raw, *Crucifixion*, p. 62.
37 See Günzel, items 51.7, 52.8, 76.7, 76.9, 76.51, and 76.60.
38 Günzel lists no corresponding prayer in her Table of Correspondences.
39 See further, Catherine E. Karkov, "Judgement and Salvation in the New Minster Liber Vitae," in *Apocryphal Texts and Traditions in Anglo-Saxon England*, ed. Kathryn Powell and Donald G. Scragg (Woodbridge: Boydell and Brewer, 2003), pp. 151–63.
40 Günzel, *Prayerbook*, item 76.60, p. 193.

senator), underscoring his role as judge as well as doorkeeper, the same dual role emphasized in the drawing of the apostle receiving Ælfwine's book.[41] Like the cross-key symbolism, the terminology may well have had a particular resonance within the Winchester community: the first verse of a hymn, possibly composed by Wulfstan when he was precentor at the Old Minster, requesting the intercession of Æthelwold uses very similar wording:

> Celi senator inclite
> Sancte pastor ecclesie:
> O Adeluuolde supplices
> Tuos exaudi seruulos.
>
> [Distinguished senator of heaven, shepherd of Holy
> Church, O Æthelwold, hear your supplicant servants.][42]

A Winchester poem addressed to Æthelwold also associates the sainted abbot with St. Peter as intercessor:

> sic quoque nos caeli dominum rogitemus, adhelphi,
>   pellat ut a famulus arbitrium sceleris,
> quatinus a uitiis et neui crimine mundi
>   conciues Petri simus in arce poli,
> clauibus inmensi reserat qui limen Olimphi,
>   cui mandauit oues altitonans niueas.
> Omnibus hoc nobis concedat gratia Christi
>   Sanguine quos proprio traxit ab hoste fero.

---

41 Raw (*Trinity*, p. 182) points out that in the drawing Peter is enthroned on a globe and the arc of the firmament, indicating his role as judge in the kingdom of heaven.

42 See *Wulfstan of Winchester Life of St Æthelwold*, ed. Michael Lapidge and Michael Winterbottom (Oxford: Clarendon, 1991), cxvi [trans. n.3]). The hymn is recorded in a collection of liturgical pieces in Alençon, Bibliothèque Municipale MS 14, fols. 30v–36r, an early twelfth-century copy of a lost Old Minster exemplar (Lapidge, *Wulfstan of Winchester*, cxiii).

[Thus let us too beseech the lord of heaven, brothers, that he may drive away from his servants the will to sin, so that, clean from sin and the evil of stain, we may be compatriots of Peter in the summit of heaven, Peter who unlocks the threshold of Olympus with huge keys, to whom God the thunderer entrusted his snowy-white flocks. Let the grace of Christ grant this to all of us whom he drew away from the savage fiend with his own blood.][43]

The drawing thus looks forward not only to Ælfwine's own salvation, but by implication also to the salvation of the Winchester community, and to their reunion with their saintly abbot. This final drawing is a fitting conclusion to the progress towards judgment and salvation documented in the program of the three drawings and their accompanying texts. The cross that signed Ælfwine in body and in mind in the miniature of the Crucifixion has in the miniature of Peter drawn him to the gates of heaven and to God.[44] In prayer and in contemplation of the image, the boundaries of time and space have been broken down. But if the Prayerbook looks forward to Ælfwine's final redemption, it also looks to the past, to Winchester images and traditions, to the reforming bishop-abbot Æthelwold, and to the role that these too will have played in that process, a role that may also be suggested in the drawings by the repeated image of the book. The pictures in Ælfwine's Prayerbook, as Raw suggests, may be independent of the prayers they accompany,[45] but they are also heavily dependent on the ideas and images those prayer express, as well as on a series of texts and images from other Winchester manuscripts.

---

43 Trans. Michael Lapidge, "Three Latin Poems from Æthelwold's School at Winchester," in his *Anglo-Latin Literature 900–1066* (London & Rio Grande, OH: Hambledon, 1993), pp. 225–77, at 275–77. For the address to Æthelwold see lines 57–68, Lapidge, "Three Latin Poems," p. 270.
44 See also Raw, *Trinity*, p. 186.
45 Raw, *Trinity*, p. 176.

Abbot Ælfwine and the Sign of the Cross

The Liber Vitae

The interrelatedness of image and text, the theme of salvation, and the role of memory and tradition in the progress towards salvation first explored in the Prayerbook, are further developed in the Liber Vitae of New Minster and Hyde Abbey (see Appendix 2). The personal devotion to the cross and concern with redemption expressed in the Prayerbook are here extended publicly to the whole of the Winchester community, something that was merely implicit in the drawings of the Prayerbook. In this manuscript, specific Winchester ideas, images, and texts are carefully combined with universal symbols like the cross in the quest for redemption. The Liber Vitae opens with the well-known drawing of Queen Ælfgifu (Emma) and King Cnut donating a golden altar cross to the New Minster (Figure 3.4).[46] The presence of the altar indicates that the setting should be understood as the east end of the abbey church, but the presence of the angels and the lack of architectural detail also give it an eternal timelessness akin to that evoked by the imagery of the Prayerbook and by the inscription of its Crucifixion drawing. At the bottom of the page the monks of the New Minster witness the donation. The open book held by the monk directly beneath the cross is this book, and is an earthly reflection of the Book of Life held by Christ in Majesty at the top of the page. Color and composition are crucial to the way in which the symbols of book and cross are related to each other. The yellow color of the book held by Christ is a sign of its heavenly nature, and marks it as different from, though related to, the earthly book. It also marks it as similar in nature to the cross at the centre of the page, indisputably the central subject of the drawing. Both the use of color and the arrangement of the figures divide the page to form a royal axis that runs horizontally across the center of the

---

46   The cross was probably donated in the 1020s; see Keynes, *Liber Vitae*, p. 35. For a discussion of the page as a double-ruler portrait see Catherine E. Karkov, *The Ruler Portraits of Anglo-Saxon England* (Woodbridge: Boydell Press, 2004), ch. 4.

page, and a vertical ecclesiastical or spiritual axis,[47] with both focused on the sign of the cross.

The location of Christ directly above the cross provides a reference back in time to the Crucifixion—Mary and Peter here flank the enthroned Christ just as Mary and John flanked Christ on the cross in the Prayerbook's drawing—and a reference forward in time to the Last Judgment, the moment at which Christ, the Judge, will open the Book of Life. The location of Mary and Peter directly over the figures of the queen and king is a sign that they act specifically as intercessors for the royal couple, whose gift of the cross has earned them their place of honor in the New Minster Liber Vitae, and thus the inscription of their names in the Liber Vitae held by Christ. The cross will open the gates of paradise for Ælfgifu and Cnut just as surely as will Peter's cross-key.[48] According to chapter XI of the New Minster Charter, composed by Æthelwold under the patronage of King Edgar in 966:[49]

> Quicumque pretitulatos monachos bonis quibuslibet locupletans ditare uoluerit . creator cunctitenens clementer eos eorumque progeniem totius ubertate proxperitatis hic et in futuro seculo ditando locupletet . Scriptis decenter eorum in libro uite nominibus cum Christo portionem in celorum habitaculis habeant qui monachos suos quos nostris congregatos temporibus possidet uel uerbis . uel factis . sanctitatis studio honorauerint.

---

47 For parallels with the composition of some of the images developed by Rabanus Maurus, see William Schipper, "Reading the Cross in Anglo-Saxon England," *Cross and Culture in Anglo-Saxon England*, ed. Karen Louise Jolly et al., pp. 321–42.

48 For the role of the sign of the cross in Anglo-Saxon models of the good king see Susan Rosser, "Ælfric's Two Homilies for May 3: The Invention of the Cross and the Martyrdom of Pope Alexander and SS Eventius and Theodolus," *Ælfric's Canonized Popes*, ed. Donald Scragg (Kalamazoo, MI: Medieval Institute Press, 2000), pp. 55–73 at 70.

49 The charter is a record of King Edgar's founding privilege to the community reformed by Æthelwold.

Abbot Ælfwine and the Sign of the Cross

[Whoever should wish to enrich the aforementioned monks, making them rich with all good things, may the creator, mercifully controlling all things, make them and their descendants rich, enriching [them] with a copiousness of property now and in a future age. Let those who shall have honoured, either in words or in deeds, with devotion to holiness, His monks whom He possesses, collected as a flock in our times, have a share with Christ in the dwellings of Heaven, their names fitly having been written in the Book of Life.]⁵⁰

The fact that it was the donation of the altar cross that was chosen for the frontispiece of the abbey's Liber Vitae is an indication of just how important it was to Ælfwine's perceptions of the role and identity of the abbey at the beginning of his abbacy. As was the case with the drawings in the Prayerbook, the image also functions intervisually, echoing the composition of the Crucifixion in the Prayerbook, the frontispiece to the New Minster Charter, and the traditional royal or donor portraits of Byzantine and Ottonian art.[51] As is the case with all six of the drawings in the two manuscripts, Ælfwine was here bringing together details from a range of different works to create a unique and multivalent image. The donation of the cross is thus set within the general tradition of royal bequests, but through its reference to the New Minster Charter frontispiece, the donation is linked to the abbey's reform and re-foundation, acts central to the salvation of the Winchester community in both this world and the next. As in the drawings of the Crucifixion, or Ælfwine and St. Peter, in the Prayerbook, the boundaries of time and space are erased and living individuals are elevated to the company of the saints through the sign of the cross.

---

50 Trans. Alexander R. Rumble, *Property and Piety in Early Medieval Winchester: Documents Relating to the Topography of the Anglo-Saxon and Norman City and its Minsters* (Oxford: Oxford University Press, 2002), pp. 84–85.
51 See Karkov, *Ruler Portraits*, chap. 4.

The page must also be understood in the context of the double-page Last Judgment sequence which follows it (Figure 3.5). The contemporary figures of the queen, king, and monks on folio 6r stand in readiness to form part of the procession of the saved into heaven depicted on the verso of the same page, a narrative continuity suggested further by the depiction of an abbot (perhaps Ælfwine) and an aristocratic lay figure dressed very like Cnut leading the group in the upper left corner of folio 6v. Below them stand two haloed ecclesiastics carrying books and a processional cross, whose figures and attributes call to mind both the altar cross on the previous page and the liturgical processions that would have taken place in the New Minster itself. The inscription +*Ælgarus* added by a later hand indicates that one of the figures was intended to represent Æthelgar, pupil of Æthelwold and the first abbot of the New Minster (964–88), or that it had at least come to represent him by the time the inscription was added.[52] Perhaps the second figure was intended to represent Æthelwold himself. The cross and the book that the figures hold are also typologically related to the books held by the angel and the devil, and to the cross-keys of Peter on the facing page. Here the keys are shown both unlocking the door of heaven and locking the door of hell, and as an active weapon in the depiction of judgment enacted in the central register of folio 7r.

In the Liber Vitae drawing Peter is depicted in his roles of both doorkeeper (*ianator*) and shepherd (*pastor*), opening the gate of heaven and guiding a soul out of the clutches of the devil, the roles in which he appears in several of the prayers in Ælfwine's Prayerbook. But the role of Peter and his key is also paralleled here by the role of the abbots of the New Minster. It is with his cross-staff that the figure who may be Æthelgar defends the souls of his flock, and it is

---

52 Æthelgar went on to become Bishop of Selsey (980–88) and Archbishop of Canterbury (988–90). On the possible relationship of this page to the space of the New Minster itself, see Karkov, "Judgement and Salvation," passim.

with the cross as both sign and physical object that Ælfwine does the same.

The role of the book itself in the process of salvation is documented in the explanation of how the book was to be used, which forms part of the preface to the lists of names of the Winchester special dead:

> Et omnium qui se eius orationibus ac fraternitati commendant hic generaliter habeantur inscripta. Quatinus cotidie in sacris missarum celebrationibus vel psalmodiarum concentibus eorum commemoratio fiat. Et ipsa nomina per singulos dies a subdiacono ante sanctum altare ad matutinalem seu principalem missam præsunter et ab ipso prout tempus permiserit in conspectu altissimi recitentur. Postque oblatam Deo oblationem dextra manu cardinalis qui missam celebrat sacerdotis inter ipse sacræ missæ mysteria supra sanctum altare posita. Omnipotenti Deo humillime commendentur, quo sicut eorum memoria agiter in terris, ita in illa uita ipso largiente qui solus qualiter ibi omnes aut sunt aut futuri sunt nouit, eorum qui maiores meriti sunt gloria cumuleter in cælis, eorum uero qui minoris sunt in occultis ipsius causa leuigeter iudiciis. Gaudete et exultate quia nomina uestra scripta sunt in cælis.

> [And may the names be entered here of all those who commend themselves to its prayers and fraternity, in the holy solemnities of Mass or in the harmonies of psalmody. And may the names themselves be presented by the sub-deacon every day before the holy altar at the Morrow or principal Mass, and may they be read out by him in the sight of the Most High, as time permits. And, after the offering of the oblation to God, placed on the holy altar at the right hand of the principal priest who is celebrating Mass, during the mysteries of the sacred Mass, may they be most humbly commended to Almighty God. So that just as commemoration of them is made on earth, so too in that life, by the bounty of Him who alone knows how all are, or are to be, there, may the glory be

augmented of those who are of greater merit in heaven, and may the cause be smoothed, in the hidden judgments, of those who are of lesser merit. Rejoice and be glad because your names are written in heaven.][53]

One must of course envisage this ceremony taking place within the Minster with the great golden cross displayed with the book on the altar.

It is evident from both manuscripts that Ælfwine had particular spiritual desires, amongst the most prominent of which were his desire for the protection of the soul at death, his desire for the wealth and security of his community and its traditions in life, and his desire to bring himself and his community to salvation. As object, image, and verbal invocation, the cross was a powerful vehicle through which his desires could be achieved. Whether as an intimate icon of personal devotion or the focus of public liturgical performance, it bound its viewers and readers to it, and to all that it symbolized and promised. In Ælfwine's prayers and in his church, the cross united heaven and earth, past and future, in an eternal present. It was through the sign of the cross that Ælfwine asserted the rights of his community, and protected it from heretics and demons, and it was the sign of the cross that in the Liber Vitae brings that community, just as it brought the abbot himself in the Prayerbook, to the gates of heaven, to Peter and to Christ.

---

53 W. de Gray Birch, ed., *Liber Vitae: Register and Martyrology of New Minster and Hyde Abbey, Winchester* (London: Simpkin, 1892), p. 12; trans. Keynes, *Liber Vitae*, p. 83.

Appendix 1

Contents of Ælwine's Prayerbook

Cotton Titus D. xxvii

2r	Lunarium for blood-letting
2v	Ides and Nones of the months
3r–8v	Calendar
9r–10	Three tables of the ages of the Moon
10v	Verses for the limits of Quadragesima
11r	Verses for the limits of Easter
11v–12r	Tables with limits of Septuagesima, Quadragesima, Easter and Rogation
12v	Horologium
13r	Calculation of the Feast limits
13v	Calculation of the Epacts and Concurrents; the four Ember Days
14r	Note in cryptographic writing naming Ælfwine as the owner of the book; the Seven Sleepers
14v–21r	Easter Tables; Obits
21v	Diagram of the relation between the moon and the sea (incomplete)
22r–23r	Critical days for blood-letting
23r	Christ's threefold becoming of Man; text on the cycle of the moon
23v	Texts on the length of the day and the calculation of the full moon at Easter

24r	Days on which the Easter Lunation cannot begin; calculation of the Easter limit and of the age of the moon on Easter Sunday; the Spring Equinox
24rv	The Fixation of Easter Sunday
24v	The leap year; the solar and lunar years; the change of Concurrents
24v–25r	The lengths of the seasons
25r	Calculation of Advent
25rv	Pseudo-Esdras
25v	The division of the year
26r–27r	Prayer: *Ante oculos tuos*
27r–29v	General Lunarium
30r–54r	Ælfric's *De Temporibus Anni*
54v	Indulgence of days; the Feast limits
55r	Calculation of the Concurrents and Epacts
55v–56r	Alphabet and sentences
56v	Relation between the sea and moon; the age of the Virgin
57r–64v	Passion according to John
64v	Prayer to the cross: *Ave alma crux*
65r	Blank
65v	Crucifixion Miniature (Figure 3.1)
66r–74r	Devotions to the cross
74v–75r	Blank
75v	Miniature of the Trinity with Mary (Figure 3.2)
76r–80r	Office of the Trinity
80r–81v	Office of the Holy Cross
81v–85v	Office of the Virgin
86r–93v	Private prayers

Abbot Ælfwine and the Sign of the Cross

Cotton Titus D. xxvi

2rv	Directions for private devotions
3r	The Six Ages of the world
3rv	Length of Christ and the wood of the cross
3v–4r	Three critical Mondays
4rv	Lucky days of birth
4v	Canicular days and certain days of a lunar month
5r	Unlucky days
5r–6r	Weather signs
6r–7r	Lunarium for blood-letting
6v–7v	Birth prognostics for weekdays
7v–8r	Lunarium for birth
8r–9r	Lunarium for illness
9rv	Lunarium for dreams
9v–10v	Thunder prognostics
10v–11v	Pseudo-Esdras
11v–16r	*Somniale Danielis*
16v	Prayers with rubric, *þis ðu scealt singan þonne ðu wytl ðwean þine handa 7 þine eagan*
17r	Recipe for boils
17v–18r	Decisions at a bishops' synod
18v–19r	Blank
19v	Miniature of Peter and Ælfwine (Figure 3.3)
20r–30r	*Commune Sanctorum*
30r–33r	*Capitula in omnem diem*
33r–37v	*Temporale*
38r–42v	Daily prayers for sinners
42v–46r	Collects for Day Hours
46v–50v	Devotions based on the penitential psalms
51r–56v	Litany of the saints
56v–79r	Private prayers
79v	Charm for finding a thief
80r	Beginning of the Gospel of John

Appendix 2

Contents of the Liber Vitae of New Minster and Hyde Abbey

1r–5r	Preliminary material by Thomas Astle (1771)
6r	Dedication drawing (Figure 3.4)
6v–7r	Last Judgment (Figure 3.5)
7v	Record of charitable act by John Suithill (1200); accounts of events in Winchester in the 1060s and 1140s
8r–12v	Early history of the New Minster
13rv	Preface to the Liber Vitae
14r	Kings of the West Saxons: Cynegils (611–42) to Æthelred II (978–1016)
	Kings of England: Edmund (916) to Henry V (1413–22)
14v	Æthelings
14v–17r	Episcopal lists
17r	Ealdormen
17rv	Deceased benefactors
17v–20r	Members of the community of the Old Minster, Winchester
20r	Additional entries of various types
20v–23v	Members of the community of New Minster 964–1290
24r	Customs of Hyde Abbey
24v	Friends of Hyde Abbey
25rv	Friends of the New Minster
26rv	Women in confraternity with the New Minster
26v–27r	Other religious houses in confraternity with the New Minster

27rv	Members of the community of Ely Abbey
27v–28r	Members of the community of Romsey Abbey
28rv	Men in confraternity with the New Minster
28v–29r	Men and women in confraternity with the abbey, 1031 to early 12th century
29v–33r	Will of King Alfred
33r–34r	Tract on the Six Ages of the world and related texts
34v–36v	The royal saints of Kent
36v–39r	The resting places of saints
39rv	West Saxon regnal lists
40rv	Letter of Eadwine (monk and "child-master" of the New Minster) to Bishop Ælfsige
41r	Charter of King William I for Abbot Riwallon
41r–49v	Gospel lectionary
50r–54v	Blessings
54v–55r	Men and women in confraternity with Hyde Abbey 12th century–ca. 1450
55v	List of relics at Hyde Abbey
56rv	Incomplete names of the saints in heaven
57rv	Vernacular text of the founding of the New Minster
57v	Relics at Hyde Abbey
58rv	Relics at the New Minster (formerly at the beginning of the manuscript)
59r	Charter of Abbot Riwallon
59v–60r	Colloquy between Damasus and Jerome
60r–61r	Liturgical texts
61v	The number of languages in the world
62r–64v	Members of the community of Hyde Abbey 13th–15th century
65r–68v	Men and women in confraternity with Hyde Abbey 1467–ca. 1530
69r	Thomas Astle's note on the history of the Liber Vitae

Fig. 3.1: The Crucifixion (London, BL Cotton Titus D. xxvii, folio 65v). Courtesy of the British Library Board.

Abbot Ælfwine and the Sign of the Cross

Fig. 3.2: The Trinity with Mary (London, BL Cotton Titus D. xxvii, folio 75v). Courtesy of the British Library Board.

Catherine Karkov

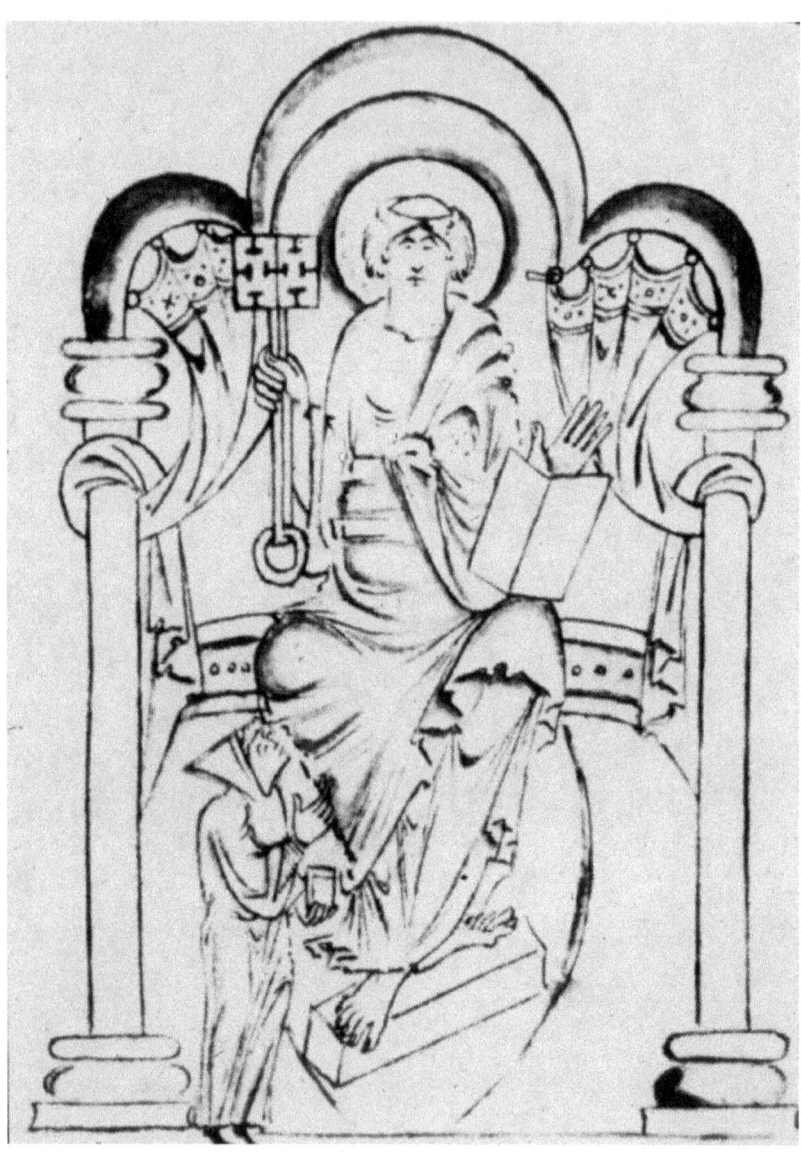

Fig. 3.3: Ælfwine before St. Peter (London, BL Cotton Titus D. xxvi, folio 19v). Courtesy of the British Library Board.

Fig. 3.4: Emma and Cnut present a Cross to the New Minster (London, BL Stowe 944, folio 6r). Courtesy of the British Library Board.

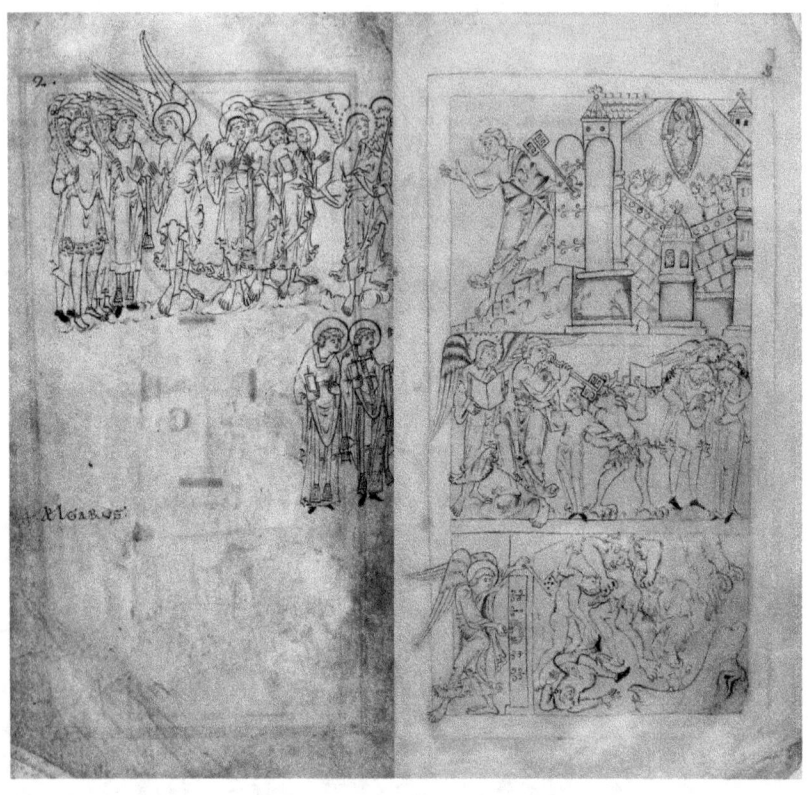

Fig. 3.5: The Last Judgment (London, BL Stowe 944, folio 6v-7r). Courtesy of the British Library Board.

II

The Cross: Meaning and Word

Sources or Analogues? Using Liturgical Evidence to Date *The Dream of the Rood*

Éamonn Ó Carragáin

I BEGIN with five general principles.
1. *The Dream of the Rood*, as we have it in the Vercelli manuscript, is a tenth-century poem. The *Dream* should be understood within an Old English verse narrative tradition of which three separate poems survive, now at Ruthwell, Brussels, and Vercelli. Each of these three poems has its own structure and coherence; and each is best understood in its immediate context which comprises, respectively, the eighth-century Ruthwell Cross; the eleventh-century Brussels Cross; and the late tenth-century Vercelli Book.[1] Thus a primary context for the *Dream* is provided by the interests of the person who copied that poem into the Vercelli Book.[2]

2. These three surviving poems are likely to be merely chance

---

1 See Éamonn Ó Carragáin, *Ritual and the Rood: Liturgical Images and the Old English Poems of the* Dream of the Rood *Tradition* (London: British Library Publications and Toronto: Toronto University Press, 2005), passim.
2 See Éamonn Ó Carragáin, "How did the Vercelli Collector interpret *The Dream of the Rood*?" in *Studies in Language and Literature in Honour of Paul Christophersen*, ed. Philip Tilling, *Occasional Papers in Linguistics and Language Learning* 8 (Coleraine: New University of Ulster, Department of English, 1981), 63–104.

survivals, fragments of a much wider tradition. It is probable that in Anglo-Saxon England there were other variant versions of such a popular poem, perhaps many of them. In suggesting that "the history that unites those three survivals must be one of movement and change that stretches the imagination," Kenneth Sisam gave this idea classic expression.[3] The surviving evidence probably gives us little idea of the original variety and plasticity of the text, whether in oral or written or sculpted versions. But we can get some idea of its extent when we compare those parts common to the Ruthwell poem and the Vercelli *Dream*.

    3. Christians have always celebrated Easter, and soon celebrated Good Friday: they have been meditating for almost two millennia on the same great narrative. Thus, the more a poet or storyteller penetrates to the core of the Christian tradition, the more his or her poem will echo central Christian traditions of every other period. When we find a liturgical or devotional text from one period echoing a version of our poem, we must beware of arguing that that echo constitutes a source. The poet or liturgist may simply be doing what Christians have done for millennia: meditating on the Passion of Christ. To take one example: the poem composed at Poitiers by Venantius Fortunatus, *Pange Lingua*, was first incorporated into the Frankish Good Friday liturgies from the late ninth century.[4] It has remained part of the Latin western liturgy down to the present day. It was thus familiar to all those modern readers of *The Dream of the Rood* who were also familiar with modern Latin liturgies. The *Pange Lingua* provides many analogies with the Old English *Dream*: above all an epic sense that Christ's life and victory over death decided a great war between God and the Devil, and reversed the defeat caused by Adam's sin. But while the *Pange Lingua* certainly provides a good analogue for *The Dream of the*

---

3   Kenneth Sisam, *Studies in the History of Old English Literature* (Oxford: University Press, 1953), p. 122.

4   See *Early Latin Hymns*, ed. Arthur S. Walpole (Cambridge: Cambridge University Press, 1922), no. 33, pp. 164–73.

Sources or Analogues?

Rood, it is much less certain that it was a source for the English poet. Venantius Fortunatus avoids the central feature of the English narrative tradition, the ethical problem that the "Lord's word" (line 35b) requires the Rood to be the slayer of its Lord. In the *Pange Lingua*, Fortunatus does not see the role of the cross as problematic in any such way. For him, the cross, the nails, and Christ are, all three, "sweet" (*dulce lignum dulce clavo dulce pondus sustinens*). In the *Dream*, the Rood cannot move or bow as long as Christ still lives; in contrast, Fortunatus appeals to the cross to "bend your boughs, lofty tree, relax your taut fibers" (*[f]lecta ramos, arbor alta, tensa laxa uiscera*), precisely in order to lessen Christ's sufferings by gently supporting his living body. The contrast with the *Dream* is stark: there, it is only after Christ is dead that the Rood can bow, to present his body to his followers.

4. Even if there are similarities between a poem and a liturgical ceremony, it does not necessarily follow that the poem was inspired by, and post-dates, that ceremony. It is possible, and even likely, that poets and storytellers could anticipate features of the crucifixion story which were reflected in liturgies in later centuries. Ritual, because it is public and communal, is usually conservative; and liturgical innovations come usually in response to needs which people in community, including their poets and storytellers, have felt for generations, perhaps even for centuries. We should not be afraid to consider whether, even if there are parallels between a poem and a particular ceremony, the poem might have been composed earlier than the ceremony, and may have inspired a community to invent it, or to adopt it from elsewhere.

5. The last general principle follows from the third: when trying to date a poem, it is best to pay attention to its overall strategy rather than to individual passages which may provide specific parallels. The first priority is to find an historical context in which the original narrative may have been composed; then we can look at the surviving versions of the narrative, and see which aspects of each are likely to date back to the original creative context, and which are likely to be later modifications of the original narrative.

A comparison of the Ruthwell poem with the Vercelli *Dream* suggests that some features of the *Dream* post-date the Ruthwell Cross. The *Dream* reflects the work of a person who might be called the "*eall*-reviser."[5] He or she intensified the poem's emotional rhetoric, no doubt to encourage an emotional response to the narrative. We can possibly see the work of this reviser in lines 9–10 of the *Dream*: "beheoldon þær engel dryht / nes // ealle fægere þurh forðgesceaft,"[6] (All fair [creatures] throughout time and creation beheld the angel of the Lord there). The formula *fægere þurh forðgesceaft* would be metrically acceptable, and is probably early. It is possible that our hypothetical *eall*-reviser, in order to encourage the readers (including him- or herself) to respond to the text more emotionally, added the initial plural *ealle*. This addition was also metrically acceptable: *ealle* is here part of the initial lift, and is not stressed metrically. But the addition has given rise to some unnecessary emendations by modern editors. We will return to the first paragraph of the *Dream* later, to see how the phrase *engel dryhtnes* fits into the strategy of the poem.

It may have been the same *eall*-reviser who gave us the first three words of the verse "eall ic wæs mid strælum for wundod,"[7] where the Ruthwell Cross, at the beginning of its fourth *sententia*, simply has the phrase *miþ strelum giwundad*.[8] If so, the *eall*-reviser effected a major

---

5 For the hypothesis of an "*eall*-reviser," see Éamonn Ó Carragáin, "Crucifixion as Annunciation: the Relation of *The Dream of the Rood* to the Liturgy Reconsidered," *English Studies* 63: (1982), 487–505, at 499.
6 Folio 104v/13-4, *Dream*, lines 9b–10a. All quotations from the *Dream* are transcribed from the Vercelli Book. Facsimiles of the relevant folios may conveniently be found in Ó Carragáin, *Ritual and the Rood*, pp. 304–7, figs. 50–53. The folio and line-numbers are first given, and then the line-numbers usually used in modern editions.
7 Folio 105v/2, line 62b.
8 Quotations from the Ruthwell poem are taken from the transcript in Ó Carragáin, *Ritual and the Rood*, xxii–xxiii and xxvi–xxvii, figs. 1 and 3: here, fig. 3, vine-scroll with the second *titulus*, line 13.

Sources or Analogues?

change in the meaning of the poem. In the second Ruthwell *titulus*, it is Christ himself who is "wounded with lances [or arrows]," clearly, a metaphor which embraces both the nails which pierced his hands and feet and the spear which pierced his side.[9] Such a metaphor made sense in the Ruthwell poem, where in the next line Christ is described as *limwœrignœ*. In heroic poetry, *wœrig* can mean, metaphorically, not merely "weary," but "dead" or "brought to death"; and Christ was precisely *limwœrig*, "brought to death by his limbs," when he was "wounded with lances," in the sense of being wounded in his hands and feet by the nails.[10] But it is the Rood which is wounded in the Vercelli *Dream*; indeed it had earlier said "on me syndon þa dolg gesiene opene inwid / hlemmas" (on me the wounds are to be seen, open wounds of malice.)[11] The *eall*-reviser seems likely to have given us yet another intensifying *eall*-phrase a few lines later: "eall ic wæs mid blode bestemed"[12] (I was all drenched in blood), intensifying Ruthwell's more laconic *"[i]c [wæs] miþ blodi bist[e]mi[d]."*[13] In such changes, we are perhaps moving away from Ruthwell's liturgical concentration on Christ to an increased devotional concentration on the cross in the Vercelli *Dream*.

The Ruthwell lines, "hweþræ þer fusæ fêârran kwomu // æþþilæ til anum ic þæt al bi[*hêâld*]"[14] (But eager ones came thither from afar / Noble ones came together. I beheld all that) have been changed in the Vercelli *Dream* to "hwæðere þær fuse feorran cwoman // to /

---

9   The syntax of this verse is discussed in Ó Carragáin, "The Ruthwell Crucifixion Poem in its Iconographic and Liturgical Contexts," *Peritia* 6-7 (1987-88): 1–71, at 27 and nos. 52–55, on 59–60.
10 *A Thesaurus of Old English*, ed. Jane Roberts and Christian Kay with Lynne Grundy, King's College London Medieval Studies XI, 2 vols (London: King's College, 1995), I:31–32, 02.02.03.02, and II:1144: *limwērig*: "state of being dead." I am grateful to Professor Jane Roberts for discussion of this word.
11 Folio 105r/21–22, lines 46–7.
12 Folio 105r/23, line 48b.
13 *Titulus* to the first vine-scroll, *Sententia* II, line 7.
14 *Titulus* to the second vine-scroll, *Sententia* III, lines 10–11.

þam æðelinge ic þæt eall be heold"[15] (But eager ones came thither from afar to the prince. I beheld all that). In the Ruthwell *titulus* there is a significant contrast between the *feorran* of line 10 and the *til anum* of line 11. The eighth-century poet may have recalled the contrast between "far" and "near" in Ephesians 2:13: *nunc autem in Christo Iesu vos qui aliquando eratis longe facti estis prope in sanguine Christi*, "But now in Christ Jesus you who once were far off have been brought near by the blood of Christ."[16] This Pauline contrast between "far" and "near" had for centuries been institutionalized in the Roman papal liturgy, where the pope and his clerics came in symbolic pilgrimage at the ninth hour on Good Friday to celebrate the death of Christ at *Hierusalem*, the basilica which in the Roman papal "stational" system symbolized Golgotha. But in the Vercelli *Dream* the older "feorran"–"til anum" balance is sacrificed to a new devotional emphasis on Christ as the young hero, "the prince" around whom his eager followers gather.[17]

The paired runic *tituli* to the vine-scrolls on the lower stone at Ruthwell are best seen as a distinct poem from the Vercelli *Dream*, and not simply as extracts from "the poem, which is preserved in toto in the Vercelli codex."[18] The Vercelli poem was equipped with a dream-vision frame, "of which there is no trace at Ruthwell."[19] While

---

15 Folio 105r/29–30, lines 56–57.
16 Robert(us) Weber, ed., *Biblia Sacra Vulgata*. 2 vols. (Stuttgart: Deutsche Bibelgesellschaft, 1969, repr. 1983); and *The Holy Bible,* Douay-Rheims Version (London: Burns Oates and Washbourne, 1914). All scriptural quotations and translations come from these texts.
17 See the discussions in Ó Carragáin, "Ruthwell Crucifixion Poem," 25–26, and in *Ritual and the Rood*, pp. 180–83.
18 Meyer Schapiro, "The Religious Meaning of the Ruthwell Cross," *Art Bulletin* 26 (1944): 232–45, at 232 (reprinted in his *Late Antique, Early Christian and Medieval Art: Selected Papers* [London, 1980], pp. 150–76 [text] and 186–92 [notes], at p. 186, note 2). Such opinions were once common: see the survey in Éamonn Ó Carragáin, "The Ruthwell Crucifixion Poem," 3–4.
19 Éamonn Ó Carragáin, "The Necessary Distance: *Imitatio Romae* and the

Sources or Analogues?

some scholars have felt that much if not all of the dream-vision frame may have been added as late as the tenth century, liturgical evidence suggests that some versions of the dream-vision frame of the Vercelli poem existed as early as the end of the seventh century (perhaps a generation before the Ruthwell Cross) in sung, oral forms.[20] The first experience that shook me from my earlier belief that the dream-vision frame should be dated to the later period was the effort to draft, for submission to *Notes and Queries*, a short article on the following lines of the *Dream*: "Hwæðere ic / þurh þæt gold ongytan meahte // earmra ærgewin / þæt hit ærest ongan // swætan on þa swiðran healfe"[21] (However, through that gold I could perceive the former struggle of wretched ones, in that it first began to sweat on the right side). The article argued that the imagery of those lines was inspired by the antiphon *Vidi aquam*: "Vidi aquam egredientem de templo, a latere dextro. Alleluia. / et omnes ad quos pervenit aqua ista salvi facti sunt et dicunt Alleluia. Alleluia"[22] (I saw water coming from the temple, from its right side, Alleluia. / and all those to whom the water came were saved, and say "Alleluia, Alleluia").

From the mid-ninth century until the liturgical reforms of Vatican II, the antiphon was used for the solemn blessing before high mass on Sundays in Eastertide. At first, I could not trace this use further

---

Ruthwell Cross," pp. 191–203, *Northumbria's Golden Age*, ed. Jane Hawkes and Susan Mills (Stroud: Sutton, 1999), pp. 191–203 at 201; compare with the discussion in Ó Carragáin, "Ruthwell Crucifixion Poem," 14–15.
20 It is possible that Old English poems were simply transmitted orally, and not written down, until the ninth century; for a concise statement of the state of discussion, with bibliography, see Andy Orchard, "Oral-formulaic Theory," *The Blackwell Encyclopaedia of Anglo-Saxon England*, ed. Michael Lapidge et al (Oxford: Blackwell, 1999), p. 345.
21 Folio 104v/20–22, lines 18–21a.
22 Michel Andrieu, ed., *Les Ordines Romani du haut moyen âge,* Spicilegium Sacrum Lovaniense, 11, 23, 24, 28, 29; 5 vols (Louvain: Spicilegium Sacrum Lovaniense, 1931–61), III:365–66 (*Ordo* XXVII, No. 77). The antiphon is based on Ezekiel 47:1–2.

back than the Carolingian period, and so the first version of the paper submitted to the *Notes and Queries* editor, Eric Stanley, stated that these lines must have been composed in the ninth century or later.[23] But before the article went to press, Andrieu's edition of the *Ordines Romani* taught me that the *Vidi Aquam* antiphon was much older than I had suspected,[24] and that its older uses were much more relevant to the echo of the antiphon in the *Dream* than the later ones. From the sixth century, the antiphon was sung in the Roman liturgy during the solemn papal vespers of Easter week, when, in the middle of the ceremony, the pope and his clerics went in procession from the font in the Lateran baptistery to the nearby chapel of the Holy Cross.[25] From the font to the cross; from baptism to eucharist: nothing could be more relevant to the opening vision of the *Dream* nor to the iconography of the Ruthwell Cross. The evidence led to the conclusion that lines 18–21 of the *Dream*, which do not appear on the Ruthwell Cross, might be as old as it is, or even older. This evidence forced me to modify my conclusions drastically, and the short paper appeared in 1983.[26]

Other pieces of disturbing evidence of an early version of the *Dream* kept turning up. I had long been impressed with the comparison, at lines 90–94 of the *Dream*, between the cross and Mary. I found that 25 March had, from early Christian times, been seen as the anniversary of Good Friday, long before the annunciation began to

---

23 In this erroneous opinion, I was relying on the Carolingian (and later) monastic use of the antiphon in Carolingian Europe for blessing the cloisters with holy water before the solemn community mass on Sundays; this use is first found in St. Gall: see Adolph Franz, *Die kirchlichen Benediktionen im Mittelalter*, 2 vols (Freiburg im Breisgau: Herder, 1909), I:633.

24 See OR XXVII, No. 77 in n. 22, above.

25 See the survey of scholarly discussion of the antiphon and its early date in Ó Carragáin, *Ritual and the Rood*, p. 175, n. 147.

26 See Éamonn Ó Carragáin, "Vidi Aquam: the Liturgical Context of *The Dream of the Rood* 20a, 'Swætan on þa swiðran healfe'," *Notes and Queries*, n.s. 30 (1983): 8–15 at 11.

be celebrated on the same day. Perhaps the early singers, who clearly intended to retell the crucifixion as a dramatic encounter (as the first Ruthwell *titulus* makes clear), intended to reshape the gospel accounts of the Passion so as to recall the dramatic encounter between Mary and Gabriel at the annunciation? The problem with any such theory was, of course, that in the *Dream* the comparison between the cross and Mary does not appear in the Ruthwell *tituli*, but forms part of the dream-vision frame. Nevertheless, the Ruthwell iconography already links the cross and Mary closely. The iconographic program of the first broad side at Ruthwell begins at the bottom of the shaft with an annunciation panel, and proceeds to a visitation panel on the first side of the upper stone. As the iconographic program of this high cross begins by celebrating the stages of Christ's incarnation, it is apparent that the links between incarnation and Passion were from the beginning an important preoccupation of the Ruthwell designer.[27] The Ruthwell Cross is to be dated to the first half of the eighth century. Its sophistication indicates a learned monastic commissioner: perhaps someone in the circle of Bishop Acca of Hexham, Bede's bishop and close scholarly collaborator. Towards the end of the eighth century or even as late as the beginning of the ninth, that is, some sixty years or more after the cross was originally erected, a later generation added a crucifixion scene below the annunciation on the base of the first side of the Ruthwell Cross: this made the visual connection between annunciation and Passion still more clear.[28] But to link incarnation and Passion was vital to seventh- and early eighth-century theology. This period saw the struggle against Monotheletism, the heretical theory that Christ did not have an independent human will. Against Monotheletism, it was vital to stress both that Christ had a full human will and therefore genuine human courage, and also that his will was never in conflict with the divine will in which he also shared. Christ's human will was incorruptible,

---

27 See Ó Carragáin, *Ritual and the Rood*, chs. 2 and 3, passim.
28 Ó Carragáin, *Ritual and the Rood*, pp. 211–13.

and always coherently united to the divine will, because he had been born incorruptibly from the Virgin Mary.[29] At the annunciation the Virgin Mary encountered an archangel whose name indicated the significance of the role he played in human history. The name "Gabriel" meant *fortitudo Dei*, "the courage or strength of God" and, as Bede expressed it (following Gregory the Great):

> Gabriel namque fortitudo Dei dicitur. Et merito tali nomine praefulget qui nascituro in carne Deo testimonium perhibet. De quo propheta in psalmo: "Dominus," inquit, "fortis et potens dominus potens in proelio." Illo nimirum proelio quo potestates aerias debellare et ab earum tyrannide mundum ueniebat eripere:
>
> [For Gabriel is called the courage [or strength] of God. And it is fitting that he should be resplendent in such a name, who gives testimony that God is about to be born in the flesh. The prophet had spoken about this in the psalm: "The Lord is strong and powerful, the Lord is powerful in battle" [Ps. 23:8], in that very battle in which He came to defeat the powers of the air and to rescue the world from their tyranny.][30]

If Gregory the Great, followed by Bede, stressed that the incarnation involved a revelation of God's courage and strength, the English poet was to transform this patristic topos into a highly original narrative which showed that Christ's heroic humility was supremely expressed in Christ's heroic decision to embrace his death upon the Rood.

It is clear that the Ruthwell runic *tituli* were an original feature of the Ruthwell Cross, and were edited for the cross with great care and sensitivity. This fact poses an urgent question: what sort of text

---

29 See Michael Hurley, "Born Incorruptibly. The Third Canon of the Lateran Council, A.D. 649," *The Heythrop Journal* 2 (1961): 216–36; see also Ó Carragáin, *Ritual and the Rood*, p. 82.
30 "Bede, *Homeliarum Euangelii Libri II*, ed. David Hurst, CCSL 122 (Turnhout: Brepols, 1955), p. 15.

Sources or Analogues?

were these Ruthwell *tituli* edited *from*? The first clue is provided by their immediate context on the cross. These *tituli* were provided for two great matched images of the Tree of Life. The centrality of the Tree of Life to the Ruthwell Cross has been memorably expressed by Jennifer O'Reilly:

> In a single unifying image the sculptural decoration of the narrow sides reveals Christ to be the Tree of Life, that is, the axis at the centre of the world joining heaven and earth and providing spiritual food and healing for all. The Tree rises the height of the towering shaft on both sides and is shown in the form of a rooted vine-scroll filled with diverse creatures feeding on its fruit. It regenerates a Mediterranean image of the incorporation of all the faithful members of the Church into the sacramental and the glorified body of Christ (John 15. 1–5; 6. 56). The form and iconography of the Ruthwell Cross, its Christology and use of the written word show the Anglo-Saxons to be a people engrafted into the universal Church and familiar with its Romanized culture but also highly creative in adapting its conventions and integrating elements from their own tradition.[31]

If so, it is likely that the Ruthwell *tituli* were carefully edited from a song (which, apart from the Ruthwell excerpts may have been passed on solely in oral tradition down to the ninth or even to the tenth century) to which the images of the "Tree of Life" were central: that is, a song which already began with some version of lines 1–33 of *The Dream of the Rood*. A further implication is that, if the original English verse narrative were inspired by the Gregorian and Bedan vision of Christ coming *ad debellandas aerias potestates,* "to defeat the powers of the air," it is likely to have included lines such as

---

31   Jennifer O'Reilly, "The Art of Authority," *After Rome: the Short Oxford History of the British Isles*, ed. Thomas Charles-Edwards (Oxford: Oxford University Press, 2003), pp. 140–89, at p. 153.

> geseah ic weruda / god
> þearle þenian þystro hæfdon
> bewrigen mid wolcnum / wealdendes hræw .
> scirne sciman sceadu forð eode .
> wann / under wolcnum weop eal gesceaft
> cwiðdon cyninges fyll / crist wæs on rode[32]

[I saw the God of armies terribly serving; the darknesses had enveloped the Ruler's body in clouds. The shadow overcame the bright shining [body], and struggled under the clouds. All creation wept, lamented the fall of the king: Christ was on the Rood.][33]

The decisive reason why I have come to suspect that the dream-vision frame may go back to songs sung in the late seventh or early eighth centuries is that monastic liturgists of that early period seem to have been perfectly aware that the coincidence of annunciation and Passion on 25 March was not a mere conceit or coincidence, but led naturally to an awareness of central facts about the theology of the Passion of Christ. To see the Passion in the context of the incarnation, and so to stress the unity of Christ's life, from incarnation to ascension to the anticipated return in glory or *parousia*, was central to the way Holy Week was celebrated in that early period. They stressed this unity in various ways. In the first place, the early liturgy had already placed at the center of Holy Week the most profound scriptural expression of

---

32 Folio 105r/25–29, lines 51b–56.
33 The translation here is one of several possible translations suggested by the manuscript punctuation and word-division. For a discussion of how the counterpointing of punctuation and word-division suggests several complementary (not contradictory) interpretations of this passage, see Ó Carragáin, *Ritual and the Rood*, pp. 317–18. It has been suggested that an early version of the phrase *weop eal gesceaft* lies behind the fragmentary inscription [-]*dægisgæf*[-] on the upper stone: see Ó Carragáin, *Ritual and the Rood*, fig. 1 on xxii, p. 48, and n. 173 on p. 72.

Sources or Analogues?

the unity between incarnation and Passion, the early Christian hymn quoted by St. Paul about C.E. 55 in his epistle to the Philippians. Philippians 2:5–11 formed the epistle for the sixth Sunday of Lent, the beginning of Holy Week (later Palm Sunday). It celebrated Christ as the model for the Christian life: "hoc enim sentite in vobis quod et in Christo Iesu" (For let this mind be in you, which was also in Christ Jesus"). The collect for that Sunday, still used as such in the Book of Common Prayer, reads that Christ "haste sente our sauior Jesus Christ, to take upon him oure fleshe, and to suffre death upon the crosse, that all mankynde shoulde folwe the example of his greate humilitie."[34] That model united incarnation and Passion as a single expedition, as a single expression of heroic humility: Christ

> qui cum in forma Dei esset
> non rapinam arbitratus est esse se aequalem Deo
> sed semet ipsum exinanivit formam servi accipiens
> in similitudinem hominum factus
> et habitu inventus ut homo
> humiliavit semet ipsum factus oboediens usque ad mortem
> mortem autem crucis
> propter quod et Deus illum exaltavit   (Philippians 2:6-9a)
>
> [Who being in the form of God, thought it not robbery to be equal with God:
> But emptied himself, taking the form of a servant, being made in the likeness of men,
> and in habit found as a man.
> He humbled himself, becoming obedient unto death, even to the death of the cross.
> For which cause, God also hath exalted him [...]]

---

34 *The First Prayer Book of Edward VI* (London: n.p., 1549): for further discussion and a facsimile of this collect, see Ó Carragáin, *Ritual and the Rood*, pp. 362–63.

That epistle was recalled throughout Holy Week, in particular by a series of antiphons which began *Christus factus obediens*, "Christ became obedient." But it was recalled in a remarkable way on Wednesday in Holy Week, when the Roman stational mass (which the Pope celebrated, on the same day each year, at particular basilicas called "stations") was at Sancta Maria on the Esquiline Hill. In the early Roman papal liturgy, this basilica was the symbolic equivalent of Bethlehem: indeed, from the mid-seventh century it was believed that, as its major relic, this basilica possessed the crib in which Christ was born. The introit for the mass of Wednesday in Holy Week reshapes three verses from Philippians 2:5–11, the epistle for the previous Sunday, so that we move from glory to suffering and back again to glory. The introit thus provides an analogue for the structure of *The Dream of the Rood*, in which we move from glory (lines 1–27) to the suffering of the Passion (lines 28–77) and back again to the glory of the cross (lines 78–156). In the following transcript of the antiphon, the scriptural verses (out of sequence, as 10-8-11) are marked, so that the reader can see how the antiphon transforms the original sequence of scriptural verses:

> Ant[iphona]. [10] In nomine Domini omne genu flectatur caelestium terrestrium et infernorum [8] quia Dominus factus oboediens usque ad mortem mortem autem crucis [11] ideo Dominus Ihesus Christus in gloriam Dei Patris. [Psalm] Domine exaudi et clamor

> [*Ant[iphon]*]. [10] In the name of the Lord every knee shall bow, of those in heaven and those on earth and those under the earth; [8] because the Lord was made obedient unto death, even the death of the cross [11] and therefore the Lord Jesus Christ is in the glory of God the Father. [*Psalm*] Lord hear me: and let my cry [come unto you].][35]

---

35 The psalm reference is to Ps. 101. See René-Jean Hesbert, ed., *Antiphonale Missarum Sextuplex* (1935; reprint Rome: Herder, 1985), no. 96, pp. 92–93.

Sources or Analogues?

The mass for Wednesday in Holy Week contains a number of other striking parallels to the imagery of the *Dream*. These have been more fully examined elsewhere,[36] but two are particularly striking, and may be briefly mentioned. The first Old Testament reading (Isaiah 62:11–63:7) presents Christ's approach to Calvary as a royal *adventus*, a king's triumphal advance into his city, Jerusalem. The Isaiah lection begins by promising "the daughter of Zion" that her salvation is coming; as the Virgin Mary was seen as "the daughter of Zion" *par excellence*, it is clear that the papal station at the basilica of Sancta Maria determined the choice of this lection. It consists of a dramatic dialogue between the hero-king and those who see his triumphant advance:

> [62:11] Ecce Dominus auditum fecit in extremis terrae; dicite filiae Sion: ecce salvator tuus venit, ecce merces eius cum eo et opus eius coram illo; et vocabunt eos Populus sanctus, Redempti a Domino; tu autem vocaberis: Quesita civitas et non Derelicta. [63:1] Quis est iste qui venit de Edom tinctis vestibus de Bosra, iste formosus in stola sua gradiens in multitudine fortitudinis suae? ego qui loquor iustitiam et propugnator sum ad salvandum.

> [Behold, the Lord hath made it to be heard in the ends of the earth. Tell the daughter of Zion: Behold, thy Savior cometh. Behold, his reward is with him and his work before him. And they shall call them: The Holy People, The Redeemed of the Lord. But thou shalt be called: A city, sought after and not forsaken. [63:1] Who is this that cometh from Edom, with dyed garments from Bosra, this beautiful one in his robe, walking in the greatness of his strength? I that speak justice and am a defender to save.]

This dramatization of a heroic *adventus* was chosen as a prelude to the gospel of the mass, the Passion according to St. Luke (Luke 22: 1–23: 53). This is the only Passion-narrative which gives an account of the

---

36 Ó Carragáin, *Ritual and the Rood*, pp. 311–16.

encounter between Jesus and the women of Jerusalem: it is clear that the papal station at Sancta Maria determined the choice of the gospel:

> Conversus autem ad illas Iesus dixit Filiae Hierusalem nolite flere super me Sed super vos ipsas flete et super filios vestros . . . quia si in viridi ligno haec faciunt in arido quid fiet.
>
> [But Jesus, turning to them, said, "Daughters of Jerusalem, weep not over me; but weep for yourselves and for your children . . . for if in the green wood they do these things, what shall be done in the dry?"]

The English *Dream*-poet retells the crucifixion in a startlingly new narrative, as a confrontation between the Rood and Christ. The dramatic narrative recalls the annunciation, in which Mary encountered *fortitudo Dei* in Gabriel. But to link incarnation and Passion in this way was also to recall central aspects of the early Roman liturgy of Holy Week: the links made between incarnation and Passion in the epistle for the Sunday before Easter (Philippians 2:5–11) and in the papal station at Sancta Maria on Wednesday in Holy Week. That mass presented Holy Week as a re-enactment of the incarnation, in which Christ had come to Mary like an advancing warrior-king. If, during that mass, Christ was seen as a green tree cut down, the mass enables us to understand why the *Dream*-poet presents the Rood also as a guiltless green tree, cut down by its enemies:

> þæt wæs geara iu . Ic þæt gyta geman .
> þæt ic wæs aheawen holtes on ende
> astyred of stefne minum . Genamon me ðær strange feondas geworhton him þær to wæfersyne heton me heora wergas hebban
>
> [That was long ago (I still remember it) that I was cut down at the edge of a wood, removed from my root. Strong enemies seized me there, made me into their spectacle, told me to raise aloft their criminals.][37]

---

37 Folio 105r/5–8, lines 28–31: translation mine.

Sources or Analogues?

The mass for the Wednesday in Holy Week was certainly celebrated before the seventh century, and lines 28–33a of the *Dream* do not occur on the Ruthwell Cross. The close parallels between those lines and the mass enable us to see that the later seventh-century Vatican liturgist (perhaps John the Archcantor), who explicitly linked annunciation and Passion in his mass for March 25 (*Adnuntiatio Domini et Passio Eiusdem*), understood that such a concept would lead them into the heart of the Easter mystery which depended on seeing Christ's life as a unity. If the cross, like Christ, is a green tree struck down, then the identification between what happens to Christ and what happens to the Rood in *The Dream of the Rood* is even closer than scholars have previously seen it to be. This identification was probably inspired by early Christian liturgy and iconography, which regularly presented the glorified cross as a symbol of Christ.[38]

The mysterious and riddling opening vision, which so closely identifies the cross as a symbol of Christ, also introduces the figure of the Dreamer. An Old English dream-vision song, which dramatized the relevance of the Rood's narrative to the fate of an individual soul, would have appealed to English monastic audiences in the final decades of the seventh century and in the first decades of the eighth. At the end of his *Historia Ecclesiastica*, Bede gives us a remarkable set of three eschatological visions, and tells us that they all took place well within the period of his own lifetime. The first is the monk Haemgisl's account of Dryhthelm's vision of the other world, which Bede tells us came to him from the circle of King Aldfrith (d. 704) and Abbot Æþelwold of Melrose.[39] This is directly followed by the second vision which the impenitent thane of King Cenred of Mercia (704–709) had of the angels who showed him an "exceedingly small" book of his good deeds, and an enormous and heavy book of his sins: Bede tells us that he got this story from Bishop Pehthelm of Whithorn who had been a pupil of the poet Aldhelm at Malmesbury and, as

---

38 Ó Carragáin, *Ritual and the Rood*, pp. 189–95 and 228–36; see also pls. 6–10, and figs. 41–43.
39 *HE* 5:12, pp. 488–89, especially pp. 496–99.

Bishop of Whithorn (731–5), was (like Bishop Acca of Hexham) a possible commissioner of the Ruthwell Cross.[40] The third vision, which immediately follows, tells of a man known to Bede himself: an impenitent monk who, before he died of despair, had a premonitory vision of the hell which awaited him.[41] It has recently been shown that these three eschatological visions circulated as a separate group of devotional texts.[42]

A monastic milieu with a taste for such urgent visions could well have also admired (and needed) a more optimistic vernacular song, in which a Dreamer tells of "the best of dreams, which [he] dreamed about midnight, when bearers of voices were at rest," and sees a wonderful tree which provides him with a pledge of salvation. Bede's circle was certainly fascinated by one famous midnight vision of the cross, that of Constantine: we know that Abbot Adomnán of Iona, and later Bede himself, reshaped the story of King Oswald's victory at Heavenfield (C.E. 634), won in the sign of the cross, in increasingly Constantinian terms.[43] Bede, indeed, went so far as to interpret Oswald's victory in terms of the Good Friday liturgy of his own day, imagining that Oswald cited the Latin introductory formula for the solemn universal prayers recited at the ninth hour on Good Friday: *Flectamus omnes genua* "Let us all bend the knee." It was only at the end of the seventh century that veneration of a cross, or of a cross-reliquary, had been introduced into the Roman

---

40 *HE*, 5:13, pp. 498–503: see also Ó Carragáin, *Ritual and the Rood*, pp. 282–98.
41 *HE* 5:14, pp. 502–505.
42 Paul Gerhard Schmidt, "Bède et la tradition des récits visionnaires," *Bède le Vénérable entre tradition et postérité / The Venerable Bede, Tradition and Posterity*, ed. Stéphane Lebecq, Michel Perrin and Olivier Szerwiniack (Lille: Ceges – Université Charles-de-Gaulle – Lille 3, 2005), pp. 260–66.
43 Jennifer O'Reilly provides a fine comparison between the accounts of Oswald's victory by Adomnán and by Bede: "Reading the Scriptures in the Life of Columba," *Studies in the Cult of Saint Columba*, ed. Cormac Bourke (Dublin: Four Courts, 1997), pp. 80–116, at pp. 81–85.

Sources or Analogues?

synaxes on Good Friday at the ninth hour. In Oswald's day, no one had yet linked the Good Friday universal prayers with public prayer around a cross (in the "Gelasian" rite, followed in basilicas run by priests) or a cross-reliquary (in the "Gregorian" ceremony, followed by the papal court at the basilica called "Hierusalem").[44] Bede imagined Oswald's action in terms of the liturgy as practiced at Wearmouth-Jarrow in the early eighth century, during the abbacy of Hwætberht.[45]

The fact that Bede often refers to his abbot as "Eusebius" also provides eloquent testimony to the fascination with Constantine's vision of the cross at Wearmouth-Jarrow during Hwætberht's abbacy.[46] But Hwætberht-Eusebius was a good Latin poet, and the collection of Latin *enigmata* attributed to him includes a *De Cruce*.[47] It has long been recognized that there is a close parallel between one of the paradoxes in this Latin riddle, "Dampnauique uirum, sic multos carcere solui" ([One] man I condemned and so I released many from prison),[48] and the third of the paradoxes through which, in *The Dream of the Rood*, the Rood explains its history to the Dreamer:

---

44 See *Liber Sacramentorum Romanae Aeclesiae Ordinis Anni Circuli (Cod. Vat. Reg. lat. 316 / Paris Bib. Nat. 7193, 41/56) (Sacramentarium Gelasianum)*, ed. Leo C. Mohlberg, Peter Siffrin and Ludwig Eisenhöfer, 3rd ed., rev. by Ludwig Eisenhöfer, Rerum Ecclesiastarum Documenta, Series Maior, Fontes, 4, (Rome: Herder, 1981), Section XLI, nos. 395–418, pp. 64–67; for the papal stational ceremony, see Andrieu, *Les Ordines Romani*, Ordo XXIII, nos. 11–19, pp. 270–71.
45 For Bede's account of Oswald's victory, see *HE* 3: 2, pp. 214–17. On Bede's phrase *Flectamus omnes genua* as a citation of the Good Friday *flectamus genua* formula, see Ó Carragáin, *Ritual and the Rood*, pp. 231–32.
46 For a list of the passages in which Bede refers to his abbot Hwætberht as "Eusebius," see *Collectiones Aenigmatum Merovingicae Aetatis*, ed. Francois Glorie CCSL 133 (Turnhout: Brepols, 1968), at p. 146.
47 "Riddle 17": CCSL 133, Part I, 227.
48 *De Cruce*, line 4: CCSL 133, Part I, 227; Daniel G. Calder and Michael J.B. Allen, trans., *Sources and Analogues of Old English Poetry* (Cambridge: D.S. Brewer, 1976), p. 55.

> iu ic wæs geworden wita heardost .
> leodum la/ðost ærþan ic him lifes weg
> rihtne gerymde reordbe/rendum."⁴⁹
>
> [Long ago I had become the hardest of tortures, most hateful to human beings, before I opened the true way of life to all those who can speak.]

A similarly close parallel has been recognized between the first of the *Dream*'s set of paradoxes:

> Nu þu miht gehyran hæleð min se leofa
> þæt ic bealuwara weorc gebiden hæbbe
> sarra sorga is nu sæl cumen
> þæt me weorðiað wide ond side
> men ofer moldan ond eall þeos mære gesceaft .
> gebiddaþ him to þyssum beacne,⁵⁰
>
> [Now can you hear, beloved warrior, that I have endured the work of criminals, terrible sorrows. Now has the time come that humans throughout the earth, and all this glorious creation, honor me; they pray to this symbol,]

and a riddle known as *De Cruce Christi* by Tatwine: "Lege fui quondam cunctis iam larbula seruis; / Sed modo me gaudens orbis ueneratur et ornat" (Once, because of the law, I was a spectral terror to all slaves; / but now the whole earth joyfully worships and adorns me).⁵¹ Tatwine was Archbishop of Canterbury from 731, and died in 734. He was thus an exact contemporary, of the same generation, as Hwætbert-Eusebius (who died about 750), Acca of Hexham (d. 740),

---

49 Folio 105v/21–23, *Dream*, lines 87–89. Translation mine.
50 Folio 105v/15–18, *Dream*, lines 78–83a. Translation mine.
51 Tatwine, *De Cruce Christi*, lines 2–3: CCSL 133, Part I, 176; see the remarks by Maria de Marco in the introduction to that volume, xiii. Trans. Calder and Allen, *Sources and Analogues*, p. 56.

Sources or Analogues?

Pehthelm of Whithorn (d. 735), and Bede (d. 735). In the *Dream*-poem, the set of three paradoxes (lines 78–89) is carefully structured to prepare for the comparison between the honor given to the Rood (above all hill-trees) and the honor given to Mary (above all women). The unique narrative of the *Dream*, and of the Ruthwell poem, was designed to retell the crucifixion as a confrontation between Christ and a horrified cross, and it is likely that from the beginning of the tradition, the English singers intended their audiences to see the parallels (and significant contrasts) between the dilemma of the Rood, which saw itself commanded to kill its Lord, and the dilemma of Mary who, exactly thirty-four years before, saw herself apparently commanded to break her vow of perpetual virginity so that Christ could be born of her womb.[52] Such highly original parallels between the Rood and Mary correspond to important christological and liturgical developments in the late seventh and early eighth centuries, developments of which Bede and his circle were certainly aware.[53] The fact that the very paragraph of the *Dream* which compares the Rood to Mary should also closely parallel riddle-poems by these two early eighth-century English monastic poets, each known to Bede, makes it likely, not merely that the explicit comparison between the Rood and Mary goes back to the earliest songs in this English narrative tradition, but that some sung version of the whole paragraph (*Dream*, lines 78–94) may go back to the beginning of the tradition. That would imply that there were some early songs in

---

52 From the late fourth century, theologians were agreed that Mary had taken a vow of perpetual virginity. This meant that at the annunciation Mary was placed briefly in a serious dilemma; until Gabriel reassured her, it seemed that she must break that vow in order to become a mother: see Augustine, *Sermon* 51:18 (PL 38–39:343); *Sermon* 215: 2 (PL 38–39:1073); *Sermon* 291: 5–6 (PL 38–39:1318–19); the theme is discussed in Kim Power, *Veiled Desire: Augustine's Writings on Women* (London: Continuum, 1995), pp. 181–82, 293. For further references to Mary's dilemma (in Gregory of Nyssa, Augustine and Bede), see Ó Carragáin, *Ritual and the Rood*, p. 86, and n. 45 on p. 113.

53 See Ó Carragáin, *Ritual and the Rood*, especially chs. 2 and 5.

which the cross explained its experience to the audience; and that the Ruthwell designer edited his or her version from a longer song in which the narrative was already adapted to the needs of individuals facing death and Judgment Day.

The paragraph of the *Dream* in which the Rood is cut down and buried (lines 73b–75) by the same enemies who originally cut it down as it grew when a green tree at the edge of a wood (lines 28–33a) may also be a feature of the earliest songs. The paragraph continues the close identification between the experience of Christ and that of the cross, which we have seen to be a central theme of the opening vision and of the beginning of the Rood's speech (*Dream*, lines 1–33). The Rood tells how its enemies cut it down at the edge of a wood, like Christ "the green tree" (Luke 23:31, intoned, as we have seen, on Wednesday in Holy Week.)[54] Christ's fate fulfilled the prophecy of Habbakuk, part of the chant with which the Roman synaxis at the ninth hour on Good Friday began: "Deus de Libano veniet / et sanctus de monte umbroso et condenso"[55] (God will come from Lebanon, and the holy one from the shaded, thickly-wooded mountain). Now, after his friends have buried the dead Christ in a sepulcher in the earth (*moldærn*, line 65b), its enemies bury the Rood, suddenly and with shocking violence:

>   þa us man fyllan ongan .
> ealle to eorðan þæt wæs egeslic wyrd
> bedealf us man on deopan seaþe
> hwæðere me þær dryhtnes þegnas freondas gefrunon
> gyredon me golde ond seolfre
>
> [Then they began to fell us all to the earth: that was a terrible experience! We were buried in a deep pit; but then

---

54 See Ó Carragáin, *Ritual and the Rood*, pp. 3 and 311–13.
55 Canticle of Habbakuk: text from the Vespasian Psalter (Canterbury, ca. 700), Henry Sweet, ed., *The Oldest English Texts,* EETS o.s. 83, (Oxford: Oxford University Press, 1885), p. 407. On the canticle, its chants and its liturgical uses, see Ó Carragáin, *Ritual and the Rood*, pp. 184–85 and notes.

Sources or Analogues?

the followers of the Lord, his friends, heard [of me]: they adorned me with gold and silver.]⁵⁶

Some sung version of this passage is likely to have featured in a seventh- or early eighth-century version of the narrative. The feast of the Invention of the Cross (3 May) was celebrated in some presbyteral basilicas at Rome (but not in the papal rite at the Lateran) in the generation before 650, even earlier than the development of the feast marking the Exaltation of the Cross (14 September).⁵⁷ The earliest gospel lection for the Invention naturally centered, like the narrative of the *Dream*, on the burial and finding of a treasure: "Simile est regnum caelorum thesauro abscondito in agro quem qui invenit homo abscondit et prae gaudio illius vadit et vendit universa quae habet et emit agrum illum" (The kingdom of heaven is like treasure hidden in a field: the man who finds it hides it, and then in his joy he goes and sells all that he has and buys that field).⁵⁸

A little later in the seventh century, when the feast of the Exaltation of the Cross began to be introduced into some Roman basilicas, initially the lection for the Invention was at times read on the new feast. The earliest Roman gospel-lection list dates from about 645, and in this list, 14 September is still simply the feast of the early martyrs

---

56 Folio 105v/11–14, lines 73b–77. Translation mine.
57 See the discussion in Antoine Chavasse, *Le Sacramentaire Gélasien (Vaticanus Reginensis 316): sacramentaire presbytéral en usage dans les titres romains au VIIe siècle*, Bibliothèque de théologie IV: Histoire de la théologie 1 (Paris and Tournai: Desclée, 1958), pp. 350–64. He points out that the earliest Roman formularies for the feast contain several clear references to the legend of St. Helena's finding of the True Cross (*Acta Cyriaci: Acta Sanctorum* Maii, I: 445–48), the Latin translation of which was certainly known at Rome from the early sixth century, when abridgements of the first edition of the *Liber Pontificalis*, drafted by this period, paraphrase the legend: *Le Liber Pontificalis*, ed. Louis Duchesne (Paris, 1892), reprinted with a third volume, *Additions et corrections de Mgr L. Duchesne*, ed. Cyrille Vogel (Paris: De Boccard, 1955–57), I: 74 and 167; see the discussion in Chavasse, *Le Sacramentaire Gélasien*, p. 353.
58 Matt. 13:44.

Cornelius and Cyprian. But after the gospel lection for that feast (Luke 11:47–54), some early manuscripts add the note "et ipsa die exaltatio scae crucis si uelis [other MSS: si uis] require euangel. ad legend. de sca cruce: Simile est regnum caelorum thesauro abscondito in agro"[59] (And on the same day [14 September] the Exaltation of the Holy Cross: if you wish, look up the gospel to be read on the Holy Cross: "The kingdom of heaven is like a treasure hidden in a field").

This note certainly goes back to the seventh century, when 14 September was still primarily "natale sci Corneli et sci Cypriani." It implies that it is still the personal choice of the celebrant (*si uelis*, *si uis*) whether instead to celebrate the new feast of the Exaltation, and which gospel to read: the feast has not yet been "officially" or traditionally assigned a gospel of its own.[60] It was only at the end of the seventh century that Pope Sergius ensured that the Exaltation of the Cross would henceforth be universally celebrated in the western Church.[61] Sergius made the feast "official" by a public act of dramatized theology. The official account of his life in the *Liber Pontificalis* tells that "by God's revelation," in the sacristy or reception hall of St. Peter's basilica (outside and to the left of the entrance to the basilica), Sergius found a silver casket lying in a very dark corner: so tarnished was it that it was not even clear that it was of

---

59 *Das römische Capitulare Evangeliorum: Texte und Untersuchungen zu seiner ältesten Geschichte*, ed. Theodor Klauser (Münster: Aschendorff, 1971), p. 38, note to no. 198.

60 At this early stage, the Invention of the Cross on 3 May also seems to have been a matter of private choice: there is no entry for that day in the list of gospel-lections from which we have transcribed the note on "euangl. ad legend. de sca cruce."

61 From this period, the feast of the Exaltation, firmly established in the papal rite, gets a new lection, John 3:1–15: see Klauser, *Das römische Capitulare Evangeliorum*, p. 84, no. 223; see also Chavasse, *Le Sacramentaire Gélasien*, p. 359. As Chavasse points out (p. 364) the mass of the Invention of the Cross (3 May) would only enter the papal liturgy, as distinct from the presbyteral liturgy ("Gelasian"), when the use of Romano-Gallican liturgical books was imposed on Rome in the post-Carolingian period.

silver. After praying, Sergius opened the reliquary and in it, under a silk cushion called *stauracis* ("of the cross"), he found a cross, "very ornate with various precious stones." Dismantling this cross, the pope "found placed inside a wonderfully large and indescribable portion of the saving wood of the Lord's Cross." Though Sergius had found the reliquary at St. Peter's, he assigned to it a liturgical function at St. John Lateran, the basilica which functioned as the cathedral of Rome: "From that day, for the salvation of the human race, this is kissed and worshipped by all Christian people on the day of the Exaltation of the Holy Cross in the basilica of the Saviour called Constantinian."[62] It is significant that this episode should be recorded in Sergius' official biography, since it makes some important points about the Roman and western cult of the cross. The feast of the Exaltation of the Cross might have been a recent import from the East, but Sergius's actions here make clear that at Rome, the cult of the cross was so ancient as to have been forgotten: covered over by the grime of ages, as it were, and consigned to a dark corner of St. Peter's treasury (like the reliquary which Sergius was inspired to find). Sergius ensured that the veneration of the cross would be understood as reviving an ancient Roman cult of the cross. The retelling of the episode is inspired by such scriptural episodes as the finding of the lost "book of the law" in the Temple at Jerusalem by Hilkia the High Priest (the word *pontifex*, which was often used as a papal title, is found in the Vulgate at II Kings 22:8–13), by the gospel parable of the treasure hidden in the field (Matthew 13: 44), and of course by the legendary finding of the True Cross by St. Helena, mother of Constantine. Bede knew of the legend that St. Helena had brought back relics of the True Cross to Rome from Jerusalem: in a list of basilicas that the Emperor Constantine built which was included in the chronicle appended to his *De Temporum Ratione*, Bede (relying

---

62 *The Book of Pontiffs (Liber Pontificalis): the Ancient Biographies of the First Ninety Roman Bishops to AD 715*, trans. Raymond Davis, Translated Texts for Historians 6 (Liverpool: Liverpool University Press, 2000), p. 88.

on the *Liber Pontificalis*) records "item basilica in Palatio Sosoriano, quae cognominatur Hierusalem, ubi de ligno crucis Domini posuit" (a basilica in the Sessorian Palace, which is known as Jerusalem, where he deposited some of the wood of the Lord's Cross).[63] Bede also paraphrased, in slightly shortened form, the account in the *Liber Pontificalis* of how, "by divine revelation," Sergius found in the sacristy of St. Peter's "a silver chest" in which was "a cross adorned with diverse precious stones," and within that, the "piece of the salvific Cross of the Lord, of marvelous size," which is venerated each year at the Lateran on the feast of the Exaltation of the Cross.[64] There is no doubt that if in this early period an English song presented the Rood as telling a terrible story of how its enemies cut it down and buried it in a deep pit on Good Friday evening, the early singer(s) would be expected to refer, however briefly, to the happy ending which so fascinated early Anglo-Saxon pilgrims to Rome: how this precious object, indeed "a treasure hidden in a field," was found by its "friends" and "adorned with gold and silver" (*Dream*, lines 75–77). By publicizing his finding of the relic at St. Peter's, and associating it with the celebration of the new Exaltation feast at the Lateran, Pope Sergius had established, for the Western Church and for England, two vital facts: first, that at Rome, the city of Constantine's victory at the Milvian Bridge, the cult of the Holy Cross was so ancient that its origins had been lost in the mist of history. Secondly, Sergius's find closely associated the new Roman papal feast of the Exaltation (14 September) with the existing feast of the Invention of the Cross (3 May), already celebrated in some Roman presbyteral basilicas though not in the papal liturgy at the Lateran. For an early English poet to emphasize that "friends of the cross" had discovered and

---

63 *De Temporum Ratione*, ch. 66, s.a. 4290: Bede, *Opera Didascalia 2*, ed. Charles W. Jones, CCSL 123B (Turnhout: Brepols, 1977), 509, para. 417. Translation from Faith Wallis, ed. and trans., *Bede: the Reckoning of Time*, Translated Texts for Historians 29 (Liverpool: Liverpool University Press, 1999), pp. 212–13.
64 *De Temporum Ratione*, ch. 66, s.a. 4652: Bede, *Opera Didascalia*, 2; CCSL 123B, 529–30.

Sources or Analogues?

adorned the buried cross was an appropriate response to that which united the two late seventh-century Roman feasts of the Cross: not only the presbyteral feast of the Invention (3 May) but also the new feast of the Exaltation (14 September), celebrated within the papal liturgy at the Lateran.

Such vivid English vernacular songs may possibly have influenced the Good Friday liturgy of late tenth-century Winchester. Jennifer O'Reilly saw a significant parallel between the narrative of the *Dream* and the liturgy of the Benedictine Revival. As she saw, in the *Dream:*

> The Creator of the cosmos is hung on a manmade object. After the Crucifixion, the wood of the Cross is felled for the second time, buried, like Christ, and then raised up. At the end of the Good Friday *Adoratio Crucis* in the *Regularis Concordia* there is provision for an additional participation in and re-enactment of the sacred drama. The ceremonial cross was "buried" in or near the altar, to be raised up on Easter Sunday.[65]

Sarah Larratt Keefer has carefully traced the increasingly elaborate, mimetic Good Friday liturgical ceremonies from the eighth to the eleventh centuries, centered on the Veneration of the Cross. She shows that, to represent the burial of Christ on Good Friday evening, some continental monasteries placed a consecrated eucharistic host in a "tomb" at the conclusion of the veneration ceremonies. But in England, in the *Regularis Concordia* and ceremonies based on it, the veneration ceremony ended by placing a wooden cross in the "tomb," not a eucharistic host.[66] The English ceremonies are distinctive and

---

65 Jennifer O'Reilly, "The Rough-Hewn Cross in Anglo-Saxon Art," *Irish and Insular Art, 500–1200*, ed. Michael Ryan (Dublin: Royal Irish Academy, 1987), pp. 153–58 at 157.

66 Sarah Larratt Keefer, "The Performance of the Cross in Anglo-Saxon England," *Cross and Culture in Anglo-Saxon England*, ed. Karen Louise Jolly, Catherine E. Karkov and Sarah Larratt Keefer (Morgantown: West Virginia

original, in that they use a cross to represent the body of Christ. As Keefer has shown, it is impossible at the present state of research to be certain whether this English variant was invented at Winchester at the time of the *Regularis Concordia*, or whether the Winchester monks adopted a variant they found elsewhere, perhaps importing the rite from the customary of some continental monastery. Whether they invented the cross-burial themselves or got it elsewhere, it is possible that the Winchester monks found such mimetic symbolism attractive and acceptable because they were already familiar with sung (or, by the tenth century, perhaps written) versions of the original English vernacular song which we know as *The Dream of the Rood*. We have seen that a central feature of that poem, from the opening vision onwards, is a close identification of the Rood and Christ.[67]

One of the strongest reasons for thinking that the vernacular songs, from which the Ruthwell designer edited the two runic *tituli*, may have included a dream-vision frame which was in some sense the ancestor of the surviving *Dream of the Rood* is the coherence of that poem's strategy. By linking the Rood and Mary, and so emphasizing that the crucifixion should be seen in the context of the incarnation as well as of the *parousia* or Second Coming, the *Dream* insists that Christ's life must be seen as a unity. Christ first appears in the poem "hastening with great valor" (*efstan elne mycle*) because he has a great cosmic expedition to perform. As the poem reminds us, this expedition led him from heaven to take on humanity in the Virgin's womb (*Dream*, lines 90–94); after his victory on the cross, to triumphantly bring joy to those who "suffered burning" in the underworld (lines 148b–9); to return to heaven with those human souls he has won from the devil (lines 150–6); and, in the future, to return in glory to judge humankind (lines 103b–21). It is likely that the earliest songs in the tradition included a reference to Christ's descent into hell: the motif was central to the Roman and orthodox arguments against

University Press, 2007), pp. 203–41 at 217–41.
67 Ó Carragáin, *Ritual and the Rood*, pp. 189–95 and 228–36; pls. 6–10, and figs. 41–43.

Sources or Analogues?

Monotheletism; thus the earliest western representations of the descent into hell come from Rome, and are dated to the early eighth century.[68] It is no coincidence that it is from this period that formulae such as *discendit ad inferos*, "he descended into the lower world," are found in an insular credal formula (in the Antiphonary of Bangor, dated to 680–91).[69] To stress the unity of Christ's achievement, rather than isolating individual episodes such as the sufferings of Good Friday, is characteristic of earlier forms of Christian liturgy. It is given memorable expression in the Ambrosian Advent hymn *Intende qui regis Israel*, also known from the first line of its second stanza as *Veni Redemptor gentium*. This hymn was incorporated into the Old Hymnal and was therefore sung by Bede and his contemporaries; like the *Dream*, it stresses that Christ's expedition, which spanned the whole cosmos from heaven to hell and back, needed to be swift (*alacris*):

v. Procedens de thalamo suo,	Going out from his bridal chamber,
pudoris aula regia,	The royal hall of modesty,
gemine gigas substantiae	A giant of twin substance,
alacris ut currat viam.	so that he may run his swift course:
vi. Egressus eius a patre,	His going forth is from the Father,
regressus eius ad patrem,	His return is to the Father,
excursusque ad inferos,	and his expedition is to hell,
recursus ad sedem Dei.	His return is to the seat of God.[70]

---

68 See Anna D. Kartsonis, *Anastasis: the Making of an Image* (Princeton: Princeton University Press, 1986), pp. 58–64; Erik Thunø, *Image and Relic: Mediating the Sacred in Early Medieval Rome*, Analecta Romana Instituti Danici, Supplementum 32 (Rome: Bretschneider, 2002), pp. 107–10; see also Ó Carragáin, *Ritual and the Rood*, p. 324 and pl. 13(d).

69 See F. E. Warren, ed., *The Antiphonary of Bangor*, 2 vols., HBS 4 and 10 (London: Henry Bradshaw Society, 1893), II: 21, no. 35, and the account of the descent into hell in the hymn *Praecamur Patrem*, II:5–7, no. 3, at stanzas xxxiii–xxxviii; see also J. N. D. Kelly, *Early Christian Creeds* (London: Longman, 1972), pp. 398–420 at 402.

70 Helmut Gneuss, *Hymnar und Hymnen im englischen Mittelalter; Studien zur Überlieferung, Glossierung und Übersetzung lateinischer Hymnen in England, Mit*

The reference in stanza v to Christ's "bridal chamber" (*thalamus*) is important. This was imagined through an identification, inspired by the Latin texts of Psalm 18, between Christ and the sun's daily course. The final lines of the *Dream* (lines 150–6) sum up Christ's cosmic expedition by citing and providing a punning English equivalent for the syntactic wordplay which associates God and the sun in Psalm 18. In Christian discourse, the syntax was seen to refer to the incarnation and life of Christ, the light of the world. It is impossible to miss the similarity between *Se sunu* ("the Son") and *seo sunne* ("the sun"), once we notice the reference to this psalm:

[6] In sole posuit tabernaculum suum et ipse tamquam sponsus procedens de thalamo suo

Exultavit ut gigans ad currendam viam: [7] a summo caelo egressio ejus et occursus ejus usque ad summum ejus nec est qui se abscondat a calore ejus.

[He hath set his tabernacle in the sun; and he, as a bridegroom coming out of his bride chamber hath rejoiced as a giant to run the way. His going out is from the end of heaven, and his circuit even to the end thereof; and there is no one that can hide himself from his heat.][71]

Apart from Psalm 18 and the Ambrosian hymn *Veni Redemptor Gentium*, the stress on the unity and swiftness of Christ's expedition may owe something to another very important early text, the preface for the Easter vigil mass which has survived in the Old Gelasian sacramentary. This prose poem was chanted by the liturgical celebrant at the most solemn moment of the liturgical year; it was certainly well known in seventh- and early eighth-century Northumbria. Like the final lines

---

einer *Textausgabe der lateinisch-altenglischen Expositio hymnorum* (Tübingen: M. Niemeyer, 1968); Inge Milfull, *The Hymns of the Anglo-Saxon Church: A Study and Edition of the 'Durham Hymnal'* (Cambridge, 1996).

71 Latin text of the Old Roman psalter from London, Britiish Library, MS Cotton Vespasian A. i, Henry Sweet, *Oldest English Texts*, p. 209.

Sources or Analogues?

of the *Dream*, the preface fuses the resurrection of Christ and his triumphant ascension into a single image: his return to his homeland with the souls he has won from hell. Like the *Dream* too, its theology is early, and profoundly Johannine in the way it closely associates Christ's raising on the cross with his exaltation and glorification:

> Adest enim nobis optatissimum tempus, et desideratae noctis lumen aduenit. Quid enim maius uel melius inueniri poterit, quam domini resurgentis praedicare uirtutem? Hic namque inferorum claustra disrumpens, carissimam nobis hodie suae resurrectionis uixillam suscepit atque hominem remeans inuidia inimici deiectum mirantibus intulit astris.

> [For the best of times has come to us, the light of the night we longed for. What greater or better could be found, than to proclaim the power of the Lord in his resurrection? For he, breaking apart the prisons of the underworld, takes up today the most precious standard of his resurrection; and winning back humankind whom the enemy's hatred brought low, carries them to the stars who look on in awe.][72]

---

72 See Mohlberg et al., *Liber Sacramentorum Romanae Aeclesiae (Sacramentarium Gelasianum)*, no. 457, lines 18–24 on p. 75; see also *Corpus Praefationum*, ed. Eugène Moeller, 5 vols., CCSL 161–161/D (Turnhout: Brepols, 1980-81), no. 17 (text at CCSL 161A (1980), p. 7; textual apparatus at CCSL 161B (1980), p. 9). A good analysis of this preface will be found in Martin Herz, *Sacrum Commercium: eine Begriffsgeschichtliche Studie zur Theologie der römischen Liturgiesprache*, Münchener Theologische Studien, II. Systematische Abteilung 15, (Munich: Fink, 1958), pp. 228–39; see also Ó Carragáin, *Ritual and the Rood*, pp. 289–91. The close association throughout St. John's Gospel between Christ being "raised aloft" on the cross, and his being "raised up" from the dead and "exalted" into heaven is fully examined by Wilhelm Thüsing, *Die Erhöhung und Verherrlichung Jesu im Johannesevangelium*, Neutestamentliche Abhandlungen, vol. 21, 3rd ed. rev. (Münster: Aschendorff, 1979).

Writing/Sounding the Cross: *The Dream of the Rood* as Figured Poetry

Helen Damico

> Nu ic þe hate, hæleð min se leofa,
> þæt ðu þas gesyhðe secge mannum,
> onwreoh wordum þæt hit is wuldres beam,
> se ðe ælmihtig god on þrowode...[1]

> [Now I command you, my beloved hero, to declare this vision, to reveal in words that it is the tree of glory on which almighty God suffered...]

I TAKE MY TITLE from the Rood's command to the Dreamer in lines 95–97 of *The Dream of the Rood*—"to reveal in words"—and from the metrical form of the poem which, by the repetitive juxtaposition of normal and hypermetric verses through line 75, produces, I suggest, a picture of the tree of glory. Generally, critics agree that these repetitive, and mostly unexpected metrical transitions

---

1 *The Dream of the Rood* in ASPR 2, pp. 61–65, at 64. In preparing this article, I have also been guided by the following editions: *The Dream of the Rood: An Old English Poem Attributed to Cynewulf*, ed. Albert S. Cook (Oxford: Clarendon Press, 1905); *The Dream of the Rood*, ed. Bruce Dickins and Alan S. C. Ross, corr. 4th ed. (London: Methuen, 1966); and *The Dream of the Rood*, ed. Michael Swanton (Manchester: Manchester University Press, 1970; repr. Exeter: University of Exeter Press, 1996).

from normal to hypermetric verse blocks constitute one of the unique characteristics of the *Dream*-poet, setting him apart from other Anglo-Saxon lyric authors.[2] The interplay between the expanded and normal lines marks the metrical signature of the poem, with its consistent use of what Michael Swanton has characterized as rapid, staccato blocks of verse in counterpoint to clusters of expanded cadences;[3] these latter, when chanted, tend to create an effect, to quote the late John C. Pope, "of deliberation or of measured solemnity" when the verse has a strong opening, and of an "impulsive outpouring of the speaker's feeling" when the verse has a retarded, polysyllabic weak opening.[4]

Though they resemble Old English normal lines, they are, again quoting Pope, "constructed whole verses of another order," although it is difficult to know what that order might be.[5] Robert D. Fulk

---

2 On the poem's stylistic and metrical distinctiveness, see, as two examples, Swanton, *Dream of the Rood*, pp. 60–62; Robert Stevick, "The Meter of *The Dream of the Rood*," *Neuphilologische Mitteilungen* 68 (1967): 149–68; and Thomas A. Bredehoft, "Old Saxon Influence on Old English Verse: Four New Cases," *Anglo-Saxon England and the Continent*, ed. Hans Sauer and Joanna Story (Tempe, AZ: ACMRS, forthcoming). I am grateful to Professor Bredehoft for showing me his article. See also nos. 4–7, below.

3 Swanton, *The Dream of the Rood*, p. 61.

4 *Seven Old English Poems*, ed. John C. Pope, 2nd ed. (New York: W.W. Norton & Company, 1981), pp. 129–33 at 132; Pope's scansion and metrical notations appear at 129–30, 132.

5 Pope, *Seven Old English Poems*, p. 131; see also Robert D. Fulk, *Eight Old English Poems: Edited and with Commentary by John C. Pope*, 3rd ed. rev. (New York: W. W. Norton & Company), pp. 150–52, at 151, and for his scansion at pp. 156–57. Among many studies on Old English hypermetric verses, see John C. Pope, *The Rhythm of Beowulf* (1942; 2nd ed. New Haven: Yale University Press, 1966), pp. 101, 121–25; A. J. Bliss, "The Origin and Structure of the Old English Hypermetric Line," *Notes and Queries* 19, o.s. 217 (1972): 242-48; and Constance B. Hieatt, "A New Theory of Triple Rhythm in the Hypermetric Lines of Old English Verse," *Modern Philology* 67 (1969): 1–8. In the "Meter of *The Dream of the Rood*," in order to address the metrical anomaly of the expanded lines, Stevick restructures them to conform to the "regular and continuous rhythmic base"

suggests that one should "think of a hypermetric verse as being like a normal one with an extra foot prefixed to it,"[6] so that a long hypermetric line contains two extra feet, three feet to the half line. Pope, on the other hand, retains the two-measure structure common to Old English verse, but doubles the value of each measure from the usual two to four.[7] In the end, both Fulk and Pope's analyses result in a considerable lengthening of the metrical line. That is to say, though their metrical rhythm does resemble that of normal verses, hypermetric verses are twice or a third again as long. Thus, the *Dream*'s metrical shape—"staccato" verses repeatedly interrupted by blocks of expanded cadences—directs the reader to discern a sound pattern that restructures time. To borrow an analogy from cinema, the metrical effect may be likened to moving from a normal speed of the camera

---

of normal lines (166). Guided by syntax and manuscript data and not by the principle of alliteration, Stevick buttresses his argument, in part, by illustrating that a similar restructuring can be effected in the mixed style of *Genesis B*, and here he uses as an example a portion of Satan's speech (lines 397–412), although he disavows any connection between the *Dream* poem and *Genesis B*, using the latter only to illustrate similarities in rhythmic and syntactical matters (see Stevick, esp. at pp. 154–61, 163). In doing so, however, Stevick has not only subordinated the principle of alliteration, on which all Old English verse is grounded, to syntax, but in effect has eliminated it completely in the off-verse of the hypermetric full line. However, see Bredehoft (above, n. 2) who upholds the *Dream*'s hypermetric clusters by tracing its alleged atypical or unmetrical forms both in normal and hypermetric verses to parallel formulaic and typically metrical forms in Old Saxon, particularly in the *Heliand*, and argues for Old Saxon influence on the composition of *The Dream of the Rood*.

6   Fulk, *Eight Old English Poems*, p. 151. In his "Hypermetric Verses: An Overview" (an unpublished paper presented at the International Congress on Medieval Studies in Kalamazoo, Michigan, 1995), Fulk maps the outline of his three-measure hypermetric half-verse and draws some pertinent correspondences between normal and hypermetric verses in order to emphasize the peculiarities of the OE hypermetric verse. My thanks to Professor Fulk for sharing his paper with me.

7   Pope, *Seven Old English Poems*, p. 131; see also Pope, *The Rhythm of Beowulf*, pp. 121–25.

to slow motion. This sound play between contrasting metrical measures, however, is in turn belied by the poem's graphic presentation in modern editions. Most modern editions adopt left-side formatting for Old English poetry. Because the blocks of hypermetrics are too long to fit the page, these are reflected as run-on lines. Unless the reader is sensitive to the poem's varying metrical pattern, he will not "hear" the sound-shaping of the poem.[8] My concern here, however, is not to offer a metrical analysis of *The Dream of the Rood*; rather, my concern lies in the reciprocity that may exist between the visual and auditory dimensions that are effected by this mixed metrical form, and may produce what John Hollander, in his book *Vision and Resonance*, has referred to as metrical "picturing of the visual world."[9]

In *Vision and Resonance*, Hollander's interest lies in the interpenetrating nature of poetry, of "utterance and inscription."[10] He investigates the interplay between the acoustical and visual elements of poems (that is, the likenesses produced by their graphemic representations with respect to genre and subject), particularly in modern poetry from sixteenth- and seventeenth-century England onwards, a period which has universally been accepted as that which produced the first English *carmina figurata*. While writing and, by extension, while reading a poem, he asserts that the poet visualizes the subject of the written utterance. The graphemic shape of a poem harmonizes with its spoken meter and—gradually in stages—reveals its *figura*, and here Hollander reaches back to Augustine to elaborate on the "interpenetrating aspects of utterance and inscription" of poems:[11]

---

8   In its manuscript context, the poem is written, as are all Old English poems, as if it were prose. See also Stevick's observation of this editorial practice in "Meter of *The Dream of the Rood*," p. 149.
9   See John Hollander, *Vision and Resonance: Two Senses of Poetic Form*, 2nd ed. (New Haven: Yale University Press, 1985), esp. chs. 1 and 12, pp. 3–43, 245–87. I follow closely Hollander's discussion which helped ground my thoughts on the composition of *The Dream of the Rood*.
10 Hollander, *Vision and Resonance*, p. 249.
11 Hollander, *Vision and Resonance*, pp. 249–50, quotes Anthony D. Nuttall's

So it is that a metrical line cannot be pronounced simultaneously. The second [syllable] is pronounced only after the first has passed, and such is the order of procedure to the end of the line, so that when the last syllable sounds, alone, unaccompanied by the sound of the previous syllables, it yet, as being part of the whole metrical fabric, perfects the form and metrical beauty of the whole. But the versifier's art itself is not dependent on time in the same way; its beauty is not portioned out in temporally measured units. It is simultaneously possessed of all those virtues which enable it to produce a line—a line which is not simultaneously possessed of all its virtues but which produces them in order. For the beautiful thing shows the last footprints of that beauty which art itself constantly and immutably watches over.

Hence for Hollander arises the importance of inscription and, by extension, of writing. All poems are at base oral: they are meant to be spoken, even as they are being conceived in the mind of the poet. As such, each utterance and, by extension, each poem is a "thing of the moment";[12] inscribing poems, then, gives them permanence. Thus, earlier "inscriptions were primarily encodings of the spoken poem," for it is only when codified, when it can be consulted and meditated upon at a later time, that a poem perfects its meaning.[13] Because of its fleeting nature, poetry cannot reach perfection of meaning (for poet or audience) until it is written down.

The difficulty that emerges in Old English oral poetry, and in the *Dream* in the present instance, it seems to me, has to do with

---

translation of Augustine's *De Vera Religione* (XXII: 42), cited in his *Two Concepts of Allegory: A Study of Shakespeare's The Tempest and the Logic of Allegorical Expression* (New York: Barnes & Noble, 1967), pp. 44–45. See also Augustine's chapters on measuring time (and its insubstantiality), using as examples the measurement of syllables and feet in verse (XI: 26–27): St. Augustine's *Confessions, with an English Translation*, trans. William Watts, trans., 2 vols. The Loeb Classical Library, vols. 26 and 27 (Cambridge, MA: Harvard University Press, 1988), II. 266–75.

12 Hollander, *Vision and Resonance*, p. 247.
13 Hollander, *Vision and Resonance*, p. 250.

the medium of the inscription, the nature of the oral encoding. Because of the peculiarity of the Old English scribal tradition that continuously copied verse as prose, and because of the apparent lack of poetic sensibility and mechanical copying habits of the Vercelli scribe in punctuation, accentuation, or capitalization (as has often been noted),[14] there is no graphemic hint that the inscription on the parchment was the encoding of a poem, let alone, as I'm suggesting, a poem with a visual dimension, a figural structure. Yet almost half the poem is given over to the Rood's command and the Dreamer's acceptance, and his petitionary prayer that he might accomplish that command (lines 78–156), that he compose an utterance, that he "declare"—speak out—and hence transform the vision, the *gesyhðe*, which is the Rood's very self, into words.[15] For the Dreamer, this

---

14 See *The Vercelli Book*, ed. Celia Sisam, EEMF 19 (Copenhagen: Rosenkilde & Bagger, 1976), esp. p. 39. *The Dream of the Rood* begins on the sixth line of folio 104v and ends at the bottom of folio 106r. The text falls in between two gatherings (14 and 15 beginning at folio 105r) and thus exhibits differences in lineation (from 24 to 32 lines per folio) and a brief change in punctuation from a general sporadic syntactical (to which it reverts in line 4) to a metrical observation at the top of folio 105r, where a punctus marks the division of the Old English metrical half-line. These first three lines reflect the passage from the end of line 22 to the end of line 25, the punctus coming after *bestemed, gange, gegyrwed, lange-hwile, hreowcearig, treo,* but missing *licgende.* There seems to be some consistency in the capitalization of the transitional words like *hwæðre* (lines 18, 24), *ac* (lines 11, 43, 115, 119, 132), *nu* (lines 78, 95), and *hwilum* (line 23). See also ASPR 2, xxviii-xxxi, xlvii; Swanton, *Dream of the Rood,* pp. 5-8, 61; Stevick, "Meter of *The Dream of the Rood*," 161; Donald G. Scragg, "The Compilation of the Vercelli Book," *ASE* 2 (1979): 189–207 at 190 and 196; Scragg, "Accent Marks in the Old English Vercelli Book," *Neuphilologische Mitteilungen* 72 (1971): 699–710; and Katherine O'Brien O'Keeffe, *Visible Song: Transitional Literacy in Old English Verse,* CSASE 4 (Cambridge: Cambridge University Press, 1990), pp. 165–72, esp. 165 and 171.

15 Within the two-part structural division of the poem, I see the sub-divisions as follows: lines 1-27, the Dreamer comments upon his spiritual dryness; lines 28–77, the vision and the Rood's lyric autobiography; lines 78–121, the Rood's exegesis of its autobiography and its command to the Dreamer; lines 122–56, the Dreamer draws forth his prayer to reunite himself with the Rood and accepts

encoding of the vision into words would be sacred work, especially since the command has been dictated by the Rood itself, as quoted in the epigraph to this essay.[16] The Dreamer's task, if he is to progress toward salvation, is simultaneously to speak and to inscribe the vision into the consciousness of the speech-bearers, so that they, being blind to thought, might see the sound of the vision and retain it whole in their mind. Thus, I suggest, the *Dream*-poem is self-reflexive, exemplifying both the inspiration for and the composition of itself. That the poem is meant to be understood as a visionary construct is suggested by the high frequency of terms (charted by Constance Hieatt) referring to sight, as, for example, *behealdan* "to behold" (five times), *seon* "to see" (seven times), *sceawian* "to gaze upon" (once), and *gesyhðe* "vision" (four times).[17] That the poem is meant to be understood as resonance is marked by the vision itself sounding out its autobiography, and the Dreamer's having been given the grace and ability to "hear" it (lines 26, 78).

In order to determine if there were an interpenetrating relationship between the *gesyhþe* "vision" and its mixed metrical resonance, I removed the text from its manuscript context, repositioned it in the center of the page (as if it were a contemporary poem) to allow space for both the normal and hypermetric verses that comprise the graphic representation of its metrical scheme (see Appendix 1). And although I did not use extreme modern electronic measures—spacing, changes in font—my modern typographical rendering of the poem approximates the outline of a cross. Admittedly, it is not as defined as is Hrabanus's double-palindrome cross in "Carmen 28" of his *De laudibus sanctae crucis* (Figure 5.1), but then the *Dream*-poet was not

---

the charge.
16 For a discussion of the renewed understanding in Carolingian poetry of writing as a sacred activity, see Ernst R. Curtius, *European Literature and the Latin Middle Ages*, trans. Willard R. Trask (Princeton: Princeton University Press, 1973), p. 314.
17 Constance B. Hieatt, "Dream Frame and Verbal Echo in *The Dream of the Rood*," *Neuphilologische Mitteilungen* 72 (1971): 251–63 at 262.

Writing/Sounding the Cross

composing in hexameters with their determined syllable count and weight, their length precisely calculated to make the prescribed pattern;[18] instead, he composed in a verse for which stress and alliteration hold primary considerations, and where certain syntactical strictures apply. Thus there is variance in syllable count in the context of meter; in a normal type-A line, for example, the syllables can vary from four to seven (e.g. lines 7, 13); this variance accounts for its ragged appearance. Nonetheless, the poem's graphic outline suggests that the poet's having cast *The Dream of the Rood* in a mixed metrical form does allow for its emergence as a poem whose shape is formed by its meter, a mixed meter that gradually reveals its *figura*.

The reader will note, for example, that out of the thirty-four expanded lines in the poem, thirty-three are contained within the "vision" part of the poem, the odd hypermetric of line 133 being spoken by the awakened Dreamer in his prayer. These thirty-three lines form seven blocks of expanded verse, with each block revealing an aspect of, or climactic moment in, the transformation of the vision from decaying substance to cosmic symbol.[19] The first hypermetric cluster of three (lines 8–10), for example, identifies the vision by metrically inscribing its most salient physical characteristic, its crossbeam; the second cluster (lines 20–23), in a mannerist style, presents the dreamer's apprehension of its dual nature as both an instrument of

---

18 See Fulk's comparision, *Eight Old English Poems*, p. 129.
19 In Old English, hypermetrics ordinarily appear in clusters. The association of the number thirty-three with the years of Christ's life is inescapable. Seven, too, is a highly symbolic number, elsewhere possibly referring to the seven degrees of sanctity, seven ages of man, seven pillars of wisdom, as examples. Here, however, within the context of the narrative, the number seven may very well symbolize the fourteen stages of the cross, halved; see Curtius's discussion (*European Literature*, pp. 503–5) on the use of number symbolism in antiquity and in the early Middle Ages, and W. F. Bolton's overview of Alcuin's theory of number symbolism in *Alcuin and Beowulf: An Eighth-Century View* (New Brunswick, NJ: Rutgers University Press, 1978), esp. pp. 74–75; and Swanton, *Dream of the Rood*, p. 101, where he associates the five gems on the cross-span with the five wounds of Christ.

evil and a gemmed, luminous beacon or *vexillum*;[20] the third (lines 30–34) delineates the path that led the vision to its fated meeting on Golgotha with Christ—a decaying natural substance, stripped of its power (that is, its trunk and/or voice), it is removed from its birthplace, transported, and replanted on a foreign hillside, poised to receive Christ. The fourth cluster (lines 39–43), which marks the center of the first half of the poem, dramatizes the moment of the first physical contact between the vision and Christ, and the vision's self-recognition and acceptance of its fate as the humiliating gallows. And thus onwards: the fifth sequence dramatizes the double crucifixion (lines 46–49); the sixth, the deposition, where the Rood/vision reaches the nadir of spiritual pain as it identifies itself as the *hefige wite* "the heavy punishment," and the *bana* "killer" of its lord; until the seventh, the final single hypermetric of line 75, which brings swift closure to the Rood's progress from natural substance to cosmic emblem: its burial in a deep pit and the beginning of its resurrection as a gemmed luminary. The way to sanctification has been completed.[21] Now, the *Dream* is an oral poem, in the sense that all poems are essentially oral, and the unusually repetitive utterance of hypermetrics at climactic moments—in sharp contrast to the rapid utterance of the normal verse—produces, I suggest, an acoustical and visual manifestation, a kind of stigmatic poem of patterned

---

20 See Swanton, *Dream of the Rood*, p. 111 (n. to line 22) where he associates the image with a royal *vexillum*.

21 Lines 8–10 [3], 20–23 [4], 30–34 [5], 39–43 [5], 46–49 [4], 59–69 [11], 75 [1]. The sixth block (lines 59–69) encompasses eleven lines, the longest sequence of hypermetrics, and marks the separation of the Rood from Christ at the deposition. Here, the Rood, afflicted with sorrows, allows Christ to be taken from it, recognizing itself as the "heavy punishment" (*hefian wite*, 61). Abandoned, it stands there dripping with blood; the wounds from the nails penetrated its body. The action of ministering to its beloved God falls to the hands of others, while it, the slayer of God, looks on. In its state of separation from Christ, the Rood becomes an onlooker, much like the Dreamer at the beginning of the poem, who likewise was "wounded through with evils" *forwundod mid wammum*, and *sorgum gedrefed* "troubled with sorrows" (line 25a).

crosses, whereby the ear, metaphorically, becomes the parchment which receives the inscription and hears it as a visual structure, in this case a cross.

Figured poems, the type to which the *Dream* may belong, are part of a class of decorative and pattern poetry that reaches back to Persian works, exemplifying the eastern tradition, and Hellenistic works, especially those of Simias of Rhodes (300 B.C.E.) and Theocritus of Syracuse (first half of the third century),[22] representing the western tradition. In his history and description of the genre, Ulrich Ernst defines the figured poem as a "lyrical text (up to modern times generally also a versified text) constructed in such a way that the words . . . form a graphic figure which in relation to the verbal utterance has both a mimetic and symbolic function."[23] The definition delimits *carmina figurata* from other visual texts like emblems, epigrams, word labyrinths, verse texts, modern manifestations like Apollinaire's "calligrammes,"[24] and contemporary concrete poetry. The heyday of English figured poetry lay in sixteenth- and seventeenth-century England with the most prominent works being those of the religious poets Richard Crawshaw, Thomas Traherne, and the adaptations of Hellenistic models by George Herbert (Figures 5.2–3). In his survey of pattern poetry in English, Dick Higgins places the corpus at about one hundred and ten pieces; these are formally conservative in their metrical forms in that they are based almost exclusively on Hellenistic

---

22   Curtius, *European Literature*, p. 187, identifies Theocritus of Syracuse as the originator of pastoral poetry.
23   Ulrich Ernst, "The Figured Poem: Towards a Definition of the Genre," *Visible Language* 20:1 (1986): 8–27 at 9; see also his *Carmen Figuratum: Geschichte des Figurengedichts von den antiken Ursprüngen bis zum Ausgang des Mittelalters* (Cologne: Böhlau, 1991), esp. pp. 9–11 on the types of *carmina figurata*.
24   Guillaume Apollinaire (1880–1918), major French modernist poet noted for his fragmentation of poetic structure, most evident in a group of poems (*calligrammes*) where he abandons linear arrangement of the letters of words in the service of design: among many dual-language editions, see *Calligrammes: Poems of Peace and War* (1913–17), trans. Ann Hyde Greet (Berkeley: University of California Press, 1980).

Greek models, found in the "Greek Anthology."[25] This collection was first anthologized by Meleager in the first century and circulated widely in France and Italy in the fifteenth and sixteenth centuries, when it apparently crossed the channel.[26] George Puttenham's *The Arte of English Poesie* from 1589, the first English Renaissance poetic treatise which discussed the form, was not influenced by "Greek Anthology," but instead by eastern, Oriental models.[27]

---

25 Dick Higgins, "The Corpus of British and Other English-Language Pattern Poetry," *Visible Language* 20:1 (1986): 28–51. Higgins offers a bibliography of books containing figured poetry in English. See also Margaret Church, "The First English Pattern Poems," *PMLA* 61:3 (1946): 636–50, for listings and discussions of English Renaissance poets who practiced the form.

26 See Church, "First English Pattern Poems," 636–37. The "Greek Anthology," which contained the first figured poetry, that of Simias of Rhodes (dated at about 300 B.C.E.), was highly popular. Church traces its manifestations that culminated in the ninth-century revision of Constantine Cephalas; from this sprang two imitations, the "Palatine Anthology" (revised and augmented in 980) and the "Planudean Anthology" (from 1303). There is no relationship between the two collections, since the "Palatine Anthology" was apparently lost soon after its revision and not rediscovered until 1606. All subsequent reworkings of the "Greek Anthology" until the eighteenth century were based on the Italian Planudean revision. According to Church, Salmasius discovered this manuscript in Heidelberg, where it had arrived by unknown means. From the eighteenth century on, Church cites it as serving as the source for all modern editions of the "Greek Anthology" and its derivatives.

27 See the facsimile reproduction of George Puttenham, *The Arte of English Poesie*, ed. Edward Arber (Kent, Ohio: Kent University Press, 1970), pp. 104–14, 268–70, for examples of shaped poetry where meter forms the *figura* in constructs of shapes (triangles signifying "air"; lozenges representing "water"; circles suggesting "perfection"). Puttenham handles meter, rhythm, and rhyme under "Of Proportion by Situation"; for Puttenham's contribution and theories, see Baxter Hathaway's introduction to this facsimile, v–xxxvii. See also Hollander's discussion of Puttenham's theories in *Vision and Resonance*, pp. 252–53, 260–65; A. L. Korn, "Puttenham and the Oriental Pattern Poem," *Comparative Literature* 6 (1954): 289–303; and Juliet Fleming, *Graffiti and the Writing Arts of Early Modern England* (Philadelphia: University of Pennsylvania Press, 2001), pp. 13–21 and notes thereto on pp. 166–68. She applies Puttenham's theories of shaped poetry

Writing/Sounding the Cross

Ernst classifies the Hellenistic or western tradition of figured poetry chronologically into different types, only three of which are relevant to this essay. The earliest type, the "outline poem," exemplified by the work of Simias of Rhodes (Figures 5.5, 5.6, 5.7), has a single textual value, and the *figura* is determined by changes in line length and meter. The "outline poem" is quite distinct from subsequent manifestations of the genre. The later poems of Optatianus Porphyrius, though influenced by the earlier form, have a double-text stratum, producing what Ernst describes as "grid" poems.[28] To illustrate his point, Ernst chooses Porphyrius's "Carmen 9" which Porphyrius sent to Constantine (Figure 5.8). In the Porphyrius poem, the *figura*—in this case a palm tree, with its branches of exactly eighteen letters—is in what Ernst calls the "intext," this *figura* is superimposed upon a base text, while at the same time forming a part of its design, which discusses its identity as it simultaneously determines its shape:[29]

> The first three lines of the intext—which are to be read in each case in descending order from the upper-left point of the branch to the trunk and, then ascending to the upper-right point of the opposite branch—contain an invocation to the muses to assist the poet in making a *palma poetica* in honor of the emperor Constantine ("Castalides, versu docili concludite palmam"). There follows an invocation of the god Apollo, whose support is particularly needed in view of the formal novelty and daring of the intextual structure ("Constantine fave; te nunc in carmina Phoebum / Mens vocat, ausa novas metris indicere leges" [Constantine, show favor: the mind now calls you, Phoebus, into my poems, daring new things,

---

to the cultural prevalence of "graffiti, tattooing, and writing on implements and clothes" in early England.
28 Ernst, "Figured Poem," 13, 15.
29 Ernst, "Figured Poem," 15–16; for a full discussion of Porphyrius's figured poems, see Ernst, *Carmen Figuratum*, pp. 95–142 (summary on pp. 135–42).

to pronounce laws into my verses]). The last pair of lines in the tree figure, which constitute the lowest two branches and the trunk, refer to the perfect symmetry of the *figura*, with its branches of exactly eighteen letters each ("Limite sub parili crescentis undique ramos/Reddat ut intextus Musarum carmine versus" [So that my verse, woven in with the song of the Muses, may produce branches growing out in every direction under a small territory]).

In contrast to the somewhat baroque complexity of the "grid" poems, the *figura* of the "outline form," precisely because it has one textual value, rises out of and is one with the simple text.

Hrabanus Maurus elaborated on Porphyrius's grid poems by an increase in pictorial techniques, and by placing the form entirely at the service of Christian doctrine.[30] The example of Hrabanus's "Carmen 28" (Figure 5.1) illustrates the connection. The "intext" is a horizontal and vertical palindrome, whereby the message that forms the *figura*—"oro te ramus aram ara sumar et oro" (I, a branch, implore you, the altar, from the altar I shall be taken up, and I implore)—is identical, read from whatever starting point. The additional pictorial element, the kneeling figure adoring the cross, is the author and penitent Hrabanus and also holds an "intext": "Hrabanum memet clemens rogo, Christe, tuere, O pie judicio" (I beseech you Christ kindly to protect me, Hrabanus, O holy one, in your judgment). Hrabanus further elaborated Porphyrius's grid poem into a highly ornate style, producing a new type of figured poetry which Ernst classifies as "imago poems,"[31] an example of which is the cruciform

---

30   Ernst discusses Hrabanus Maurus in *Carmen Figuratum*, pp. 222–323 (summary, pp. 323–32; on extant manuscripts of Hrabanus, pp. 309–23); see also Celia Chazelle, *The Crucified Christ in Carolingian Art and Thought: Theology and Art of Christ's Passion* (Cambridge: Cambridge University Press, 2001), pp. 99–100; and William Schipper's "Reading the Cross in Anglo-Saxon England: Cambridge, Trinity College MS B.16.3," *Cross and Culture in Anglo-Saxon England*, ed. Karen Louise Jolly, Catherine E. Karkov, and Sarah Larratt Keefer (Morgantown: West Virginia University Press, 2008), pp. 321–42.

31   Ernst, *Carmen Figuratum*, pp. 277–92; Chazelle, *Crucified Christ in Carolingian*

design (Figure 5.9) shaped by symbols of the four evangelists (with "intexts"), holding tablets (with biblical quotations), which has been interpreted by Ernst as containing four levels of interplay between sign and language.[32]

It is no wonder that Ernst Curtius, in his discussion of the varieties of formal mannerism, sees figured poetry as representing the triumph of "mannerist virtuosity" in its combination of "grammatical [i.e. exegetical] with metrical trifling,"[33] alluding to the Greek name for the type, *technopaignia*, "games or tricks." As is apparent, the genre possesses a mixed nature, first, in its juxtaposition of profound content and dazzling metrical form, and second, in its appeal to the pictorial and aural senses, to Hollander's "vision and resonance." It seems to me that the *Dream*-poet, given his own tendency toward a high mannerist style, might have chosen such a mixed form, with its interplay of meter and figure, in which to embody the double nature of God and the mixed nature of his hero, the Rood itself.

In the context of Anglo-Saxon literary culture of the eighth to tenth centuries (the tenth century being the latest given for the composition of the *Dream*-poem),[34] figured poems as a genre were most probably known to the Anglo-Saxons. Ecclesiastical though literary, the culture was a blend of native Anglo-Saxon and British ideologies and those of Ireland, Rome, and, after the coming of Theodore of Tarsus and the African Hadrian to Canterbury, of the

---

Art and Thought, pp. 99–118.

32 In addition to the base text in hexameters, Ernst sees three textual levels: (1) "the intext and its explication of the evangelists' symbols plus quotation," (2) "colored pictures of the evangelists' symbols plus inscribed tablets," and (3) "the order of figures in cruciform layout," with its appropriate allegorical meaning: Ernst, "The Figured Poem," 17.

33 Curtius, *European Literature*, pp. 282–91 at 284.

34 See the discussion in Éamonn Ó Carragáin's essay "Sources or Analogues? Using Liturgical Evidence to Date *The Dream of the Rood*, in this volume, pp. 135–65 above; see Bredehoft's metrical argument for a ninth-century dating for the poem (above, n. 2).

Greco-oriental territories as well.[35] Aldhelm (?640–709), who may be identified as the first English mannered poet, is a product of this mixed culture, falling under the influence of Irish and eastern teachings, and appropriating the Christian-Latin theory of art, including poetry, as handmaiden to Christian subjects.[36] Writing in a mannerist style that later emerged in Alcuin, Aldhelm cultivated Latin figures and metrics, producing, in addition to his larger works (including *De virginitate*), a hundred *enigmata*, riddling poems, whose style celebrates artifice and whose content contemplates God's creation.[37] Alcuin (?735–804), the teacher of Hrabanus Maurus and himself apparently influenced by Porphyrius's work, composed in the form of cruciform acrostics, following the panegyrics on the cross of Venantius Fortunatus.[38] In the last decade of the eighth

---

35 See Michael Lapidge, "The Anglo-Latin Background," *A New Critical History of Old English Literature*, ed. Stanley B. Greenfield and Daniel G. Calder (New York: New York University Press, 1986), pp. 9–10, 15; see also Lapidge, "The School of Theodore and Hadrian," *ASE* 15 (1986): 45–72, esp. at 52–62; Wilhelm Levison, *England and the Continent in the Eighth Century* (Oxford: Clarendon Press, 1946), pp. 132–46; *HE*, Book IV, esp. chs. 1–2; Curtius, *European Literature*, pp. 45, 457–58.

36 Lapidge, "Theodore and Hadrian," 46, 52-59; Vivien Law, "The Study of Latin Grammar in Eighth-Century Southumbria," *ASE* 12 (1983): 43–71, esp. 44–57; Curtius, *European Literature*, p. 458.

37 Lapidge discusses the influence and innovation of Aldhelm's work in "Aldhelm's Latin Poetry and Old English Verse," *Comparative Literature* 31 (1979): 209–31, and in Greenfield and Calder, *A New Critical History*, pp. 10–13; see also Cook, *Dream of the Rood*, xlvii–l; W. F. Bolton, *A History of Anglo-Latin Literature: 597–1066. Vol. 1: 597–740* (Princeton: Princeton University Press, 1967), pp. 68–100, 186–91; and Andy Orchard, *The Poetic Art of Aldhelm*, CSASE 8 (Cambridge: Cambridge University Press, 1994), pp. 239–83.

38 For recent studies on the reception of figured poems in Anglo-Saxon England, see Ernst, *Carmen Figuratum*, pp. 160–67; on Alcuin's influence, see Lapidge in *A New Critical History*, ed. Greenfield and Calder, pp. 22–25; Levison, *England and the Continent*, pp. 152–70; Chazelle, *Crucified Christ in Carolingian Art and Thought*, chs. 2 and 3 passim, and for a discussion of his cruciform poems, see pp. 14–18, 20–23, 99–100, and 110–111; Ernst, *Carmen figuratum*, pp. 168–78 at

century, Alcuin collected his Porphyrius poems, and along with grid poems by other Carolingian writers, presented the anthology to Charlemagne.[39] Porphyrius's and Fortunatus's poems were in circulation in Anglo-Saxon England. J.D.A. Ogilvy observes that Porphyrius's *carmina* were noted by Bede in his *Arte Metrica*, and refers to a letter written to Lul by Milret of Worcester, who protests that he had not yet sent "Porphyrius because Cuthbert [Bishop of Canterbury, 740-58] had not yet returned him." Extant also is a manuscript, Durham Cathedral Library MS B. iv. 9, containing a poem by Porphyrius to Constantine.[40] Finally, the appearance of Hrabanus's work in Anglo-Saxon manuscripts indicates that the *Dream*-poet, in composing in the genre of figure poetry, was working within the poetic production of his time.[41] In line with the mannerist

---

174–78. For Alcuin and Venantius Fortunatus, see Ernst, *Carmen figuratum*, pp. 149–57; Michael Lapidge, "Appendix: Knowledge of the Poems in the Earlier Period," in Richard W. Hunt, "Manuscript Evidence for Knowledge of the Poems of Venantius Fortunatus in Late Anglo-Saxon England," *ASE* 8 (1979): 279–95 at 291–95; Swanton, *Dream of the Rood*, pp. 49–50; Joseph Szövérffy, "Crux Fidelis . . . Prolegomena to a History of the Holy Cross Hymns," *Traditio* 22 (1966): 1–41 at 15–16. Generally, on Fortunatus's poems, see Venanti Honori Clementiani Fortunati, Presbyteri Italici, *Opera Poetica*, ed. Frederich Leo, MGH, Auctorum Antiquissimorvm 4 (Berlin: Weidmann, 1881), at 30–33, 116–17, 381.

39 Ernst, "Figured Poem," 20; see also Chazelle, *Crucified Christ in Carolingian Art and Thought*, p. 14 n. 1 and p. 15.

40 J. D. A. Ogilvy, *Books Known to the English, 597–1066* (Cambridge, MA: The Mediaeval Academy of America, 1967), p. 225; and *Books Known to Anglo-Latin Writers From Aldhelm to Alcuin (670–804)* (Cambridge, MA: The Mediaeval Academy of America, 1936), pp. 146–48; but see more closely, Gneuss, p. 52, no. 246, "Optatianus Porphyrius, carm. 15 (SK605): s. x. med., (prov. Durham)." For Fortunatus, see Lapidge, "Appendix," in Hunt, "Venantius Fortunatus in Late Anglo-Saxon England," 291–95; and Michael Lapidge, "Surviving Booklists from Anglo-Saxon England," in *Learning and Literature in Anglo-Saxon England: Studies Presented to Peter Clemoes on the Occasion of his Sixty-Fifth Birthday*, ed. Michael Lapidge and Helmut Gneuss (Cambridge: Cambridge University Press, 1985), pp. 33–89 at 46, 48, 89.

41 See Simon Keynes, *Anglo-Saxon Manuscripts and Other Items of Related Interest*

tradition, the *Dream*-poet can be viewed as the first to appropriate the mannerist style into the vernacular elegy.

I am not equating the *Dream*-poem to Porphyrius's grid poems or Hrabanus's image poems in their mannered virtuosity, although Matti Kilpiö has hypothesized that Hrabanus's *De laudibus* poems may be a possible source for *The Dream of the Rood* in the choice of imagery, where he finds suggested pictorial, spatial, and typological relationships.[42] I am, however, suggesting that *The Dream of the Rood*, with its mixed metrical form and single text base, partakes of the tradition and exemplifies, in particular, the type classified by Ernst as the Hellenistic outline poem and discussed by Hollander. The difficulty in supporting this hypothesis is that, to my knowledge, there are apparently no other examples of outline poems in the vernacular by Anglo-Saxon authors. One reason may have to do with their not having access to the "Greek Anthology," or its later manifestation as the "Palatine Anthology" (revised and augmented in 980).[43] But, as discussed above, they knew Porphyrius's work, although his poetry

in the Library of Trinity College, Cambridge, Subsidia 18 (Binghamton: Center for Medieval and Early Renaissance Studies, 1992), pp. 11–14, for a description and discussion of Cambridge, Trinity College MS B. 16. 3, 30v [see Figure 5.1], which contains *De laudibus sanctae crucis* (ca. second quarter of the tenth century). Keynes also discusses a later Anglo-Saxon manuscript of *De laudibus* (Cambridge, University Library MS Gg. 5. 35); a copy in London, British Library MS Cotton Tiberius B. v, pt. 1; and Oxford, Bodleian Library MS Auct. F. 4. 32 [St. Dunstan's Classbook], wherein is found a "figure clearly modelled on that of Hrabanus," suggesting (on p. 13) that a copy of Hrabanus was available at Glastonbury in the mid-tenth century; for the date of the Trinity manuscript, see also Gneuss, p. 45, no. 178.

42   Matti Kilpiö, "Hrabanus' *De Laudibus Sanctae Crucis* and *The Dream of the Rood,*" *Neophilologica Fennica* 45 (1987): 177–91 at 181 and 189–90 for the imagery in lines 4–12 and 18–20; see also Swanton, *Dream of the Rood*, pp. 49, 51, 106, 111 (also cited by Kilpiö). Professor Kilpiö's article, which I had not seen before writing this essay, adds support to my thesis that *The Dream of the Rood* is a poem composed in the tradition of figured poetry.

43   Church, "The First English Pattern Poems," 636–37; see n. 25, above.

following the earlier Hellenistic works of Simias and Theocritus seems not to have been of interest to Anglo-Saxon authors working in the mannerist style. The reason may also lie in their work being in Latin and, in conception, written for presentation on parchment, whereas the *Dream*-poet composed orally what was at base a "poem for the ear" (the phrase is Hollander's), and in the vernacular. With this in mind, I suggest that the *Dream*-poem has some affinity with the Hellenistic outline poem, particularly since it possesses one textual value, and its *figura*—as I see the structural movement of the poem—arises out of its mixed metrical form. As noted above, the distinctive characteristic of the outline poem, in which classification only the work of Simias and Theocritus strictly apply, is that the poem itself was the *figura*, and the shape of the *figura* was brought about by a patterned lengthening and shortening of metrical verse.

Simias's "wings," "egg," and "axe" as three of many examples (see Figures 5.5, 5.6, 5.7; my discussion of these depend on Hollander and W. R. Paton)[44] are texts that gradually uncover the visual meaning of their own poetic devices (recalling Augustine's description of the relationship between vision and resonance noted above). Moreover, the "axe" and the "egg" are to be read from the top to bottom, and thus toward the center. The "axe"'s diminishing couplets (shaped as two triangles), for example, end in the shortest central lines through which the handle of the two-edged axe was to be inserted.[45] Eros's wings, similar in metrical style, form their shape in like manner: in the center section of his biographical statement, Eros reveals that he came into being under Necessity, when

---

44 See Hollander, *Vision and Resonance*, pp. 253–58; Ernst, "Figured Poem," 13; *The Greek Anthology*, ed. and trans. W. R. Paton, 5 vols., Loeb Classical Library 112 (New York: G. P. Putnam's Sons; London: William Heineman, 1916–18), V, 124–29, 134–35.

45 Hollander (*Vision and Resonance*, p. 254) suggests that the poem was composed to be inscribed on a votive copy of a bladed axe that was apparently used in making the Trojan horse.

> all creatures were kept
> far apart, moved they,
> in Air,
> or Chaos.
> The swift-flying son
> of Kypris and of Achilles.[46]

The gap in the wings comes between Air and Chaos, where the wings would be attached to the body. Again, the shape emerges from the verse.

Simias's "egg" is likewise self-revelatory. The text increases from a one-foot measure to a decameter, as it identifies itself as the egg of the "Dorian nightingale," which Hollander suggests is a reference to the poet or the poem itself: "The poem is about poetry, about creation and tradition . . . about its own shape (one that "grows" as one reads it—from top to bottom "out" toward center). It is also about what the shape represents, the egg of generation."[47]

The final example of an outline poem that reveals its shape by the manipulation of meter is the Syrinx, "the pipe," of Theocritus, the shape brought about by diminishing meter (Figure 5.10).[48] Like the "egg," the poem is mannerist in style, containing a riddling aspect that requires prior knowledge of mythology (i.e., Odysseus as "no man"; Pan as the offspring of Hermes and Penelope). Hollander notes that Theocritus himself is referred to in the poem as "Paris, son of Simmias"—Paris, "because he was a judge among gods (Theo+kritos, or Theocritus), and "[follower of] Simmias as inventor of the shaped poems."[49] Most of the outline poems are stanzaic. In the case of the "egg" and "wing" poems, the stanzas are repeated to create the form. In this regard, the seven metrical cruciform

---

46 Hollander, *Vision and Resonance*, pp. 254–55.
47 Hollander, *Vision and Resonance*, p. 256.
48 Syrinx is one of the nymphs pursued by Pan, like Echo and Pitys.
49 Hollander, *Vision and Resonance*, p. 258.

patterns that make up the "vision" of the Rood can be thought of as repeated stanzaic structures.

All these sophisticated poetic characteristics—mannerism in style, the interpenetration of metrical form and content, riddling aspects, and allusions to religious thought—resemble those found in *The Dream of the Rood*. The *Dream*-poet's mannerist style in his ready use of Latin rhetorical devices, especially that of *prosopopoeia*, was extensively argued by Margaret Schlauch some time ago;[50] its complex doctrinal philosophy and its underlying allegorical significance explicated by Rosemary Woolf and Faith H. Patten;[51] its relationship to the monastic experience elucidated by John V. Fleming;[52] and, lastly, its evocations of liturgical hymns, poetic addresses to the cross and the Latin and vernacular cross riddles that were features of Anglo-Saxon religious and literary thought were first amply discussed by Howard Patch and A. C. Cook, among others.[53] Finally, a host of the poem's editors and interpreters, from the end of the nineteenth century to the beginning of the

---

50 Margaret Schlauch, "'The Dream of the Rood' as Prosopopoeia," *Essays and Studies in Honor of Carleton Brown* (London: Oxford University Press, 1940), pp. 23–34. Speaking inanimate or inhuman beings—door posts, parrots, statues, trees—were a literary device that reached back to the epigrams of the Hellenistic age and were prevalent in Latin literature and inscriptions. Arguing that Latin rhetorical devices (e.g., *prosopopoeia, ethopoeia, purgatio*) form the appropriate genre for *The Dream of the Rood*, Schlauch discusses a number of literary pieces, and singles out the lamenting "De Nuce" (The Nut Tree), attributed to Ovid, as being closest to *The Dream of the Rood*, but does not consider it a source (esp. pp. 28–29, 30–33). See also Cook, *Dream of the Rood*, xliii–lii; and Swanton, *The Dream of the Rood*, pp. 66–67.

51 Rosemary Woolf, "Doctrinal Influences on *The Dream of the Rood*," *Medium Ævum* 27 (1958): 137–53; Faith H. Patten, "Structure and Meaning in *The Dream of the Rood*," *English Studies* 49 (1968): 385–401.

52 See John V. Fleming, "'The Dream of the Rood' and Anglo-Saxon Monasticism," *Traditio* 20 (1966): 43–72, esp. 56–67.

53 Howard R. Patch, "Liturgical Influence in *The Dream of the Rood*," *PMLA* 34 (1919): 233–57; on Cook, see notes 37 and 50, above.

twenty-first, have discoursed on the poem's ornate and polysemous language which fuses the personae of the Rood, Christ, and the Dreamer, and displays an unusual tendency towards wordplay (*gealgan heanne* "the high and the humiliating gallows").[54] Likewise prevalent is the use of the literary conceit—the yoking of discordant or disparate elements—as exemplified by the vibrant discordant image of Christ's corpse (*hræw*) as a bright radiance (*scirne sciman*, line 54a) and as a beautiful fortress of life (*fæger feorhbold*, line 73a), and of the cross's form as alternatively drenched with blood and gems, a painterly image of its identity as a "heavy punishment" (*hefian wite*, line 61) and a healer (*ic hælan mæg*, line 85). The most striking conceit of all is the *figural* dramatization of the kenning "tree of battle"—the disparate yoking of man and wood—placed in a mystical and religious context.[55]

If one concedes that the vision part of the poem through line 77 may be an Anglo-Saxon adaptation of the Hellenistic outline poems, the second part of the poem may have some affinity with *De laudibus* and its accompanying commentary, a hypothesis also put forward by Kilpiö.[56] The second part of *The Dream of the Rood* (lines 78–156),[57]

---

54 As for example, in lines 14a–62b; 39–41, 51b–58a, 60b–64a; 78b–95a; 84–85, and 101b–102. See esp. J. A. Burrow's, "An Approach to *The Dream of the Rood*," *Neophilologus* 43 (1959): 123–33; and Greenfield and Calder, *New Critical History*, pp. 138–39; Schlauch, "'Dream of the Rood' as Prosopopeia," p. 32; Woolf, "Doctrinal Influence," 149; Patten, "Structure and Meaning," 392, 394, and passim; and Hieatt, "Dream Frame," passim, and for graphs charting the lines in the poem that effect the connections between the personages.

55 Other examples of parallel disparate yoking are those exemplified by the conjoining of an idea with a material substance: for example in such terms as *sigebeam* "victory timber" (lines 13, 127), or "timber of glory," *wuldres beam* (line 97), and its variation *wuldres treow* (line 14).

56 Kilpiö, "Hrabanus's *De laudibus* and *The Dream of the Rood*," at 182, 185.

57 Although the more prevalent division is three parts, Hieatt ("Dream Frame," 258–259) gives the poem five: Prologue lines 1–27, Vision 1 (lines 28–77), Vision 2 (lines 78–94), Vision 3 (lines 95–121), Epilogue (lines 122–156). The change in form from monologue to direct address and the absence of distancing make me hesitant to accept this division; see also Dickins and Ross, *Dream of the*

which begins with the first direct address to the Dreamer, has had a mixed press, perhaps because the poem has dispensed with its form, has shed its dramatic distance,[58] and the Rood abruptly turns to accost the Dreamer directly, articulating and adjudicating the defense for its adoration in doctrinal terms, ideas that have been previously presented allusively, and experientially, in monologue. Here, the *Dream*-poet has set aside his mannerist style: there is no fresh wordplay, no juxtaposition of disparate images, save the repetitions of familiar phrases and images that are meant to be self-referential. Finally, gone is the utterance of mixed meter, that repetitive pattern of complex metrical shifts from expanded to normal lines that engaged the hearer acoustically and visually. With the first direct address to the Dreamer, the Rood abandons its visionary persona that has been shaped through sound, to become a monophonic exegesis on its own revelation. It is a type of structural self-reflexivity which Constance Hieatt expresses as "cyclical" in explaining the effect of the *Dream*'s highly repetitive diction at the poem's closure that points to and recapitulates phrases and events that have occurred in the vision's poetic monologue.[59] It is as if the Dreamer-poet, startled awake from his dream, were at once recovering the remembered phrases as he utters the meaning of his poetic vision.

Structurally, it is possible to liken this doctrinal self-explication that concludes the speech of the Rood (lines 78–121) to the prose doctrinal commentary that accompanies Hrabanus Maurus's poems, "Carmen 28" as an instance,[60] but with this striking difference: the

---

Rood, p. 18.

58 On this point, see Edward B. Irving, Jr., "Crucifixion Witnessed, or Dramatic Interaction in *The Dream of the Rood*," *Modes of Interpretation in Old English Literature: Essays in Honour of Stanley B. Greenfield,* ed. Phyllis Rugg Brown et al. (Toronto: University of Toronto Press, 1986), pp. 101–13.

59 Although Hieatt is not alone in commenting upon and using structural parallelism in diction as an argument for the poem's unity, she is to my knowledge the only critic who has charted the regularity and high percentage of the poem's verbal parallelism: see "Dream Frame," esp. 258–59.

60 See also Kilpiö, n. 42, above.

Dream-poet gives the doctrine an immediate and emotional authority by placing it in the utterance of the suffering cross. The awakened *Dream*-poet can do nothing else but accept the sacred task placed before him when it has been offered to him by the Rood whose suffering he has heard and witnessed.

Further, *The Dream of the Rood* holds similarities with Hrabanus's double palindrome, in that both works are devotional texts, presenting an abject and penitent author in prayer. True, Hrabanus's prayer is in direct address, whereas the awakened poet speaks to the reader (lines 122–56); yet both penitents have a joyful spirit in prayer (*Dream*, line 122 and *De Laudibus sanctae crucis,* line 15), with a deep desire and expectation to be transported by the cross to eternal bliss (*Dream*, lines 135–140, and *De Laudibus sanctae crucis*, lines 16–22, 38), and to offer themselves as sacrifice (directly stated in Hrabanus, lines 21–22, but indirectly in *Dream*, lines 126–28). In this respect, *The Dream of the Rood* and Hrabanus's poem are in line with the widespread iconographic tradition of a figure in *proskynesis*, "prostrated" before the cross, a type that hearkens back to the fourth century and Constantine's vision before the battle of the Milvian Bridge (C.E. 312). In early Christian art, this tradition, Robert Deshman tells us, was "associated with authors, donors, or dedications."[61] Although there is no explicit description in the second part of *The Dream of the Rood* that the poet is in *proskynesis*, it can be assumed that this was his physical position,[62] since his first utterance after the Rood-vision falls silent is "then I prayed to the cross" (line 125), expressing thanks of having been granted grace to have witnessed the vision.

Hrabanus bids adieu to the cross; the *Dream*-poet will not let the vision go. Now that he has experienced an inner spiritual reality, he

---

61 Robert Deshman, "The Exalted Servant: The Ruler Theology of the Prayerbook of Charles the Bald," *Viator* 11 (1980): 385–417 at 387.
62 In its broadest sense, *proskynesis* means worship of God in a number of ways starting with daily prayer, but generally it is associated either with prostration or genuflection (as I suggest here) before God.

wants nothing more than to be alone, in his privacy, to seek out the cross often, worship it well (lines 126–31), and gaze on it (line 137), to hang on to the vision, to relive it, so to speak. This is the hope of his life (line 126). Yet visions, like poems, are "things of the moment," for neither has any materiality. It is only when they are inscribed that they attain permanence. Carolingian artists, Deshman tells us, were able to translate mystical visions into material form, in crosses of stone, and in crucifix iconography realized in prayer books.[63] But in the case of a poet whose prayer is song, how can a poet materialize his vision, bear the sign in his breast like an insignia of the martyr (in the sense of a witness) he has just become, other than by inscribing its shape in figured song?

With this in mind, I return to Hollander's view of the dual nature of poetry as "utterance and inscription" and the importance of inscription, in the case of a poem's achieving a kind of permanence. For the *Dream*-poet to accomplish his sacred work, it may be that only by his metrically inscribing the figure of the Rood and repeating the metrical figure, can he be able, in turn, to reveal the tree of glory as an immediate reality for the speech-bearers, those who are blind to thought, and need to be spoken to. It may also be the only means by which he himself can continue to bear the insignia of the cross on which to hang and perhaps revive his own languishing spirit.[64]

Concentrating as it has on trying to come to terms with the mixed form of *The Dream of the Rood* and its interplay with content, this essay has not touched upon a number of other issues—audience, dating (except generally), or possible influences the inscriptions of the Ruthwell Cross may or may not have had on the poet.[65] But it

---

63 Deshman, "Exalted Servant," 388–95.
64 See Fleming's discussion on the Dreamer's state of mind and spirit and its parallel movement with the state of the cross in "'The Dream of the Rood' and Anglo-Saxon Monasticism," 61–67.
65 On Old Saxon parallels, see Stevick and Bredehoft, n. 2, above; see also Cook, *Dream of the Rood*, pp. 30, 31, 35. Lines 39, 40b–41a, 42b, 44b, 45, 48, 49a,

has begun tentatively to answer the question of the *Dream*-poet's choice of mixed meter, which, as we have seen, is considered its metrical signature. The essay also proposes something of a corrective on received opinion regarding figured poetry: if my reading of *The Dream of the Rood* has validity, then it would seem that the *Dream*-poet's construction of the Rood-vision, with the shape of its *figura* rising out of its metrical form, is the first example of a figured poem in English, and that the proper history of figured poetry in British and American literature should begin with the Anglo-Saxons.

56b–59, 62–64a of *The Dream of the Rood* are inscribed into the top horizontal and both vertical edges of the narrow sides of the Ruthwell Cross: see ASPR 6, pp. 114–15; see also Dickens and Ross, *Dream of the Rood*, pp. 1–13, 25–29; and Éamonn Ó Carragáin's essay "Sources or Analogues?" in this volume, and "Vision Transfigured into Prayer: the Crucifixion Narrative in *The Dream of the Rood*," ch. 7 of his *Ritual and the Rood: Liturgical Images and the Old English Poems of the Dream of the Rood Tradition* (Toronto: British Library and University of Toronto Press, 2005), pp. 308–38.

Appendix 1

The *Dream of the Rood*
(adapted from The Vercelli Book, ed. G.P. Krapp. ASPR 2)

Hwæt! Ic swefna cyst secgan wylle,
hwæt me gemætte to midre nihte,
syðþan reordberend reste wunedon!
Þuhte me þæt ic gesawe syllicre treow
on lyft lædan, leohte bewunden, 5
beama beorhtost. Eall þæt beacen wæs
begoten mid golde. Gimmas stodon
fægere æt foldan sceatum, swylce þær fife wæron
uppe on þam eaxlegespanne. Beheoldon þær engel dryhtnes ealle,
fægere þurh forðgesceaft. Ne wæs ðær huru fracodes gealga, 10
ac hine þær beheoldon halige gastas,
men ofer moldan, ond eall þeos mære gesceaft.
Syllic wæs se sigebeam, ond ic synnum fah,
forwunded mid wommum. Geseah ic wuldres treow,
wædum geweorðode, wynnum scinan, 15
gegyred mid golde; gimmas hæfdon
bewrigene weorðlice wealdendes treow.
Hwæðre ic þurh þæt gold ongytan meahte
earmra ærgewin, þæt hit ærest ongan
swætan on þa swiðran healfe. Eall ic wæs mid sorgum gedrefed, 20
forht ic wæs for þære fægran gesyhðe. Geseah ic þæt fuse beacen
wendan wædum ond bleom; hwilum hit wæs mid wætan bestemed,
beswyled mid swates gange, hwilum mid since gegyrwed.
Hwæðre ic þær licgende lange hwile
beheold hreowcearig hælendes treow, 25
oððæt ic gehyrde þæt hit hleoðrode.
Ongan þa word sprecan wudu selesta:
"Þæt wæs geara iu, (ic þæt gyta geman),
þæt ic wæs aheawen holtes on ende,
astyred of stefne minum. Genaman me ðær strange feondas, 30
geworhton him þær to wæfersyne, heton me heora wergas hebban.
Bæron me ðær beornas on eaxlum, oððæt hie me on beorg asetton,
gefæstnodon me þær feondas genoge. Geseah ic þa frean mancynnes
efstan elne mycle þæt he me wolde on gestigan.
Þær ic þa ne dorste ofer dryhtnes word 35
bugan oððe berstan, þa ic bifian geseah
eorðan sceatas. Eale ic mihte
feondas gefyllan, hwæðre ic fæste stod.
Ongyrede hine þa geong hæleð, (þæt wæs god ælmihtig),
strang ond stiðmod. Gestah he on gealgan heanne, 40

Writing/Sounding the Cross

modig on manigra gesyhðe, þa he wolde mancyn lysan.
Bifode ic þa me se beorn ymbclypte. Ne dorste ic hwæðre bugan to eorðan,
feallan to foldan sceatum, ac ic sceolde fæste standan.
    Rod wæs ic aræred. Ahof ic ricne cyning,
    heofona hlaford, hyldan me ne dorste.   45
Þurhdrifan hi me mid deorcan næglum. On me syndon þa dolg gesiene,
opene inwidhlemmas. Ne dorste ic hira nænigum sceððan.
Bysmeredon hie unc butu ætgædere. Eall ic wæs mid blode bestemed,
begoten of þæs guman sidan, siððan he hæfde his gast onsended.
    Feala ic on þam beorge gebiden hæbbe   50
    wraðra wyrda. Geseah ic weruda god
    þearle þenian. Þystro hæfdon
    bewrigen mid wolcnum wealdendes hræw,
    scirne sciman, sceadu forðeode,
    wann under wolcnum. Weop eal gesceaft,   55
    cwiðdon cyninges fyll. Crist wæs on rode.
    Hwæðere þær fuse feorran cwoman
    to þam æðelinge. Ic þæt eall beheold.
Sare ic wæs mid sorgum gedrefed, hnag ic hwæðre þam secgum to handa,
eaðmod elne mycle. Genamon hie þær ælmihtigne god,   60
ahofon hine of ðam hefian wite. Forleton me þa hilderincas
standan steame bedrifenne; eall ic wæs mid strælum forwundod.
Aledon hie ðær limwerigne, gestodon him æt his lices heafdum,
beheoldon hie ðær heofenes dryhten, ond he hine ðær hwile reste,
meðe æfter ðam miclan gewinne. Ongunnon him þa moldern wyrcan   65
beornas on banan gesyhðe; curfon hie ðæt of beorhtan stane,
gesetton hie ðæron sigora wealdend. Ongunnon him þa sorhleoð galan
earme on þa æfentide, þa hie woldon eft siðian,
meðe fram þam mæran þeodne. Reste he ðær mæte weorode.
    Hwæðere we ðær greotende gode hwile   70
    stodon on staðole, syððan stefn up gewat
    hilderinca. Hræw colode,
    fæger feorgbold. Þa us man fyllan ongan
    ealle to eorðan. Þæt wæs egeslic wyrd!
Bedealf us man on deopan seaþe. Hwæðre me þær dryhtnes þegnas,   75
    freondas gefrunon,
    ond gyredon me golde ond seolfre.
    Nu ðu miht gehyran, hæleð min se leofa,
    þæt ic bealuwara weorc gebiden hæbbe,
    sarra sorga. Is nu sæl cumen   80

þæt me weorðiað wide ond side
menn ofer moldan, ond eall þeos mære gesceaft,
gebiddaþ him to þyssum beacne. On me bearn godes
þrowode hwile. Forþan ic þrymfæst nu
hlifige under heofenum, ond ic hælan mæg 85
æghwylcne anra, þara þe him bið egesa to me.
Iu ic wæs geworden wita heardost,
leodum laðost, ærþan ic him lifes weg
rihtne gerymde, reordberendum.
Hwæt, me þa geweorðode wuldres ealdor 90
ofer holmwudu, heofonrices weard!
Swylce swa he his modor eac, Marian sylfe,
ælmihtig god for ealle menn
geweorðode ofer eall wifa cynn.
Nu ic þe hate, hæleð min se leofa, 95
þæt ðu þas gesyhðe secge mannum,
onwreoh wordum þæt hit is wuldres beam,
se ðe ælmihtig god on þrowode
for mancynnes manegum synnum
ond Adomes ealdgewyrhtum. 100
Deað he þær byrigde, hwæðere eft dryhten aras
mid his miclan mihte mannum to helpe.
He ða on heofenas astag. Hider eft fundaþ
on þysne middangeard mancynn secan
on domdæge dryhten sylfa, 105
ælmihtig god, ond his englas mid,
þæt he þonne wile deman, se ah domes geweald,
anra gehwylcum swa he him ærur her
on þyssum lænum life geearnaþ.
Ne mæg þær ænig unforht wesan 110
for þam worde þe se wealdend cwyð.
Frineð he for þære mænige hwær se man sie,
se ðe for dryhtnes naman deaðes wolde
biteres onbyrigan, swa he ær on ðam beame dyde.
Ac hie þonne forhtiað, and fea þencaþ 115
hwæt hie to Criste cweðan onginnen.
Ne þearf ðær þonne ænig anforht wesan
þe him ær in breostum bereð beacna selest,
ac ðurh ða rode sceal rice gesecan

of eorðwege æghwylc sawl, 120
seo þe mid wealdende wunian þenceð."
Gebad ic me þa to þan beame bliðe mode,
elne mycle, þær ic ana wæs
mæte werede. Wæs modsefa
afysed on forðwege, feala ealra gebad 125
langunghwila. Is me nu lifes hyht
þæt ic þone sigebeam secan mote
ana oftor þonne ealle men,
well weorþian. Me is willa to ðam
mycel on mode, ond min mundbyrd is 130
geriht to þære rode. Nah ic ricra feala
freonda on foldan, ac hie forð heonon
gewiton on worulde dreamum, sohton him wuldres cyning,
lifiaþ nu on heofenum mid heahfædere,
wuniaþ on wuldre, ond ic wene me 135
daga gehwylce hwænne me dryhtnes rod,
þe ic her on eorðan ær sceawode,
on þysson lænan life gefetige
ond me þonne gebringe þær is blis mycel,
dream on heofonum, þær is dryhtnes folc 140
geseted to symle, þær is singal blis,
ond me þonne asette þær ic syþþan mot
wunian on wuldre, well mid þam halgum
dreames brucan. Si me dryhten freond,
se ðe her on eorþan ær þrowode 145
on þam gealgtreowe for guman synnum.
He us onlysde ond us lif forgeaf,
heofonlicne ham. Hiht wæs geniwad
mid bledum ond mid blisse þam þe þær bryne þolodan.
Se sunu wæs sigorfæst on þam siðfate, 150
mihtig ond spedig, þa he mid manigeo com,
gasta weorode, on godes rice,
anwealda ælmihtig, englum to blisse
ond eallum ðam halgum þam þe on heofonum ær
wunedon on wuldre, þa heora wealdend cwom, 155
ælmihtig god, þær his eðel wæs.

Helen Damico

Fig. 5.1: "De Laudibus sanctae crucis" by Hrabanus Maurus (Cambridge, Trinity College B.16.3, folio 30v). Courtesy of the Master and Fellows of Trinity College, Cambridge

Writing/Sounding the Cross

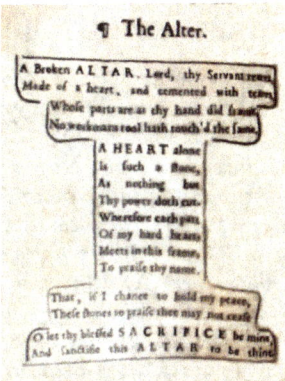

Fig. 5.2: "The Altar" of George Herbert. Reproduced from *The Temple* (1656), PR3507.A1. Courtesy of the Center for Southwest Research, University Libraries, University of New Mexico.

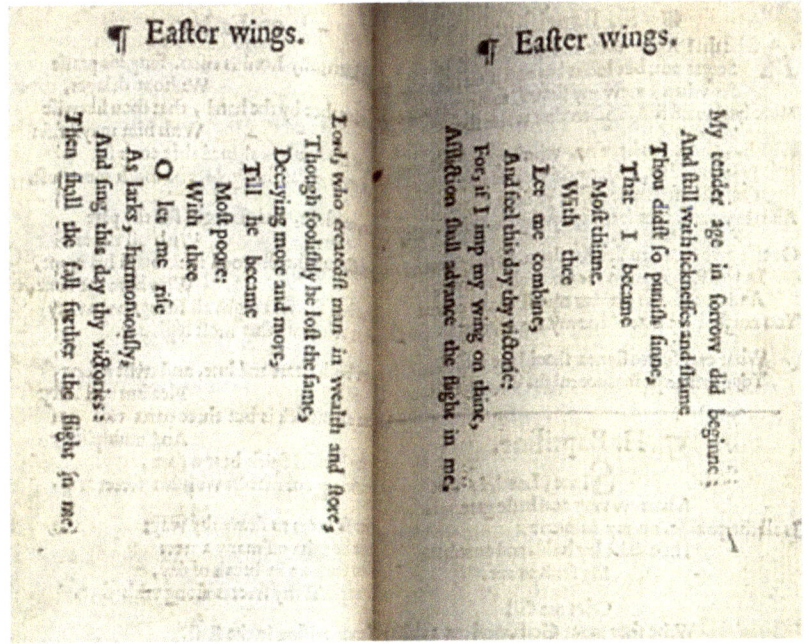

Fig. 5.3: "Easter Wings" of George Herbert. Reproduced from *The Temple* (1633). Digital scan provided courtesy of the CCEL (Christian Classics Ethereal Library: *http://www.ccel.org/*). Source of original photograph unknown.

Helen Damico

—ΒΗΣΑΝΤΙΝΟΥ ΒΩΜΟΣ

Ὀλὸς οὔ με λιβρὸς ἱρῶν
Λιβάδεσσιν, οἷα κάλχη
Ὑποφοινίῃσι τέγγει·
Μαύλιες δ' ὕπερθε πέτρης Ναξίας θοούμεναι
Παμάτων φείδοντο Πανός· οὐ στροβίλῳ λιγνύϊ
Ἰξὸς εὐώδης μελαίνει τρεχνέων με Νυσίων.
Ἐς γὰρ βωμὸν ὁρῇς με μήτε γλούρου
Πλίνθοις, μήτ' Ἀλύβης παγέντα βώλοις·
Οὐδ' ὃν Κυνθογενὴς ἔτευξε φύτλη
Λαβόντε μηκάδων κέρα,
Λισσαῖσιν ἀμφὶ δειράσιν
Ὅσσαι νέμονται Κυνθίαις,
Ἰσόρροπος πελοιτό μοι.
Σὺν Οὐρανοῦ γὰρ ἐκγόνοις
Εἰνάς μ' ἔτευξε γηγενής·
Τάων ἀείζωον τέχνην
Ἔνευσε πάλμυς ἀφθίτων.
Σὺ δ' ὦ πιὼν κρήνηθεν, ἣν
Ἶνις κόλαψε Γοργόνος,
Θύοις τ' ἐπισπένδοις τέ μοι
Ὑμηττιαδᾶν πολὺ λαροτέρην
Σπονδὴν ἄδην· ἴθι δὴ θαρσέων
Ἐς ἐμὴν τεῦξιν· καθαρὸς γὰρ ἐγὼ
Ἰὸν ἱέντων τεράων, οἷα κέκευθ' ἐκεῖνος
Ἀμφὶ Νέαις Θρηϊκίαις, ὃν σχεδόθεν Μυρίνης
Σοί, Τριπάτωρ, πορφυρέου φὼρ ἀνέθηκε κριοῦ.

Fig. 5.4: "The Altar Poem" of Besantinus. Reproduced from W. R. Paton, ed. and trans., *The Greek Anthology* (1918).

—ΣΙΜΙΟΥ ΑΙ ΠΤΕΡΥΓΕΣ ΕΡΩΤΟΣ

Λεῦσσέ με τὸν Γᾶς τε βαθυστέρνου ἄνακτ', Ἀκμονίδαν τ' ἄλλυδις ἑδράσαντα,
μηδὲ τρέσῃς, εἰ τόσος ὢν δάσκια βέβριθα λάχνᾳ γένεια.
τᾶμος ἐγὼ γὰρ γενόμαν, ἁνίκ' ἔκραιν' Ἀνάγκα,
πάντα δὲ Γᾶς εἶκε φραδαῖσι λυγραῖς
ἑρπετά, †πάνθ' ὅσ' ἕρπει
δι' αἴθρας.
Χάους δέ,
οὔτι γε Κύπριδος παῖς
ὠκυπέτας οὐδ' Ἄρεος καλεῦμαι·
οὔτι γὰρ ἔκρανα βίᾳ, πραϋλόγῳ δὲ πειθοῖ·
εἶκε δέ μοι γαῖα, θαλάσσας τε μυχοί, χάλκεος οὐρανός τε·
τῶν δ' ἐγὼ ἐκνοσφισάμαν ὠγύγιον σκᾶπτρον, ἔκρινον δὲ θεοῖς θέμιστας.

Fig. 5.5: "Wing Poem" of Simias of Rhodes. Reproduced from W. R. Paton, ed. and trans., *The Greek Anthology* (1918).

—ΣΙΜΙΟΥ Ο ΠΕΛΕΚΥΣ

Ἀνδροθέᾳ δῶρον ὁ Φωκεὺς κρατερᾶς μηδοσύνας ἦρα τίνων Ἀθάνᾳ
τᾶμος, ἐπεὶ τὰν ἱερὰν κηρὶ πυρίπνῳ πόλιν ἠθάλωσεν
οὐκ ἐνάριθμος γεγαὼς ἐν προμάχοις Ἀχαιῶν,
νῦν δ' ἐς Ὁμήρειον ἔβα κέλευθον,
τρὶς μάκαρ, ὃν σὺ θυμῷ
ὅδ' ὄλβος
ἀεὶ πνεῖ.
Ἵλαος ἀμφιδερχθῇς.
σὰν χάριν, ἁγνὰ πολύβουλε Παλλάς·
ἀλλ' ἀπὸ κρανᾶν ἱθαρὰν νᾶμα κόμιζε δυσκλής·
Δαρδανιδᾶν, χρυσοβαφεῖς τ' ἐστυφέλιξ' ἐκ θεμέθλων ἄνακτας·
ὥπασ' Ἐπειὸς πέλεκυν, τῷ ποκὰ πύργων θεοτεύκτων κατέρειψεν αἶπος.

Fig. 5.6: "Axe Poem" of Simias of Rhodes. Reproduced from W. R. Paton, ed. and trans., *The Greek Anthology* (1918).

Helen Damico

—ΣΙΜΙΟΤ ΩΟΝ

Κωτίλας
τῆ τόδ' ἄτριον νέον
πρόφρων δὲ θυμῷ δέξο· δὴ γὰρ ἁγνᾶς
τὸ μὲν θεῶν ἐριβόας Ἑρμᾶς ἔκιξε κάρυξ
ἄνωγε δ' ἐκ μέτρου μονοβάμονος μέγαν πάροιθ' ἀέξειν
θοῶς δ' ὕπερθεν ὦκα λέχριον φέρων νεῦμα ποδῶν σποράδων πίφαυσκεν
θοαῖς ἴσ' αἰόλαις νεβροῖς κῶλ' ἀλλάσσων ὀρσιπόδων ἐλάφων τέκεσσιν
πᾶσαι κραιπνοῖς ὑπὲρ ἄκρων ἱέμεναι ποσὶ λόφων κατ' ἀρθμίας ἴχνος τιθήνας
καί τις ὠμόθυμος ἀμφίπαλτον αἶψ' αὐδὰν θὴρ ἐν κόλπῳ δεξάμενος θαλαμᾶν μυχοιτάτῳ
‹ᾇτ›' ὦκα βοᾶς ἀκοὰν μεθέπων· ὅγ' ἄφαρ λάσιον νιφοβόλων ἀν' ὀρέων ἔσσυται ἄγκο
ταῖσι δὴ δαίμων κλυτᾶς ἴσα θοοῖς δονέων ποσὶ πολύπλοκα μετίει μέτρα μολπᾶ
ῥίμφα πετρόκοιτον ἐκλιπὼν ὅρουσ' εὐνάν, ματρὸς πλαγκτὸν μαιόμενος βαλίας ἑλεῖν τέκος
βλαχαὶ δ' οἴων πολυβότων ἀν' ὀρέων νομὸν ἔβαν τανυσφύρων ἐς ἀν' ἄντρα Νυμφᾶν
ταὶ δ' ἀμβρότῳ πόθῳ φίλας ματρὸς ῥώοντ' αἶψα μεθ' ἱμερόεντα μαζὸν
ἴχνει θένωι . . ταν παναίολον Πιερίδων μονόδουπον αὐδὰν
ἀριθμὸν εἰς ἄκραν δεκάδ' ἰχνίων κόσμον νέμοντα ῥυθμῶν
φῦλ' ἐς βροτῶν, ὑπὸ φίλας ἑλὼν πτεροῖσι ματρός
λίγειά μιν κάμ' ἶφι ματρὸς ὠδίς
Δωρίας ἀηδόνος
ματέρος.

Fig. 5.7: "Egg Poem" of Simias of Rhodes. Reproduced from W. R. Paton, ed. and trans., *The Greek Anthology* (1918).

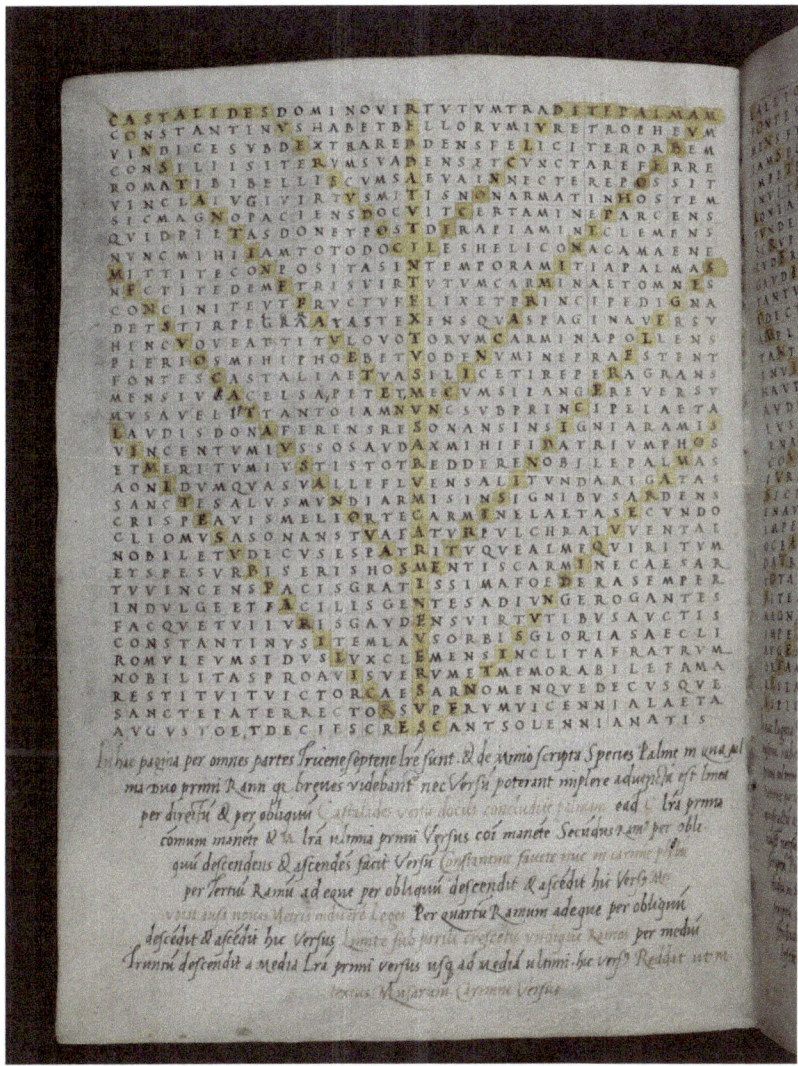

Fig. 5.8: "Grid Poem" of Optatianus Porphyrius, in the form of a palm with commentary (Codex Guelferbytanus, 9" Aug. 40, folio 12v). Courtesy of Herzog August Bibliothek, Wolfenbüttel.

Fig. 5.9: "Imago Poem" of Hrabanus Maurus, with symbols of the evangelists and of the lamb of God (Codex Bernensis 9, folio 11v). Courtesy of Bürgerbibliothek Bern.

—ΣΤΡΙΓΞ ΘΕΟΚΡΙΤΟΤ

Οὐδενὸς εὐνάτειρα, Μακροπτολέμοιο δὲ μάτηρ,
μαίας ἀντιπέτροιο θοὸν τέκεν ἰθυντῆρα,
οὐχὶ Κεράσταν, ὅν ποτ' ἐθρέψατο ταυροπάτωρ,
ἀλλ' οὗ πιλιπὲς αἶθε πάρος φρένα τέρμα σάκους,
οὔνομ' ὅλον, δίζων, ὃς τᾶς Μέροπος πόθο.
κούρας γηρυγόνας ἔχε τᾶς ἀνεμώδεος·
ὃς Μοίσᾳ λιγὺ πᾶξεν ἰοστεφάνῳ
ἕλκος, ἄγαλμα πόθοιο πυρισμαράγω·
ὃς σβέσεν ἀνορέαν ἰσαυδέα
παπποφόνου Τυρίαν τ' . . .,
ᾧ τόδε τυφλοφόρων ἐρατὸν
πᾶμα Πάρις θέτο Σιμιχίδας.
ψυχάν, ᾇ βοτοβάμων,
στήτας οἴστρε Σαέττας,
κλωποπάτωρ, ἀπάτωρ,
λαρνακόγυιε, χαρείς
ἁδὺ μελίσδοις
ἔλλοπι κούρᾳ,
Καλλιόπᾳ,
νηλεύστῳ.

Fig. 5.10: "The Pipe" of Theocritus (the outline of the panpipies). Reproduced from W. R. Paton, ed. and trans., *The Greek Anthology* (1918).

Old English "Cross" Words

Rolf H. Bremmer Jr.

"CROSS, KREUZ, KRUIS, KRÚS, KROES/KRUS, KORS," or "croix, cruce, cruz." Here is a sample of words in Modern English, German, Dutch, Frisian, Low German, and Scandinavian, and in French, Italian, and Spanish, respectively, denoting the instrument of execution on which Christ suffered his death. All forms are cognates and descend from *cruc-em*, the accusative form of the Latin word *crux*, or in any case from an inflected form of *crux*. Moreover, the fact that they all end in a sibilant shows them to have been borrowed into the respective Germanic languages at some point in time after the medial consonant in *crucem* was no longer pronounced with a plosive but had been palatalized to /tʃ/, sometime in the fourth or fifth century. The distribution of the reflex of the Latin word over the Romance languages is not really surprising, while its presence in the Germanic languages today would suggest a wholesale adoption of the loan at the time of the conversion of its speakers, that is, from the late sixth up to and including the eleventh century.

However, the picture is not as simple as we may think at first glance. In particular, the Anglo-Saxons appear to have had a strategy of their own in giving a word to the cross. By the time that the exciting project "Sancta Crux/Halig Rod" had reached its third year, it seemed to me high time to take a lexicological view of the problem.[1]

---

1 A version of this paper was presented at the 37th International Congress of

Old English "Cross" Words

In this paper I therefore present a critical survey of the many Old English "cross" words. Together and individually, it appears to me, these words pose problems that have not yet been coherently addressed in the scholarship.

THE "CROSS" IN GREEK AND LATIN

For some it may be common knowledge, for others it may be new, but the idea that Christ was fixed on a wooden structure consisting of a vertical post with a transverse bar about two-thirds from the bottom, so as to form †—what we call a cross—is not necessarily in accordance with what the Bible tells us. The Greek texts of the Old and New Testaments use two words for the instrument of execution: *stauros* and *ksulon*. Gk *stauros* primarily means "stake, pole" and, by extension, any kind of elevated structure on which criminals were executed, including the time-honored representation of the cross, but also, for example, the CHI-shaped cross X, on which the apostle Andrew allegedly suffered his death, and the TAU-shaped cross T. Gk *ksulon*, "wood," refers primarily to the material of which the instrument is made. The verb "to crucify" in the New Testament is *stauroo* "to fix on a stake or pole," and is derived from the noun.[2] Bible exegetes and classical scholars tell us that basically a *stauros* was utilized in a number of ways, the most common ones being that the victim could be (1) impaled by a sharpened pole flat on the ground; (2) impaled by having the sharpened pole forced through his breast, then the pole being raised and fixed in the ground so that he hangs from it;

Medieval Studies at Kalamazoo, MI, in 2003. I would like to thank Stephen Laker, Alan Griffiths, Ursula Lenker, and an anonymous referee for their helpful suggestions on pre-final versions of this paper.

2   Greek also knew the compound verb *anestauroo*; see Martin Hengel, *Crucifixion in the Ancient World and the Folly of the Message of the Cross* (London: SCM Press / Philadelphia: Fortress Press, 1977), p. 26 and n. 17, in his quotations from Josephus.

(3) lifted up, with his hands bound behind his back and thus hung from the pole; and, finally, (4) nailed to the pole through his hands over his head and his feet nailed as well, or, alternatively, nailed with his arms outstretched on a cross-beam. The gospel narratives suggest that Christ was executed in the last manner. Although crucifixion and impalement were the most common, if the most ignominious methods of execution in ancient times, detailed descriptions are wanting in extra-biblical sources. In fact, the evangelists provide the most detailed of all narratives. "No ancient writer wanted to dwell too long on this cruel procedure."[3] It also appears that there is no way of giving an accurate account of the crucifixion *per se* in ancient times, because there was such an abundance of possibilities for the executioner to carry out his brutal task.

The Latin word *crux*, too, originally had little to do with our word "cross," but signified, like Greek *stauros*, a "pole" or "stake." However, like *stauros*, its meaning had come to include, more generally, "any wooden structure for execution" by the time of Christ's life on earth.[4] As in Greek, the Latin verb denoting "to execute on a cross" included the noun itself, but unlike in Greek, was extended with a verb, *cruci-figo* "to fix on the cross."[5]

THE "CROSS" IN GOTHIC

It is instructive to see how Bishop Wulfila dealt with the word when he translated the Bible from Greek into his Gothic language around

---

3 Hengel, *Crucifixion*, p. 25.
4 *OLD*, s.v. *crux* (with uncertain etymology). For an exhaustive treatment with extensive documentation of the semantic range of both *stauros* and *crux*, see Sarah J. Roberts, "Jehovah's Witnesses and the Cross" (1990), *http://www.forananswer.org/Top_JW/jwcross.pdf*, a scholarly polemic against the Jehovah's Witnesses' claim that Christ suffered not on a cross but on a stake.
5 Sometimes written as two words, see *OLD*, s.v. The "simple," denominative verb *crucio* never signifies "to crucify," but only more generally "to torment," *OLD*, s.v.

the year A.D. 350. His version of the Bible is the oldest we have in any Germanic language. Each time he encountered a form of *stauros* in his text, Wulfila used *galga* for its translation.[6] The question with Gothic *galga* is, of course, why Wulfila chose that word in particular. The literature on this problem is quite unanimous: crosses were unknown to the Goths—or to any ancient Germanic tribe, for that matter—and therefore Wulfila would have opted for the instrument of execution that came closest to a cross, the gallows. With this structure for execution the Goths, and indeed all Germanic tribes, were quite familiar. There is plenty of documentary evidence to show that hanging was the way *par excellence* of executing criminals amongst the German tribes.[7] They even associated the god Woden/Óðinn in particular with this practice as the "god of the hanged."[8] However, Gothic *galga* seems to have originally indicated a "pole" or "stake" rather than a specific instrument of execution by hanging.[9]

Unlike Greek *-stauroo* and Latin *crucifigo*, Gothic has no denominative verb for "to crucify," nor had any other early Germanic language.[10] Instead, Wulfila used *(us-)hramjan*, formally related to Old English *hremman*, "to hinder, cumber," but semantically less easily so.[11] In

---

6 *Die gotische Bibel*, ed. Wilhelm Streitberg, 5th edn (Darmstadt: Wissenschaftliche Buchgesellschaft, 1965), II: 45, s.v. *galga*; cf. Wolfgang Krause, *Handbuch des Gotischen*, 3rd edn (Munich: C. L. Beck, 1968), § 28.4, Anmerkung 3.
7 Adalbert Erler, "Galgen," in Adalbert Erler et al., eds., *Handwörterbuch zur deutschen Rechtsgeschichte*, 5 vols (Berlin: Erich Schmidt, 1971–1998), I: cols. 1375–78.
8 See my "Mercury–Hermes and Woden–Odin as Inventors of Alphabets: a Neglected Parallel," *Old English Runes and Their Continental Background*, ed. Alfred Bammesberger (Heidelberg: Carl Winter, 1991), pp. 409–19 at 409–10, with further bibliographical references.
9 Winfred P. Lehmann, *A Gothic Etymological Dictionary* (Leiden: Brill, 1986), s.v. *galga*. The lexeme in cognate Indo-European languages likewise points to "pole, stake" being the original meaning.
10 Excepting verbs with the loan word, such as Old High German *krūzigōn*, Old Frisian *kriūsga*, Middle Dutch *crucigen*.
11 Lehmann, *Gothic Etymological Dictionary*, s.v.; in this semantic context, cf.

general, the German tribes denoted the act of fixing someone to the cross with the verb "to hang," e.g. Old English *(ā)hōn* and *hangian*. Like so many words related to the Christian faith, *galga*, "(Christ's) cross," was in all likelihood passed on to the West Germanic speaking tribes from Gothic, an assumption which seems more likely to me than the Germans, Anglo-Saxons, and Scandinavians having all independently opted for this word.[12]

Reflexes of Latin *crux*

When the Vulgar Latin-speaking missionaries set out to preach the cross to the Germanic tribes in the western parts of Europe, not only had the word *crux, cruc-* undergone palatalization of the medial consonant, but it had also seen lengthening of the stem vowel. Hence, sometime before the seventh century, such South-German tribes as the Bavarians and Alemanni, but also the Franks who were living on the borders of the Rhine further north, adopted the word as *kriuze, krūzi*, although detailed accounts of the earliest efforts at converting these tribes are not available. In any case, the word had so firmly established itself that the Old Saxons, too, adopted *krūci*, as did the Frisians with *kriūse, kriōse*, both sometime in the ninth to tenth centuries.[13] The word competed with and eventually

---

Old Frisian *hrem-band* "fetter." All Old Frisian references in this article are to Ferdinand Holthausen, *Altfriesisches Wörterbuch*, rev. ed. Dietrich Hofmann (Heidelberg: Carl Winter, 1985).

12 Piergiuseppe Scardigli, *Die Goten. Sprache und Kultur* (Munich: C. H. Beck, 1973), chapter 9, "Die Einflüsse des Gotischen auf die übrigen germanischen Sprachen," provides plenty of such examples but does not mention *galga*. Dennis Howard Green, *Language and History in the Early Germanic World* (Cambridge: Cambridge University Press, 2000), p. 348, assumes that *galga* was an independent translation in Gothic, Old High German, Old Saxon, and Old English.

13 Green, *Language and History in the Early Germanic World*, pp. 213, 214, 348–49. Green overlooked the Old Frisian evidence. See also Wilhelm Braune, "Althochdeutsch und Angelsächsisch," *Beiträge zur Geschichte der deutschen Sprache*

usurped the indigenous *galgo, galga* (Old High German) and *galgo* (Old Saxon) for "cross."

For the conversion of the Anglo-Saxons we are much better informed than we are for the early missionary activities amongst the continental Germans, owing to Bede's detailed account.[14] At his first encounter with the missionaries in 597, Æthelberht, king of Kent, cannot have escaped the impressive procession of Augustine and his companions that was headed by *crucem pro vexillo argenteam,* "a silver cross as their standard," and the likeness of "our Lord and Savior painted on a panel."[15] We do not know in what way Christ was depicted on the panel, whether with his face only or crucified or in glory, but the standard unmistakably served to make clear to King Æthelberht that the cross was all-important in the new faith that was going to be preached to him. Actually, Æthelberht must have been familiar with that sign through his wife Bertha, a Christian Frankish princess, who had been allowed to practice her faith in Kent with the help of the Frankish Bishop Liudhard. The Latin word *crux, cruc-em* or the Frankish word *krūzi* or the like, must have been heard in Æthelberht's vicinity long before his meeting with St. Augustine on the Isle of Thanet. If this had not been the case, then the Frankish interpreters in Augustine's company would have used it in their conversations with the king.[16] Much further to the north, in Northumbria, Irish monks would soon be active, some decades after Augustine's arrival, in spreading the news of the (Old Irish) *cros.* Quite remarkably, neither in the south nor in the north of England did the Anglo-Saxons adopt this Celtic descendent of Latin *cruc-.*[17]

---

und Literatur 43 (1918): 361–445 at 390–91.
14 *HE*, I, 25, pp. 72–75.
15 *HE*, pp. 74–75.
16 On the intelligibility of speakers of continental Germanic languages by Anglo-Saxons, see Rolf H. Bremmer, Jr., "Continental Germanic Influences," *A Companion to Anglo-Saxon Literature*, ed. Phillip Pulsiano and Elaine Treharne (Oxford: Blackwell, 2001), pp. 375–87, with further references.
17 Alistair Campbell, *Old English Grammar* (Oxford: Clarendon Press, 1957),

Whatever evidence we have of the Irish loanword points to a very late adoption in Old English.

The DOEC yields seven occurrences of Old English *crūć*, the majority of which—four examples—are found in "Charm 19." On closer consideration of these seven attestations, it appears that most forms can barely be called Old English. They instead are the Latin term used in a vernacular context. Let us consider the evidence.

The first example comes from the Old English translation of Bede's *Historia Ecclesiastica*, commonly dated to the late ninth century and hence the earliest of these seven occurrences of OE *cruc*: "Ða aðenede se biscop hine in cruce & hine gebæd" (then the bishop stretched himself out in the form of a cross and prayed). The bishop stretched himself *in cruce* (the phrase is purely Latin), instead of (in Old English) *on cruce*, "in the form of a cross."[18] The form *cruce* cannot therefore be considered to be Old English. Moreover, there is nothing in Bede's Latin text to suggest in what posture the bishop prayed. The addition was apparently made by the translator who may have been thinking of the Irish "Céli Dé" monks who prayed cruciform or knew about praying *aþenedum earmum* "with outstretched arms."[19]

Another example of *cruc* is found in the *Vision of Leofric*, at the

---

§565. No attestations of an Old English loan of early Irish *croch* have been found either.

18 Thomas Miller, ed. and trans., *The Old English Version of Bede's Ecclesiastical History of the English People*, EETS o.s. 95, 96, 110, 111 (London: Trübner, 1890–1898), I: 372, lines 14–15 (= Oxford, Bodleian Library, MS Tanner 10). The text in Cambridge, Corpus Christ College MS 41, however, has the hybrid phrase *on cruce*.

19 See, respectively, Sandra McEntire, "The Devotional Context of the Cross before A.D. 1000," *Sources of Anglo-Saxon Literary Culture: A Trial Version*, ed. Paul E. Szarmach and Virginia D. Oggins, *Studies in Medieval Culture* 20 (Kalamazoo: Medieval Institute Press, 1986), pp. 345–56 on the Irish *Céli Dé* practice, and Anselm Hughes, ed., *The Portiforium of St. Wulfstan* (Corpus Christi College, Cambridge Ms. 391), HBS 89–90 (Leighton Buzzard: The Faith Press, 1958–1960), II:24 (three times in a prayer to the cross). I owe these references to Sarah Larratt Keefer.

point where Leofric, earl of Mercia, has entered the church of St. Clement in Sandwich to attend mass. Behind the altar hangs a beautiful woven curtain and in the northeast corner of the church is a cross of moderate size (*medmycel rod*). Remarkably the account relates that *se preost mæssode be cruce*, "the priest celebrated mass near the cross" (i.e. not at the altar).[20] Again, *cruc* is preceded by a preposition without a determiner, but unlike in the phrase *in cruxe* that we saw in the Old English Bede, the preposition in the phrase *be cruce* is clearly vernacular which gives us confidence to interpret *cruce* likewise as an Old English word here.

"Charm 19" ("Against Elf-sickness or Elf-disease") is one of seventy-six such recipes included in the third, anonymous part of the *Leechbook*, thought to have been composed in the late ninth century.[21] It is a complex charm, consisting of four parts (numbered "A" to "D" by Storms) in which writing and writing material figure prominently. In part B, the celebrant/liturgist is told among many other things: "And hine eac ymbwrit mid sweorde on IIII healfa on cruce" (and also write in cross manner [?] around him [the patient] with a sword on four sides). Unlike the phrase in the Old English Bede which features the Latin preposition, we find Old English *on* preceding the word *cruce* in the charm. The latter form is perfectly good Latin (ablative),

---

20 A.S. Napier, "An Old English Vision of Leofric, Earl of Mercia," *Transactions of the Philological Society* (1907–1910), 180–88 at 186, line 74. On this vision, see Milton McC. Gatch, "Miracles in Architectural Settings: Christ Church, Canterbury and St. Clement's Sandwich in the Old English Vision of Leofric," *ASE* 22 (1993), 227–52 for the cross here, also called *treow*, 246–48.

21 London, British Library, MS Royal 12 D. xvii. The first two collections in this mid tenth-century manuscript are known as Bald's Leechbook. See Ker, item 264; and Gneuss, no. 479. See also Karen Louise Jolly, *Popular Religion in Late Saxon England: Elf Charms in Context* (Chapel Hill: University of North Carolina Press, 1996), pp. 156–67, and "Cross-Referencing Anglo-Saxon Liturgy and Remedies: The Sign of the Cross as Ritual Protection" in *The Liturgy of the Late Anglo-Saxon Church*, ed. Helen Gittos and M. Bradford Bedingfield, HBS Subsidia 5 (London: Boydell Press, 2005), pp. 232–35, 239–42.

but it could just as well represent the natural outcome of sound-laws of a loan into Old English. For the time being I will consider it to be an ambiguous case. Beside many other actions, in part D of "Charm 19" the celebrant is instructed to first write the following:

> Scriptum est rex regnorum et dominus dominantium. byrnice. beronice. lurlure. iehe. aius. aius. aius. Sanctus. Sanctus. Sanctus. Dominus Deus Sabaoth. Amen. Alleluiah.

> [It is written: King of kings and Lord of lords. byrnice. beronice. lurlure. iehe. Holy, holy, holy [Greek]. Holy, holy, holy [Latin]. Lord. God. Sabaoth. Amen. Halleluiah.]

Whether he is supposed to write these phrases on a piece of parchment or perhaps on a waxed writing tablet, we are not told. Having next recited a long Latin prayer over the writing and the potion he has to concoct, the celebrant is instructed to write a cross, presumably on the piece of parchment or writing tablet. He is told to do so in the Latin accusative form *crucem*: "Writ III crucem mid oleum infirmorum, and cweð: Pax tibi" (write three times a cross with oil for the sick [i.e. of extreme unction], and say: Peace be with you). Note that unlike the Latin inflected *crucem*, the Old English preposition *mid* does not affect *oleum* (one would have expected dative *oleo*). Immediately after this instruction, he has to continue:

> Nim þonne þæt gewrit, writ crucem ofer þam drince, and sing þis þær ofer: "Deus omnipotens, pater domini nostri Jesu Cristi, per inpositionem hius scriptura et per gustum huius expelle diabolum a famulo tuo N."

> [Then take the piece of writing, write a cross [or: write "cross"] over the drink, and sing this over it: "God almighty, father of our Lord Jesus Christ, by imposing this writing and by this taste expel the devil from your servant N."]

Old English "Cross" Words

Interestingly, the celebrant is not actually required to write a cross on the bottle or container which holds the potion he has just prepared, but to represent the word *crucem* by signing the cross in the air. After he has performed this exorcism within the charm, and has recited the *Credo* and *Pater Noster*, the celebrant is told to proceed as follows:

> Wæt þæt gewrit on þam drence and writ crucem mid him on ælcum lime and cweð: "Signum crucis Christi conserva te in vitam eternam. Amen."
>
> [Wet the writing in the drink and write a cross [or: "cross"] with it on each limb and say: "May the sign of Christ's cross preserve you for the life everlasting. Amen."][22]

With respect to the thrice recurring form *crucem*, to find a Latin grammatical form here, i.e. accusative singular, is not surprising, because "Charm 19" is larded with other Latin terms and, indeed, is interspersed with long passages in Latin.

Only the sample from Bald's Leechbook unequivocally seems to present the Old English accusative form *cruc*:

> Gif mon eac of his gewitte weorðe þonne nime he his dæl & wyrce cristes mæl on ælcre lime, butan cruc on þam heafde foran, se sceal on balzame beon & oþer on þam heafde ufan.
>
> [Also if a man becomes witless, then let him take a part of it [i.e., oil] and make Christ's sign on every limb, but [make] a cross upon his forehead which must be in balsam [not in oil], and the other one on the top of his head].[23]

---

22 Quotations from Godfrid Storms, *Anglo-Saxon Magic* (The Hague: Martinus Nijhoff, 1948), p. 226, lines 62–91. The translations from Old English are Storms's, those from Latin are mine.

23 Thomas O. Cockayne, ed., *Leechdoms, Wortcunning and Starcraft of Early England* (London: The Holland Press, 1864–66; repr. with new introd. by Charles Singer. London: The Holland Press, 1961), II: lxiv (on 288–89).

The author seems to distinguish in meaning between *Cristes mæl* and *cruc*, as indicated by the contrastive conjunction *butan*. Alternatively, the two phrases may both indicate "the sign of the cross," as argued by Ursula Lenker.[24] Syntactically, in any case, *cruc* in the last quotation is in concordance with *Cristes mæl* ("Christ's sign," i.e. "sign of the cross"), the object of the verbal predicate *wyrce*. It must have been on the meager evidence of this last single instance that Bosworth-Toller assigned the word its masculine gender, as opposed to neuter in Old High German, Old Saxon, and Old Frisian.[25]

In conclusion, then, the evidence for the existence of OE *crūċ* is slender, if it is there at all. On the face of it, I would almost suggest that it be struck from our Old English dictionaries or at least marked as dubious, were it not for the fact that Middle English seems to testify to *crūċ* as having been a reality in Old English. The presence of *crouch* (preserved in Present Day English "to crouch") suggests that perhaps the word had come into use in Old English after all, but that it was at first confined to limited circles. Alternatively, after the Conquest the word was borrowed anew from Latin, and Old French *croche* played a part in its coinage, as the *Middle English Dictionary*, s.v. *crouch*, tentatively suggests.[26] Significantly in this respect, the Toronto *Dictionary of Old English* does indeed feature an entry *cruc*,[27] however,

---

24 On *Cristes mæl* and *cruc*, see Ursula Lenker, "Signifying Christ in Anglo-Saxon England: Old English Terms for the Sign of the Cross" in this volume, below, passim.

25 BT and BTS, s.v. *crúc* (p. 135). Old Saxon *krūci* actually had both the masculine and the neuter gender, the latter more frequently so than the former.

26 Hans Kurath, et al. ed., *Middle English Dictionary* (Ann Arbor: University of Michigan Press, 1952–2001), s.v. *crouch*: "[OE crūc (ult. L) & OF croche (vr. of croce)]." Otto Funke, *Die gelehrten lateinischen Lehn- und Fremdwörter in der altenglischen Literatur von der Mitte des X. Jahrhunderts bis um das Jahr 1066* (Halle/S: Max Niemeyer, 1914), p. 127, thinks of a mixed Latin-native form for Old English and a new loan from Latin in Early Middle English.

27 *Dictionary of Old English*: C, ed., Ashley Crandell Amos, Antonette di Paolo Healey et al., (Toronto: Pontifical Institute of Medieval Studies, 1988).

without assigning a gender to this noun. The Toronto lexicographers also add that the form *crucem* shows a Latin inflected ending, but have left it to the user of the dictionary to decide whether the entire form *crucem* is Latin or not. I think it is, which reduces the total number of seven occurrences to four, with some of the four occurrences being of dubious weight.

We are on slightly firmer ground with the lexeme *cros*, which is usually found not as a simple form, but in compound place-names: the DOEC gives *Nor(ð)mannescros, Grætecros, æt Wyrðreðe crosse* (not a compound here but a simple dative form with *Wyrðreðe* in the genitive) and *Crosfleot*.[28] All attestations are post-Conquest and the places referred to are all situated within the borders of the Danelaw. For that reason, these place-names must contain the Scandinavian form *kros(s)*, itself a loan from Old Irish *cros*. In addition to the DOEC material, I can mention such place-names as Crosby, Crosthwaite, and others, all from within former Danelaw territory.[29] Remarkably, the *DOE* does not include *cros* in its microfiche pages. Would this omission be an oversight or is it a sign that the editors did not consider the word a true Old English word?[30]

Old English *rod*

If the two reflexes of Latin *crux* in Old English, *crūc̓* and *cros*, are rare or dubious Johnnies-come-lately, what then did the Anglo-Saxons call the cross when they first accepted it? Like so many other technical terms

---

28 DOEC, Simple Search, fragmentary, "cros": *http:/ets.umdl.umich.edu/o/oec*
29 A. H. Smith, *English Place-Name Elements*, 2 vols, English Place-Name Society 25–26 (Cambridge: Cambridge University Press, 1956), s.v. *cros* and *cruc*³.
30 On the basis of a preliminary version of this paper which I sent to Toronto in May 2003 at the request of Antonette di Paolo Healey, the dictionary editors appear to have rewritten the entries on *cruc* and *cros*, and, on the basis of my discussion, have adopted my reading of these words. See *Dictionary of Old English*. A–F on CD-ROM (2004), s.vv., which now differs in this respect from the earlier microfiche edition.

related to the Christian faith, suitable candidates were looked for in their native language and quite a few were found. The first choice, it seems, fell on *rōd*. The word, a good Germanic one at that, originally signified "pole" or "stake." As such, it semantically parallels Greek *stauros* and Latin *crux*, something that Ælfric, for example, was well aware of: in his *Glossary* he included "*crux* oððe *staurus* : *rod*."[31]

Occasionally the word seemed to have indicated a spar or yard, as in the compound *seglrōd* "sail-yard," a *hapax legomenon* recorded in the poem *Exodus*:

> hæfde witig god
> sunnan siðfæt   segle ofertolden,
> swa þa mæstrapas   men ne cuðon,
> ne ða seglrode   geseon meahton
> eorðbuende.   (*Exodus*, lines 80b–84a)[32]

[The wise God had covered the course of the sun with a sail/veil, so that men could neither know the halyards nor dwellers on earth were able to see the sailyard.]

The lines occur at the point in which the poet describes the pillar of cloud which guided the Israelites through the desert. In a set of illuminating notes to this passage, Peter Lucas explains how the poet has been extensively weaving into his narrative all kinds of patristic interpretations of the pillar of cloud. One of these was the use of nautical terms so as to suggest that the Israelites were on board the ship of the Church; another was that the pillar was a pre-figuration of the cross. Together, the mast and the sail-yard make a cross, although the Israelites could not yet see the significance of this sign.[33]

---

31 Julius Zupitza, ed., *Ælfric's Grammatik und Glossar,* Sammlung englischer Denkmäler in kritischer Ausgabe (Berlin: Weidmann, 1880), p. 313, line 15.
32 ASPR 1, p. 93. Translation mine.
33 Peter J. Lucas, ed., *Exodus*, rev. ed., Exeter Medieval English Texts and Studies (Exeter: University of Exeter Press, 1994), pp. 88–91.

Old English "Cross" Words

In all probability, the poet coined the compound for the occasion to suit his typological mode of narration.[34]

Furthermore, *rōd* also seems to have been used as a yard stick, because in charters land measures are occasionally expressed in "roods," i.e. "rods":

> Þæt is þonne þæt Werfrið biscop & se hired æt Wigraceastre syllað & gewritað Æþelrede & Æþelflæde heora hlafordum þonæ hagan binnan byri æt Wigraceastre se is fram þære ea sylfre bi þæm norðwalle eastwardes *XXVIII* roda lang & þonon suþwardes *XX IIII* roda brad & eft þonon westwardes on Sæferne *XIX* roda long.[35]

> [That is then that Bishop Werfrith and the community at Worcester give and grant by charter to Æthelred and Æthelflæd, their lords, the messuage within the town [wall] of Worcester which is 28 rods in length from the river itself along the north wall eastwards, and from there southwards 24 rods in breadth and then from there westwards to the Severn 19 rods in length.]

However, differing from its use in continental Germanic languages, linear measurement is rare and late for Old English.[36] This observation can be confirmed by the fact that, according to the DOEC, Latin *virga* "rod (also for measure), stick" is never translated by or glossed with *rōd*, but always with *gierd* and varying spellings (*gerd*, *gyrd*), the ancestor of "yard."

What all the meanings of Old English *rōd* have in common is that they basically signify "an elongated, round piece of wood." The

---

34 The more common word seems to have been *seglgyrd*, attested in glossaries, once as the translation of *antemna* (BrGl 1) and twice (related) as a paraphrase for *cornua* (AntGl 6 and BrGl 1): "þa twegen endas þaere seglgyrde" and "þa ytemystan endas þære seglgyrde," respectively; see the DOEC.
35 A. J. Robertson, ed., *Anglo-Saxon Charters* (Cambridge: Cambridge University Press, 1939), no. XIX, lines 5–10.
36 See also *MED*, s.v. *rode* (n. (5)).5.

most common sense for *rōd* before the conversion to Christianity must have been "instrument for execution by hanging." In this sense, the word is also recorded in cognate languages, e.g. Old Frisian *rōde*, Old Saxon *rōde*, and Old High German *ruote*.

Thus, when the Pharaoh's chief butler and chief baker are thrown into prison and tell their dreams to Joseph, Joseph explains that the butler will be restored to his office, whereas the baker is to be hanged in three days *in cruce*, as the Vulgate here translates the Septuaginta words *epi ksylou*, "upon the wood" or "upon the tree," a phrase which appears as *on rode* in Ælfric's Old English prose translation of Genesis 40:19.[37] Yet this instance of *rōd* as "instrument of execution" is one of the very few in which it does not specifically denote Christ's cross. The latter sense holds an overwhelming majority in the DOEC.

The Christian sense of *rōd* as Christ's cross apparently usurped the generic meaning of "instrument for execution" to such a degree, that it was evidently necessary for speakers to coin the compound *wearhrōd* in order to avoid confusion. The first element *wearh* is the typical Old English (Germanic) word for "criminal, outcast,"[38] and serves to distinguish the object from a "cross" put up in the landscape for devotional purposes. *Wearhrōd* is twice attested in border

---

37 Samuel J. Crawford, ed., *The Old English Translation of the Hexateuch, Ælfric's Treatise on the Old and New Testament*, and *His Preface to Genesis*, EETS o.s. 160 (London: Oxford University Press, 1922), p. 181. The "pole" which Haman erected for Mordechai also appears as *ksylos* in the Septuaginta, but this Greek word was for some reason or other translated by the Vulgate with *trabs* "beam" in the Book of Esther—it was nevertheless interpreted by Ælfric as *gealga* in his homily on Esther (e.g. line 69): see Stuart D. Lee, ed., *Ælfric's Homilies on Judith, Esther, and the Maccabees*, line 69 (on-line edition, 1999): http://users.ox.ac.uk/~stuart/kings/, the only edition available of William L'Isle's unique seventeenth-century transcript in Oxford, Bodleian Library, MS Laud Misc. 381, folios 140v–148, from a manuscript now lost).

38 Michael Jacoby, *"Wargus, vargr" "Verbrecher", "Wolf." Eine sprach- und rechtsgeschichtliche Untersuchung*, Studia Germanistica Upsaliensia 12 (Upssala: Almqvist and Wiksell, 1974).

descriptions in charters, once being located, whether significantly or not in view of Woden's association with the hanged, on *Wodnes dic*.[39] *Wearhrōd* is also found more than once for the *interpretamentum* of *furca* as a gloss word, as early as in the eighth-century *Épinal Glossary*.[40] Latin *furca*, the source for our "fork," is found once glossed as *genus ligni bicipitis*, that is "a kind of two-headed or two-peaked wood/tree."[41] The term was used for a fork-shaped structure—originally the pole of a cart to which the horses or oxen were fastened—to the ends of which the arms of the criminal were tied. Interestingly, Emperor Constantine had introduced the *furca* as the instrument for executing criminals to replace the "ordinary" cross,[42] since the latter had even then become too closely associated with Christ's passion. Association of *furca* with the cross is also suggested by the gloss *furcifer : cruci dignus*, "(one) worthy of the cross," i.e., a criminal.[43] It is to be observed, however, that nowhere have I found the term *furca* in connection with Christ's crucifixion. To me, this observation confirms that the *furca*, or indeed the *wearhrōd*, was an instrument that the Anglo-Saxons must have imagined as being dissimilar in shape to Christ's cross.

---

39 W. de Gray Birch, ed., *Cartularium Saxonicum. A Collection of Charters Relating to Anglo-Saxon History*, 4 vols (London: Whiting & Co., 1885–1899), III: nos. 998 and 1053 (different Latin texts but similar border description).
40 J. D. Pheifer, *Old English Glosses in the Épinal-Erfurt Glossary* (Oxford: Clarendon Press, 1974), p. 23, no. 409. See also in the Latin–Old English glossaries in London, British Library, MSS Cotton Cleopatra A. iii, and Harley 3376.
41 Cambridge, Corpus Christi College MS 144 (Ker, no. 36: s. viii/ix; Gneuss, no. 45: s. ix1); see Jan Hendrik Hessels, *An Eighth-Century Latin–Anglo-Saxon Glossary* (Cambridge: Cambridge University Press, 1890), F.372/3 (p. 58).
42 *Der neue Pauly. Enzyklopädie der Antike*, ed. Hubert Cancik and Helmut Schneider (Stuttgart: J. B. Metzler, 1997), s.v. *crux*.
43 Hessels, *An Eighth-Century Glossary*, F.373 (p. 58). Other Anglo-Saxon glosses of *furcifer* include the bilingual *furca* [!] *dignus, feondulf*, i.e. "criminal" (PrudGl 1), *wearh* (HlGl), while *furcifera* (pl.) is glossed by "þa weargberendan" (ClGl 1).

OLD ENGLISH (*RŌDE-*)*HENGEN*: "CROSS" OR "CRUCIFIXION"?

In his dictionary, Clark Hall included the meaning "cross" for *hengen*, and for this meaning cites "Æ[lfric]."[44] The other meanings given by Clark Hall are "hanging," "rack, torture," and "imprisonment." The word is derived from the verb *hangian* "to hang." As we have seen, this verb was commonly used in Old English for "to crucify." The DOEC yields only one instance of this word: "Þæt Iudeisce folc. nolde on Crist gelyfan ðone ðe hi mid hospe on hengene fæstnodon" (The Jewish people did not want to believe in Christ but fixed him disgracefully to the cross).[45] There is also the compound *rōdehengen*, which Clark Hall glosses as "hanging, crucifixion." Besides denoting the act of crucifying, however, this word also specifically denotes Christ's cross itself, as appears, for example, from the following quotations: "þa ða he on rodehengene mancyn alysde" (when he [Christ], on the cross, redeemed mankind), and "Ne com he to þy þæt he wære on mærlicum cynesetle ahafen: ac ðæt he wære mid hospe on rodehengene genægalod" (He [Christ] did not come in order to be raised to a glorious throne, but to be nailed disgracefully to the cross).[46] Translating *rodehengen* in these two cases with "hanging, crucifixion" makes no sense. Nine out of the ten occurrences of this compound, according to the DOEC, are found in works by Ælfric, so that we may conclude that *rōdehengen* was his own coinage. The tenth occurrence is found in the prayer *De patientia*: "Eala ðu ælmihtiga God, þu ðe dydest þæt ðin leofa sunu, ure hælend Crist, underfeng menniscnysse, and rodehengene underbeah" (O you almighty God, you who brought about that your beloved son, our savior Christ, received human nature, and submitted to the cross).[47]

---

44 J. R. Clark Hall, *A Concise Anglo-Saxon Dictionary*, 4th ed. (Cambridge: Cambridge University Press, 1960), p. 177.
45 Godden II, p. 146, line 261.
46 Clemoes, pp. 206, line 18 and 219, line 85, respectively.
47 Thorpe, II: 600.

Old English "Cross" Words

The phrase *rodehengene underbeah* translates the Latin *crucem subire*.[48] This prayer, one of ten that were written immediately after the conclusion of Ælfric's *Catholic Homilies* at the end of Cambridge, University Library MS Gg. 3. 28, is marked as an anonymous piece of liturgical text by the DOEC. However, according to Kenneth Sisam, these ten prayers "may safely be assigned to [Ælfric] on grounds of style and of aptitude to the purpose of the whole collection."[49] To style and aptitude—two admittedly rather general kinds of evidence—we can now add, on account of *rodehengene*, a piece of solid lexical evidence of Ælfric's authorship.

Clark Hall lists four more compounds with *rōd-*, viz. the nouns *rōdbīgenga* "worshipper of the cross," *rōdbora* "cross bearer," and *rōdetācen* "sign of the cross," and the adjective *rōdewyrðe* "deserving hanging." In view of the compounds with the linking element "-e-," I think that *rōde cwealm* (in *Fates of the Apostles*, line 39) should likewise be taken as a compound "death on the cross" and be given a separate dictionary entry as such.[50] Finally, attention should be paid to yet another compound, viz. the verb *rōdfæstnian*, of which the past participle is found once, in an interlinear glossed *Credo* in the Lambeth Psalter. The word has every appearance of being

---

48 Donald G. Bzdyl, "The Sources of Ælfric's Prayers in Cambridge University Library MS. Gg. 3. 28," *Notes & Queries* 222 (1977), 98–102, at 100.

49 Kenneth Sisam, *Studies in the History of Old English Literature* (Oxford: Clarendon Press, 1953), pp. 166–67 [repr. of "MSS. Bodley 340 and 342: Ælfric's Catholic Homilies," *Review of English Studies* 7 (1931), 7–22; *RES* 8 (1932), 51–68; and *RES* 9 (1933), 1–12]. Sisam's attribution of these prayers to Ælfric has widely been accepted; see e.g. Peter Clemoes, "The Chronology of Ælfric's Works," in Clemoes, ed., *The Anglo-Saxons: Studies in Some Aspects of their History and Culture Presented to Bruce Dickins* (London: Bowes & Bowes, 1959), pp. 212–47 at 215; and John C. Pope, *Homilies of Ælfric: A Supplementary Collection*, EETS o.s. 259 and 260 (London: Oxford University Press, 1967–68), I: 145 (6 [b]).

50 On the problem of distinguishing syntactic phrases from compounds with "-e-," see Hans Sauer, *Nominalkomposita im Frühmittelenglischen. Mit Ausblicken auf die Geschichte der englischen Nominalkomposition* (Tübingen: Niemeyer, 1992), §2.4.3.1., esp. p. 94.

a spontaneous calque of Latin *crucifixus*: "Geðrowad under þam Pontiscan Pilate gerodfæstnad dead & bebyrged Passus sub Pontio Pilato crucifixus mortuus et sepultus."[51] (He suffered under Pontius Pilate, [was] crucified, dead and buried.) The Lambeth Psalter belongs, whether directly or indirectly, to what is called the "Winchester group," a number of texts dating from the first half of the eleventh century and characterized by a striking uniformity in vocabulary.[52] Like Ælfric's coinage of *rōdehengen*, the verb *rōdfæstnian* may reflect a conscious attitude towards creating a specific terminology when it came to referring to the cross and to crucifying.

How to cope with Latin *patibulum*?

The picture so far established becomes different when we turn our attention to Latin *patibulum*. This word denoted in Classical Latin "a fork-shaped yoke or gibbet to which criminals were fastened." More specifically, *patibulum* was also used in classical Latin to indicate the cross-beam onto which the arms of the convicts were tied or nailed. Usually, convicts were forced to carry to the place of execution the *patibulum* on which they were tied or nailed and then hoisted up on the pole.[53] For example, in a sermon on Abraham's sacrifice of Isaac, Ambrose compared Isaac's carrying the bundle of fire wood to Christ

---

51 U. Lindelöf, ed., *Der Lambeth-Psalter: Eine altenglische Interlinearversion des Psalters in der Hs. 427 der erzbischöflichen Lambeth Palace Library*, Acta Societatis Scientiarum Fennicae 35, i and 43, iii (Helsinki: n.p., 1909–1914), canticle 13, verse 3.

52 London, Lambeth Palace Library MS 427 (s. xi1); Gneuss, no. 517. On this text and the "Winchester group," see Walter Hofstetter, "Winchester and the Standardization of Old English Vocabulary," *ASE* 17 (1988): 139–61 at 141.

53 *OLD*, s.v. *crux*; cf. a quotation there: "Patibulum ferat per urbem, deinde adfigatur cruci" (Pl[autus]). Fr[agment], 48) "Let him carry the cross-beam through the city, let him next be fixed to the cross." For further ample evidence, see Roberts, "Jehovah's Witnesses," 12–14.

carrying the *patibulum crucis*.⁵⁴ By the time of the church fathers, *patibulum* seems to have become somewhat old-fashioned. According to Isidore of Seville, the word had been replaced in popular parlance by *furca*,⁵⁵ yet in church Latin *patibulum* managed to persist. For example, in the first stanza of Venantius Fortunatus' famous hymn *Vexilla regis prodeunt*, line 2 mentions the *crucis mysterium* "mystery of the Cross," while in line 4, the flesh (i.e. body) of Christ is said to be *suspensus in patibulo* "hanging on the cross-beam."⁵⁶ Thus, in a late Roman, pseudo-Augustinian sermon, Christ is said to be *iustus in patibulo*, which Rosemary Woolf translated as "righteous on the gibbet."⁵⁷ Problematic with this translation is that "gibbet" has acquired other connotations. According to the *OED*, s.v. *gibbet* n.¹, the word was originally synonymous with "gallows," but in later use it has come to signify "an upright post with a projecting arm from which the bodies of executed criminals were hung in chains or irons *after* [my emphasis] execution."⁵⁸ Translation of *patibulum* as "gibbet" is therefore liable to cause confusion and is best avoided. On

---

54 "Ligna Isaac sibi uexit, Christus sibi patibulum portauit crucis," Ambrosius Mediolanensis, Sancti Ambrosii opera pars primi qua continentur libri [. . .] De Abraham [. . .], ed. Karl Schenkl, CSEL 32 (Vienna: Tempsky, 1897), I: viii. 72 (on 549, line 20).
55 Isidore of Seville even equated patibulum with furca—"patibulum enim vulgo furca dicitur," Etymologiae V: 27–34 in *Etymologiarum sive Originum libri XX*, W. M. Lindsay, ed., 2 vols (Oxford: Clarendon Press, 1911). According to Isidore, death on the *patibulum* was a lesser punishment because the victim died at once, whereas on the cross his suffering was protracted. As noted, I have found no instances of *furca* denoting Christ's cross.
56 Venanti Honori Clementiani Fortunati, Presbyteri Italici, Opera Poetica, ed. Frederich Leo, MGH, Auctorum Antiquissimorvm 4 (Berlin: Weidmann, 1881), p. 34.
57 Rosemary Woolf, "Doctrinal Influences on The Dream of the Rood," *Medium Ævum* 27 (1958): 137–53 at 149. For further references to patristic *patibulum* = *crux*, see Bremmer, "Hermes/Mercury," p. 411, n. 7.
58 Cf. OED, s.v. *jib* n²: "the projecting arm of a crane; also applied to the boom of a derrick." This word is derived from "gibbet."

more than one occasion we find the collocation *crucis patibulum* in Anglo-Saxon charms and prayers. In a charm, Christ is addressed as "fili dei, qui per crucis patibulum uim et fortitudinem Satane destruxisti" (Son of God, you who through the transverse of the cross have destroyed Satan's force and power). A prayer implores Christ, "qui pro humano genere crucis patibulum sustinuisti" (you who have suffered for mankind the transverse of the cross).[59] In the collocation *crucis patibulum*, we are dealing with the two components that make up the cross: the upright post and the transverse beam. A proper translation for *patibulum* in this collocation would therefore be "transverse, cross-beam" or even, as we shall see, "gallows," although this word too presents its problems.

OLD ENGLISH G(E)ALGA

First of all, Old English *gealga* or *galga* "gallows," the former of which is usually found in southern texts, were used from the eighth to eleventh century, though infrequently, to denote Christ's cross. But what precisely do we see in our mind's eye, when we hear or see the word "gallows"? Speaking for myself, I see something very similar to the *OED*'s description of a gibbet: an upright post with an arm projecting at right-angles, supported by a strut at an angle of 45 degrees. But is this what an Anglo-Saxon associated a gallows with? The one Anglo-Saxon illustration of a gallows that I know is to be found in the *Illustrated Old English Hexateuch* (London, British Library, MS Cotton Claudius B. iv) on folio 59, at the point when the Pharaoh has the baker hanged (Genesis 40: 22). The picture (Figure 6.1). shows a structure that consists of two upright posts—hence the plural in Present Day English, according to the *OED*—ending in forks upon which a horizontal pole has been placed and from which a hanged man is dangling. The upright posts have been provided with rungs to

---

59 Both quotations from Julius Zupitza, "Kreuzzauber," *Archiv* 88 (1882): 364–65.

allow the hangman to climb them in order to carry out his gruesome duty.[60] This construction seems to be the original form of a handmade gallows.[61] Christ, however, is never to my knowledge depicted as hanging from a structure that resembles in any way a gallows in this sense. And yet, he is often said to "hang on the gallows." How can this be explained? Is it because the pictorial tradition of Christ hanging on a cross was already so firmly fixed that it allowed no room for him to be depicted as hanging from a gallows-like structure? Or are we being misled by the modern sense of "gallows," and should we translate *galga* prosaically with something like "wooden frame, wooden structure on or from which to hang something" or maybe, more specifically, "cross-beam, transverse bar"?

As I have briefly pointed out, on the continent in Old High German, the word *galga* was also used in connection with Christ's cross, if very rarely so. In Otfrid's *Evangelienbuch*, for example, it occurs only when the scribes and elders deride Christ on the cross: "Nu helf er imo selben / ufan themo galgen" (Now let him help himself on the gallows); otherwise Otfrid consistently uses *kruci*.[62] The word is also found in sermons in the phrase "an deme galge des kriuzes," where it seems to indicate the transverse of the cross. This assumption becomes firmer in the following passage "den galgen des kriuzes er selber truoc" (he himself carried the transverse of the cross).[63] These last two examples come very close to a similar

---

60 Peter Clemoes and C. R. Dodwell, ed., *The Illustrated Old English Hexateuch* (British Museum Cotton Claudius B. IV), EEMF 18 (Copenhagen: Rosenkilde and Bagger, 1974).
61 Erler, "Galgen," col. 1376.
62 Oskar Erdmann, ed., *Otfrids Evangelienbuch*, 3rd ed. Ludwig Wolff, Altdeutsche Textbibliothek 49 (Tübingen: Max Niemeyer, 1957), IV.30.15 (on p. 208).
63 Wilhelm Wackernagel, *Altdeutsche Predigten und Gebete aus Handschriften* (Basel: Hugo Richter, 1876; repr. Darmstadt: Wissenschaftliche Buchgesellschaft, 1964), pp. 6, line 28 and 61, line 20, respectively. Compare "daz er den galgen des crvces vf sich nam" (that he took the transverse of the cross upon himself),

collocation in Old English, to wit *rode g(e)algan* "the gallows of the cross." Here we are dealing with a straight translation of Latin *crucis patibulo/-um*. In early Middle High German, the word also carried the meaning of "construction over a well with which to draw up a bucket," presumably consisting of two upright posts with a cross-beam. This meaning is even more explicitly expressed in the compound *wazzargalge*, literally "water-gallows," glossing Latin *antlia* "bucket."[64] Do we here have the solution to the meaning of Old English *g(e)alga* "cross beam, transverse"? Further Old High German evidence for a narrower meaning for *galga* is found in glossaries and glosses: *patibulum : galga* and *gabulum* (fork) *: patibulum*. A wider sense than "cross-beam" is suggested by the gloss *patibulum : crux*. But in this case we might be dealing with a clarifying gloss.[65] All in all, then, I would suggest that Old English *g(e)alga* does not only mean "gallows" in general but also signifies more specifically "transverse, cross-beam," especially in the collocation *rode g(e)alga* as a translation for Latin *crucis patibulum*. The earliest example of this collocation in Old English, according to the DOEC—which gives seventeen instances of the collocation when queried—is to be found in the Alfredian translation of Gregory's *Regula Pastoralis*:

Berthold von Regensburg, *Deutsche Predigten*, ed. Dieter Richter, Kleine deutsche Prosadenkmaler des Mittelalters 5 (Munich: Wilhelm Fink, 1968), no. 4, lines 62–63 (at 59).

64 Matthias Lexer, *Mittelhochdeutsches Handwörterbuch*, vol. A–M (Leipzig: S. Hirzel, 1872), s.v. Alternatively, a *wazzergalgen* indicates a construction consisting of an upright post ending in a fork, over which a long beam (German *Brunnenschwengel*, Low German *sodwippe*, Dutch *puthaal*) is resting at an angle of about 45° that can be lowered into the well with a bucket. If this is so, then my argument is not valid, of course. In seventeenth-century German, Galgen also denoted the beam in a loom from which the batten is hanging, so again it suggested a construction resembling the two-posted gallows: see Hans Strigl, "Einiges über die Sprache des P. Abraham a Sancta Clara," *Zeitschrift für deutsche Wortforschung* 8 (1906–07): 206–312 at 283–84.

65 Taylor Starck and J. C. Wells, *Althochdeutsches Glossenwörterbuch* (Heidelberg: Carl Winter, 1972–90), s.v. *galgo*.

"He nolde beon cyning, & his agnum willan he com to rode gealgan," translating "rex fieri noluit, ad crucis uero patibulum sponte conuenit" (he did not want to be king, but of his own will came to the transverse of the cross).[66]

As a final note, attention should be drawn to the nonce-word *eaxlgespann* [MS *eaxle ge spanne*] in *The Dream of the Rood*. The word has offered notorious difficulties to lexicographers. BT translated it literally (and nonsensically) with "shoulder-span," and Clark Hall assigned it the meaning of "place where the two beams of a cross intersect." In his glossary, Swanton gives "cross-beam, junction of the cross" and he is followed in this, if hesitatingly, by the *DOE* in fascicle E, with "cross-beam?, intersection?" In an explanatory note, Swanton dwells on this crux and glosses its second element as "that which links or stretches," to continue "It might therefore simply refer to the beam of the gallows along which Christ's arms were stretched."[67] Swanton's hunch could well be right. Support for the "simple" suggestion cannot be found from within Old English, but is readily available in a closely kindred language: Middle Dutch. One of the meanings of Middle Dutch *gespan* was "cross-beam," especially in roof constructions.[68] The sense of "intersection," at least from an art-historical point of view, does not make sense, as Annemarie Mahler has demonstrated. She suggests that *eaxlgespann* is "simply a translation of the Latin *patibulum*, but then referring to the whole cross."[69] I concur with the first part of her "simple" suggestion, but in

---

66 Henry Sweet, ed. and trans., *King Alfred's West-Saxon Version of Gregory's Pastoral Care*, EETS 45, 50 (London: Oxford University Press, 1871), I. iii. 19–20 (on 33); Bruno Judic, Floribert Rommel and Charles Morel, eds. and trans., *Grégoire le Grand, Règle Pastorale,* Sources Chrétiennes 381–82 (Paris: Cerf, 1992), I. iii. 18–19. The editors translate the collocation with "le supplice de la croix."
67 Michael Swanton, ed., *The Dream of the Rood* (Manchester: Manchester University Press, 1970), pp. 102–3, line 9.
68 Eelco Verwijs and Jacob Verdam, *Middelnederlandsch Woordenboek* (The Hague: Martinus Nijhoff, 1885–1971), s.v. *gespan*.
69 Annemarie E. Mahler, "Lignum Domini and the Opening Vision of The Dream of the Rood: A Viable Hypothesis?," *Speculum* 53 (1978), 441–59 at 446–48.

the light of my discussion of *patibulum* I see no compelling reason to accept Mahler's claim for translating *eaxlgespann* with "cross" when "cross-beam" suits the context equally well.

OLD ENGLISH *BĒAM* AND *TRĒOW*

Less specific words used for the cross are *bēam* and its synonym *trēow*, both meaning "tree"—Old Frisian *bām* and *trē* also have the meaning of "gallows"[70]—as well as *wudu* "wood," if rarely so. Particularly in poetry, the first two words were popular. In *The Dream of the Rood*, for instance, we find, besides the now familiar terms *rod* and *g(e)alga*, the following: *syllicre treow* (line 4) "a very marvelous tree," *beama beorhtost* (line 6) "brightest of trees," *sigebeam* (lines 13, 127) "tree of victory" (also in *Elene*), *wuldres treow* (line 14) "tree of glory," *Hælendes ~* , *Wealdendes treow* (lines 25, 17) "tree of the Savior, of the Ruler," *wudu selesta* (line 27) "the best tree," *wuldres beam* (line 97) "tree of glory," and simply *beam*. Once in this poem, we encounter the compound *gealgtreow* (line 146). It is a so-called *dvanda*, a compound consisting of two stems without a linking element, as is *wynbeam* "tree of joy" in *Elene* (line 842), likewise a *hapax legomenon*. But whether *gealgtreow* "normally means simply 'gallows,'" as Swanton remarks in an explanatory note,[71] is questionable. This word too is *hapax*, so there can be no normal and simple meaning for it. An almost similar form as *gealgtreow* is *galgatre*, this time, however, not a *dvanda*-formation but with a linking element; it is a Scandinavian loan, found only twice in the late tenth-century gloss to the *Durham Ritual*. Significantly, in the latter text this loan occurs precisely in the collocation *rodes galgatre* as a gloss for Latin *crucis patibulo*:

---

70 In the phrase *northhalde tre, ~ bam* "northerly directed tree," a metaphor for "gallows."
71 Swanton, *The Dream of the Rood*, p. 134.

Old English "Cross" Words

> Domine iesu christe qui hora nona in crucis patibulo confitentem latronem intra menia paradisi transi te supplices confitentes peccata nostra deprecamur ut post obitum nostrum paradisi portas introire nos gaudentes concedas . . .
>
> driht' hæl' crist ðv ðe tiid non on rodes galgatree ondettende sceaðe bionna vallas nerxnawong' of'fara eft gihriordest ðec boensando ondettendo synna vs' ve biddað þætte æft' giliornise vsa' neirxnavongas gætto inngeonga vsig gifeando f'let . . . [72]
>
> [Lord Jesus Christ, (you) who on the ninth hour when on the crossbeam entreated the confessing thief to follow you into the confines of paradise, we, confessing our sins, beg you to allow us to enter rejoicing the gates of paradise after our death . . .]

Rather than simply meaning "gallows," the translation in the *Durham Ritual* of *in crucis patibulo* by "on rodes galgatree" once more supports the meaning "transverse, cross-beam" for *galgtreow* in *The Dream of the Rood*.

Conclusion

These native words, then—*rod, hengen, g(e)alga, beam, treow, wudu*—and their respective compounds—*rodehengen, gealgtreow, sigebeam, wynbeam*, so excluding words compounded with *wudu*—as well as *eaxlgespann,* were current as appellatives for the cross or components

---

72   U. Lindelöf, ed., *Rituale Ecclesiae Dunelmensis*, Surtees Society 140 (Durham: Andrews and Co, 1927), p. 124, translation mine; see also "Deus qui pro nobis filium tuum crucis patibulum subire uoluisti vt inimici a nobis expelleres potestatem concede nobis famulis tuis ut resurrectionis gratiam consequamur per eundem," glossed as "god ðv ðe f'e vs svnv ðin rodes galgatre vndergaa ðy waldest þætte fiondas from vsig afirdest mæht gilef vs ðiwvm ðinvm þætte erestes gefe we gifylgað," (Lord, (you) who wished your son to undergo the cross-beam for us so that you would expel enemies from us, concede to us, your servants, that we follow the grace of resurrection thereby), p. 23, translation mine.

thereof throughout the Old English period. By far the commonest was *rod*.[73] Most of them are found in prose and poetry alike. But *g(e)alga* "cross" is restricted to poetry, while *gealga* "cross-beam" is found in prose and then only in the combination *rode gealga*. Prosaic, too, is *hengen* and its compound *rodehengen*, the latter, as we have seen, being confined to Ælfric's writings. The words *beam* and *wudu* for "cross" are confined to poetry; *treow* is found in prose, but only occasionally so, e.g. "Eala þu scinende rod swiþor þonne tungla, mære on middanearde, micclum to lufigenne, halig treow and wynsum"[74] (Oh, you shining cross, brighter than stars, famous on earth, greatly to be loved, holy and joyful tree). Perhaps the lyrical nature of this address to the cross elicited the use of the word *treow* in this piece of prose. More often, *treow* refers to the material of the cross.[75]

The Latin loans *crūć* and *cros* and the Scandinavian loan *galgatre*, however, appear to be late and hence were no longer given a chance to enter the realm of poetry.[76] A table may illustrate the distribution of the various words over prose and poetry:

---

73 Jane Roberts and Christian Kay with Lynne Grundy (*A Thesaurus of Old English*, 2 vols., improved ed. [Amsterdam and Atalanta, GA: Rodopi, 2000], I: 698: 16.02.05.11 "The cross [as a Christian image]") miss *g(e)alga*, *gealgtreow*, *galgatre*, *hengen* and *rodehengen*. For *eaxelgespann* [sic], marked as hapax and poetic, the *Thesaurus*, under the rubric "Item providing support" (17.03.02), gives "axis, axle-tree," a sense I have not encountered elsewhere in the current lexicographic literature. On *cristelmæl* "sign of the cross," see Lenker, "Signifying Christ in Anglo-Saxon England," in this volume, pp. 261–70, below. The *Thesaurus of Old English* is also available on-line: http://libra.englang.arts.gla.ac.uk/oethesaurus.

74 Skeat, II: 150, lines 117–18 (Exaltation of the Cross).

75 Clemoes, Hom. I. 30: "þa ða heo stod dreorig forn angean cristes rode & hire leofe cild geseah mid isenum næglum on heardum treowe gefæstnod" (when she [Mary] stood sorrowfully before Christ's cross and saw her dear child being fixed with iron nails to the hard wood).

76 Hence, *cruc* and *cros* are not included in the somewhat enumerative but hardly analytical treatment in Albert Keiser, *The Influence of Christianity on the Vocabulary of Old English Poetry*, University of Illinois Studies in Language and Literature 5 (Urbana: University of Illinois, 1919), §§ 249–55, pp. 79–81.

Old English "Cross" Words

	Prose	Poetry
rod	+	+
rodehengen	+	-
hengen	+	-
g(e)alga	+	+
gealgtreow	-	+
galgatre(e)	+	-
eaxlgespann	-	+
cruc	+	-
cros	+	-
beam	-	+
sigebeam, wynbeam	-	+
treow	+	+
tre	+	-
wudu	-	+

Table 1. Distribution over prose and poetry of the various words for "cross" and "transverse, cross-beam."

A saying has it that "A child that is loved has many names." If there is truth in this popular wisdom, the Anglo-Saxons must have loved the cross and what it represented—Christ's act of redeeming mankind. Whether the fact that present-day English today possesses only one current word, "cross," is indicative of the depth of love for what the cross represents today, is something I would rather leave the reader to decide.

Fig. 6.1: The Baker is Hanged on the Gallows. Drawing (detail) by Femke Prinsen, after London, BL Cotton Claudius B.iv, folio 59r.

Signifying Christ in Anglo-Saxon England: Old English Terms for the Sign of the Cross

Ursula Lenker

AT THE END OF HIS HOMILY for the fifth Sunday in Lent, Ælfric summarizes the central properties of Christian worship of the cross. In a typological reading based on interpretations of the Fathers,[1] he contrasts the Old Testament Tree of Life, which brought death, with its New Testament counterpart, the "tree of redemption," which brought life and salvation. In a synopsis of Christian faith, he highlights the core elements of the Christian belief in salvation through Christ's sacrifice on the cross:

> (1) Mine gebroðru uton behealdan þone ahangenan crist . . . Swa micel is betwux þære gehiwodan anlicnysse. and ðam soðan ðinge . . . Þurh treow us com deað. þa ða adam geæt þone forbodenan æppel. and ðurh treow us com eft lif. and alysednyss. ða ða crist hangode on rode for ure alysednysse; Ðære halgan rode tacn. is ure bletsung. and to ðære rode we us gebiddað. na swa þeah to ðam treowe. ac to ðam ælmihtigum drihtne. ðe on ðære halgan rode for us hangode.[2]

---

1 This typological interpretation is, for instance, found in Hippolyt, Gregory of Nyssa and Augustine; see Godden I, p. 473.
2 Godden II, ii, 136, homily 13, lines 277–94 ("Fifth Sunday in Lent"). Most of

[My brothers, let us behold the crucified Christ ... so great is the difference between the apparent likeness and the true thing. Through a tree death came to us when Adam ate the forbidden apple; and through a tree life came again to us and redemption when Christ hung on the rood for our redemption. The sign of the holy cross is our blessing and to the rood we pray, though not to the tree, but to the Almighty Lord who for us hung on the holy rood.]

At the beginning and the end of this passage, probably reflecting on practices in contemporary orthodox Christian worship, Ælfric stresses that the cross as a material object must not itself be an object of worship, and emphasizes that the cross is in its essence symbolic: one must not pray to a tree or a material object of any kind, but to "Christ who for us hung on the holy rood," that is, to Christ himself in the culmination of his redemptive mission. In essence, the cross signifies Christ.

The cross is thus intrinsically a sign. And though cross-forms, i.e., two lines intersecting in one of the most basic of geometrical patterns, go back to a very remote period of human civilization and were used as symbols, religious or otherwise, long before the Christian era,[3] the cross has unquestionably become the principal symbol and emblem of the Christian religion itself.[4]

---

the translations in the present chapter basically follow the translations given in Thorpe, here p. 241; yet, some of the phrases have been changed to correspond to the findings of the present chapter.

3 See *Lexikon des Mittelalters*, 9 vols. (Stuttgart: Metzler, CD-ROM version, 2000), s.v. *Kreuz / Kruzifix* (various authors) and the detailed articles "The Archæology of the Cross and Crucifix," "The Cross and Crucifix in Liturgy," and "Sign of the Cross" in *The Catholic Encyclopedia, www.newadvent.org/cathen/c.htm*. Most important and also influential for Christian faith are the ancient Egyptian hieroglyphic symbol of life—the "ankh"—which was adopted and extensively used by Coptic Christians, and the "swastika," which was marked on many early Christian tombs as a veiled symbol of the cross. For TAU as a precursor of the Christian tradition, see Bremmer, "Old English 'Cross' Words" in this volume, p. 205, and below, pp. 258–260.

4 The cross and its interpretation attest to the radical transformation of the

Signifying Christ in Anglo-Saxon England

The Sign of the Cross as a Performative Manual Gesture

The centrality of this symbol in Christianity is made explicit in the various manual acts and their specific performative functions in liturgy and daily devotional life which have developed in the course of Christianity—the different forms of the "sign of the cross." Basically, this term is "applied to various manual acts, liturgical or devotional in character, which have this at least in common: that by the gesture of tracing two lines intersecting at right angles they indicate symbolically the figure of Christ's cross."[5] It is an engagement of the body that affirms what the faithful professes, and it is also a sign to others of what one professes oneself. There are three variants of this gesture which I shall examine here.

Variant 1: Little Cross Traced on the Forehead

Of all the methods of employing this symbol as an emblem, the most ancient is a little cross, which is traced as a very personal gesture upon a part of the body, most often the forehead. From the second century onwards,[6] this practice is attested to by numerous allusions

---

image in the history of Christianity: the cross as an instrument of torture was replaced by the cross as a symbol of triumph. Jesus's sacrifice on the cross has never been easy for believers expecting the triumphant Messiah, since crucifixion was reserved for slaves and common criminals in Roman law and was thus considered to be extremely degrading. Accordingly, Christians were at first very reticent about portraying the cross because too open a display of it might have exposed them to ridicule or even danger. The cross only became a popular symbol after Constantine converted to Christianity and abolished crucifixion as a death penalty. Pauline theology which interprets the crucifixion as "the paradox of the crucified Christ's victory in defeat" (1 Corinthians 1:23–28; see also 2 Cor. 10:7–10; and 2 Cor. 12:9), is central for its positive understanding of the cross's ambiguity. For Paul, the crucifixion is the perfect sign for a fundamentally paradoxical divinity—strong in its weakness, glorious in its ugliness. See also Robert Baldwin, "'I slaughter Barbarians:' Triumph as a Mode in Medieval Christian Art," *Konsthistorisk Tidskrift* 59/4 (1990): 225–42.

5 *Catholic Encyclopedia*, s. v. "Sign of the Cross."
6 For one of the earliest examples from the beginning of the third century,

in patristic literature. In idea, it is clearly associated with references in scripture, notably Ezechiel 9:4: "And the Lord said to him: Go through the midst of the city, through the midst of Jerusalem: and mark Thau upon the foreheads of the men that sigh, and mourn for all the abominations that are committed in the midst thereof."[7]

This little cross, the oldest variant of the manual gesture, is used as the fundamental ensign and symbol of Christianity and is thus traced on the forehead of the infant in baptism as a mark that the child is baptized in Christ:

> (2) Mid þam haligan ele ge scylan þa hæþenan cild mearcian on þam breoste and betwux þæm <gesculdru> on middeweardan mid rode tacne [2a], ærþanþe ge hit fullian on þam fantwætere. And þonne hit of þæm wætere cymð, ge scylan wyrcan rode tacen [2b] upp on þæm heafde mid þam haligan crisman.[8]

> [With the holy oil you shall mark the heathen child on the breast and in the middle between the shoulders with the sign of the cross before you baptize it in the baptismal water. And when it has come out of the water, you shall trace the sign of the cross on the head with the holy chrism.]

---

see Tertullian (*De corona militis* 3: 4, *Tertullianus, Quintus, Septimius Florens: De corona*, ed. Jacques Fontaine [Paris: Presses Université de France, 1966]): "Ad omnem progressum atque promotum, ad omnem aditum et exitum, ad uestitum, ad calciatum, ad lauacra, ad mensas, ad lumina, ad cubilia, ad sedilia, quacumque nos conuersatio exercet, frontem signaculo terimus," (In all our travels and movements, in all our coming in and going out, in putting on our shoes, at the bath, at the table, in lighting our candles, in lying down, in sitting down, whatever employment occupies us, we mark our foreheads with the sign of the cross).

7 Translation from Douay-Rheims, *http://www.drbo.org/* (October 16, 2008).

8 *Die Hirtenbriefe Ælfrics*, ed. Bernhard Fehr, Bibliothek der angelsächsischen Prosa 9 (Hamburg, 1914; repr. with supplement, ed. Peter Clemoes, Darmstadt: Wissenschaftliche Buchgesellschaft, 1966), p. 148, lines 5–6.

Signifying Christ in Anglo-Saxon England

Variant 2: Large Cross Traced from Shoulder to Shoulder
From the fourth or fifth century, we also find another variant of the sign of the cross as a performative manual gesture, namely a large cross traced from forehead to breast and from shoulder to shoulder. It is made today, for instance, by Catholics upon themselves when they begin their prayers or by the priest at the foot of the altar when he commences mass with the words: "In nomine Patris et Filii et Spiritus Sancti." The *pectorale* (a large cross over the breast on the liturgical vestments) has become one of the emblems of bishops, derived from their wearing of a pectoral cross as a sign of their office, and the sign for the bishop in the Old English monastic sign list accordingly comprises this large sign of the cross: (3) "Bisceopes tacen is þæt þu strice mid þinre hande ofer æðere eaxle niþerweard ofer þine breost on rode tacne,"[9] (The sign for the bishop is that you stroke with your hand over each shoulder down over your chest in the sign of the cross).

Variant 3: Blessing
The sign of the cross, as many quotations from the Fathers in the fourth century show, also passed very early on into a gesture of benediction. Thus another important variant of the sign of the cross is made in the air, mainly by bishops or priests (but usually people of authority), in blessing persons or material objects. Although this act in a Christian context always comprises the sign of the cross, this connection is not openly expressed in English (cf. Old English *bletsian*, Present Day English "bless").[10] The Old English verb *bletsian* generally used for this act is—like Old English *rod*[11] "cross"—not

---

9 *Monasteriales Indicia: The Anglo-Saxon Monastic Sign Language*, ed. and trans. Debby Banham (Pinner: Anglo-Saxon Books, 1991), p. 46, no. 120.
10 See the entries in the *OED*, s.v. "bless" and *DOE*, s.vv. *bletsian* and *gebletsian*, which establishes the central Old English meanings "to bless (1a. of God, Christ), (1b. of a bishop, priest, saint, etc.), (1c. of a parent)" and "to bless (ritually)" (2.); other much less frequent meanings are "to praise, extol" (3.), or "to be pleased" (4).
11 On the etymology and history of rod, see Rolf H. Bremmer, Jr's "Old

found elsewhere in the Germanic languages: being—like *rod*—of a somewhat uncertain etymology, the *OED* relates *bletsian* to Old English *blōd* "blood," so that its etymological meaning would be "to mark . . . with blood; to consecrate."¹²

The other Germanic languages do not use a native Germanic word, but choose a loan formed on Latin *signare* "to mark" (cf. *signum* "sign"). Thus we find the forms Old High German *seganon*, Old Frisian *seininge*, Old Saxon *segnon*, Old Norse *signa:* "to mark with the sign of the cross."¹³ Only in the earliest of extant Anglo-Saxon witnesses, mainly in manuscripts of the translations of King Alfred's circle, do we meet a loan Old English *(ge)segnian*.¹⁴ See, for instance, (4) "Segna þe & sete þe on þæt tacen ðære halgan rode"¹⁵ (Bless yourself and set on yourself the mark of the holy cross). *Segnian*, however, is eventually ousted by the native formation *bletsian* and is, for example, only rarely attested to in Ælfric's writings.¹⁶

English 'Cross' Words" in this volume, above pp. 215–221.

12 See *OED*, s.v. "bless." As an "equally satisfactory" suggestion, the *OED* mentions the derivation of *blētsian* from *blōt* "sacrifice." The derivation from *blōd* is favored by the OED because the form *blōedsian* occurs earlier and because the change of *ds* to *ts* is seen to be phonetically natural in Germanic languages, while the reverse is not.

13 See Friedrich Kluge, *Etymologisches Wörterbuch der deutschen Sprache*, ed. Elmar Seebold, 24th rev. ed. (Berlin/New York: Mouton de Gruyter, 2002), s.v. *segnen*.

14 See BT, s.v. *segnian*. Old English is also special in that it not only borrows reflexes of Latin *signum/signare* in a Christian sense, but more often uses the noun to express the military meaning "sign; banner." See Alfred Wollmann, *Untersuchungen zu den frühen lateinischen Lehnwörtern im Altenglischen. Phonologie und Datierung*, Texte und Untersuchungen zur Englischen Philologie 15 (Munich: Fink, 1990), pp. 297–323.

15 *Bischof Waerferths von Worcester Übersetzung der Dialoge Gregors des Grossen*, ed. Hans Hecht, Bibliothek der angelsächsischen Prosa 5 (Leipzig and Hamburg 1901–07: repr. Darmstadt: Wissenschaftliche Buchgesellschaft, 1965), p. 325.

16 See, for example, the tautological phrase *senian and bletsian* in "Mid þrym fingrum man sceall senian and bletsian for þære halgan þrynysse," (With three

While Latin explicitly connects the act of blessing with tracing the sign of the cross by the expression *facere signum crucis,* "make the sign of the cross," Old English communicates this concept only implicitly. The different cognitive effects of these two ways of expression are clearly seen when we compare the Old English description for the sign of the sacramentary in the monastic sign list with its Latin counterpart: compare (5) "Gif þu mæsse boc habban wille þonne wege þu þine hand [and] do swilce þu bletsige,"[17] ([i]f you want a sacramentary, then you move your hand and make as if you were giving a blessing) with (6) "Pro signo libri missalis: generali signo premisso adde, ut facias signum crucis" ([f]or the sign of the sacramentary: the general sign being made, add as if you make the sign of the cross).[18]

In order to compensate for this loss of transparency, the actual act and meanings of *segnian* as well as *bletsian* are (as already seen in quotation [4]) made more explicit by a following prepositional phrase *mid tacne þære halgan rode* "with the sign of the holy cross."[19]

---

fingers must a man make the sign and bless himself for the Holy Trinity), Skeat, II: 154, line 155 ("Exaltation of the Holy Cross"). Two further occurrences are attested to in Ælfric's homily on Palm Sunday: "Eft swa gelice gelæhte ænne calic. senode mid swiðran. and sealde his gingrum" (Afterwards in like manner he took a cup and blessed [Thorpe: signed] it with his right hand and gave it to his disciples) and "and he syððan senode husel," (and he then blessed [Thorpe: signed] the Eucharist), but they refer to Jesus's blessing of wine and bread on the occasion of the Last Supper and therefore obviously can *not* comprise the sign of the cross. See Godden II, p. 139, lines 50 and 66 ("Palm Sunday"; cf. Thorpe, p. 245).

17 Banham, *Monasteriales Indicia,* p. 24, no. 9.
18 "List of Signs from Cluny" (s. xi); see Walter Jarecki, *Signa Loquendi. Die cluniacensischen Signa-Listen eingeleitet und herausgegeben,* Saecula Spiritualia 4 (Baden-Baden: Koerner, 1981), p. 133, no. C 65.
19 BT, s.v. *segnian,* lists this as a separate meaning: "III. without reference to the sign of the cross." The twenty-six occurrences with such a prepositional phrase are, however, only a small fraction of the total of about 1350 occurrences of the forms *(ge)bletsian* and *(ge)bledsian* in Old English; see *DOE,* s.v. *bletsian,*

In the following quotation, it is used to specify the act in the first instance of *segnian* in 7a: (7) "genom hine ða bi his cinne & mid tacne ðære halgan rode hio gesegnade [7a]. Ða he ða hio gesegnad hæfde [7b], ða heht he . . . "[20] (He then took him by the chin and blessed him with the sign of the holy cross. Then, when he had blessed it, then he commanded . . .).

In these cases, the manual gesture of the sign of the cross involved in the act of blessing is spelled out verbally: (8) "þa com him to se costnere; Witodlice an blac þrostle; . . . ac he hine bletsode mid þære halgan rodetacne. and se fugol sona aweg gewat,"[21] (then the tempter came to him. . . indeed, a black throstle. . . but he blessed him with the sign of the holy cross; and the bird instantly went away). It is again Ælfric who most explicitly summarizes the decisive aspects of the holy cross in its relation to the act of blessing. In his homily on the feast-day of the Exaltation of the Holy Cross he states:

> (9) Is swa-þeah to witenne þæt heo [= the holy cross] is wide todæled mid gelomlicum ofcyrfum to lande gehwilcum. ac seo gastlice getacnung is mid gode æfre a unbrosnigendlic. þeah þe se beam beo to-coruen. þæt heofonlice tacn þære halgan rode is ure guðfana wiþ þone gram-lican deofol. þonne we us bletsiað gebylde þurh god mid þære rode tacne. and mid rihtum geleafan. Þeah þe man wafige wundorlice mid handa ne bið hit bletsung

---

(ge)bletsian.
20 *The Old English Version of Bede's Ecclesiastical History of the English People*, ed. Thomas Miller, 4 vols., EETS 95, 96, 110, 111 (London: Oxford University Press, 1890–1898, repr. 1959–63), I: 2 and 388, lines 25–26. Interestingly, Miller tries to resolve the loss of transparency in *segnian* and translates both instances of *segnian* by "make the sign of the cross:" "and then took him by the chin and made over it the sign of the holy cross. When he had thus made the sign of the cross over it . . . " (p. 389).
21 Godden II, ii, 93, homily 11, lines 45–49 ("The Feast of Saint Benedict the Abbot"); Thorpe renders *mid þære halgan rodetacne* as "with the holy sign of the cross," ii, 157.

buta he wyrce tacn þære halgan rode. and se reða feond biþ sona afyrht for ðam sige-fæstan tacne. Mid þrym fingrum man sceall senian and bletsian for þære halgan þrynysse.[22]

[It is, however, to wit that it [the cross] is widely distributed, by means of frequent sections, to every land. But the spiritual token (signification) is always with God, ever incorruptible, though the tree be cut in pieces. That heavenly sign of the Holy Rood is our banner against the fierce devil, when we bless ourselves boldly through God with the sign of the cross and with right belief. Though a man may wave about wonderfully with his hand, nevertheless it is not a blessing except he make the sign of the holy cross; and forthwith the fierce fiend will be terrified on account of the victorious token. With three fingers must a man make the sign and bless himself for the Holy Trinity.]

As we saw in the homily for the Fifth Sunday in Lent, Ælfric again highlights the difference between the material object and the cross as a symbol: while the actual instrument of torture, as well as its relics, are basically a tree which has been cut into pieces and has been widely distributed to every land, its spiritual signification is always incorruptible. One of the main functions of this sign—protection against the fierce devil—can only be fulfilled when we bless ourselves with the sign of the cross in the right belief. And so it seems necessary to Ælfric to point out that the act of blessing has to encompass the manual gesture of the sign of the cross: "Þeah þe man wafige wundorlice mid handa ne bið hit bletsung buta he wyrce tacn þære halgan rode" (a man may wave about wonderfully with his hand, nevertheless it is not a blessing except he make the sign of the holy cross). Without the central symbol of Christianity—the sign of the cross—the act is no performative act, no blessing at all.

---

22 Skeat, ii, 152 and 154, lines 143–155 ("Exaltation of the Holy Cross").

Old English Terms for the Sign of the Cross: *rode tacen*, *cristes mæl*, *(cruc)*

These inherent properties of the cross as (a) a symbol representing Christ and, consequently, the salvation of mankind through Christ's sacrifice on the cross, and (b) a sign used in various concrete, manual gestures in specific liturgical and devotional contexts, are nicely mirrored in the Old English lexicon. Two Old English terms denoting the sign of the cross contain lexical elements designating "sign:" *tacen* "token, sign" in *rodetacen* "sign of the cross," and *mæl* "sign" in *cristes mæl* (and its variant *cristelmæl*) "sign of Christ."[23]

First of all, it is intriguing that Old English should have two different terms for the concept "sign of the cross," the central symbol of Christ and Christianity. The point of reference of these two forms, as can be seen at first glance, is entirely different: *rodetacen* "sign of the cross" refers to the instrument of crucifixion (*rod* "cross") and requires a transfer from the material object to its symbolic meaning, Christ and salvation. The term *cristes mæl* "Christ's sign," on the other hand, already refers to the central referent, Christ (and salvation), and thus calls for a "step-down" transfer to the material object, the cross.

Both *rodetacen* and *cristes mæl*, however, also pose another question. Modern German, a language typologically similar to Old English, differentiates between the syntactic group *(das) Zeichen des Kreuzes* ("sign of the cross") and the lexicalized compound *(das) Kreuzzeichen* ("cross-sign"). While the first one generally refers to the cross as a symbol for Christ and Christianity, the lexicalized

---

23 For Old English expressions for "sign," see Jane Roberts and Christian Kay, *A Thesaurus of Old English in Two Volumes*, (London: King's College, 1995; now also http://libra.englang.arts.gla.ac.uk/oethesaurus), 09.04.01. *Beacen*, another central Old English term meaning "sign," is used in the figurative *sigebeacen* "sign of victory" (for *sigebeacen* denoting "cross"). OE *mearc* "mark, sign" is not employed for compounds denoting the "sign of the cross"; for the use of its derived verb *mearcian*, a frequent collocate with *rodetacen*, see below, pp. 252–255.

compound more specifically denotes the concrete manual gestures used in liturgical and devotional practice, i.e., the little or large cross traced on parts of the body in its various functions.[24] The present study, which is designed to complement Rolf H. Bremmer's study on the words for "cross" proper elsewhere in this volume, will therefore now take a closer look at the Old English formations *rodetacen* and *cristes mæl*, in particular their morphological make-up and, consequently, their meaning. Both *rodetacen* and *cristes mæl* would certainly deserve separate entries in the dictionaries of Old English if they could be established as lexicalized compounds, similar to German *Kreuzzeichen*, and denoting not only the "cross as a sign," but more specifically the concept of the sign of the cross which serves specific functions in the Christian liturgy and devotional practice.

Old English Words Designating "Cross as a Material Object"
The short summary of the inherent nature of the cross as a sign, above, shows that first of all we have to differentiate between words denoting the cross as a material object on the one hand, and those referring to the sign of the cross on the other. The most general word employed for both these concepts is Old English *rod* (Present Day English "[holy] rood").[25] While other Germanic languages borrow

---

24 Accordingly, German dictionaries and encyclopedias list *Kreuz* ("cross") and the compound *Kreuzzeichen* ("cross-sign") in two separate entries. In the *Lexikon für Theologie und Kirche*, 11 vols. (Freiburg: Herder, 1993–2001, 3rd ed.) for example, the symbolic functions and art history of the cross are described in the headword *Kreuz*, while the headword *Kreuzzeichen* ("cross-sign") is defined more specifically as "Zugehörigkeitszeichen zu Christus und spezifisch christliche Segensgebärde," (sign of affiliation to Christ and specifically Christian gesture of blessing), s. v. *Kreuzzeichen*.

25 See BT and BTS, s.vv. *rōd*; see also *MED*, s.v. *rōde* (n. 5) and *OED*, s.v. "rood." For more detailed information on the etymology and use of *rod* and its compounds and *gealga*, see Bremmer, "Old English 'Cross' Words" in this volume, above, pp. 215–220 and pp. 224–228.

the Latin word together with the new concept very early (i.e., in the eighth century) and create loans based on a late Latin form of *crux, crucis* (see Old High German *kruzi, kriuze*, Old Saxon *kruci*, Old Frisian *krioze, kriose*),[26] Old English employs the native word *rod*, whose original meaning "yard," however, is basically only attested in the compound *segl-rod* "sail-yard," a hapax legomenon (see BT, s.v. *rōd* I.) or in contexts referring to "a measure of land" (see BT, s.v. *rōd* II).[27] Denoting a material object, *rod* principally refers to the instrument of crucifixion, the cross on which Jesus was tortured and eventually killed, and also its relics (see BT[S], s.v. *rōd* III). In order to separate the cross of Christ, which had by Anglo-Saxon times become the central symbol of Christianity, from the instrument of punishment on which criminals were tortured ("gibbet," "gallows") and which is thus only in very specific eschatological contexts an object of veneration, Old English uses the compound *wearg-rod* "the accursed tree, a gallows, gibbet"[28] or chooses—like Old High German—an entirely different lexeme, namely OE *g(e)alga* "gallows," "gibbet" or more specifically "traverse; cross-beam."[29]

In addition to referring to the original instrument of crucifixion and its relics, *rod* designates a replica of the original instrument,[30] i.e.,

---

26 See Kluge, *Etymologisches Wörterbuch*, s.v. *Kreuz*. For the occasional occurrences of a loan *cruc* in Old English, see below, pp. 270–274 and Bremmer, "Old English 'Cross Words'," in this volume, above pp. 208–15.

27 See also Bremmer, "Old English 'Cross' Words," in this volume, above, pp. 215–218.

28 Cf. *wearg* "evil, vile, malignant, accursed." See BT, s.v. *wearg-rōd*, and the discussion in Bremmer, "Old English 'Cross' Words," above, p. 219.

29 See BT, s.v. *gealga*, MED, s.v. *galwe*; see also Kluge, *Etymologisches Wörterbuch*, s.vv. *Kreuz* and *Galgen;* and Bremmer, "Old English 'Cross' Words," above, pp. 224–228.

30 Among the oldest of these are processional crosses—commonly a staff surmounted by the figure of a cross (see *OED*, s.v. "cross" 6.)—whose use seems to have been general in early times, since the Roman *ordines* suggest that one belonged to each church. Altar-crosses, on the other hand, can hardly be traced farther back than the thirteenth century.

a model or figure of Christ's cross as a religious emblem, employed for ritual use (nowadays often called "crucifix").[31] These models of Christ's cross may be found "in a church" (BTS, s.v. *rōd* IV a), and the lexeme *rod* is accordingly used for the signs for a large or small cross in the Old English monastic sign list: (10) "Ðonne þu micelan rode abban wylle þonne lege þu þinne finger ofer þinne swyðran finger and rær up þinne þuman. Litelere rode tacen is ealswa rær up þonne litlan finger,"[32] (When you want a large cross, then lay your finger over your right finger and hold up your thumb. The sign for a small cross is just the same; raise the little finger).

Rod may further denote a small-sized model of Christ's cross suspended from the neck (BTS, s.v. *rōd*, IV c),[33] but also a large-sized figure "out-of-doors" (BTS, s.v. *rōd* IV b), i.e., "a monument in the form of a cross, or having a cross upon it, erected in places of resort, at crossways etc., for devotional purposes, or as a devout or solemn memorial of some event" (*OED*, s.v. "cross," 7). The term *rod* is thus used for the large stone crosses which were one of the distinctive features of Christianity in pre-Norman England,[34] and is generally employed for all kinds of crosses set up as tokens and memorials—thus, for instance, in praise of God by King Oswald before his battle against Ceadwalla:

---

31 The Present Day English term "crucifix" is ambiguous. In its technical sense, it is reserved for "an image or figure (formerly also a pictorial representation) of Christ upon the cross" (see *OED*, s.v. "crucifix," 2.), though this distinction is not always drawn; see *OED*, same entry: "The misuse of crucifix for 'cross, figure of the cross,' is frequent in writers of the 18–19th c."

32 Banham, *Monasteriales Indicia*, p. 28, nos. 35 and 36.

33 For these, we also find the compounds *sweor-rod* "neck-cross"(cf. *swēora* "neck;" see BT, s.v. *swēor-rōd*) and the hapax *bisceop-rod* "bishop's pectoral cross or crosier" (see *DOE*, s.v. *bisceop-rōd*).

34 See, for instance, the self-denotation of the cross in *The Dream of the Rood*. For these crosses, see Richard N. Bailey, "Crosses, Stone," in *The Blackwell Encyclopaedia of Anglo-Saxon England*, ed. Michael Lapidge et al., (Oxford: Blackwell, 1999), pp. 129–130.

(11) Oswold þa arærde ane rode sona Gode to wurðmynte ær þan þe he to ðam gewinne come, and clypode to his geferum, Uton feallan to ðære rode, and þone ælmihtigan biddan þæt he us ahredde wið þone modigan feond þe us afyllan wile.[35]

[Then Oswald raised a cross quickly to the honour of God before he came to battle, and cried to his companions, "Let us fall down before the cross, and pray the Almighty that he will save us against the proud enemy who desires to kill us."]

Words for the Sign of the Cross: Old English rodetac(e)n

OLD ENGLISH *RODETACEN*: COMPOUND OR SYNTACTIC GROUP?

Similar to Old English *rod* for "cross," Old English *rodetacen*—a loan translation of Latin *signum crucis (Christi)*—is the most central, frequent, and versatile word signifying the different aspects and functions of the sign of the cross. In the Dictionary of Old English Corpus, the forms *rodetacen* and *rode tacen* are attested to 157 times.[36] Yet in BT, the most comprehensive dictionary of Old English covering the letter *r*, *rodetacen* is not given a separate entry but is listed as one of the meanings of *rod* "cross," though with the

---

35 Skeat, ii, 126, lines 17–21 ("Oswald"). The *vita* later refers to the healing powers of the cross (lines 30–32) and its moss (lines 36–39) and to the fact that it *on wurðmynte stod* "stood there for worship" (line 31).

36 See DOEC: the spelling most frequently attested is *rodetac(e)n* (117 occurrences) followed by *rode tac(e)n* with separation of determinant and determinatum (34 occurrences). Other attested spellings are *rodetaken* (4 occurrences in manuscript H of the translation of Gregory's *Dialogues*), *rodentacen* (1 occurrence in the "Life of Saint Margaret" in Cambridge, Corpus Christi College MS 303) and *rodætacæn* (1 occurrence in a Charter (S 427)). Charter and wills are quoted from the database *Regesta Regum Anglorum* at http://www.trin.cam.ac.uk/chartwww (S refers to the number in the *Electronic Sawyer*, an online version of the revised edition of Peter H. Sawyer, *Anglo-Saxon Charters: an Annotated List and Bibliography* [London: Royal Historical Society, 1968]).

commentary: "*Rode tacen* seems hardly a compound to judge by the numerous phrases in which *rōde* is qualified by an adjective or genitive, but may be such in instances like *He mearcode him on heafde halig rode-tacen.*"[37]

The delimitation of syntactic groups (nominal head *tacen* preceded by a genitive modifier *rode*) and compounds (one single noun *rodetacen*) is notoriously difficult for Old English.[38] Generally, the distinction between syntactic groups and compounds is based on certain kinds of "isolation" in the compound—orthographical, phonological, morphological, and/or semantic isolation. As criteria for this isolation, word division (orthography), stress pattern (two major stresses = syntactic group, one major stress = compound), morphological reasons, and semantic specification involving loss of transparency are considered to be decisive. It has been convincingly shown, however, that the stress pattern of Old English elements cannot be established from our extant sources, not even in poetry.[39] The same is true for spelling, which was even more erratic in this respect than it is in Modern English. In the case of *rodetacen*, however, one might wonder whether the overwhelming preponderance of the single form *rodetacen* (123 occurrences)[40] in contrast to *rode tacen*—with division of determinant and determinatum (34 occurrences)—might not be an indicator that Anglo-Saxon scribes took the syntagm as a compound. But an analysis of spelling with respect to word division is, of course, much impeded by editorial practices which are often oriented on the forms found in dictionaries.[41]

---

37 See BTS, s.v. *rōd*, III (3).
38 See Dieter Kastovsky, "Semantics and Vocabulary," in *The Cambridge History of the English Language, Volume 1: The Beginnings to 1066*, ed. Richard Hogg, (Cambridge: Cambridge University Press, 1992), 356–63; and Hans Sauer, "Die Darstellung von Komposita in altenglischen Wörterbüchern," *Problems of Old English Lexicography. Studies in Memory of Angus Cameron*, ed. Alfred Bammesberger (Regensburg: Pustet, 1985), pp. 267–315.
39 Sauer, "Komposita," pp. 269–70.
40 Including the spellings *rodetaken*, *rodentacen* and *rodætacæn*.
41 See, for instance, the remarks on the editorial procedure in the editions of

Thus morphological isolation remains as the most valid criterion to distinguish the compound from the corresponding syntactic group. In the case of genitive compounds,[42] the whole noun phrase has to be inspected: if the article and/or adjective agree in morphological form with the determinatum (in our case the neuter *tacen*), we have a compound. If they refer to the determinant (in our case the feminine *rod*), we have a syntactic group. Thus the feminine article *þære* in the first quotation of the paper from Ælfric, above,—"*Ðære* halgan rode tacn is ure bletsung"—establishes the syntagm as a syntactic group, which is to be translated as "the sign of the holy cross is our blessing."[43] Other instances of this use we have met so far are "Segna þe & sete þe on þæt tacen *ðære* halgan rode" (quotation 4), "mid tacne *ðære* halgan rode hio gesegnade" (quotation 7a), "ac he hine bletsode mid *þære* halgan rodetacne" (quotation 8), and "ne bið hit bletsung buta he wyrce tacn *þære* halgan rode" (quotation 9).

By contrast, a neuter modifier is also attested throughout the Old English period. See, for instance, the second instance of *rodetacen* in the translation of Gregory's *Dialogues*:

Ælfric's *Catholic Homilies*: "Word-division has been standardized on the basis of normal practice in dictionaries and grammars, supplemented where necessary by the precedents set by Pope's edition of Ælfric and by evidence (such as syntactic usage) of Ælfric's own views" (Clemoes, p. 169). In the glossary to the two series of Ælfric's *Catholic Homilies* we then find "*rodetac(e)n* n. 'sign of the cross'; as two words II: 13. 290" (see Godden I, p. 756).

42 Both *rodetacen* and *cristes mæl* are genitive compounds. As concerns *rodetacen*, OE *rōd* is a feminine noun (*ō*-declension) and so the first component of a compound *rodetacen* – {rode} – can be seen as the genitive *rōde*; Kastovsky, however, points out that in "a number of cases, e.g. *hildecalla* . . . the internal vowel should not be regarded as a genitive ending, but as a linking element like the German Fugen-s," (Kastovsky, "Semantics and Vocabulary," p. 363); see also pp. 369–370 commenting on *restedæg* "rest-day, Sabbath," or *hellefyr* "hell-fire."

43 The weak adjective *halgan* is of no help here because weak adjectives are not inflected for gender in the oblique cases.

(12) Eac he me sæde, þæt he mihte þis wundor wyrcan, þæt in swa hwilcre stowe swa he gemette nædran . . . þæt he hi acwealde sona gif he hi gesegnode *mid Cristes rodetacne* [12a], swa þæt heo toborstenum þam innoðum swulte for þam mægne þære halgan rode, þonne se Godes wer *þæt rodetacen* awrat [12b] mid his fingre.[44]

[He also told me, that he was able to work this wonder, that in whichever place he met a serpent . . . that he killed it instantly if he blessed it with the sign of Christ's cross [12a], so that it died from burst insides because of the power of the holy cross then, when the man of God wrote the cross-sign [12b] with his finger.]

While in the first instance (12a) the genitive modifier *Cristes* seems to indicate that the syntagm should be taken as a syntactic group (Latin *signum crucis Christi*, "the sign of the cross of Christ"), the neuter article *þæt* (instead of feminine *þære*) in the second instance *þæt rodetacen* (12b) shows that it is used as a compound.[45]

In its analysis of *rodetacen*, BTS implicitly also refers to this decisive factor for the differentiation between a syntactic group (German *Zeichen des Kreuzes*) and a compound (German *Kreuzzeichen*): the strong neuter adjective *halig* instead of the feminine *haligu*[46] shows that the syntagm is considered to be a compound. So the passage should be taken as ". . . with the holy sign of the cross" and not "with the sign of the holy cross." The full text of this quotation from Ælfric

---

44 Hecht, *Bischof Waerferths von Worcester Übersetzung der Dialoge Gregors des Grossen*, ch. 35, pp. 246–47. Manuscript O does not give the compound form, but the syntactic group *ðare haligan*.

45 For another of these occurrences of *þæt*, see "hi wæron gemetfæste on geleafan þæs lifigendan Godes suna, and his ðæt halige rode tacn on heora lichoman getreowlice bæron" (they were modest in their faith in the son of the living God, and carried that (his) cross-sign [literal translation, U.L.] steadfastly on their bodies), translation mine: *The Anonymous Old English Legend of the Seven Sleepers*, ed. Hugh Magennis, Durham Medieval Texts 7 (Durham: Durham Medieval Texts, 1994), line 106.

46 Alistair Campbell, *Old English Grammar* (Oxford: Clarendon, 1959), § 643.

runs as follows: (13) "and he awoc ða bliðe. for ðære gesihðe. and for ðan behatenan sige. and mearcode him on heafde halig rodetacn,"[47] (and he awoke in a happy mood because of this vision and because of the promised victory, and traced on his head the holy sign of the cross).

This morphological means of delimitation by the different forms of modifiers seems fairly straightforward at first glance. A closer look at all the Old English occurrences reveals, however, that it is in fact only applicable in a very small number of cases.

	rodetacen (123 occ.)[48]	*rode tacen* (34 occ.)
without modifier /determiner	40	9
Determiner	6	2
feminine (> syntactic group)	4	1
neuter (> compound)	2	1
Adjective	9	7
feminine (> syntactic group)	6	5
neuter (> compound)	3	2

---

47 Godden II, ii, 174, homily 18, lines 16–17 ("Invention of the Holy Cross"). Manuscript T has the variant *þæt halige*, in which the neuter demonstrative *þæt* stresses the grammatical gender neuter. For another use of the compound, see the version "he awoc þa bliþelice for þære fægeran gesihðe and for þære mæran behatenan sige. and mearcode him on heafde halig rode tacen. and on his guðfanan gode to wurðmynte," (he then awoke blithely because of the fair sight and for the great promised victory; and he marked on his head and on his banner the holy cross-sign in honor to God), "Discovery of the Sacred Cross," *Legends of the Holy Rood*, ed. Richard Morris, EETS o. s. 46 (London: Trübner, 1871), pp. 4–5.

48 Including the isolated attested spellings *rodetaken, rodætacæn* etc. (see above, n. 36), all of which do not divide the determinant and the determinatum.

	rodetacen (123 occ.)⁴⁸	*rode tacen* (34 occ.)
Cristes	61	16
drihtnes ~	1	
þæs hælendes ~	1	
his ~	1	
þære halgan Cristes ~	3	
~ *Cristes*	1	

This table shows that only about 15 percent of the attestations (24 occurrences) allow a precise morphological analysis with respect to grammatical gender. In about a third of all instances (49 occurrences), a morphological test is not applicable because the forms are used without any modifier.⁴⁹

In about half of the cases (77 occurrences), *rodetacen* or *rode tacen* are modified by the genitive *Cristes*, yielding the form *Cristes rodetacen*,⁵⁰ a phrase which explicitly relates the cross with Christ and thus further stresses the fact that the sign of the cross signifies Christ. BT take the many occurrences of the collocation *Cristes rodetacen* as an indicator that the syntagm was considered a syntactic group and not a compound, because *Cristes* is seen as modifying *rod*, i.e., "the sign of Christ's cross." As a loan translation of Latin *signum crucis Christi*, it is, however, such a frequent collocation in Old English that it seems possible to regard the whole phrase as a fixed expression for the specific concept "sign of the cross" with a first element *Cristes*, similar to *cristes-bōc* "book containing all or part of the gospels" or *cristes-mæsse* "Christmas Day,"⁵¹ and in particular

---

49 See quotations (2a), (2b) above and (16), (17) below.
50 See quotations (14), (15), (21) and (24) below.
51 See *DOE*, s.vv. *Cristes-bōc* and *cristes-mæsse*. For *cristes-mæl*, see below, pp. 261–270.

to *cristes mæl* "sign of the cross." Both these terms highlight the intrinsic nature of the "sign of the cross" as a sign for Christ and salvation. This relation becomes most evident in the one instance of a post-posed instead of pre-posed genitive[52] in the F-Version of the Anglo-Saxon Chronicle (London, British Library MS Cotton Domitian A. viii; s. xi/xii) for the year 796. Here, *Cristes* modifies the whole compound *rodetacen* and not only its first constituent *rod*: (14) "& ic Aðelhard arcebiscop mid twelf biscopan & mid þrim & twentigan abbodan þis ylce mid rodetacne Cristes getrimmað & <gefæstnað>"[53] (and I, Archbishop Aðelhard, confirm and validate this here with Christ's sign of the cross, together with twelve bishops and twenty-three abbots).

The formal analysis also shows that instances of the compound marked by a neuter modifier are attested to during the whole Old English period in different authors, and not only those who are marginal or later (see the quotations from the Old English translation of Gregory's *Dialogues* [12b] and Ælfric [13]). Thus the syntagm was obviously regarded as a compound by certain Anglo-Saxon authors and scribes, especially in contexts which refer to the concrete marking or tracing (OE *writan* or *mearcian*) of a cross on a part of the body (often the forehead). These are also the contexts in which German employs the compound *Kreuzzeichen*. The forms which are grammatically explicitly feminine are, by contrast, in about half of the cases (seven instances) used in contexts of "blessing," an

---

52 Genitival modifiers can be placed before or after the head they modify: while the numbers are almost even for early texts (52% pre-posed vs. 48% post-posed around 900), there is a strong tendency for pre-position in late Old English (77% pre-posed vs. 22% post-posed in the eleventh century); see Manfred Görlach, *Einführung in die englische Sprachgeschichte*, 5th ed. (Heidelberg: Winter, 2002), p. 79.

53 Peter S. Baker, ed., *The Anglo-Saxon Chronicle. A Collaborative Edition. Volume 8: MS. F* (Cambridge: Boydell & Brewer, 2000), for the year 796, p. 56. The Latin text of this passage only says "Et subscripsit Aðelardus archiepiscopus . . ." (p. 57).

act which, as shown above, has to be performed *mid þære (halgan) rode tacne*. Here again, the comparison with Modern German shows that the typologically similar language may use both forms, but would prefer the syntactic group when designating the act of blessing, probably for reasons of explicitness and intensity: "Ich segne Dich mit dem Zeichen des Kreuzes" (I bless you with the sign of the [holy] cross) is preferred to "Ich segne Dich mit dem (heiligen) Kreuzzeichen" (I bless you with the cross-sign). In more general contexts, however, Old English, like Modern German, uses *(Cristes) rodetacen* as a compound.

OLD ENGLISH *RODETACEN*: SEMANTICS

Since the morphological analysis suggests a diversified use of the syntactic group *(þære) rode tacen* and the compound *(þæt) rodetacen* or *Cristes rodetacen*, the semantics of *rodetacen* will now be analyzed with respect to the question of semantic isolation or lexicalization. This survey account of the different meanings of *rodetacen* will then also provide the background for the following analysis of *cristes mæl* and *cruc*, both of which show some overlap with *rodetacen* in the referents they denote, i.e., are also Old English expressions for the "sign of the cross."

When dealing with a historical period, it is not always easy to determine whether a given formation is lexicalized or not, in particular in a form like *rodetacen* which—in contrast to *cristes mæl*[54]—has never adopted meanings that are not predictable from the meaning of the constituents and the pattern underlying the compound.[55]

A survey of all the attestations to the forms *rodetacen* and *rode tacen* in Old English (here ordered by their relative frequency) establishes essentially four broad meanings:

---

54 See below, p. 262.
55 For this criterion of lexicalization, see Kastovsky, "Semantics and Vocabulary," p. 356.

Meaning	Collocate verb(s)
A) the little sign of the cross as a manual gesture (89 occ.)	*wyrcean (ofer)*,
A1) traced on something concrete ~ a person, a part of the body (37 occ.) ~ an animal (6 occ.) ~ a concrete object (door, loaf of bread; 11 occ.)	*(a)writan* *mearcian (mid)*, *(wæpnian [mid])*, *(agrafan)*
A2) the sign of the cross written on a (legal) document to validate solemn declaration (25 occ. in formulaic use)	*trymman mid, fæstnian mid, strangian mid*
A3) traced in the air (10 occ.)	
B) the sign of the cross used in the act of blessing (26 occ.)	*segnian mid,* *bletsian mid*
C) a material object, a model or figure of a cross as a religious emblem; a crucifix (21 occ.)[56]	
~ for liturgical or devotional use (processional cross etc.) set up within a building or in the open air (an outdoor cross or crucifix) (17 occ.) ~ as a vision or apparition of Christ's cross (3 occ.)	
D) used in general reference to Christ's suffering on the cross and salvation (6 occ.)	

---

56 Including one—perhaps erroneous, because late—occurrence where *rodetacen* refers to Christ's cross itself, i.e., the instrument of crucifixion: "þa nolde se

This survey shows that in most of the occurrences, *rodetacen*, as in Modern German, indeed refers to the oldest variant of the sign of the cross (Variant 1), i.e., the little sign of the cross traced as a performative manual gesture in the air or, more typically, on something specific (a person, an animal, a concrete object or such), most often on parts of the human body (A1) or written—in formulaic use—on (legal) documents (A2). The character of this tracing of the sign of the cross as an emblem is highlighted in the frequent collocation with the verb *mearcian* "to mark," i.e., *mearcian rodetacen* or *mearcian mid rodetacen* "to mark (with) the sign of the cross." This collocation is typically but not exclusively used in the writings of Ælfric.[57]

At all times, the Church has attributed to this mark not only effects of grace, but also of power against physical and spiritual destruction and death:

(15) And we sceolon mearcian ure forewearde heafod. and urne lichaman mid cristes rodetacne. þæt we beon ahredde fram forwyrde. þonne we beoð gemearcode ægðer ge on foranheafde. ge on heortan mid blode þære drihtenlican ðrowunge.[58]

[And we should mark our foreheads and our bodies with the sign of Christ's rood, that we may be saved from destruction, when we are marked both on the forehead and on the heart with the blood of the divine Passion.]

---

mildheorta drihten geþafigen þe on hire self willes þrowode. and on þam rode tacne eall mancyn alysde . . ." (but the merciful Lord would not permit that the cross on which he himself had willingly suffered and redeemed all mankind . . .): Morris, "Discovery of the Sacred Cross," p. 17.
57   *Mearcian* is only rarely (ca. five times) used in the texts of the Alfred circle which commonly employ *(a)writan* "write" (see *DOE*, s.v. *awrītan*, A.8.a.). For more general references, Old English authors use the verb *wyrcean* "make."
58   Godden II, ii, homily 15, p. 151, lines 55–60 ("On Easter Sunday").

This power of the sign of the cross manifests itself in particular when it is traced (by saints or priests) in the act of healing,[59] when it serves as a weapon against fierce might, a concept made explicit in the frequent collocation *wæpnian mid rodetacen* "arm with the sign of the cross:"

> (16) Syððan se hæþengylda eac sealde þone attorbæran drenc þam apostole: & he mid rodetacne his muð & ealne his lichaman gewæpnode. & þane unlybban on godes naman halsode. & syððan mid gebyldum mode. hine ealne gedranc.[60]

> [Then the idolater gave the venomous drink also to the apostle, and he armed his mouth and all his body with the sign of the cross, and exorcised poison in God's name and then he drank all of it with bold heart.]

From the earliest period, it has thus also been employed in exorcisms and conjurations as a weapon against all kinds of dark spirits.[61]

While the little sign of the cross employed in the performative acts depicted so far is mainly traced by priests, it can also extend its functional realm beyond the liturgy and rites of the Church. The most prolific use of the "sign of the cross" in a non-religious context is its employment as a written figure entered in a document to validate solemn declaration. It serves as a signature and kind of "seal in Christ" when charters, wills, or documents are signed and thus ratified "with the sign of the cross." Here it features as a material drawing on the parchment. The act of signature itself is accompanied by certain

---

59 "Ne beo ge afyrhte þurh his gesihðe: ac mearciað rodetacen on eowerum foreheafdum. & ælc yfel gewit fram eow" (Be not afraid at the sight of him, but mark the sign of the cross on your forehead, and every evil shall depart from you): Clemoes, i, 445, homily 31, lines 184–86 ("Passion of St. Bartholomew").

60 Clemoes, i, 214, homily 4, line 222 ("Assumption of St. John the Apostle").

61 In the contexts of exorcism and popular medicine, we often find the term *cristes mæl* and also some instances of *cruc*; see below, pp. 261–270.

Signifying Christ in Anglo-Saxon England

performative formulae[62] employing the Latin terms *signaculum (sanctae) crucis* or *signum (sanctae) crucis,* or an Old English term for the "sign of the cross," such as *rodetacen*.[63] This practice is amply attested in the Anglo-Saxon Chronicle and particularly in the witness lists of charters and wills. As performative verbs used in the formulas, we most often find the verb *fæstnian* "to confirm, ratify," often in pair formulas such as *writan and fæstnian* or, even more frequent, with *getrymman* "to strengthen, confirm," *getrymman and fæstnian*.[64] See as illustrative examples for different formulas (i.e., "I, King X, confirm/ratify Y with the sign of the holy cross"):[65]

(17) Ic Offa þurh Cristes gyfe Myrcena kining ðas mine geoue *mid rodetacne gefæstnige* (S 126)[66]

---

62 The formulas are generally of the form "1st person personal pronoun (*ic/we* + (name)) + performative verb in present tense + *mid rodetacen/crystesmæl.*" The 1st person personal pronoun and the verb in the present tense are indicators that these formulas are performative speech acts, i.e., utterances that explicitly denote the action to be carried out.

63 For an employment of this act in an age of widespread illiteracy, see ch. 58 of the *RSB* which commands: "Write he þa fæstnunge mid his agenre handa, gif he þonne writan ne cunne, bidde oþerne, þe writan cunne, þæt hine aspelige, and he sylf on þam gewrite rodetacn mearcige and hy swa fæstniende mid his agenum handum uppan þone altare alecge" (He shall write the confirmation in his own hand; if he is, however, not able to write, he shall ask some other person who can write that he should be a substitute for him; and he himself shall mark the sign of the cross on the document and confirm it, with his own hands placed upon the altar): Arnold Schröer, ed., *Die angelsächsischen Prosabearbeitungen der Benediktinerregel*, Bibliothek der angelsächsischen Prosa (Kassel, 1885–1888; repr. with appendix by Helmut Gneuss [Darmstadt: Wissenschaftliche Buchgesellschaft, 1964]), p. 101, lines 3–7.

64 See *DOE*, s.v. *fæstnian* B.2.

65 Note the different morphological forms of *rodetacen* in these three examples: (17) uncertain: no modifier, (18) syntactic group: feminine *þære* in the prepositional phrase *mid þære halgan rodetacne*, and (19) compound: masculine premodifier *ðam*.

66 786 or 589 for ? 779 or 789 x 790. Offa, king of Mercia, to the monks of St.

(18) Ic Æþelbreht cyning *mid þære halgan rodetacne* þis het swiþe geornlice *getrymman & gefæstnian* (S 333)⁶⁷

(19) + Ic Ælfric se erceb*iscop* of Euerwic ðas ilces kinges godne wille *mid ðam halege rode tacne gefæstni* (S 959).⁶⁸

In this formulaic use, the sign of the cross is not only a manual, transitory gesture, but is written in ink at the bottom of treaties and charters in a performative act of validating a document.

As is to be expected from Ælfric's exposition in quotation (1), the term *rodetacen* is also used in more general contexts to denote the cross figuratively as the ensign and symbol of Christianity and the central fact of the Christian religion, the atonement wrought on the cross (see meaning D in table):⁶⁹ (20) "He soðlice þone dead oferswiðde .

Mary's, Worcester (MS from s xi²).
67 864 (Dorchester, Dorset, 26 Dec.). Æthelberht, king of Wessex, to the church of Sherborne; grant of privileges, with note that Æthelberht placed the charter on the high altar at Sherborne (865, Good Friday). English (MS from s. xii^med).
68 1023. King Cnut to Christ Church, Canterbury; grant of the port of Sandwich (diverse MSS from s. xii¹ and later).
69 This context might also explain Ælfric's anachronistic use of the term *rodetacen* in an Old Testament context: "God sette on ðære ealdan. æ. and het niman anes geares lamb æt ælcum hiwisce. and sniðan on eastertide. and wyrcan mid þæs lambes blode rodetacn on heora gedyrum" (God appointed in the old law and commanded a lamb of one year to be taken of every family, and slain on Easter-tide, and to make with the blood of the lamb the sign of the cross on their door-posts), Godden II, ii, 21, homily 3, lines 81–82 ("On the Epiphany of Our Lord"); "Hi mearcodon mid ðæs lambes blode on heora gedyrum. and oferslegum. TAU. þæt is rodetacen" (They marked with the blood of the lamb, on their door-posts and lintels, the letter TAU, that is, the sign of the cross), Godden II, ii, 151, homily 15, lines 52–54 ("On Easter Day"); and "God bebead moyse on egypta lande. þæt he & eall israhela folc sceoldon offrian æt ælcum hiwisce gode an lamb. anes geares & mearcian mid þam blode rodetacen on heora gedyrum and oferslegum" (God commanded Moses in Egypt that he and all the people of Israel should offer, for every household, a lamb of one year to God, and mark with the blood the sign of the cross on their door-posts and lintels), Clemoes, i, 354, homily 22, lines 6–8 ("On the Day of Pentecost").

.. & on þam þriddan dæge sigefæst aras & sealde his rodetacen his apostolum"⁷⁰ (But he overcame death . . . and on the third day he rose victorious, and gave the sign of his cross to his apostles).

This use probably yields a more surprising, distinct meaning of the compound *rodetacen* in Old English. *Rodetacen*, which explicitly employs the constituent *tacen* "sign" as its determinatum, can also denote a model or figure of a cross, i.e., a material object (see meaning C). It thus serves as a synonym for its determiner *rod*, and not—as would be regular—its determinatum *tacen*. This use of *rodetacen* instead of the simple noun *rod* thus shows that the form *rodetacen* is indeed lexicalized and, in accordance with Ælfric's exposition in quotation (1), highlights that the cross is always a symbol. Christ's cross is never just a gibbet: (21) "Towurpað þis deofolgild and tocwysað. and ærærað cristes rodetacn on ðære stowe"⁷¹ (Cast down this idol, and crush it, and raise up the sign of Christ's rood on this place).

The same idea motivates the use of *rodetacen* (and, in the first place, *signum crucis* in the Latin exemplar) in the A-version of the *Gospel of Nicodemus*. *Rodetacen* here three times refers to a material object, which can be carried (cf. *berende*). This text, however, is somewhat idiosyncratic in that the feminine premodifiers *anre* (22a), *þysse* (22b), and *þysse* (22c) seem to indicate that *rodetacen* is not used as a neuter, but a feminine compound:

(22) Ac onmang þam ðe Enoh and Elias þus spræcon, heom þær to becom sum wer þe wæs earmlices hywes and wæs berende *anre*

While the identification of the letter TAU with the sign of the cross is common in allegorical patristic literature, Godden could not find any parallel for the detail that the Israelites marked their doors with the sign of the cross (see Godden I, p. 490). For Ælfric, it is obviously not absurd to use the inherently Christian *rodetacen* ("the salvation of Christ on the cross") in a description of the rites of the Jewish *pascha*.
70 Clemoes, i, 443, homily 31, lines 119–121 ("Passion of St. Bartholomew").
71 Godden II, ii, 169, homily 18, lines 14–16 ("The Apostles Philip and James").

rodetacen [22a] onuppan hys exlum . . . He hym andswarode and cwæð: " . . . And he me *þysse rodetacen* [22b] sealde and cwæð: ga on neorxnawang myd þysum tacne and gif se engel, þe ys hyrde to neorxnawanges geate, ðe inganges forwyrne, ætyw hym *þysse rodetacen* [22c] and sege to hym þæt se hælenda Cryst, Godes sunu, þe nu wæs anhangen þe þyder asende."[72]

[But while Enoch and Elias were saying these things, there came to them a certain man who was of a wretched appearance, and carrying a (sign of the) cross on his shoulders . . . He answered them and said: " . . . and He [the Savior] gave me the (sign of the) cross and said: "Go into paradise with this sign, and if the angel who is the keeper at the gate of Paradise does not allow you to enter, show him this (sign of the) cross, and say to him that Christ the Savior, the Son of God who has been crucified, sent you there."]

Instances of a lexicalized compound *rodetacen* designating a "material object" are also attested to in the Vercelli Homilies. In quotation (23), *rodetacna*[73] are listed together with *oðre halige reliquias* "other holy relics" which have to be venerated with appropriate humility on Rogation Days: (23) "ær he mæssan hæbbe gehyred, & barefotum Cristesbec & his rodetacna & oðre halige reliquias eadmodlice gegret hæbbe"[74] (before he has heard the mass, and has greeted the gospels, his crosses and other holy relics in a humble way with bare feet). In the second occurrence from the Vercelli Homilies, *Cristes rodetacen* refers to a material object, a procession cross, which is carried over the land on the Rogation Days: (24) "& we sculon beran usse reliquias ymb ure land, þa medeman Cristes

---

72 "*Euangelium Nichodemi*: Text and Translation," *Two Old English Apocrypha and Their Manuscript Source: "The Gospel of Nichodemus" and "The Avenging of the Saviour*," ed. James E. Cross et al, CSASE 19 (Cambridge: Cambridge University Press, 1996), pp. 234–36, ch. 26, lines 1–13.

73 Note the plural form *rodetacna* which only makes sense if *rodetacen* refers to a concrete object, and not the cross as a general symbol for the salvation.

74 *The Vercelli Homilies*, ed. Donald Scragg, EETS o. s. 300 (Oxford: Oxford University Press, 1992), [homily] XIX, p. 320, lines 93–94.

rodetacen þe we Cristes mæl nemnað, on þam he sylfa þrowode for mancynnes alysnesse"[75] (and we shall carry our relics over our land, the precious Christ's crosses which we call *Cristes mæl* on which he himself suffered for the salvation of mankind). Since both of the occurrences in the Vercelli Homilies designate a material object, Scragg even gives "crucifix" as the single meaning for *rodetacen* in this text.[76]

The morphological and semantic analysis of *rodetacen* has thus shown that the term *rodetacen* and also the fossilized *Cristes rodetacen* should indeed be considered lexicalized compounds with concrete, distinct meanings in Old English. While the syntactic group *þære rode tacen* is mainly employed in general reference to Christ (and his salvation) or in contexts of blessing, the neuter compound *(þæt) rodetacen* distinctly refers to the oldest variant of the sign of the cross, the little cross traced on something concrete, most typically a part of the body or parchment, or to a crucifix.

Words for the Sign of the Cross: Old English Cristes mæl

In the passage from the Vercelli Homilies quoted above (24), we not only see that *rodetacen* is indeed a lexicalized compound with a specific meaning, but also that it is not the only Old English term used to denote the concept "sign of the cross." In this passage, the phrase "þa medeman Cristes rodetacen" (the precious Christ's crosses) is glossed by "þe we Cristes mæl nemnað" (which we call *Cristes mæl*). As mentioned above, *cristes mæl*, which here denotes a crucifix, is structurally similar to *rodetacen*, because it also incorporates a linguistic element meaning "sign"—OE *mæl*—as its determinatum.[77] Its status as a lexicalized compound, is—like that of *rodetacen*—disputed in the dictionaries of Old English.

---

75 Scragg, *Vercelli Homilies*, [homily] XII, p. 228, lines 16–18.
76 Scragg, *Vercelli Homilies*, p. 455, s.v. rodetacen.
77 OE *mæl* is synonymous with *tacen* and generally refers to a kind of "sign" or "mark;" see BT, s.v. *mæl*.

OLD ENGLISH *CRISTES MÆL*: STATUS

Cristes mæl is attested to forty-four times in Anglo-Saxon sources.[78] In contrast to other Old English dictionaries,[79] it is not given a separate headword in the *DOE*, but is discussed in the head entry *Crist* in the section "in particular genitival constructions," together with *Cristes geleafa*, *Cristes lagu*, *Cristes bebod*, *Cristes godspel*, and also *Cristes rod* and *Cristes rodetacn* (1.b.ii.).

In view of the discussion on Old English compounds above,[80] this lemmatization does not seem to grasp fully the word formation of *cristes mæl* as a lexicalized genitive compound. Expressions like *Cristes bebod*, *Cristes godspel* and the like are fully transparent genitive constructions in which the genitive *Cristes* functions as a modifier of the head, i.e., naming the originator in *bebod* or *lagu* ("Christ's law;" "genetivus subjectivus") or the object in *Cristes geleafa* ("belief in Christ;" "genetivus objectivus"). *Cristes mæl*, by contrast, should be regarded as a lexicalized compound similar to *cristes-boc* "gospels" or *cristes-mæsse* "Christmas Day."[81] It clearly exhibits an advanced stage of lexicalization, because, in contrast to *rodetacen*, it has adopted meanings that are not predictable from the meaning of the constituents, i.e., it has undergone a restriction of meaning.[82] The

---

78 In the DOEC, we find 31 occurrences of *cristes mæl*, 11 matches for *cristes mel* and 2 for *criste mæl*.

79 J. R. Clark Hall, *A Concise Anglo-Saxon Dictionary*, 4th ed. (Toronto: University of Toronto Press, 1984), for instance, has a cross-reference from *crīstelmǽl* to *Cristes-mǽl* "Christ's mark," "the cross;" the latter is thus given priority. BTS only has entries for *cristel-mæl* (with a variant *crystel-*) "I. a cross" and "II. the sign of the cross" and *cristelmæl-bēam* "a tree on which a cross is fixed." Holthausen, on the other hand, sees *cristelmæl* as a derived form of *cristes mæl*; see Friedrich Holthausen, *Altenglisches etymologisches Wörterbuch* (Heidelberg: Winter, 1934): "*cristel-mæl* mn. "Kreuz" < *Cristes mæl*," p. 60.

80 See pp. 246–253.

81 See *DOE*, s.vv. *cristes-bōc* and *cristes-mæsse*.

82 Morphologically, determiners, adjectival modifiers as well as cataphoric and anaphoric references to *cristes mæl* agree in all instances with the neuter noun *mæl*.

form does not generally refer to a sign for/of Christ, but to the most important emblem of Christianity, the cross. An understanding of the full symbolic meaning and interpretation of *cristes mæl* as the "cross" requires the ideas stressed by Ælfric in the first quotation above, i.e., that the holy rood is a sign for Christ. Without this interpretative support in a theological background, *cristes mæl* could, for instance, also denote baptism (cf. German *Christusmal* "baptism" in theological discourse) or be taken to refer to the stigmata of Christ (cf. German *Wundmal*).

This advanced stage of lexicalization is also documented in occurrences which show phonological attrition. In addition to two instances of *criste mæl* with loss of the genitival -*s* in the first element of the compound,[83] we find nine occurrences of a form *cristelmæl* or *crystelmæl*.[84] Clearly this term also refers to the "sign of the cross," as the description of the sign for the *pistolboc* in the Old English monastic sign list shows:

(25) "Ðære pistol boce tacn ys þæt mon wecge his hand and wyrce crystelmæl on his heafde foran mid his þuman forþon þe mon ræt god spel þær on and eal swa on þære cristes bec"[85]

---

83 Some of these cases of phonological attrition are not easy to find because of (undocumented) emendations by the respective editors. The most recent editor of the *Lacnunga*, for example, provides a new occurrence by giving the text of line 804 as "Weorc Criste[s]mæl of cassuce fifo." In his critical apparatus, he explains the square brackets by "MS. *cristemæl* with the first part of the -*m*- resembling the top part of a low s;" see Edward Pettit, *Anglo-Saxon Remedies, Charms, and Prayers from British Library MS Harley 585: The Lacnunga*, 2 vols. (Lewiston: Mellen, 2001), p. 96 (804).

84 See also the structurally similar attrition and assimilation to nasal [n] in the attested spelling *cristenmælbeam* (s. xii) for *cristelmælbeam*. See *DOE*, s.v. *cristelmæl-bēam*.

85 Banham, *Monasteriales Indicia*, p. 24, no. 10. For an identification of the *pistolboc* as a "full mass lectionary" and not an "epistle lectionary," see Helmut Gneuss, "Liturgical Books in Anglo-Saxon England and their Old English Terminology," *Learning and Literature in Anglo-Saxon England*, ed. Michael

[The sign for the *pistolboc* is that one moves one's hand and makes the sign of the cross on the front of one's head with one's thumb, because one reads the word of God in it, and likewise in the gospels.]

The use of the sign is justified by the causal clause "forþon þe mon ræt god spel þær on," and thus establishes a strong link between the sign of the cross and the gospels, i.e., the book documenting Christ's life, death, and resurrection. The bodily movements described resemble the ritual preparation of the *diacon* who, before reading the gospel of the day, kisses the book and crosses himself. He also traces another sign of the cross in the liturgical book at the verse where the lesson begins.[86] Accordingly, the sign for the deacon in *Monasterialia Indicia* is (26) "Ðonne þu diacon abban wille þonne stric þu ealgelice mid þinum scyte fingre and wyrc cristes mæl on þin heafod foran on þæs halgan godspelles getacnunge"[87] (When you want a deacon, then stroke with your index finger just the same, and make the sign of the cross on the front of your head in indication of the holy gospel). The description again explicitly stresses, in the prepositional phrase *for þæs halgan godspelles getacnunge* "in indication of the holy gospel," why this sign is chosen, but does not use *cristelmæl* but its full form *Cristes mæl*.[88]

Lapidge and Helmut Gneuss (Cambridge: Cambridge University Press, 1985), p. 110; see also Ursula Lenker, *Die westsächsische Evangelienversion und die Perikopenordnungen im angelsächsischen England*, Texte und Untersuchungen zur Englischen Philologie 20 (Munich: Fink, 1997), pp. 128–132, and "The Gospel Lectionary in Anglo-Saxon England: Manuscript Evidence and Liturgical Practice," *ASE* 28 (1999): 158–159.

86 See Josef Jungmann, *Missarum Sollemnia. Eine genetische Erklärung der römischen Messe*, 2 vols., 5th ed. (Freiburg: Herder, 1962), I: 566–567; and Karl Young, *The Drama of the Medieval Church*, 2 vols. (Oxford: Clarendon, 1933; corr. repr. 1962), I: 27–28.

87 Banham, *Monasteriales Indicia*, p. 48, no. 124, and p. 59 (commentary).

88 Interestingly, the Anglo-Saxon monastic sign list also employs the synonymous

In view of these occurrences, it is surprising that the *DOE* lists *cristelmæl*, but not *Cristes mæl* as a separate headword, and that merely a cross-reference "cristes mæl *s.v. crist*" is given at the end of the entry *cristel-mæl*. I would, by contrast, like to support the view of Holthausen and Clark Hall that *cristelmæl* is a (colloquial) variant of *cristes mæl*, showing phonological attrition and assimilation.[89] Accordingly, the form *cristelmæl* should not appear as a headword, but in the section "attested spellings" for the headword *cristes-mæl*. With respect to word formation, *cristelmæl* only at first glance shows similarities to Old English patterns of word formation ending in Old English *-el* or Present Day English *-le* in Germanic languages (such as are attested to in Present Day English *beetle* or *girdle*) or Frisian compounds with *–l*;[90] it is, however, not akin to these coinages because they are basically derived from verbs. *Cristelmæl* is thus not formed on a pattern of the kind {*Crist*}+ {*el* } + {*mæl*}; the element {el} must rather be considered an assimilation of the final genitival *s* to the following nasal. This process of phonological attrition, which is quite common in lexicalized compounds, leads to a loss of transparency of the original compound: the determiner

---

term *rodetacen* in the description of another sign related to the gospels, namely for a homiliary containing the exposition of the gospels for the Night Office: "Gyf þu hwylce oþre boc habban wylle þe godspelles traht on sy þonne lege þu þine swyðran hand under þin hleor. and werc rode tacen on þin heafod foran" (If you want any other book in which there is a gospel text, then lay your right hand under your cheek and make the sign of the cross in front of your head), Banham, *Monasteriales Indicia*, p. 28, no. 31.

89 See n. 79.

90 For the Germanic pattern of word-formation by the suffix *-el/-il/-ol/-ul/-l* (> PDE *-le*), see Hans Sauer, "The Old English Suffix *-el/-il/-ol/-ul/-l* (> PDE *le*; cf. *beetle, girdle, thistle*) as Attested in the Épinal-Erfurt Glossary," *Innovation and Continuity in English Studies. A Critical Jubilee*, ed. Herbert Grabes, Bamberger Beiträge zur Englischen Sprachwissenschaft (Frankfurt: Lang, 2001), pp. 289–313. For *-l* as a *Fugenelement* (empty morph) in compounds in Frisian, see Volkert F. Faltings, "Die Kompositionsbildung mit L-Einschub im Friesischen," *NOWELE* 25 (1995): 3–23.

cristel is no longer fully motivated, i.e., no longer necessarily connected to the proper noun *Crist*, so that language users may even have lost the feeling for the original meaning of the compound ("Christ's mark").

Old English Cristes mæl: *Semantics and Register*
It is especially interesting that the terms *cristes mæl* and *cristelmæl* are—in contrast to *rodetacen*—never used in the context of blessing (cf. meaning B for *rodetacen*), one of the core fields of the "sign of the cross." Neither are they employed in general reference to Christ's suffering on the cross (cf. meaning D for *rodetacen*). *Cristes mæl* and its variants are only used for the (sign of the) cross that can be seen or touched, i.e., for a model or figure of a cross, a crucifix (cf. meaning C for *rodetacen*),[91] or for the sign of the cross as a manual gesture traced on something concrete (cf. meaning A for *rodetacen*). It is thus employed in exactly the contexts where we find the compound—and not the syntactic group—*rodetacen*.

Another prototypical example of *cristes mæl* designating a procession cross—in addition to the passage in the Vercelli Homilies quoted above in (24)—is attested to in the famous passage of the Anglo-Saxons' first encounter with the (sign of the) cross from Bede's *Ecclesiastical History*. Here *sylfrene Cristes mæl* (translating "[veniebant] crucem [pro vexillo] ferentes [argenteam]") denotes the silver cross carried in the impressive procession of Augustine and his companions, (27) "Ac hi nalæs mid deofulcræfte ac mid godcunde mægene gewelgade coman: bæron Cristes rode tacen, sylfrene Cristes mæl mid him & anlicnesse Drihtnes Hælendes on

---

91 Including references to visions or apparitions of the cross, as in "and men gesegon read Cristes mel on heofenum æfter sunnan setlan gange" (and the people saw a red (sign of the) cross in the sky after sunset): Susan Irvine, ed., *The Anglo-Saxon Chronicle. A Collaborative Edition. Volume 7: MS E* (Cambridge: Boydell & Brewer, 2004), for the year 774, p. 39 [MS F: read *Cristes mæl*; MS D: read *Cristes mel*].

brede afægde & awritene"[92] (But they came not endowed with devilcraft, but virtue from heaven: they bore the emblem of Christ's cross, and had a silver crucifix with them and a likeness of the Savior drawn and colored on a panel). As in quotation (24), *cristes mæl* is here again placed as a kind of gloss next to the expression *Cristes rode tacen* and explicitly refers to the actual material object made of silver, a procession cross with the "likeness of our Lord," i.e., a *crucifix* in the narrow sense of the word. The wording of both this passage and in particular the Vercelli Homilies' "þe we Cristes mæl nemnað" indicates that *rodetacen* and *cristes mæl* belong to different registers. The loan translation *rodetacen* seems to be the official term for something which is—as the authors/translators insinuate—in colloquial language also called *cristes mæl*.

This prototypical use of *cristes mæl* designating objects or concepts that can be seen and touched by everyone in colloquial language, is also found in the five occurrences of *cristes mæl* in Old English charter bounds, where it obviously refers to outdoor crosses serving as roadside or boundary crosses: (28) "And syððan ... to þæm Criste mæle. And swa fram þam Cristes mæle of dun weard ondlang anre ealde dic."[93] (And then ... to the sign of the cross. And then from the sign of the cross on downwards along an old trench). This setting of *cristes mæl* in colloquial or at least everyday language may also account for the assimilated form *cristelmæl*. This kind of "sloppy pronunciation" is related to spoken language and we accordingly find the *cristelmæl* form mainly in the kind of sources we might expect, in functional texts such as the Anglo-Saxon monastic sign list (quotation 25) and in particular in Old English charter bounds:

---

92   Miller, *Old English Version of Bede's Ecclesiastical History*, Bk. I, ch. 1, p. 58, lines 23–25.

93   S 201: C.E. 851. Berhtwulf, king of Mercia, to St. Mary's, Worcester; grant of 3 hides (*cassati*) at Grimley, Worcester. Latin with English bounds. [lost original; MSS s. xi[2] and s. xvii (incomplete)]; see also the occurrences listed in the *DOE*, s.v. *cristelmæl*.

(29) Þis sint þa gemæru . . . þær þæt cristel mæl stod of þan up . . . oþ þære ealdan byrig. [94] (There are the bounds . . . there where the sign of the cross stands, from there up . . . to the old town)

(30) . . . þonne on þa ealdan dic on þæt cristelmæl. Of þam cristelmæle . . . [95] (. . . then on the old trench to the sign of the cross. From the sign of the cross . . .)

This view is corroborated by the two occurrences of a term *cristelmælbeam* unfortunately only attested in late charter manuscripts (s. xii; s. xiii) which probably refers to a "tree with a crucifix attached to it."[96]

While about half of the occurrences of *cristes mæl* (twenty-one instances) designate a material object, a kind of crucifix, the other twenty-three attestations refer to the little sign of the cross traced on something concrete, often a part of the human body: (31) "Wid blodrine of nosu, wriht on his forheafod on cristes mel"[97] (Against bleeding from the nose, write on his forehead a sign of the cross). Analogous to *rodetacen*, *cristes mæl* is also used for the sign of the cross written on parchment in the formulas of witness lists and thus employed for the ratification of charters and similar documents:

(32) Ðet wæs first seo kyning Wulfere þe þet feostnode first mid his worde & siððon mid his fingre gewrat on Cristes mel & þus cwæð: Ic Wulfere kyning mid þas kyningas & mid eorles & mid

---

94   S 738: 966. King Edgar to Ælfgifu, his kinswoman; grant of 10 hides (*cassatae*) at Newnham Murren, Oxon. Latin with English bounds. [MSS s. xi and s. xvii].

95   S 684: 960. King Edgar to Eanulf, his faithful *minister*; grant of 9 hides (cassati) at Tywarnhayle in Perranzabuloe and St Agnes, and 2 (*mansae*) at Bosowsa in Ladock, Cornwall. Latin with English bounds. [MSS. s. x med, s. vii].

96   See BTS and *DOE*, s.v. *cristelmæl-bēam*.

97   Chapter heading in Oxford, St. John's College MS 17 + London, British Library, MS Cotton Nero C. vii, folios 80–4: see Ker, p. 435.

heorotogas & mid þægnas þas gewitnesse mines gifes, toforan þone ærcebiscop Deusdedit ic hit festnia mid Cristes mel. And ic Oswi Norþhimbre kyning þeos mynstres freond & þes abbotes Saxulf hit loue mid Cristes mel. And ic Sighere kyning hit tyðe mid Cristes mel. And ic Sibbi kyning hit write mid Cristes mel. And ic Sighere kyning hit tyðe mid Cristes mel. And ic Sibbi kyning hit write mid Cristes mel.[98]

[That was first the king, Wulfere, who confirmed it first with his word, and afterwards wrote with his finger on the cross of Christ, and said thus: "I, Wulfere, king, in the presence of kings, and of earls, and of captains, and of thanes, the witnesses of my gift, before the Archbishop Deusdedit, I confirm it with the cross of Christ." "And I, Oswy, king of the Northumbrians, the friend of this minster, and of this Abbot Saxulf, commend it with the cross of Christ." "And I, Sighere, king, ratify it with the cross of Christ." "And I, Sibbi, king, subscribe it with the cross of Christ."]

In sum, it is evident that *cristes mæl* (and its variant form *cristelmæl*) is only used for a restricted range of the meanings found for *rodetacen*, but precisely for those which could be established as the core meanings of the compound *rodetacen*, i.e., (A) "little sign of the cross" and (C) "crucifix." *Cristes mæl* is, however, only used in a certain group of texts, those that are basically early and which mainly document "colloquial" language to a larger extent than others: "Charm 1" (2 occ.); the Vercelli Homilies (1 occ.); the translation of Bede's *Ecclesiastical History* (7 occ.); confessional and penitential texts (Conf 1.1, Conf 5; 3 occ.); "Rubrics and Directions for the Use of Forms of Service" (Lit 5; 2 occ.); Charters (4 occ.); versions D (1 occ.), E (9 occ.) and F (1 occ.) of the Anglo-Saxon Chronicle; the Leechbook I and II (6 occ.); "Charm 15" (1 occ.); "Charm 16" (1 occ.)' "Charm 19" (3 occ.); and the Old English monastic sign list (1 occ.).[99]

---

98 Irvine, *Anglo-Saxon Chronicle: MS E*, for the year 656, pp. 28–29.
99 For the abbreviations and the editions of the texts, see *DOE* and DOEC.

Ursula Lenker

By contrast, *cristes mæl* is very rarely found in texts of the theological or religious register, and thus, for instance, never attested to in the writings of Ælfric.[100] While *rodetacen* is, for instance, used in the Saints' Lives denoting the healing power of the sign of the cross, *cristes mæl* is employed in a similar function and meaning in texts related to medical practice, chiefly popular cures and liturgical healing formulas (commonly classified as "charms"). The charm "Against Elf-Sickness or Elf-Disease," for instance, uses *cristes mæl* to designate a cross-shaped object (the lichen is taken from a cross) and also the little sign of the cross traced on a body part:

> (33) Nim bisceopwyrt, finul, elehtre, ælfþonan nioþowearde, and gehalgodes Cristes mæles ragu and stor, do ælcre handfulle . . . And writ him Cristes mæl on ælcum lime . . . Awæsc siþþan, do to drence, and bisceopwyrt and Cristes mæles ragu, awyl þriwa on meolcum.[101]

> [Take bishop's wort, fennel, lupine, the lower part of enchanter's nightshade, and lichen from a hallowed cross/crucifix, and incense, take a handful each . . . And inscribe the sign of the cross on each limb . . . Wash it afterwards, make it a drink, together with bishop's wort and lichen from a crucifix, boil them three times in several kinds of milk.]

This distribution of occurrences as well as the wording of the attestations, above, suggests that *cristes mæl* was a very common term in Old English, but was probably more often used in everyday language than in written texts.[102]

---

100   Neither does Ælfric use *mæl* as an expression for "sign; mark," a concept which he generally expresses by *tacen* (106 occurrences in the *Catholic Homilies*) or, occasionally, *beacn*, as in *fore-beacn* "portent" or *sigebeacn* "emblem of victory," s.v in Godden I.
101   Godefrid Storms, ed., *Anglo-Saxon Magic* (The Hague: Nijhoff, 1948), p. 222, lines 1–2, 10 and 29–30.
102   This view is also corroborated by attestations from the early Middle

Old English (?) cruc

Even more restricted in its meaning and textual distribution is Old English *cruc*—a loan based on Latin *crux, crucis*—which is specifically used to denote the "sign of the cross" in texts documenting popular and liturgical healing practices. *Cruc* can without doubt be established as a synonym of *cristes mæl* by an attestation in the second book of Bald's Leechbook, which singles out two of the "signs of the cross" called *cristes mæl* and refers to them as *cruc*.

(34) and he [se petraoleum] is god gif hwam seo spræc opfylð, nime þonne & wyrce cristes mæl under his tungan & his an lytel swelge. Gif mon eac of his gewitte weorðe þonne nime he his dæl & wyrce cristes mæl on ælcre lime, butan cruc on þam heafde foran, se sceal on balzame beon & oþer on þam heafde ufan.[103]

[and it [petroleum] is good if the speech of someone fails, then he shall take it and make the sign of the cross under his tongue, and swallow a little of it. Also if a man loses his mind, then he shall take part of it and make the sign of the cross on every limb, except the sign of the cross on the forehead, that shall be in balsam, and [also] the other one on the top of his head.]

Loans coined on Latin *crux, crucis* were borrowed as the common term for "cross" in the other Germanic languages. In Old English, which commonly renders this term by *rod*, we only find seven instances of *cruc*. It has been rightly pointed out by Käsmann in his study on the Middle English religious vocabulary,[104] however, that it is

---

English period: the *MED*, s.v. *mēl* (n. 2) lists the meaning "4. A written figure of the cross (entered in a document to validate a solemn declaration); on (mid) Cristes ~" (two occurrences from the Peterborough Chronicle for 1121) and is used as a place name element (5).

103 Oswald Cockayne, ed., *Leechdoms, Wortcunning and Starcraft of Early England*, Rolls Series 35, 3 vols. (London: Longman, 1864–1866), II: 88–89.

104 Hans Käsmann, *Studien zum kirchlichen Wortschatz im Mittelenglischen. Ein Beitrag zum Problem der Sprachmischung* (Tübingen: Niemeyer, 1961), p. 113.

remarkable that *cruc* has survived into Present Day English in *crouch* and *crouchmas*,[105] in particular since Middle English soon adopted another word modeled on Latin *crux*, the French term *crois*.[106] This indicates that the rarely attested form Old English *cruc* was much stronger than today's evidence seems to suggest.[107]

Two of the seven occurrences of *cruc*, which are analyzed in detail by Bremmer in this volume, are of an idiosyncratic and somewhat accidental character. Once *cruc* refers to the material object and is used as a synonym for *rod*,[108] the other from the translation of Bede—also unique in its meaning—is more difficult to interpret but most probably refers to the shape of the cross, in which the bishop prostrates himself, i.e., the sign of the cross made on the ground.[109]

The other five attestations are taken from texts relating chiefly

---

105   Cf. *OED*, s.v. "crouch" and *MED*, s.v. *crouche*. The form *cros* appeared—probably at an earlier date—in the north and east of England from the Norse *kross* (adopted from Old Irish *cros* and ultimately Latin *crux*; see *OED*, s.v. "cross;" *MED*, s.v. *cros*). In Old English, this is only known in topological nomenclature, mainly northern place-names such as "Crosby," "Crosthwaite." The *OED* also mentions that Wace (ca. 1175) cites *Olicrosse* (apparently referring to the Holy Rood of Waltham) as the battle-cry of Harold at Hastings.

106   See *MED*, s.v. *crois*. The *OED* does not list the form in a separate entry, but generally states "English has had several types of this word, derived by different channels from L[atin] *cruc-em*" (s.v. *cross*).

107   For a fuller discussion of *cruc*, see Bremmer, "Old English 'Cross' Words" in this volume, above, pp. 208–215, and *DOE*, s.v. *cruc*. *DOE* only considers four occurrences as native, and regards the three attestations of the accusative form *crucem* in "Charm 19" (Storms's no. 17) as "Latin forms in Old English context."

108   "and stod þær an medmycel rod on ðære eorðan on ðam norðeasthyrnan . . . & se preost mæssode be cruce. Ða geseah he ofer þa rode ane hand swylce heo bletsode" (and there stood a moderate-sized cross on the ground in the north-east corner . . . And the priest was saying mass near the cross. And then he saw above the cross a hand as though it were blessing): Arthur S. Napier, ed., "An Old English Vision of Leofric, Earl of Mercia", *Transactions of the Philological Society* 1907–1910 (London, 1909), 184–86.

109   See *DOE*, s.v. *cruc* b. and Bremmer, "Old English 'Cross' Words," above, pp. 208–215.

to popular medical practice, namely from the Charms and the Leechbook. Four of them are found in "Charm 17" preserved in the third part of the Leechbook ("Against Elf-Sickness or Elf-Disease").[110] These clearly refer to either the little sign of the cross employed as a performative act and written/traced in a certain way (cf. the verb *writan*) or—like (34) from the second book of Bald's Leechbook—to a little cross traced on body parts functioning as an exorcism:

(35) Writ III crucem mid oleum infirmorum, and cweð: . . . Nim þonne þæt gewrit, *writ* crucem ofer þam drince, and sing þis . . . Wæt þæt gewrit on þam drence and writ crucem mid him on ælcum lime and cweð: Signum crucis Christi conserva te in vitam eternam. Amen.[111]

[Write three signs of the cross with oil of the extreme unction and say . . . Then take the writing, trace the sign of the cross over the drink and sing over it . . . Wet the writing in the drink and write a sign of the cross with it on each limb and say: The sign of Christ's cross preserve thee in eternal life. Amen.]

These attestations of the loan *cruc* in specific performative contexts suggest that the reason why *cruc* (probably pronounced /kru:tʃ/)[112] was borrowed, probably lies in the fact that it commonly carried a very special force due to its foreign or even "learned" character as a loan. It may have been used on purpose, because it gave the charm or recipe a special power similar to other Latin or foreign formulas used in this text type.[113] This would also account for the fact that the

---

110   See Storms, *Anglo-Saxon Magic*, pp. 17–232.
111   Storms, *Anglo-Saxon Magic*, p. 226, lines 80–81, 82–83, 88–91.
112   The Present Day English form *crouch*/krautʃ/ suggests a pronunciation /kru: tʃ/ in Old English. In the *OED*, the palatalization of the final *c* /tʃ/ is explained by the "probability . . . that it is a late learned adaptation of L. *cruci-*, as pronounced by Italians or other Romanic people, just like Italian *croce*" (see *OED*, s.v. "crouch").
113   See, for instance, the end of the exorcism in "Sing ðis gebed on ða blacan blegene IX <syðan>, ærest 'pater noster', Tigað tigað tigað calicet aclu cluel

word has proved to be rather strong in spite of the small number of Old English attestations. It may have carried a special force, as it was accompanied by manual and other gestures in special circumstances—usually highly emotional situations, such as cases of emergency, not necessarily documented in our extant written sources.

Quotation (35) also demonstrates that we have to take into account that the inflected forms of Latin *crux, crucis*—pronounced in its Romance way with a /tʃ/—were much more frequently heard in Anglo-Saxon times than our Old English sources document. It is a word used very frequently, not only in all kinds of Latin religious and liturgical texts but also in prayers and charms. In (35), the gesture of tracing the sign of the cross is accompanied by reciting the Latin formula "Signum crucis Christi conserva te in vitam eternam. Amen" (The sign of Christ's cross may safeguard you in the eternal life. Amen). A similar context showing how the Latin term may have entered the Old English language is seen in an Old English "Cross Charm:" (36) "And wyrc swyþe gelome Cristes rode tacen on ðinum heafde and cweð þis gelome: Ecce crucem domini, and cweþ ðis þonne: Hoc signaculo sancte crucis"[114] (And trace the sign of the cross over

---

sedes adclocles acre earcre arnem nonabiuð ær ærnem niðren arcum cunað arcum arctua fligara uflen binchi cutern nicuparam raf afð egal uflen arta arta arta trauncula trauncula, querite et inuenietis, adiuro te per patrem et filium et spiritum sanctum non amplius crescas sed arescas, super aspidem et basilliscum ambulabis et conculcabis leonem et draconem, crux matheus, crux marcus, crux lucas, crux iohannes;" "Sing this prayer upon the black blains nine times; Firstly, Paternoster; "Tigað tigað tigað calicet aclu cluel sedes adclocles acre earcre arnem nonabiuð ær ærnem niðren arcum cunað arcum arctua fligara uflen binchi cutern nicuparam raf afð egal uflen arta arta arta trauncula trauncula [no meaning can be attached to most of these words; Fn. 1]. Seek and ye shall find. I adjure thee by Father, Son and Holy Ghost that thou grow no greater but that thou dry up. Upon the asp and basilisk shalt thou tread and upon the lion and the dragon shalt thou trample. Cross Matthew, cross Mark, cross Luke, cross John." *Anglo-Saxon Magic and Medicine*, ed. John Gratton and Charles Singer, Publications of the Wellcome Historical Medical Museum n.s. 3 (London: Oxford University Press, 1952), ch. 25, pp. 106–7.

114 Julius Zupitza, ed., "Kreuzzauber," *Archiv* 88 (1892): 364–365, line 26.

and over again on your head and say this over and over again: Ecce crucem domini, and then say this: Hoc signaculo sancte crucis).

SIGNIFYING CHRIST—OLD ENGLISH TERMS FOR THE SIGN OF THE CROSS: CONCLUSIONS

For the most important emblem and ensign of Christianity—the sign of the cross, the sign of Christ—Old English employs three different terms, two of which are genitive compounds with a determinant meaning "sign." *Rodetacen* is the most general term and is used for all shades of meaning of this concept in all kinds of religious and secular texts. The syntactic group *(þære) (halgan) rode tacen* "sign of the holy cross" is mainly employed in general reference to Christ (and salvation) and, for reasons of explicitness, in the context of "blessing," i.e., in collocations with the verbs *segnian* and *bletsian* which do not make explicit—in a Christian context—that the act of blessing must encompass the sign of the cross. The lexicalized compound *þæt rodetacen* (and its variant *Cristes rodetacen*), on the other hand, explicitly designates a crucifix or the oldest variant of the sign of the cross, the little sign of the cross traced on a part of the body or on parchment or the like. *Cristes mæl* "Christ's mark > sign of the cross" (and its variant *crystelmæl* with phonological attrition) is exclusively used for these two core meanings of the compound *rodetacen*, and is further restricted to colloquial (and early) texts. While these terms are fully established in the Old English lexicon, the loan *cruc*, which was borrowed in the other Germanic languages as the central term for "cross," is mainly used in very specific medical contexts for the sign of the cross traced on parts of the body and has, at least in Old English, never lost its "foreign character."[115]

---

115 I would like to thank Helmut Gneuss, Lucia Kornexl, Rolf Bremmer, the anonymous readers and, in particular, Sarah Larratt Keefer for their most helpful comments on an earlier version of this paper.

III

The Cross: Gesture and Structure

The Staff of Life: Cross and Blessings in Anglo-Saxon Cereal Production

Debby Banham

Non... in ludis et equorum cursibus, et epulis majoribus; sed magis, cum timore et tremore, signo passionis Christi nostræque æternæ redemptionis, et reliquis sanctorum Ejus coram portatis.

[Not... in games and horse-races, and great feasts, but rather, with fear and trembling, with the sign of Christ's passion and our eternal redemption, and the relics of his saints, carried in front.]

BY THE END OF THE ANGLO-SAXON PERIOD, no aspect of life in England can have been free from Christian influence. This paper will explore one of the most fundamental aspects of Anglo-Saxon life, the feeding of the people, and the role in it of Christian ideas and ritual, and especially of the cross. Most studies of the cross in Anglo-Saxon England are well grounded in known manifestations of that symbol, whether in literature or the visual arts, and offer to explain, analyze, or interpret those manifestations. By contrast, the intention here is to do something that might be considered foolhardy: to look for crosses where hitherto they have rarely been identified, in the production of food in Anglo-Saxon England.

Debby Banham

My conclusions will be fairly tentative because, apart from the few examples of such rituals which formed part of the "orthodox" liturgy (for instance at Rogationtide), it is impossible to establish beyond doubt what role the cross did play, since the less orthodox the practice, the less likely it is to have been recorded.[1] What seems to me beyond doubt is that some kind of ritual must have accompanied practically every stage of the vital and fundamental process of food production, even where no evidence survives for us to study. This was the case in later medieval England, as indeed it is and was in every traditional society whose practices are recorded.[2] Only with the industrialization of agriculture, starting in western Europe in the eighteenth century, did customs such as harvest homes and Plow Monday begin to disappear, as farmers transferred their trust from the supernatural to "science" to ensure the success of their labors. Customs relating to food-production must therefore have played a vital part in the lives of most Anglo-Saxons. The fact that there is so little evidence for them should not lead us, living in a culture where both ritual and food production can easily be ignored, to suppose that the same was true in Anglo-Saxon England, with its predominantly subsistence economy and its implicit faith in supernatural explanations of the workings of the universe.

We can be confident then that some such rituals did exist in Anglo-Saxon England, but, for reasons already mentioned, little is recorded of them in writing. This may suggest that some of the practices in use were not of a type to recommend themselves to the literate classes, or perhaps to the ecclesiastical establishment. If this was the case, the part played by the cross, or indeed by orthodox blessings in general,

---

1 See Ursula Lenker's "Signifying Christ in Anglo-Saxon England: Old English Terms for the Sign of the Cross" in this volume, pp. 233–275 above, for the complexities of concept "cross" (and "blessing") in Old English.
2 For a comprehensive discussion of the rituals of the farming year in later medieval and early modern England, see Ronald Hutton, *Stations of the Sun* (Oxford: Oxford University Press, 1996), passim.

might be supposed to have been relatively limited. However, as I shall show, at various points in the agricultural cycle, there were significant interventions by the Church. These are the most fully attested and understood of Anglo-Saxon farming rituals, and it is generally in these that the cross plays the most prominent part. What is much more difficult to establish is what other, less "official" rituals were also in use, and what part the cross, and indeed orthodox religion in general, played in these. The evidence, then, typically for the early Middle Ages, is both deficient and unevenly weighted. It should also be pointed out that nearly all the evidence discussed below is late, some of it not even certainly pre-Conquest. Thus we are looking mainly at a period when all aspects of life were conditioned by generations of Christianity (even if not all its manifestations were of the most impeccable orthodoxy), when the rituals of even the least educated classes must have changed considerably since, say, the days of Bede, let alone the settlement period. We must therefore beware of generalizing about "Anglo-Saxon England" as though it were a homogeneous and static whole, especially since farming too had changed a great deal, at least in some parts of the country.[3] Nonetheless, it is worth drawing together the evidence, however fragmentary, exiguous, or unsatisfactory. This will enable us at least to try to establish the relative importance of orthodox and more informal religious practices in what does survive (not

---

3 The most important changes, taking a very general view, were the reorganization of arable land into open fields, the displacement of barley by wheat as the main bread-corn, and possibly an increase in the numbers of sheep kept, driven by a growing trade in wool and cloth. For the open fields, see Tom Williamson, *Shaping Medieval Landscapes: Settlement, Society, Environment* (Macclesfield: Windgather Press, 2003), especially ch. 1, "Debating the Open Fields"; for changing cereal preferences, see also Banham, *Food and Drink in Anglo-Saxon England* (Stroud: Tempus Publishing, 2004), pp. 13–15, and for livestock, Sebastian Payne, "Animal husbandry," *The Blackwell Encyclopaedia of Anglo-Saxon England*, ed. Michael Lapidge et al. (Oxford: Blackwell, 1999), pp. 38–39). All these issues will be discussed in my study (with Rosamond Faith), *Anglo-Saxon Farms and Farming* (forthcoming Oxford University Press).

to mention the possible survival of pre-Christian ideas or practices). More to the point for our purposes in this collection, we may then be in a better position to assess the importance of the cross itself in rituals associated with food production, even if the picture we finish up with is patchy, and in places frustratingly out of focus.[4]

Despite the paucity of the evidence, food production is a broad field, encompassing the majority of economic activity in Anglo-Saxon England, and I have therefore confined my researches for this paper to its most basic manifestation, the staff of life, taking the production of cereals from plowing through sowing, harvesting, milling, and baking to the loaf on the table.[5] Like the Anglo-Saxon farmer, who had no choice, I propose to start at the beginning, with plowing. It is characteristic of the very limited representation of such down-to-earth tasks in Anglo-Saxon sources that there is no record of what rituals, if any, surrounded this basic procedure in the normal course of events. The Plowman in Ælfric's *Colloquy*, for instance, merely says that he leads out his oxen, fixes the metal parts to the plow, and is expected to plow a whole acre in a day. He mentions that it is hard work, but not that any rituals go with it.[6] Nor do the two main estate management texts, the *Rectitudines singularum personarum* and *Be gesceadwisan gerefan*, tell us of any customs that might accompany or precede what is clearly for their compilers one of the major winter tasks.[7] However, the long and complex "charm" known as *Æcerbot*

---

4 A more general discussion of the relationship between informal and "official" religion is that of Karen Louise Jolly in her *Popular Religion in Late Anglo-Saxon England: Elf Charms in Context* (Chapel Hill: University of North Carolina Press, 1996), especially pp. 18–27, where she moves the paradigm away from "pagan survivals" to the contemporary meanings and uses of the practices concerned.

5 I hope to investigate rituals associated with livestock farming at a later date.

6 G. N. Garmonsway, ed., *Ælfric's Colloquy* (Exeter: University of Exeter Press, 1991), pp. 20–21.

7 F. Liebermann, *Die Gesetze der Angelsachsen*, 3 vols. (Halle: Niermeyer, 1903), I. 444–53 and 453–55, respectively. It has been argued that these texts owe more

("field remedy"), intended to ward off supernatural interference with the fertility of farmland, does concern itself quite clearly with the initial breaking of the ground.[8] The instructions for the final part of the ritual read:

> Nim þonne ælces cynnes melo and abacæ man innewerdre handa bradnæ half and gecned hine mid meolce and mid haligwætere and lecge under þa forman furh.
>
> [Then take every kind of flour, and a loaf is to be baked the width of the inside of a hand and kneaded with milk and with holy water and laid under the first furrow.][9]

This makes quite explicit the connection between plowing and its eventual end product, and thus the cyclical nature of the agricultural process. Presumably the "sacrifice" of this one loaf is intended to ensure that many more will eventually be produced, and the inclusion of all types of cereal crop is to make sure the effects will not be restricted to particular grains. The verse accompanying this part of the ritual looks forward to a "Ful æcre fodres . . . growende gife, þæt us corna gehwylc cume to nytte" (field full of food . . . a growing gift so that every kind of corn may come to our need).[10]

---

to a literary tradition than to Anglo-Saxon farming practice, and they would certainly be inadequate as agricultural instruction manuals, but that is not their purpose; nor is such a manual likely to have been needed in the eleventh century. For a recent summary of the debate, with bibliography and some interesting new suggestions, see Mark Gardiner, "Implements and Utensils in *Gerefa* and the Organization of Seigneurial Farmsteads in the High Middle Ages," and John Hines, "*Gerefa* §§15 and 17: a Grammatical Analysis of the Lists of Nouns," in *Medieval Archaeology* 50 (2006): 260–67 and 268–70, respectively.
8   ASPR 6, pp. 116–18. My translation of the complete text is given as an appendix to this paper.
9   ASPR 6, p. 118, lines 72–74.
10 ASPR 6, p. 118, lines 75 and 79–80.

Æcerbot may not in fact be originally all one text (there is at least a possibility that only the second half concerns arable land, the first part dealing with pasture), but taken as a whole, the charm makes extensive use of the cross and cross symbolism.[11] The first set of instructions begins "Genim þonne on niht, ær hit dagige, feower tyrf on feower healfa þæs landes, and gemearca hu hy ær stodon" (then at night, before it gets light, take four turfs from four parts of the land, and mark [or notice] where they came from).[12] These *feower healfa* may be the four corners of the field, or the four cardinal points, and may therefore form a cross. After a ritual over the places the turfs were taken from, the instructions continue:

> And bera siþþan ða turf to circean, and mæssepreost asinge feower mæssan ofer þan turfon, and wende man þæt grene to ðan weofode, and siþþan gebringe man þa turf þær hi ær wæron ær sunnan setlgange.
>
> [And then take the turfs to church, and let a priest sing four masses over the turfs, and let the green be turned to the altar, and then let the turfs be brought where they were before, before sunset.][13]

In this context, the significance of the number four is much more likely to relate to the cross than, say, the four elements or humors, concepts unlikely to have been familiar to people concerned with the cultivation of the land.[14] They may have been familiar with the

---

11 As far as I have been able to establish, the first to suggest that there were two charms was A. R. Skemp, in a review of Grendon's *Anglo-Saxon Charms* in *Modern Language Review* 6 (1911): 262–66. He would divide the text immediately after the first passage of verse, whereas I think it more likely that the instructions following belong with this verse, and the part concerned with arable land begins with "Ðonne þæt eall sie gedon" (which certainly looks like a linking phrase) on line 45 in Dobbie's edition.
12 ASPR 6, p. 116, lines 3–5.
13 ASPR 6, p. 116, lines 14–17.
14 For a thorough analysis of the Christian symbolism of the "fours" in this

four seasons, but even that idea may not have penetrated the whole of English society by the first half of the eleventh century when this text was written down.[15] Bede says that the Anglo-Saxons "originally used to divide the whole year into two seasons, namely winter and summer," *Principaliter totum annum in duo tempora, hiemis videlicet et aestatis, dispertiebant*, and such old conceptions may have persisted far longer among the farming population than in the learned circles that he inhabited, and that we mainly read about.[16]

Whatever all these fours mean, however, the next stage of the procedure brings in the cross much more explicitly: before the four turfs are replaced in their holes,

> ... hæbbe him gæworht of cwicbeame feower Cristes mælo and awrite on ælcon ende: Matheus and Marcus, Lucas and Iohannes. Lege þæt Cristes mæl on þone pyt neoþeweardne cweðe ðone: Crux Matheus, crux Marcus, crux Lucas, crux sanctus Iohannes.[17]
>
> [... have four crosses made for them out of quickbeam, and write on each end, Matthew and Mark, Luke and John. Lay the cross in the bottom of the hole, then say: Crux Matheus, crux Marcus, crux Lucas, crux sanctus Iohannes.]

After the recitation of a fairly orthodox Christian verse (by the standard of charms, at least), the celebrant is enjoined to "dedicate

---

charm, see Thomas D. Hill, "The Æcerbot Charm and its Christian User," *ASE* 6 (1977): 213–21 at 215–18.

15 The manuscript, London, British Library MS Cotton Caligula A. vii (the Heliand manuscript), is dated by Helmut Gneuss (Gneuss, p. 61) to s. x^2, but the charm is regarded as an addition of s. xi^1.

16 Bede, *De temporum ratione*, ch. 15, *Bedae opera didascalica*, ed. C. W. Jones, CCSL 123B (Turnhout: Brepols, 1977), II. 330–31. Linguistic support for his statement is provided by Earl R. Anderson, "The Seasons of the Year in Old English," *ASE* 26 (1997): 231–63.

17 ASPR 6, pp. 116–17, lines 17–21. *Cwicbeam* may be hawthorn or a *Sorbus* species, but possibly just living wood (or perhaps in this context, the living tree).

it to the praise and glory and grace of Christ and Saint Mary and the holy cross," *bebeod hit Criste and sancta Marian and þære halgan rode to lofe and to weorþinga and to are.*[18] In this first part of *Æcerbot*, then, the cross explicitly plays a major role, whether as physical object, or as a symbol invoked either orally or visually. However, it seems to me more likely that this part, with its turfs, relates not to plowing or arable land but to pasture or meadowland, and it may therefore not belong in the arable food production sequence that is the concern of this paper.

The second half of *Æcerbot*, which does unquestionably deal with plowing, is where all the most unorthodox, even "heathen" elements of the text are to be found: the references to earth as "mother" and the repeated but otherwise unknown word *erce*, which has often been read as an epithet of "mother earth."[19] Here also are most of the references to the supernatural practices and practitioners that might have made the counter-measures described in the charm necessary. But the central appeal even here is to "ece dryhten / and his halige" (the eternal lord and his saints),[20] without question the Christian God, so this half of the text cannot be said to be "pagan," either. The framework of its ideas is Christian, and it no doubt belongs to a social context where "many phenomena . . . which historians now recognize as 'pagan survivals' were simply taken for granted as part of the fabric of existence and of a common inherited culture."[21]

What is missing from this latter half of the charm, however, is any explicit reference to the cross. It does seem to me that the character of the two halves is rather different, and the reason for this may be that the second half is derived from more generalized plowing rituals, perhaps performed every year, in a prophylactic

---

18 ASPR 6, p. 117, lines 42–44.
19 ASPR 6, p. 117, line 51.
20 ASPR 6, p. 118, lines 59–60.
21 Hutton, *Stations*, p. 418, referring to the work of R. A. Markus on the Christianization of the Roman Empire.

rather than remedial capacity.²² If that is the case, then such rituals certainly seem to place more emphasis on "mother earth" than on the cross. This would lend support to the idea that agricultural rituals owe rather little to "official" religion, and may indeed have been performed continuously, if not unchanged, since before the conversion. It is not clear, however, whether the somewhat different registers of the two parts, in terms of supernatural content and attitudes, are related to the different aspects of farming concerned. In terms of the practical operations involved, there is no obvious reason why livestock raising should be more orthodox in this respect than arable farming, especially in an economy where the same farmers normally practiced both. Cattle were however the main form of movable wealth in Anglo-Saxon England, and therefore of considerable interest to the upper levels of society, which seem to have concerned themselves very little with cereal production.²³ It may be that the compiler, looking for an arable ritual to go with a pastoral one, could only find one that did not quite match. It is possible that the first part belongs to a management regime closely controlled by the social and economic elite, while the second may have been used by peasant farmers left largely to their own devices

---

22 John D. Niles takes the view that *Æcerbot* itself was performed regularly every year, and associates it with the later customs of Plow Monday (the Monday following the first Sunday after Epiphany), but the text itself does not demand such an interpretation (see Niles, "The Æcerbot Ritual in Context" in his *Old English Literature in Context: Ten Essays* [Cambridge: D. S. Brewer, 1980], pp. 44–56, esp. 45–49).

23 Nearly all the provisions of Anglo-Saxon law dealing with theft, for instance, are concerned primarily with livestock, according to the late Patrick Wormald (personal communication). The Old English word *feoh* is also indicative, meaning as it does either "wealth" or "cattle," or in many cases no doubt both, as does *ceap* in the homilies quoted below. For lack of interest in arable farming on the part of the Anglo-Saxon elite, see also my forthcoming paper, "Race and Tillage: Scandinavian Influence on Anglo-Saxon Agriculture?" *Anglo-Saxon England and the North: Proceedings of the 2003 Conference of the International Society of Anglo-Saxonists*, ed. Matti Kilpiö et al. (Tempe: ACMRS, forthcoming).

by their superiors, even though such a distinction cannot be demonstrated from the texts.

Returning to what the texts do tell us, the *Rectitudines singularum personarum* says that "on sumre ðeode gebyreð ... gytfeorm for yrðe" (among some people is owed ... a pouring [i.e., of drink, presumably] feast for plowing).[24] Presumably this took place on completion of the plowing, or main plowing, whereas the *æcerbot*-type ritual, if it was in fact in more general use, would belong to the beginning rather than the ending of the task. What took place at this "drinking-feast," apart from the obvious elements, and whether any other ritual may have preceded it, for instance before the plow-team left the field, we will probably never know, let alone whether references to the cross may have been involved. This feast may in fact have been a fairly straightforward party, with little in the way of supernatural or religious content. There is no evidence, either, of ceremonies, other than the *Æcerbot* ritual, involving the plow itself: nothing, for instance, analogous to the later Plow Sunday and Monday, marking the return to work after the midwinter holiday with blessings and processions.[25]

The next stage in arable operations, after the ground has been broken, is to sow the seed. This part of the process is less prominent in our sources than plowing, but there are some indications that this was because it was seen as closely connected with that procedure: *Æcerbot* B, if I may so term it, certainly involves seed as well as the plow:

> Nime man uncuþ sæd at ælmesmannum and selle him twa swylc, swylce man æt him nime, and gegaderie ealle his sulhgeteogo togædere; borige þonne on þam beame stor and finol and gehalgode sapan and gehalgod sealt. Nim þonne þæt sæd, sete on þæs sules bodig

---

24 *Rectitudines* 21.4, Liebermann, *Die Gesetze*, I: 452.
25 For some early modern customs at this season, see Ronald Hutton, *The Rise and Fall of Merry England* (Oxford: Oxford University Press, 1994), pp. 16–17.

> [Unknown seed is to be taken from beggars, and they are to be given twice as much as is taken from them, and all the plowing gear is to be gathered together; then bore into the beam incense and fennel and blessed soap and blessed salt. Then take the seed, place it on the body of the plow.]

This is done before the first furrow is driven.[26] Presumably the seed is not "unknown" in the sense that people are uncertain what species it belongs to, but instead that they do not know where it comes from. David Hill has suggested that this is a rational procedure, in that seed brought in from outside is likely to produce a better crop than if it had been saved from the same land.[27] However, that would still be the case if it were swapped with a neighbor or relation; what matters more in this context, I suspect, is that this seed effectively "comes from nowhere," having been supplied by chance, if not some more personal supernatural force, rather than by those enacting the ritual.

There is also no doubt about the sexual symbolism in this part of *Æcerbot*: the plow pushing into the soil and the placing of seed in the furrow literally inseminate the earth, addressed explicitly as "mother," linking the fertility of the soil with animal fecundity.[28] The requirements of this symbolism may be the main reason for associating plowing and sowing so closely in the text. In real life the connection may not have been quite so close. However, once the soil has been cleared by the plow, in the absence of chemical herbicides it does save work to get the crop growing as soon as possible, rather than leave the ground bare and have to keep it weed-free. This is also the situation, for what it is worth, presented by the two eleventh-century

---

26 ASPR 6, p. 117, lines 46–50.
27 Personal communication, but see also his "Sulh: the Anglo-Saxon Plough c. 1000 A.D.," *Landscape History* 22 (2000): 5–19, and "Eleventh Century Labours of the Months in Prose and Pictures," *Landscape History* 20 (1999): 29–40.
28 ASPR 6, pp. 117–18, lines 50–51 and 67–68.

English "labors of the months" cycles of illustrations: the plow is shown being followed very closely by a man broadcasting seed.[29] Once again this picture may owe more to artistic exigencies or models than to the actual organization of Anglo-Saxon agriculture, and it is admittedly a problem that the calendars show these tasks for January, when it would be risky in the extreme to sow even hardy cereals in England.[30] However, given that we have no clear evidence that sowing did *not* follow closely upon plowing, it might be unwise to dismiss out of hand what evidence we do have on this matter.

The only ritual specific to sowing recorded in Anglo-Saxon sources is this *Benedictio seminis*, "Blessing of Seed," from the earliest of the "Claudius Pontificals" (?Worcester or York, s. x/xi) and the *Missal of Robert of Jumièges* (Christ Church, Canterbury, s. xi¹):

> Omnipotens sempiterne deus creator generis humani. suppliciter tuam celementiam exoramus. ut hoc semen quod in tuo nomine serimus in agros nostros. celesti tua benedictione benedicere et multiplicare digneris. atque ad maturitatem perducas. ut per uniuersum orbem terrarum conlaudentur dextera tua. per dominum.
>
> [Almighty everlasting God, on bended knee we beg your clemency, that you may deign to bless with your heavenly blessing this seed which in your name we sow in our fields, and bring it to ripeness,

---

29 London, British Library MSS Cotton Julius A. vi and Tiberius B. v, folios 3r–8v in both manuscripts: *An Eleventh-Century Anglo-Saxon Illustrated Miscellany: British Library Cotton Tiberius B. v, Part 1* (ed. Patrick McGurk et al., EEMF 21 [Copenhagen: Rosenkilde and Bagger, 1983]) also reproduces the equivalent illustrations from Julius A. vi, with discussion by McGurk, "The Labors of the Months," at pp. 40–43. The two series are extremely closely related.

30 The English climate was similar in the late Anglo-Saxon period to that of the later twentieth and early twenty-first centuries. See Petra Dark, *The Environment of Britain in the First Millennium AD* (London: Duckworth, 2000), pp. 19–28, for an examination of the evidence; for some new data, see S. K. Solanki et al., "Unusual Activity of the Sun during Recent Decades Compared to the Previous 11,000 Years," *Nature* 431 (2004): 1084–87.

The Staff of Life

so that throughout the world your right hand may be praised. Through the Lord.][31]

The wording does not allow us to decide whether the blessing was used in the field as the seed was being sown, or the seed was brought to church to be blessed before sowing started. Practice may have varied in different localities. However, it is not at all clear how commonly such "quasi-liturgical" blessings were used at all.[32] Most of them only appear in one or two English books, nor are they particularly common on the continent. One might speculate that blessings like this would be used in contexts where the production of food was under the control of people with strong religious interests, as might be expected at monastic home farms or granges, rather than by the average Anglo-Saxon peasant farmer, or even on the estates of secular landlords. We can at least say that where it was used, although the text does not mention the cross explicitly, the person making the blessing is likely to have made the sign of the cross over the seed.

Once the seed is in the ground, the main thing is to leave it to grow, but some tasks were necessary between sowing and harvest to encourage a large and successful crop. It is probable that the seed was harrowed in after sowing (at least in the later period), and

---

31 Text from *The Claudius Pontificals*, ed. D. H. Turner, HBS 97 (Chichester: Moore and Tillyer, 1971), p. 72; my translation. Also found in *The Missal of Robert of Jumièges*, ed. H. A. Wilson, HBS 11 (London: Harrison and Sons, 1896), p. 282. I have not to date found this blessing in any other English liturgical book, and I am not aware of any studies of its sources. See n. 32, below.

32 These "blessings of things" have received very little attention from liturgists, no doubt because it is not clear if they were in fact in liturgical use (or, if so, how widely). It appears that they are in general of continental origin, and may go out of use in England during the eleventh century (Sarah Larratt Keefer, pers. comm.). I am extremely grateful to Professor Keefer for helping me to find them. There is a brief discussion in *The Leofric Missal*, ed. Nicholas Orchard, 2 vols., HBS 113–14 (London: Boydell, 2002), I: 89–94.

cereals were probably weeded one or more times, depending on the weather and consequent weed growth, and on available labor. If any ceremonies were attached to these jobs, however, we know nothing of them. Harrowing will have followed very quickly on sowing, to stop the seed being eaten by birds, so if plowing and sowing were covered by the same rituals, harrowing may have been included too. Weeding is unlikely to have been regarded as an important task; it was traditionally carried out by women and children on a piecemeal basis, when time could be spared from other work. It is one of those tasks that is never conclusively finished, and thus would not provide an obvious single occasion for celebration. The Venerable Bede says that the Old English name for August was *weodmonath*, so that may have been the main weeding season in his time.[33] However, later evidence suggests that August was the major harvest period,[34] so weeding, in the arable fields at least, may have been more or less over by that time of year in the tenth or eleventh century. Another job for children, almost certainly, was bird-scaring, to protect the sown seed and later the ripening crop.[35] This was even more of a never-ending task than weeding, and its completion could only finally be celebrated with the harvest.

While the crops were still growing, however, one event took place which the authorities certainly thought should involve the cross. This is also one of the few such rituals that we can trace back before the late Anglo-Saxon period: the Rogationtide perambulation of the fields and blessing of the crops.[36] This is the subject of a chapter in the *acta* of the

---

33 *De temporum ratione*, ch. 15 in Jones, *Bedae opera*, II: 330, with interpretation at 331–32: "Weodmonath mensis zizaniorum quod ea tunc maxime abundant" (Weodmonath, month of weeds, because they are most abundant then).

34 For instance, the Latin versions of the *Rectitudines* and *Gerefa* in the *Quadripartitus* (Liebermann, *Die Gesetze*, I: 450–51) consistently give *A(u)gustus* where the Old English has *hærfest*.

35 See Karen Louise Jolly, "Prayers from the Field: Practical Protection and Demonic Defense in Anglo-Saxon England," *Traditio* 61 (2006), 95–147.

36 I would like to thank Karen Louise Jolly for her help with this part of the

The Staff of Life

Clofesho synod of 747, framed in terms showing that it was already traditional by that date. The text of the chapter runs as follows:

> Ut Lætaniæ, id est, rogationes, a clero omnique populo his diebus cum magna reverentia agantur, id est, die septimo kalendarum Maiarum, juxta ritum Romanæ Ecclesiæ: quæ et Lætania major apud eam vocatur. Et item quoque secundum morem priorum nostrorum, tres dies ante Ascensionem Domini in coelos cum jejunio usque ad horam nonam et Missarum celebratione venerantur: non admixtis vanitatibus, uti mos est plurimis, vel negligentibus vel imperitis, id est, in ludis et equorum cursibus, et epulis majoribus; sed magis, cum timore et tremore, signo passionis Christi nostræque æternæ redemptionis, et reliquis sanctorum Ejus coram portatis, omnis populus genu flectendo Divinam pro delictis humiliter exorat indulgentiam.

> [That the litanies, that is the rogations, should be performed with great reverence by the clergy and the whole people on these days, that is, on the seventh day before the kalends of May [25 April], according to the rite of the Roman church, which is also called the Greater Litany there, and also likewise, according to the custom of our forefathers, let the three days before the Ascension of our Lord into heaven be venerated with a fast until the ninth hour and the celebration of masses, not with vanities intermingled, as is the custom for very many people, either negligent or ignorant, that is, in games and horse races and great feasts, but rather, with fear and trembling, with the sign of Christ's passion and our eternal redemption, and the relics of his saints, carried in front, the whole people should pray humbly, on bended knee, for divine indulgence for their sins.][37]

paper.
37 *Councils and Ecclesiastical Documents relating to Great Britain and Ireland*, ed. and trans. Arthur W. Haddan and William Stubbs, 3 vols. (Oxford: Clarendon Press, 1871), III: 368 (capitalization and such are presumably editorial).

What is unfortunately glaringly obvious by its absence here is any mention of crops or their blessing. The people are not enjoined to ask for a good harvest, but forgiveness for their sins. It might be supposed that a good harvest would be a sign of God's forgiveness, but if so, that is not specified. Presumably a perambulation or procession of some kind is envisaged, since cross and relics are to be *portatis coram*, "carried in front," though the people are evidently stationary while actually praying since they have to do so *genu flectendo*, "on bended knee." This would be in accordance with what we know of Rogationtide processions in the later Middle Ages: the community halted at various points on the circuit for prayers led by the parish priest.[38] But how much of this existed by C.E. 747, we can hardly guess. Did the congregation "beat the bounds" of their territory, as was standard in the later Middle Ages? Did they actually go out into the fields at all? There is comparative evidence from the continent to suggest that these processions, probably derived from pre-Christian practice, were indeed undertaken for the sake of the crops, in fact mainly to ensure rain, although this last is unlikely to have been such an important consideration in England.[39] If this aspect was not imported from the continent at a later date, protection for crops is likely to have been at least one of the purposes of Anglo-Saxon Rogationtide rituals, too. This does leave us with a rather skeletal sense of eighth-century English practices, but we do at least have enough of a picture to be confident that there were Rogationtide practices, and that variations existed among them.

Later Anglo-Saxon evidence shows, however, that much of what was understood by "Rogationtide customs" in the later Middle Ages was already familiar before the Conquest.[40] For instance, a homily

---

38 For later medieval and early modern Rogationtide customs, see Hutton, *Stations*, pp. 277–78.
39 For the continental evidence, see Valerie I. J. Flint, *The Rise of Magic in Early Medieval Europe* (Oxford: Clarendon Press, 1991), p. 186.
40 M. Bradford Bedingfield, in his study of the Anglo-Saxon Rogationtide liturgy, is confident that the texts do describe a procession, involving the people

The Staff of Life

in the eleventh-century manuscript, Oxford, Bodleian Library MS Hatton 14, drawing on both Ælfric and Wulfstan, tells us that

> we sculon beon Gode lof secgende, and Cristes rodetacen forð beran and his þa halige godspell and oðre halignessa, mid þam we sceolan bletsian ure þa eorðlican speda, þæt sind æceras and wudu and ure ceap and ealle þa þing þe us God forgyfen hafað to brucanne þe we bileofian sceolan
>
> [we must be saying praise to God, and carry the sign of Christ's cross outside, and his holy gospel, and other relics (*halignessa*), with which we must bless our earthly possessions, that is to say fields and woods and our cattle and all the things that God has bestowed on us to enjoy so that we may have faith.][41]

Likewise, the "popular" homily number 12 in the Vercelli Codex (from the second half of the tenth century) states that

> ... we sculan berian usse reliquias ymb ure land, þa ... Cristes rodetacen þe we Cristes mæl nemnað ... 7 urne ceap 7 urne eard 7 urne wudu 7 eal ure god we sculon Gode bebeodan, 7 him þancian þara gesynte þe forþgewitene syndon.
>
> [... we must carry our relics around our land, [and] the ... sign of Christ's cross, which we call *Cristes mæl* ... And we must commend to God our cattle and our land and our woods, and all our goods, and thank him for the prosperity that has already been experienced.][42]

---

at large, with prayers at stopping-places. Unfortunately, the only English texts that specify these stopping-places describe those in the city of Rome, rather than an English rural community, so it cannot be established whether or not these were in the fields (see Bedingfield, *The Dramatic Liturgy of Anglo-Saxon England* [Woodbridge: Boydell Press, 2002], pp. 191–209, especially pp. 195–97).

41 Joyce Bazire and James E. Cross, ed., *Eleven Old English Rogationtide Homilies* (Toronto: University of Toronto Press, 1982), p. 112.

42 Donald G. Scragg, ed., *The Vercelli Homilies*, EETS 300 (London: Oxford

Another anonymous homily, found in the early eleventh-century manuscript, Cambridge, Corpus Christi College MS 162, lists among other rituals of *þas halgan gangdagas*, "holy procession days":

> ... þæt we mid þære halegan Þrynnysse rode and mid his halegra reliquium, þe we mid gangað, and mid haligum sangum we sceolon bletsian ure land and Drihten biddan þæt þa wæstmas, þe on eorðan syndon, geþeon moton mannum to gode and brice.
>
> [... that with the cross of the Holy Trinity and with the relics of his saints, that we process with, and with holy song, we must bless our land, and ask the Lord that the crops that are on the land may flourish for people's benefit and use.][43]

Other homilies also emphasize cross and relics, although not necessarily in such strong association with the fields or crops. In fact, the usual context of this emphasis is an exhortation to adhere to orthodox modes of observing Rogationtide, as opposed to the *idle spellunge and hlacerunge*, "vain tales and unseemly behavior,"[44] that laypeople might feel tempted to substitute. But we can see that, by the later Anglo-Saxon period, when these homilies were being composed and preached, the protection of the growing crops by means of the cross and blessings was recognized as one of the functions of the Rogationtide processions, even if not the most important one for the homilists.[45]

University Press, 1992), pp. 228–29.

43 Bazire and Cross, *Rogationtide Homilies*, p. 48.

44 This characterization comes from another anonymous homily, recorded in an eleventh-century manuscript, Cambridge University Library MS Ii. 4. 6; see Bazire and Cross, *Rogationtide Homilies*, p. 96. The editors discuss Rogationtide customs as evidenced in Old English homilies in general in their introduction, at xxii–xxiii.

45 There are two blessings *In campo*, where God is asked to protect "fines et fruges famulorum tuorum" (your servants' boundaries and crops), in the tenth-century *Sacramentary of Fulda*, which shares much material with Anglo-Saxon liturgical books, but I have not found these or similar blessings in English

The Staff of Life

What is also interesting is that by C.E. 747 Rogationtide was already an established custom with alternative traditions, as it continued to be throughout the Anglo-Saxon period and beyond. The Greater Litany on St. Mark's day is identified as Roman, while the Lesser, on the Monday to Wednesday before Ascension Day, is "secundum morem priorum nostrorum" (following the custom of our ancestors).[46] One would very much like to know whether these *priores* are envisaged as Christian ones, or whether these late spring activities are seen as originating before the conversion in England as well as on the continent. Unfortunately we are not told whether the "intermingled vanities" (*admixtis vanitatibus*) deplored by the Synod of Clofesho were also practiced by these ancestors, but presumably the alternative procedure, involving the cross and relics, would at least meet with the approval of the *romana ecclesia*. More than one school of thought about what was an appropriate way to behave at this season evidently continued to exist right through the Middle Ages, suggesting that the laity had a strong and persistent feeling that these occasions in some sense "belonged" to them, and it was not up to the Church to prescribe how they should be celebrated.[47] It is therefore quite possible that the cross in fact played a rather less widespread part in Rogationtide practices than the religious hierarchy would have liked, and than the texts might lead us to expect, or indeed that, where it was employed, it was not in a way the authorities approved.

The next major point in the agricultural year is harvest. Indeed, harvest is *the* major point, when all the year's efforts, both practical and

---

collections: *Sacramentarium Fuldensis saeculi X*, Gregor Richter and Albert Schönfelder, eds. (Fulda: Druck der fuldaer Actiendruckerei, 1912), p. 368.

46 Indeed, it was the three days before Ascension Day that continued to be celebrated in England, although frequently called *Letania major* ("greater litany").

47 For such disagreements in later periods, see Hutton, *Stations*, p. 277, and Keith Thomas, *Religion and the Decline of Magic* (Harmondsworth: Penguin Books, 1973), p. 74.

ritual, come to fruition, and it becomes clear whether the following year is likely to be a comfortable, well-fed one, or a lean and hungry one. Not surprisingly, then, some celebrations are known to attach to this season. The list of feasts in the *Rectitudines* includes "bendform for ripe . . . æt cornlade hreaccopp" (a binding entertainment for reaping . . . at corn carrying, a rick cup).[48] The harvest is important enough to be divided into two stages, with celebrations for each. The reaping and binding of the crops, and presumably stooking the sheaves in the field, are worth celebrating in themselves, and then there is a further feast when the fruits of the earth are carried home and made safe in a rick near the house, ready to be threshed and used during the winter. There is no mention of the cross here, nor should we expect one from what is essentially a list of meals. The list as a whole gives very little detail; it is there to remind people, mainly landlords, of their obligations. We are not told whether any rituals preceded the feasts, either in the fields or at the stack-yard. On the evidence of more recent harvest customs, we might certainly suppose activities, for instance, surrounding the last sheaf to be carried home. This was after all no less important a moment for the Anglo-Saxons than for later English farming communities.

We might equally wonder about the fashioning of objects like the modern "corn-dollies" from the harvested cereals, and whether they might take the form of the cross or other religious symbols. In fact there is some evidence on this, if rather oblique: the Latin version of the *Rectitudines* has at the time of corn carrying, not a rick cup, but a "rick top," *caput macholi*, implying something like the "topping-out" ceremony, still observed on some building sites when the highest point of a structure is reached. This may not mean anything very different from "rick cup": a drink to celebrate the completion of the rick. But, on the other hand, it may suggest that the completion itself was attended with some ceremony or decoration, as has more recently been the case. There is a little evidence for the tops of ricks

---

48 Liebermann, *Die Gesetze*, I. 452B3 at section 21.4.

The Staff of Life

in more recent times being decorated with crosses, for instance in nineteenth-century lowland Scotland.[49] It is not clear whether this represents a specific local tradition or a more widespread one, but it does at least constitute a comparative example from within the British Isles, and a fairly traditional society, for what might have been done in Anglo-Saxon England.

Be all that as it may, drinking is definitely not the only way that harvest was celebrated in our period. The feast of Lammas, 1 August, at which bread baked from the first fruits was traditionally consecrated, certainly goes back to the Anglo-Saxon period.[50] The name of the feast is Old English, *hlafmæsse*, "bread-mass," and this word occurs in a number of surviving Old English texts, usually simply as a date, showing the degree to which it was taken for granted in the period. In Bald's Leechbook, the dog-days, when conventional wisdom forbade bloodletting, are described as "fiftyne nihtum ær hlafmæsse and æfter fif and thritig nihtum" (for fifteen nights before Lammas and for thirty-five nights afterwards).[51] The translator of the Alfredian *Orosius* used it to explain the kalends (1st) of August: "Þæt [wæs] on þære tide calendas Agustus, 7 on þæm dæge þe we hatað hlafmæsse," (that was on the date the calends of August, and on the day that we call Lammas).[52] Furthermore, a fragmentary charm to stop rodents spoiling crops in store ("[U]t surices garbas non noceant"), belonging to the second half of the eleventh century, prescribes that pieces "of ðam gehalgedan hlafe þe man halige on hlafmæsse dæg" (the blessed bread that is blessed on Lammas day)

---

49 One at an unnamed location in Fife (late nineteenth century?) is illustrated by Alexander Fenton, *Scottish Country Life* (Edinburgh: John Donald, 1976), pl. 36a on p. 75. The photograph is undated, and devoid of datable artifacts other than barbed wire.
50 See Hutton, *Stations*, pp. 330–31.
51 Thomas O. Cockayne, ed., *Leechdoms, Wortcunning and Starcraft in Early England*, 3 vols., Rolls Series 35 (London: Longman, 1864–6), I. 146 at ch. 72.
52 See Janet Bately, ed., *The Old English Orosius*, EETS s.s. 6 (London: Oxford University Press, 1980), V. xiii. 2 on p. 130.

should be crumbled in the four corners of the barn,[53] suggesting that something like the later Lammas ritual was already in use soon after the Conquest, if not before.

What form the Lammas blessing might have taken at this early period is not certain, but there are blessings for bread in surviving Anglo-Saxon service-books. For example, the following benediction for new bread appears in the tenth century *Claudius Pontifical*, the *Leofric Missal* (?Christ Church, Canterbury, s. ix^{ex} or s. x^{in}), the *Durham Collectar* (this part southern England, s. x^{in}) and the *Missal of Robert of Jumièges*:

> Benedic domine hanc creaturam nouam panis, sicut benedixisti quinque panes in deserto, quinque milibus hominum saturatis, ut sit dominis eiusdem abundans in annum alimentum, gustantesque ex eo, accipiant tam corporis quam anime sanitatem.
>
> [Bless, Lord, this new creation of bread, as you blessed the five loaves in the desert, five thousand people being fed, so that food may be abundant for its owners during the year, and those tasting of it may receive health of body and soul.][54]

This "new bread" (the *Durham Collectar* has *creaturam noui panis*) could well be the Lammas bread made from the first fruits,[55] and the reference to abundance "during the year" also suggests a harvest

---

53   London, British Library MS Cotton Vitellius E. xviii, folio 16r. The instructions are in Old English, and the two "blessings" in Latin. See Ker, p. 300, for full text.

54   Text from Orchard, *The Leofric Missal*, II. 417; my translation. Orchard shows that the phrase "quinque milibus hominum saturatis" is unique to Leofric (I. 91–92), but otherwise its version is the best of the English ones, supposing that the original core of the collection, in which this blessing is found, is in fact English, as Orchard argues (I. 131).

55   This is the context envisaged for the blessing in *The Durham Collectar*, ed. Alicia Côrrea, HBS 107 (London: Boydell Press, 1992), p. 214, n. to no. 594. She also mentions there the possibility of its being used for the eucharistic bread.

The Staff of Life

context, looking forward to a whole year's good feeding until the next year's crops are ready. Other blessings for bread in English collections have less specific wording, but might also have been used at the Lammas celebrations.

Also found in some English service books are blessings for "new crops" (*fruges nouas* or *nouos*), in texts that vary, but seem to be related.

> Domine sancte pater omnipotens aeterne deus, qui caelum et terram mare et omnia creasti, te supplices quesumus, ut hunc fructum nouum benedicere et sanctificare digneris, et multiplicare habundanter offerentibus tibi, et impleas eorum cellaria cum fortitudine frumenti et uini, ut laetantes in eis, referant tibi deo omnipotenti laudes et gratias.
>
> [Lord holy Father almighty everlasting God, who has created the heaven and the earth, the sea and all things, we beg you humbly that you may deign to bless and sanctify this new fruit, and multiply it abundantly for those offering it to you, and fill their storehouses with the strength of corn and wine, so that, rejoicing in them, they may render to you, God almighty, praises and thanks.][56]

Such a blessing could be used for other crops apart from cereals, as the reference to *fortitudine uini* shows, and might perhaps be used on several occasions through the year as different crops were brought in. This might explain the request to the deity to multiply the crops of those making the offering; if they were all already gathered in, such an increase would constitute a miracle. As a blessing for crops in general, we cannot assume that this one was used at Lammas; there is certainly no suggestion that the crops concerned, even if they happened to be cereals, were in the form

---

56 Orchard, *The Leofric Missal*, II. 417: my translation. *The Missal of Robert of Jumièges*, ed. Wilson, p. 280, has a similar text. *The Claudius Pontificals*, ed. Turner, p. 64, has a shorter text with less specific detail.

of bread. But the reference to an offering does suggest that the blessing was used in church, rather than in the *cellaria* mentioned in the text, or in the fields.

Once the crops were gathered in, it was of course vital that they should not be spoiled during storage, and this is the purpose of the charm against the depredations of *surices* ("mice" or "shrews") mentioned above. Here the cross features prominently. Not only is the bread to be crumbled in the four corners of what was perhaps the barn and itself divided into four pieces, but this is to be done after two sticks (possibly square in section) have been laid on the floor of the barn in the form of a cross. The four-quarters symbolism is emphasized heavily here, even though the cross does not feature explicitly in either of the two blessings that follow. Furthermore, the instruction to take four parts of the loaf suggests that it is itself marked with a cross. If it was cut deeply in so doing, it would break easily and naturally into quarters, but even a light scoring would produce a loaf clearly marked into four portions.[57] As in the *Æcerbot* charm, the end-product of the agricultural cycle is used in a ritual to ensure its eventual success, but here we can be much more confident that the cross is employed in bringing that success about.

A more orthodox method of protecting the stored grain would be the blessing for a granary given in the *Missal of Robert of Jumièges* as part of a perambulation of a monastery, which includes prayers for various buildings, some of them quite humble.

> Omnipotens et misericors deus. qui benedixisti horrea ioseph. aream iedeonis. et adhuc quod maius est. iacta terrae semina surgere facis cum foenore messis. te humiliter quesumus ut sicut ad petitionem famuli tui helie non defuit uiduae farina ita ad nostrae

---

57 See below, pp. 307–311, for more on the possible marking of Anglo-Saxon loaves with the cross. Any such marking would almost certainly be done with a knife before baking, rather than for instance with strips of paste, as frequently found on hot cross buns today.

partuitatis suffragia. huic horreo famulorum tuorum non desit benedictionis tuae habundantia.

[Almighty and merciful God, who has blessed Joseph's storehouses [and] Gideon's threshing-floor, and, what is still greater, makes the seed cast upon the earth to grow up, with increase of harvest, we humbly beseech you that, just as, at the request of your servant Elias, the widow's flour did not run out, so, at the prayers of our littleness, the abundance of your blessing will not be missing from this storehouse of your servants.][58]

Here the heading *In granario*, as well as the references to the growing crops and to the widow's flour, make it clear that cereal stores are the specific object of the blessing.

Before the stored grain can finally be ground and baked into bread, it needs to be threshed. Although a good deal of labor went into this, it is another job that would be fitted in whenever there was time, or when the weather was too bad to work outside, so it is unlikely to be attended by any prescribed ceremony. There is a blessing for a threshing-floor in the *Missal of Robert of Jumièges*, in the context of the perambulation of a monastery already mentioned.[59] Whether non-monastic threshing-floors were also blessed with this or other, perhaps less orthodox, formula, we unfortunately have no evidence.

Again, there seems to be no ritual associated with milling. The perambulation just mentioned also contains a blessing for a *pistrinum*, but, although this word originally meant a mill, in medieval Latin it is a bakehouse.[60] Milling was also a major task, in terms both of the labor expended and of the results: the Anglo-Saxons certainly preferred to eat their corn in the form of bread (to which end it had to be ground into flour) rather than in potages and porridges.[61] But

---

58 Wilson, *Missal of Robert of Jumièges*, p. 279; my translation.
59 Wilson, *Missal of Robert of Jumièges*, p. 279.
60 Wilson, *Missal of Robert of Jumièges*, p. 279.
61 I have discussed these preferences, and the circumstances that may have influenced them, in *Food and Drink in Anglo-Saxon England*, pp. 17–20.

before it was mechanized, this work was carried out by women, and in larger households by slaves, so it is unlikely to have been highly valued.[62] It is also another of the tasks that would be going on more or less all the time (King Æthelberht of Kent had a whole category of female slaves devoted to the task in the seventh century),[63] so there was no obvious point in the year to celebrate or reward it, even if there had been the desire to do so. With the building of mechanical mills, the grinding of flour passed into the realm of commerce, and thus arguably beyond the traditional, communal world in which rituals such as we have been discussing would be considered appropriate.[64]

Baking, similarly, seems according to our sources to have been without ceremony, although we may imagine the baker taking some measures intended to guarantee the success of his or her enterprise. We have already seen a blessing for a monastic bakehouse (*pistrinum*), and we might expect some, perhaps more "popular," procedures in a secular context.[65] Similarly, successful baking was presumably to be

---

62 A lunary added in the twelfth century to Oxford, Bodleian Library MS Hatton MS 115 has a "grinder" (masculine) who is apparently free to decide when to get out his quern (the fourth night of the moon is recommended), but conditions may have changed by then; certainly there were plenty of water mills in existence. See Max Förster, "Beiträge zur mittelalterlichen Volkskunde, VIII," *Archiv für das Studium der neueren Sprachen und Literaturen* 129 (1912), 16–49 at 43, for the text of the lunary, and H. C. Darby, *Domesday England* (Cambridge: Cambridge University Press, 1977), pp. 270–75, for the mills.

63 See Æthelberht's law-code, clause 11, in Liebermann, *Die Gesetze*, I: 3.

64 A mill was a major technological undertaking, and therefore an expensive one, even for wealthy landlords. The reason that mills appear so consistently (not just whole ones, but fractions of mills, too, presumably where they were jointly owned) in Domesday Book is that they were regarded as sources of income: the owners would hope at the very least to recoup their investment. See Darby, *Domesday England*, pp. 270–75.

65 As far as I am aware, none are recorded to compare, for instance, with those to protect beer and dairy foods given in *Bald's Leechbook* I, chapter 67 (Cockayne, *Leechdoms*, II: 142).

The Staff of Life

celebrated, and bread was valuable enough, both in nutritional terms and in terms of the labor that went into it, to require supernatural protection. We have seen blessings for "new bread" already, in our discussion of Lammas, but it is possible that they were not confined to that feast. Fresh bread may have been worth celebrating at any time of the year, and certainly would not have been taken for granted as it is today. Even the wealthiest households in the late Middle Ages only baked between six and twelve times a month, and others even less frequently.[66] In our period, when ovens and bakehouses were even less common (and probably less sophisticated, too), fresh bread would have been an even rarer treat. Hearth-baked bread, which is denser and therefore keeps better, might be made even less often than that baked in ovens.[67] New bread might thus need blessing to preserve it for quite an extended period from vermin, damp, mold, and generally reduced palatability.

Likewise, there are other blessings for bread which do not specify it as "new," such as this one, which often travels with the "five loaves in the desert" formula quoted above:

> Benedico te creatura panis, in nomine patris, et filii, et spiritus sancti per uirtutem dominice passionis et resurrectionis a mortuis, ut sanctificata uerbo dei, benedictionem assumas aduersus omnes nequitias spiritales, et uniuersas ualitudines infirmitatesque membrorum, ut quicumque te sumpserint, sis eis in tutelam mentis et corporis, in honorem domini nostri iesu christi qui est benedictus in saecula saeculorum. Amen.
>
> [I bless you, creation of bread, in the name of the father, and of the son, and of the holy spirit, through the power of our Lord's passion and resurrection from the dead, so that, blessed by the

---

[66] D. J. Stone, "The Consumption of Field Crops in Late Medieval England," *Food in Medieval England: Diet and Nutrition*, ed. C. M. Woolgar, D. Sergeantson and T. Waldron (Oxford: Oxford University Press, 2006), pp. 11–26, at p. 14.
[67] See Banham, *Food and Drink*, pp. 18–22.

word of God, you may take up blessing against all spiritual evils, and all conditions and diseases of the limbs, so that, whoever consumes you, you may be a protection for them in mind and body, in honor of our Lord Jesus Christ who is blessed for ever and ever. Amen.][68]

This blessing, conferring as it does power to cure ills both bodily and spiritual, might well be thought more appropriate to the host than to everyday bread, but the whole question of the relationship between eucharistic and ordinary bread in Anglo-Saxon England remains to be explored.

Now we have arrived at the point of bread-making, the question arises of the form of the Anglo-Saxon loaf.[69] Until recently, our knowledge of this depended on the Old English monastic sign language, which prescribes a sign Ðonne þu laf habban wylle, "when you wish to have bread," as follows: "sete þu þine twegen þuman to gædere and þine twegen scyte fingras æðerne foran ongean oþerne" (put your two thumbs together, and your two index fingers one against the other in front).[70] This somewhat enigmatic description is illuminated by its counterpart in the Latin sign-list from Cluny, which is at least the partial source for the Old English one: "fac unum circulum cum utroque pollice et his duobus digitis, qui sequuntur, pro eo, quod et panis solet esse rotundus" (make one circle with either thumb and these two fingers that come next, because a loaf is usually round too).[71] This suggests something probably small as well as round, but taken by itself there is nothing to tell us if the Old English sign describes at

---

68 Text from Orchard, *The Leofric Missal*, II: 416; my translation. See also Turner, *The Claudius Pontificals*, p. 64, and Wilson, *The Missal of Robert of Jumièges*, p. 281.
69 See Banham, *Food and Drink*, pp. 21–22 for bread-making.
70 See Debby Banham, *Monasteriales indicia: The Anglo-Saxon Monastic Sign Language* (Pinner: Anglo-Saxon Books, 1991), p. 32.
71 Walter Jarecki, *Signa loquendi: die Cluniacensischen Signa-Listen*, Saecula spiritalia 4 (Baden-Baden: Koerner, 1981), p. 121; my translation.

The Staff of Life

all accurately the form of the Anglo-Saxon loaf, or merely reproduces Cluny practice. Its evidence is now supported, however, by a recent find of several loaves of precisely the form it leads us to expect. These were preserved by carbonization in a house burnt down in the eleventh century in the Buttermarket at Ipswich.[72] They were about four inches across when excavated, but since they were heavily charred, they may have been intended to be somewhat bigger. The report describes them as small, round, and flat. Compared with modern loaves baked in tins, they are indeed flat, but their domed form shows that they had been raised, either with fresh yeast or a sourdough. More to the point for our purposes, there is no sign that any of them was marked with a cross, but their preservation is not good enough to be absolutely certain of this.

I have been unable to find any other Anglo-Saxon evidence of whether or not loaves were marked with a cross, although there is a fair scatter of information from both Ireland and the Continent in the same period.[73] In particular, the monastic sign-list from Cluny, mentioned above, shows more variety and sophistication than appears to have been available to Anglo-Saxon monks. The first gesture, *Pro signo panis* "for the sign for bread" (already quoted), is recognizably the same one as in the Old English list, but this is followed by three more signs for different kinds of bread, which are not found in the

---

72 I should like to thank Keith Wade and Peter Murphy for information about this find. A photograph of the loaves, kindly provided by Suffolk County Council Archaeological Service, can be found in Banham, *Food and Drink*, pl. 5.

73 In particular, Sarah Larratt Keefer informs me that the Cracow Pontifical (a redaction of the Roman-German Pontifical originating in Mainz in the mid-tenth century, and perhaps copied in Tyniec in the middle of the eleventh century) includes bread marked with the Lord's Prayer for liturgical use; however such an inclusion in this book may be regional practice. In any event, the Roman-German Pontifical, while known in Anglo-Saxon England, was not apparently used prior to ca. 1050. See *The Cracow Pontifical: Pontificale Cracoviense Saeculi XI (Cracow, Jagellonian Library MS 2057)*, ed. Z. Obertyński, HBS 100 (Manchester: Philips Park Press, 1967–71), p. 89, #341.

English text. The second of these, sign 3, is "Pro signo panis sigalini et qui torta vulgariter appellatur" (for the sign of fine-flour bread, and that which is commonly called *torta*), and the directions for the gesture read thus: "iterum generali signo panis hoc adde, ut crucem per medium palme facias, pro eo, quod id genus panis dividi solet per quadrum" (again, add this to the general sign for bread, that you make a cross across the middle of the palm, because this kind of bread is usually divided into four).[74]

This raises a number of questions. First of all, was marking with the cross confined, or originally confined, to special kinds of bread? If so, were these breads, and the cross upon them, only brought into England after the Anglo-Saxon period? It is in fact likely that there were changes in English diet, possibly quite important ones, at or soon after the Norman Conquest, but it is certainly not the case that only one basic kind of bread was known to the Anglo-Saxons. We know from food rents that as well as ordinary bread there were white bread and "alms bread," and that monastic landlords were particularly fussy about the type of bread they received.[75] Alms bread may have been especially coarse, suitable for giving away to the poor, while white bread, if not intended solely for the mass, may have been precisely the kind of "fine-flour bread" identified by a cross in the Cluny sign-list. If that is so, however, there is no mention of it being so marked in England. On the other hand, white bread might have been normal on monastic tables, and thus indicated by the sign in the *indicia*. Alms bread might equally be expected to have borne a cross to indicate its charitable purpose, but again there is no evidence for this.

This brings us to the other group of questions, concerning the cross itself: why was it put on the loaf? Although the Cluniac sign

---

74 Jarecki, *Signa loquendi*, p. 121.
75 Some of these rents are discussed at pp. 74–75 in Debby Banham, "The Knowledge and Uses of Food Plants in Anglo-Saxon England" (unpubl. thesis), University of Cambridge, 1990. I hope to publish on food-rents and related payments in the not-too-distant future.

is described as making a cross, *ut crucem . . . facias*, it does not seem to be its spiritual significance that is important here. We are not told that this kind of bread is dedicated to the Lord or even blessed, merely that it is divided *per quadrum*, "on the square" or "into quarters." And this is in a text deriving from Cluny, a powerhouse of the Benedictine reform at this time.[76] If any religious implications were there, presumably they would be emphasized, even in a practical text like this.[77] We are led to conclude, therefore, that the marking of the loaf or *torta* in this way may also have been practical. It would enable the loaf to be broken in four when baked, and in the baking it would allow it to rise more easily. This does imply fine wheat flour: anything with large lumps of bran would not rise well, whatever you did with it, and the same applies to grains other than wheat.[78] It may be that the "ordinary" loaf was too coarse to be worth marking with a cross; only those breads regarded as a treat would benefit from this treatment, in terms of improved rising and lightness, but of course the cross would also be a visible signal of their special status.

The idea of marking loaves with the cross was certainly not unknown in Anglo-Saxon England, for this procedure forms the

---

76 Although the Cluny sign-list is only recorded in two related texts of the later eleventh century, the introduction of sign-language to that house is attributed to Abbot Odo (927–42), and the textual relationship between the early continental lists, as well as the Old English one, makes it clear that Cluny was the original from which the others were adapted. See Jarecki's "Introduction" in *Signa loquendi*, pp. 5–78.

77 It should not be assumed that these sign-lists were purely utilitarian texts divorced from contemporary theological thinking: see Scott G. Bruce, *Silence and Sign Language in Medieval Monasticism: The Cluniac Tradition, c. 900–1200* (Cambridge: Cambridge University Press, 2007), chapter 1, "Uttering No Human Sound," pp. 13–52.

78 See Jane M. Renfrew, *Paleoethnobotany: The Prehistoric Food Plants of the Near East and Europe* (London: Methuen, 1973), pl. 48a for a graphic demonstration of this.

basis of a miracle story in Gregory the Great's *Dialogues*, translated into English under the aegis of King Alfred by bishop Wærferth of Worcester.[79] The miracle is said to have taken place in the province of Valeria, not in England, and unfortunately Wærferth does not tell us explicitly whether the practice was also familiar to him and his readers. His translation does however depart from the Latin in two ways which may give us some clues on this matter. In the first place, whereas Gregory describes the marking as being applicable to *panes crudi*, most naturally read as meaning "loaves before they were cooked," Wærferth renders this as *þeorfhlaf*, "unleavened bread." While this might be a legitimate translation (if not classical), his choice may reveal some assumptions based on English experience. In the first place, this was a loaf baked on the hearth, under the ashes (Old English *heorðbacen*, Latin *subcinerarius*), and it may be that such bread was always unleavened in Anglo-Saxon England, or indeed more widely (it would not rise as much as oven-baked bread, even if made with yeast). On the other hand, it may have been the mention of the cross that made Wærferth think that this was unleavened bread: he may have assumed that bread so marked was destined for the eucharist (although neither he nor Gregory says so), and for that reason, not raised. The second departure is an addition by Wærferth to Gregory's story: when the saint asks the bakers why they have not marked the bread with a cross, in the Old English version he adds "as is the custom," *swa swa hit þeaw is*. Was this addition necessary because Wærferth's audience would not otherwise know that this was a normal thing to do, or did he include it to make the story accord more closely with their experience in England? Taking this passage in isolation, I might think the former more likely, but in conjunction

---

79   The story constitutes Book 1, ch. 11 of *Gregorii magni Dialogi libri IV*, ed. Umberto Moricca, Fonti per la storia d'Italia, Scrittori secolo VI (Rome: Istituto Storico Italiano, 1924), p. 67. See also Hans Hecht, ed., *Bischofs Wærferth von Worcester Übersetzung der Dialoge Gregors des Grossen*, Bibliothek der angelsächsischen Prosa 5 (Leipzig: Wigand, 1900), pp. 86–87 for the Old English.

with Wærferth's interpretation of *crudi*, it suggests that the bishop had communion bread in mind, which was marked with the cross in England in his time. If this interpretation is correct, the cross, which originally distinguished bread to be dedicated to God, may have extended its application over time to mark bread meant for mortal sustenance, but perhaps originally only on those occasions dedicated to God or his saints. Eventually, the use of the cross evidently spread to bread for any occasion, but whether this happened in England before the Conquest, cannot currently be established.[80]

When our loaf, even if it did not itself bear a cross, finally reached the table, would it have encountered the cross there? In other words, did the Anglo-Saxons say grace at meals? There are surprisingly few Anglo-Saxon descriptions of feasts (those in *Beowulf* form the largest group), and none involve blessing food.[81] While ecclesiastics would presumably have blessed food before eating, whether at their own table or someone else's, there is no reason to think that lay people, unless particularly pious, would have done so when dining without benefit of clergy. A neat, if not strictly Anglo-Saxon comparison appears between the two feasting scenes in the Bayeux Tapestry. In the second, showing Duke William's al fresco but not frugal meal after landing in England, the bishop has his fingers raised in blessing over the table, as is confirmed by the caption.[82] He is admittedly not

---

80 For hot cross buns, the main survivor of this practice in modern England, see Laura Mason and Catherine Brown, *Traditional Foods of Britain: An Inventory* (Totnes: Prospect Books, 1999), pp. 235–36.

81 See Hugh Magennis, *Images of Community in Old English Poetry*, CSASE 18 (Cambridge University Press, 1996), esp. pp. 42–48 and chs. 3 ("Hall and Feasting in Beowulf") and 4 ("Hall and Feasting: Transformations and Alternative Perspectives"), pp. 60–103, as well as his *Anglo-Saxon Appetites: Food and Drink and their Consumption in Old English and Related Literature* (Dublin: Four Courts Press, 1999), ch. 1, "Food, Drink and Feast in Anglo-Saxon and Germanic Literary Tradition," at pp. 17–45.

82 See David M. Wilson, *The Bayeux Tapestry: The Complete Tapestry in Colour*, (London: Thames and Hudson), 1985, pl. 48: "hic episcopus cibum et potus

an Anglo-Saxon bishop, but on the assumption that the "tapestry" was made in England, he may be portrayed in a manner reflecting Anglo-Saxon expectations of a man in his position. The earlier scene shows an Anglo-Saxon meal without clerical presence, that of Harold Godwineson and his companions about to set out on their ill-fated trip across the Channel.[83] No one is doing any blessing or praying here. Clearly these scenes are in no sense representative of general practice in late Anglo-Saxon England, let alone of earlier periods.

If we turn to Anglo-Saxon pictures of feasting, we find that they fall into three groups.[84] The largest by far consists of biblical scenes, often including angels, patriarchs, and other such figures whose attitudes and gestures are unlikely to represent Anglo-Saxon practice. Then there are three in manuscripts of Prudentius's *Psychomachia*, all showing Luxuria feasting, and not, in accordance with her characterization, blessing her food. Thirdly, there is a small calendar group. The illustration for April in the two "Labors of the Month" cycles already mentioned (pp. 288–289, above) shows a feast, in which, again, no blessing is taking place.[85] These two depictions are closely related, the Tiberius image almost certainly being copied from the Julius picture, which in turn is probably modeled on a continental exemplar. Finally, there is a feasting scene, not attached to a calendar but to computistical material, in London, British Library MS Cotton Tiberius C. vi, a psalter of the later eleventh century. This is

---

benedicit" (here the bishop blesses food and drink).

83   Wilson, *Bayeux Tapestry*, pls. 3–4.

84   All these scenes are identified as such in Thomas Ohlgren, ed., *Insular and Anglo-Saxon Illustrated Manuscripts: An Iconographic Catalog, c. A.D. 625 to 1100* (New York: Garland, 1986), index s.v. "feasting". I have not discovered any further examples myself, and in fact Ohlgren may overestimate the number depicted, since he appears to include all scenes with people eating at table, however informal they appear.

85   The feasting scenes are found on folio 4v in both manuscripts. See McGurk, *An Eleventh-Century Anglo-Saxon Illustrated Miscellany*, for reproductions, and McGurk, "The Labours of the Months" for discussion.

The Staff of Life

not particularly close to the two calendar illustrations already mentioned, but it has been suggested that it, too, derives from a "Labors of the Month" cycle, and thus belongs to my third group.[86] If so, it too almost certainly has continental origins. Again, no figure seems to be performing a blessing. The Anglo-Saxon depictions of people eating are therefore not very productive in terms of telling us about contemporary feasting practice, either because they depict biblical or allegorical figures, or because their models are not English, or in some cases, probably both. Nevertheless, it can be stated that no figure not part of a biblical narrative is making a blessing in any of them.

The evidence that Anglo-Saxons blessed their bread at table is thus not very substantial, nor do we know for sure what formula they used when they did do so. It is possible that one of the blessings for bread given above would be used, but perhaps more likely that one of the traditional blessings *pro cibum* or *ante cibum* ("for food" or "before food") would be considered appropriate. The problem is that I have not been able to find these blessings in any liturgical book that is certainly from Pre-Conquest England. They are given in the original part of the *Leofric Missal*, conventionally supposed to be a continental book although the latest editor believes it was made for Christ Church, Canterbury.[87] This collection shares a great deal with liturgical books compiled in Anglo-Saxon England, including the blessings for bread already given, but if the ancient formula for blessing meals were more widely known in the Anglo-Saxon church, it is surprising that other collections do not have them. Alternatively,

---

86 Francis Wormald, "An English Eleventh-Century Psalter with Pictures, British Library, Cotton MS Tiberius C. vi," in his *Collected Writings*, ed. J. J. G. Alexander, T. Julian Brown and Joan Gibbs, 2 vols. (London: Harvey Miller, 1984), I: 123–37 at 126. The illustration is reproduced at plate 124 and described at p. 131.

87 Text from *The Leofric Missal*, Orchard, ed., II.19–20, with brief discussion at I.31–2.

it is possible that an independent tradition of blessings for the table existed in England, perhaps unrecorded because it was not strictly liturgical. Of the benedictions that are preserved, none, either specific to bread or for food generally, mentions the cross in its wording, but we can assume that a gestural cross normally went with them. Thus it is likely that the Anglo-Saxons, at least those in the habit of making blessings, usually made the sign of the cross over their bread before breaking it.

To sum up, in its journey from field to table, it seems likely that the Anglo-Saxon loaf or the corn it was made from would have encountered the cross at some point, but some doubt remains about the specific role of the cross, or even of Christian blessings more generally, at most stages of that journey, as is true of many aspects of everyday life in the early Middle Ages. Only when it came into contact with the Church, whether at Rogationtide, at Lammas or at table, can we be certain that the cereal production process was graced by the symbol of our redemption. The cross may have played a somewhat smaller part in the other, less orthodox customs associated with the growing of grain and the manufacture of bread, but the charm against rodent attack and the first half of the *Æcerbot* are examples of the cross being used in rituals at some distance from official religion, and there are plenty of other examples of this phenomenon not associated with food production. Of course, we know much less about these less orthodox customs than about those approved by the Church. Many, undoubtedly, were never written down, or, if they were written down, were not thought worth preserving. It may be true that those involving the cross or other orthodox elements were disproportionately likely to have been valued by the literate classes, but, equally, they may have had little interest in practices in which they themselves played no part, regarding them as the province of the peasantry whose job it was to produce food. Thus it is probable that, among food-production rituals which have not come down to us, at least some involved the cross in some form. The significance of the cross to the non-literate, working classes of Anglo-Saxon was probably more various and complex than the contemporary ruling classes, let alone modern scholars, could comprehend. There is also evidence that the Church (in its capacity as landlord) was taking more notice of agricultural processes towards the end of our period, if not always for strictly religious reasons, which may have led to an injection of orthodoxy into farming rituals.[88] These factors between them mean that, in addition to the recorded blessings, orthodox and less so, which we have already looked at, there was almost certainly a large hinterland of unrecorded practices associated with Anglo-Saxon bread and cereal production, which featured the cross in many guises. Thus, although we cannot identify all its manifestations, we can be sure that there was a close and complex connection in Anglo-Saxon England between the staff of life and the rood of our Lord.[89]

---

88 In addition to the presence of the *Rectitudines* and *Gerefa* in a Wulfstanian manuscript like Cambridge, Corpus Christi College MS 383, the most striking piece of evidence is the Ely farming memoranda, a piece of genuine Anglo-Saxon account-keeping, London, British Library MS Additional 61735, edited in *Anglo-Saxon Charters*, ed. A. J. Robertson (Cambridge: Cambridge University Press, 1939), pp. 252–57.

89 I am especially grateful to Sarah Larratt Keefer and Karen Louise Jolly for their help and advice while I was writing both the original paper delivered in Winchester and this revised version. I was very much aware of breaking, if not new ground exactly, then ground that was only partly mine. I would also like to thank the other participants in the Winchester conference for a stimulating discussion of my paper, and apologize for not being able to incorporate all their suggestions. Martha Bayless, Rosamond Faith and Kathryn Rudy all read the paper at various stages, and I would like to thank them for their comments and encouragement.

Appendix 1

Translation of *Æcerbot* Charm

Here is the remedy with which you can improve your fields if they will not grow well, or any disagreeable thing is done to them by magic(ian) or witch(craft).

Then at night, before it gets light, take four turfs from four parts of the land, and mark where they came from. Then take oil and honey and leaven, and the milk of every animal that is on the land, and part of every kind of tree that grows on the land, except for hard trees(?), and part of every plant that is known by name, except for *glappa* only, and then put holy water on them, and then drip it three times on the place the turfs came from, and then say three times these words: *Crescite*, grow, *et multiplicamini*, and multiply, *et replete*, and fill, *terre*, the earth. "In nomine Patris et Filii et Spiritus Sancti sit benedicti." And Pater Noster as many times as the other one. And then carry the turf to church, and let the priest sing four masses over the turfs, and let the green side be turned towards the altar, and then let the turfs be brought back to where they were before, before sunset.

And have four crosses made for them out of quickbeam (*or* living wood), and write on each end, Matthew and Mark, Luke and John. Lay the cross in the bottom of the hole, then say: "Crux Matheus, crux Marcus, crux Lucas, crux sanctus Iohannes." Then take the turf and place it on top and then say nine times these words, *Crescite*, and Pater Noster the same number of times, and then turn to the east and bow humbly nine times, and then say these words:

The Staff of Life

> I stand facing east,   I pray for grace,
> I pray to the mighty *domine*   I pray to the great lord,
> I pray to the holy   ruler of the heavenly kingdom,
> I pray to the earth   and heaven above,
> and to the true   Saint Mary,
> and the power of heaven   and the high hall,
> that by the lord's gift   I may utter this song
> through my teeth,   with sound thought,
> awake the growing things   for our earthly need,
> fill the country,   with my firm belief,
> beautify this meadow,   as the psalmist says,
> that he may have grace in the earthly kingdom,   who distributes
> his alms with judgment   according to the lord's will.

Then turn three times in the direction the sun goes, then stretch out at full length and count the litanies and then say: *Sanctus, sanctus, sanctus* to the end. Then sing *Benedicite* with arms outstretched, and Magnificat and Pater Noster three times and dedicate it to the praise and glory and grace of Christ and Saint Mary and the holy cross for the one who owns the land and all those who are dependent on him.

When all that has been done, then unknown seed is to be taken from beggars, and they are to be given twice as much as is taken from them, and all the plowing gear is to be gathered together; then bore into the beam incense and fennel and blessed soap and blessed salt. Then take the seed, place it on the body of the plow, then say:

> Erce, Erce, Erce,   mother earth,
> may the almighty,   the eternal lord, grant you
> fields growing   and flourishing,
> increasing   and reviving,

tall stalks,	bright crops,
and the broad	barley crops,
and the white	wheat crops,
and all	the fruits of the earth.
May the eternal lord,	and all his saints
who are in heaven,	grant him
that his land be kept safe	from all enemies whatsoever
and protected	from all injury whatsoever,
from the witchcraft	sown throughout the land.
Now I pray to the ruler	who created the world
that there may be no woman so loquacious nor man so powerful	
that they may change	the words so spoken.

When the plow is driven forward and the first furrow cut, then say:

Wellbeing to you, earth,	mother of people!
May you grow	in God's embrace,
filled with food	for people's needs.

Then take every kind of flour, and a loaf is to be baked the width of the inside of a hand and kneaded with milk and with holy water and laid under the first furrow. Then say:

Field full of food	for the human race,
flowering brightly,	may you be blessed
in that holy name	that created heaven
and the earth	that we live on;
may the God who made these lands	grant us a growing gift
so that every kind of corn	may come to our need.

Then say three times "Crescite in nomine patris, sit benedicti. Amen" and Pater Noster three times.

The Anglo-Saxon Chapel at Bradford-on-Avon, Wiltshire

David A. Hinton

> "To an archaeologist, this unique building must
> ever be one of the deepest interest."[1]

THE CHAPEL OF ST. LAURENCE at Bradford-on-Avon, Wiltshire, is one of the best-known and least understood Anglo-Saxon buildings; its date, function, and founder are all open to question. As its plan is cruciform, a discussion of it is appropriate in the Proceedings of the Cross and Cruciform conference. Furthermore, the two carved angels high above its chancel arch show that it once had an Anglo-Saxon rood similar in size to the larger of the two at Romsey Abbey, and to those at Headbourne Worthy and Breamore, all in Hampshire and visited by conference delegates in 2003 (Figure 9.1).

The symbolism of the use of the cross as the pattern for the ground-plan of many medieval churches has Early Christian roots, and was expounded to an English audience in the ninth-century *De Abbatibus*, which describes a church that was "fairly laid out in the shape of a cross . . . the building was supported all the way round

---

1 W. H. Jones, "On the Finding of the Saxon Church of St Laurence, Bradford-on-Avon," *Journal of the British Archaeological Association* 31 (1875): 142–52, at 151.

the wall by large and small porticuses. Of these, twice two looked towards the four corners of the world, and above touched the top of the wall."[2] The *Vita Sancti Oswaldi* of 995 x 1005 explained that Ramsey Abbey, Cambridgeshire, was built "in the fashion of a cross: a porticus on the East, on the South and on the North, a tower in the middle . . . supported by the porticus butting against it; then in the West he annexed a tower."[3] This description has a precise physical counterpart at Breamore, where the church even has evidence of a western annex, no longer surviving but shown by quoin scars.[4] Bradford is less obviously cruciform, for it has no crossing, so that its porticuses are appended to its nave; they are effectively central to it, so that the "shaft" of the cross is very short (Figure 9.2).[5] This is not unlike H. M. Taylor's preferred reconstruction of the *De Abbatibus* church, which he thought best described a nave flanked on each side by a long porticus, rather than a "transeptal" plan like Breamore or Romsey (Figure 9.3).[6] Another "transeptal" church visited by the 2003 conference was the Old Minster, Winchester, where the cross pattern used in the seventh century was later obscured physically on the outside by the addition of other annexes;[7] presumably its

---

2   Alastair Campbell, ed., *De Abbatibus* (Oxford: Oxford University Press, 1967), section XXII, lines 714–17; see too Harold M. Taylor, "The Architectural Interest of Aethelwulf's *De Abbatibus,*" *ASE* 3 (1974): 163–74 at 165–69.

3   Richard Gem, "Towards an Iconography of Anglo-Saxon Architecture," *Journal of the Courtauld and Warburg Institute* 46 (1983): 1–18 at 12–13; see too James Raine, ed. and trans, *Historians of the Church of York and its Archbishops, 1* (London: Rolls Series LXXI, 1879), 434.

4   Warwick Rodwell and E. Clive Rouse, "The Anglo-Saxon Rood and Other Features in the South Porch of St Mary's Church, Breamore, Hampshire," *Antiquaries Journal* 64 (1984): 298–325 at 299–300.

5   On the outside, the length of nave wall east of the porticuses is marginally greater than to the west.

6   Taylor, "Architectural Interest," 169–73.

7   Birthe Kjølbye-Biddle, "The Seventh-Century Minster at Winchester Interpreted," *The Anglo-Saxon Church. Papers on History, Architecture and Archaeology in Honour of Dr H. M. Taylor*, ed. Lawrence A. S. Butler and Richard K. Morris, Council for British Archaeology Research Report 60 (London: Council for British

significance could still be expounded inside.

The discovery of the angels was the first indication that there might survive at Bradford an ancient building; its subsequent recognition as ecclesiastical, its rescue from use as a school and cottage, and its restoration as a chapel, are a tribute both to Victorian perseverance and willfulness.[8] The study presented here results from a small excavation undertaken in the year 2000; not only was that the international millennium, but it preceded the more local celebration of the millennium of the donation of Bradford to the nuns of Shaftesbury Abbey by King Æthelred II in 1001.[9] The excavation aimed to discover whether there had been a chamber or crypt below the south porticus, part of the chapel that is demolished and identifiable only by the scar of its roof-line against the nave, from which it was entered by a narrow opening that is now used as the principal door into the building. The nineteenth-century architect J. T. Irvine observed ashlar under that opening which contrasted to the rubble foundations under the south wall of the nave at its west end. This had been visible in a cellar that was infilled during the 1870s restoration work. Enough of the infill was removed in 2000 to re-expose the ashlar, which was clearly part of the original fabric of the chapel (Figures 9.4 and 9.5).[10] Because the ground slopes steeply southwards where the chapel was built, the upper room in the south porticus would have been on a suspended floor, with the space under it only semi-subterranean, so that it was not like a normal crypt. How it

---

Archaeology, 1986), pp. 196–209; Martin Biddle, "Archaeology, Architecture and the Cult of Saints in Anglo-Saxon England," in Butler and Morris, *Anglo-Saxon Church*, pp. 18–25.

8 The sculptures were found in the 1850s, and moved to a new position before being replaced more or less where they had been found: see Harold M. Taylor, "J. T. Irvine's Work at Bradford-on-Avon," *Archaeological Journal* 129 (1972): 89–118, at 91.

9 Peter H. Sawyer, *Anglo-Saxon Charters: an Annotated List and Bibliography* (London: Royal Historical Society, 1968), no. 899.

10 I am grateful to the Trustees of the chapel, notably the incumbent Canon W. A. Matthews, who made the excavation possible.

was used is open to interpretation, but it shows how important the cruciform plan was, because of the extra time and cost involved in creating it. No other church has a space below the floor level of a side porticus, so it was not liturgically essential.

Another reason for the 2000 excavation was to see if the chapel could be more closely dated, as a seventh-century date for it has often been argued, whereas the 1001 charter provides a much later context for its construction. There was almost certainly a church of some sort at Bradford before it passed into Shaftesbury Abbey's ownership. The record of a foundation by Aldhelm, who by C.E. 680 was abbot of Malmesbury and subsequently bishop of Sherborne from 705 to 709/10,[11] was recorded by William of Malmesbury writing in the early twelfth century;[12] William also stated that in his day there was a "little church" (*ecclesiola*) at Bradford said to have been built by Aldhelm and dedicated to St. Laurence, and the assumption that the chapel was that building was soon made by those trying to save it—hence its present dedication.[13] That it was of quite such an early date began to be doubted as knowledge of Anglo-Saxon architecture developed, but was still advocated in the 1950s and 1960s by E. D. C. Jackson and Lord Eric Fletcher, whose arguments were undermined by various writers, notably H. M. Taylor.[14] Taylor's demonstration

---

11 Michael Lapidge, "Aldhelm," *The Blackwell Encyclopaedia of Anglo-Saxon England*, ed. Michael Lapidge et al. (Oxford: Blackwell Publishers, 1999), p. 25.

12 *William of Malmesbury: The Deeds of The Bishops of England (Gesta Pontificum Anglorum)*, trans. David Preest (Woodbridge: Boydell Press, 2002), p. 236. It should be stressed that William of Malmesbury was prone to exaggerate the achievements of Aldhelm: see Antonia Gransden, *Historical Writing in England, c. 550 to c. 1307* (London: Routledge and Kegan Paul, 1974), pp. 176–78.

13 Jones, "Bradford-on-Avon," p. 12.

14 E. D. C. Jackson and E. G. M. Fletcher, "The Saxon Church at Bradford-on-Avon," *Journal of the British Archaeological Association*, Third Series 16 (1953): 41–58; Harold M. Taylor, "The Anglo-Saxon Chapel at Bradford-on-Avon," *Archaeological Journal* 130 (1973), 141–75 at 171.

The Anglo-Saxon Chapel at Bradford-on-Avon, Wiltshire

that the whole chapel had been built in a single operation, apart from the widening of a window, was augmented by Eric Fernie's work on the consistency of its measurements.[15]

Nevertheless, that a church of some importance existed at Bradford towards the end of the seventh century is assured by the large stone slab now in the chapel but taken there after its discovery in the 1860s from the nearby parish church, where part of it had been reused as a lintel in the south door.[16] The panels carved overall with small relief crosses are reminiscent of the early seventh-century Sutton Hoo shoulder-clasps, and the interlaced scrolls in its borders could derive from "Celtic" hanging-bowl escutcheons.[17] Both motifs, however, continue to occur for another hundred years in such manuscripts as the Durham Cassiodorus, attributed to the second quarter of the eighth century.[18]

Whatever the slab's purpose, it must have come from a church on which considerable patronage was bestowed, perhaps Aldhelm's. Also to be considered is royal interest, since the Anglo-Saxon Chronicle records a battle fought by King Cenwealh of the Gewisse in C.E. 652 at *Bradanforde be æfna*; neither the opponent nor the outcome are named,[19] but presumably it was a Wessex success or it would

---

15 Eric Fernie, *The Architecture of the Anglo-Saxons* (London: Batsford, 1983), pp. 146–51.
16 T. J. Pettigrew, "On Antiquities in the Parish Church of Bradford-on-Avon," *Journal of the British Archaeological Association* 22 (1866): 160–65 at 164.
17 See Rupert Bruce-Mitford, *The Sutton Hoo Ship-Burial, Volume 2: Arms, Armour and Regalia*, 3 vols. (London: British Museum Publications, 1978), p. 586, Figure 429.
18 Durham, Cathedral Library MS B. II. 30: see folio 172b, illustrated in color in *The Making of England Anglo-Saxon Art and Culture A. D. 600–900*, ed. Leslie Webster and Janet Backhouse (London: British Museum Press, 1991), p. 125.
19 *The Anglo-Saxon Chronicle: a Revised Translation*, ed. and trans., Dorothy Whitelock (London: Eyre and Spottiswoode, 1961), p. 20. Although the Chronicle was compiled in the late ninth century, the mid-seventh century entries seem to derive from earlier annals, so the date is not as unreliable as earlier ones, and the record was probably made before memory of an important battle had faded.

have been tacitly omitted. The ruling family might well have had a particular interest in fostering a place associated with one of its dynasty's origin stories.

Bradford was almost certainly a royal estate in the mid-tenth century, when King Eadred's will provided for land there to go to the nunnery at Winchester[20]—it is more likely that this referred to Bradford-on-Avon than to any other "Bradford" in Wessex, as the will also provided for the donation of another north Wiltshire estate, Calne. The transfer may never have taken effect, as no other record of Nunnaminster's ownership exists, and the choice of Bradford as the meeting-place of a royal council in 957 or 958 would certainly be easier to understand if it was still a royal estate, with a royal residential complex in which it was appropriate for a council to meet. The chapel might therefore have been built as part of that tenth-century establishment, and as the charter of 1001 states that there was then a *coenobium*, a church community of some sort, at Bradford, at least one ecclesiastical building must already have existed. A community suggests a "minster," however, for which the likely site is the present Holy Trinity, a few meters south of the chapel. Similar arrangements are known at Cheddar palace, Somerset, where the Period II chapel was certainly stone-footed and quite probably stone-walled.[21] Another example is Deerhurst, where in 1056 Earl Odda built a *regiam aulam*, a chapel dedicated to the Holy Trinity;[22] this was almost certainly not the early church there but the two-celled building found in 1885, which has roughly coursed rubble stone walls with ashlar dressings. The lengths of both its nave and its chancel are within twenty centimeters of those at Bradford, though both are a little wider. Neither Cheddar nor Deerhurst had porticuses.

---

20 Sawyer, *Anglo-Saxon Charters*, no. 1515, dated 951 x 955.
21 Philip Rahtz, *The Saxon and Medieval Palaces at Cheddar*, British Archaeological Reports, British Series 65 (Oxford: British Archaeological Reports, 1979), pp. 193–233.
22 David Parsons, "Odda's Chapel, Deerhurst: Place of Worship or Royal Hall?" *Medieval Archaeology* 44 (2000): 225–28, passim.

The Anglo-Saxon Chapel at Bradford-on-Avon, Wiltshire

Because excavations rarely provide evidence that can be used to date an ecclesiastical building to within fifty years, it was not to be expected that the 2000 excavation at the Bradford chapel could show definitively whether it was a mid-tenth or an early eleventh-century structure. The two carved angels that undoubtedly flanked a crucifixion are not definitive either, partly because they cannot be proved to be coeval with the fabric, although their later insertion seems fairly improbable. Stylistic comparisons point towards a post-950s date; they are comparable to angels in the New Minster charter of ca. 966, in the slightly later Benedictional of St. Æthelwold, and, more specifically, because of the napkins over their arms to wipe the sweat and blood from Christ's face, in one of the drawings in the manuscript known as the Sherborne (or Dunstan) Pontifical,[23] which has recently been ascribed to a date between 985 and 991x3, rather than broadly to the second half of the tenth century.[24] The garments that the angels wear are similar to those shown in art works well into the eleventh century, however, with those in the Tiberius Psalter allowing a date even as late as the 1070s.[25]

The angels may therefore be a guide to a later date for the chapel than that of the council meeting, but they are of less use in settling a

---

23 As noted by Elizabeth Coatsworth, "Late Pre-Conquest Sculptures with the Crucifixion South of the Humber," *Bishop Aethelwold: his Career and Influence*, ed. Barbara Yorke (Woodbridge: Boydell Press, 1997), pp. 161-95 at p. 177.
24 Joel Rosenthal, "The Pontifical of St Dunstan," *St Dunstan: his Life, Times and Cult*, ed. Nigel Ramsay et al. (Woodbridge: Boydell Press, 1992), pp. 143–63 at pp. 159–62; see also Elżbieta Temple, *Anglo-Saxon Manuscripts 900–1066* (London: Harvey Miller, 1976), pls. 84–85 and 134 for illustrations. Other parallels are ivory panels, perhaps from book-covers, attributed to the late tenth/early eleventh centuries, but only on stylistic grounds; these have half-length angels in relief, with similar napkins: see John Beckwith, *Ivory Carvings in Early Medieval England* (London: Harvey, Miller, and Medcalf, 1972), nos. 17 and 78.
25 On the basis of the Easter Tables in that manuscript (London, British Library MS Cotton Tiberius C. vi), see T. A. Heslop, "A Dated 'Late Anglo-Saxon' Illuminated Psalter," *Antiquaries Journal* 72 (1992): 137–54 for its late dating; and Temple, *Anglo-Saxon Manuscripts*, pl. 302 for an example, though its drawing may be thought more inert than the earlier examples.

recent controversy that has arisen because of doubts raised about the true nature of the 1001 charter, which have implications for the building. The document is known only through the copy in Shaftesbury's fifteenth-century cartulary, but whether it was copied accurately was called into question by the late Patrick Wormald in a review, a matter that he amplified in his book on English law.[26] The nub of the problem is not the veracity of the date ascribed to the donation; 1001 is quite credible. The difficulty is partly in the phraseology of the Latin used, which Wormald regarded as suspiciously clumsy in places, but which others consider may merely be due to the processes of transcription into the fifteenth-century cartulary.[27] Wormald's other concern was that those passages about which he had grammatical doubts say that in the event of a threat by barbarians, i.e., the Vikings, the nuns were to take to Bradford the relics of King Æthelred's half-brother Edward, and those of their other saints.[28] The difficulty with this is, firstly, lack of other evidence of the king's support of the cult and secondly, the very precise date of composition of the charter. As late as 1014 Archbishop Wulfstan made no mention of Edward's cult, and although the law-code of 1008 states the saint's mass-day, the relevant sentence may be an interpolation.[29]

26 See Patrick Wormald, "Review of S. Ridyard, *The Royal Saints of Anglo-Saxon England* (Cambridge 1988)," *Journal of Ecclesiastical History* 42 (1991): 101–2; and *The Making of English Law: King Alfred to the Twelfth Century. Volume I: Legislation and its Limits* (Oxford: Blackwell Publishing, 1999), pp. 343–4; see also Susan E. Kelly, ed., *Charters of Shaftesbury Abbey*, Anglo-Saxon Charters V (Oxford: Oxford University Press for British Academy, 1996), pp. 114–22 accepting the possibility that references to Edward could have been added later.

27 Ann Williams, *Æthelred the Unready: the Ill-Counselled King* (London: Hambledon and London, 2003), p. 16.

28 Edward had been killed at Corfe in Dorset, and after a year his supposed body was taken to Wareham and then to Shaftesbury Abbey: see Williams, *Æthelred the Unready*, pp. 1–17; and Barbara Yorke, *Nunneries and the Anglo-Saxon Royal Houses* (London: Continuum, 2003), pp. 115–16 for all that was involved. Although he was only the king's half-brother, *germanus* was used of him in the charter.

29 Wormald, *English Law*, pp. 343–44. At the 2003 Cross Conference, Patrick

The second difficulty is that the charter must have been written before 7 October 1001, as it was signed by Bishop Ælfgar who died on that day, yet according to Edward's probable biographer, who presumably had direct access to records and traditions at Shaftesbury, the royal corpse was translated to a new shrine in the sanctuary of the abbey church there on 20 June 1001.[30] That a new refuge, albeit a temporary one, was already being planned for Edward, even as he was being moved to a more conspicuous position at Shaftesbury, has been a difficulty for some commentators, but alternatively it can be seen as a sensible precaution, the donation not only giving the nuns a valuable estate for their maintenance, but a place to go to if north Dorset came under threat.[31]

Other points made in support of the authenticity of the whole text of the 1001 charter have included the possibility that Queen Ælfthryth died on 17 November 1000, so that her death would have freed her son to commemorate his half-brother, whom she was popularly believed to have murdered; but she may not in fact have died until 17 November 1001, after the issue of the charter.[32] Æthelred was certainly supporting the cult of St. Edith, another of Edgar's children by someone other than Ælfthryth, at Wilton before 1001;[33] the Shaftesbury nuns

---

Wormald spoke on this issue after my lecture, and subsequently set his views out in an e-mail message to me; he remained convinced that in 1014 Wulfstan would not have failed to mention the cult of Edward if the king had sanctioned it by 1008. This clarification was the last of many benefits that I had from Patrick's scholarship, learning and general conversation in an intermittent acquaintance going back more than thirty years to our first meeting, appropriately at a conference that I had arranged to mark the 1100th anniversary of the accession of King Alfred.

30   Christine E. Fell, *Edward King and Martyr*, Leeds Texts and Monographs New Series (Leeds: University of Leeds, 1971), p. 12; see also Kelly, *Charters of Shaftesbury Abbey*, p. 119.
31   Williams, *Æthelred the Unready*, pp. 16 and 84.
32   Simon Keynes, *The Diplomas of King Æthelred 'the Unready', 978–1016: a Study in their Use as Historical Evidence* (Cambridge: Cambridge University Press, 1980), p. 210 n. 203.
33   Yorke, *Nunneries*, pp. 122 and 173.

would have known of this concern for a family member,[34] and whoever instructed that the Bradford charter should be drawn up, may have thought to please the king by stressing their care for his half-brother, whatever Æthelred himself might actually have thought.

The importance of all this for St. Laurence's chapel is of course that the interpretation generally favored for it in recent years has been that its very high-quality masonry, design, and sculpture are because it was built by Shaftesbury in the years immediately following the nuns' acquisition of the Bradford estate to house the relics of Edward in the splendor that their king expected.[35] A slightly later date is not precluded by architectural features, however, and the floor-space is no less than that of some small late Anglo-Saxon parish churches, such as St. Martin at Wareham, Dorset. On the other hand, the very narrow openings, especially into the east end, do not suggest congregational use, and Wareham St. Martin and others do not have porticuses.[36] Could the chapel still have been intended as a setting for Edward's shrine after Æthelred's death in 1016, after which the boy-martyr's cult was undoubtedly acceptable? It seems unlikely, because the only evidence that the nuns contemplated such a move are the suspect phrases in the charter, and if these are additions to the original, after Cnut's accession in 1017, Shaftesbury would not

---

34 Pauline Stafford ("Queens, Nunneries, and Reforming Churchmen: Gender, Religious Status and Reform in Tenth- and Eleventh-Century England," *Past and Present* 163 [1999]: 3–35 at 29) suggests that Shaftesbury also had links to Edith and Wulfthryth, and would therefore have had an internal reason to favor Edward's cult if he were also the latter's son—but he may not have been: see Williams, *Æthelred the Unready*, pp. 1–5.

35 Richard Gem, "Church Architecture in the Reign of King Æthelred," *Ethelred the Unready*, ed. David Hill, British Archaeological Reports, British Series 59 (Oxford: British Archaeological Reports, 1978), pp. 105–27 for a succinct summary.

36 David A. Hinton and C. J. Webster, "Excavations at the Church of St Martin, Wareham, 1985–6, and Minsters in South-East Dorset," *Proceedings of the Dorset Natural History and Archaeological Society* 109 (1987): 47–54 at 47–48.

have expressed a need to protect the relics against barbarians—and there would scarcely have been time to get anything done in the brief interlude of Edmund Ironside's rule. Any post-Æthelredian intention to move Edward's shrine is more likely to have resulted in some memory of the possibility, yet no part of Edward was ever associated with Bradford, even though bits of him were spread with surprising liberality.[37] The architecture of the chapel certainly fits better with having been intended to have a role as a shrine, and the below-floor chamber was perhaps to serve as a crypt for some of the other Shaftesbury relics for which the charter made provision.

One further problem about the precise date of the chapel at Bradford is that the charter seems to allow for Shaftesbury Abbey as a whole to be relocated, and the small nave hardly seems big enough for the whole community to have been contained within it. So little survives of the late Anglo-Saxon nunnery churches of Wessex, however, that quite what provision was made for worship in them is uncertain. The Nunnaminster at Winchester has only the foundations of the west end of the second church on the site, attributed to Æthelwold's reforms in the later tenth century,[38] and recent geophysical work by the University of Southampton at Wherwell has established the possibility of an eastern apse, as well as much of the layout of the post-Conquest abbey.[39] At Shaftesbury there are

---

37 *William of Malmesbury*, trans. Preest, p. 125; William of Malmesbury did not pick up any hint of a cult based at Bradford or he would surely have mentioned it, since he wrote about what he found of it at Shaftesbury. The charter stated that the nuns were to leave a *familia* at Bradford, but there is no evidence that they did so; Blair notes similar uncertainty over what was intended for the elaborate tower at Barton-on-Humber where no community is recorded but which was on land associated with the community at Barrow: John Blair, *The Church in Anglo-Saxon Society* (Oxford: Oxford University Press, 2005), p. 360.

38 G. Scobie and K. Qualmann, *Nunnaminster: a Saxon and Medieval Community of Nuns* (Winchester: Winchester Museums Service, 1993), unpaginated.

39 Wherwell: see Edward Roberts, with K. Clark, "The Rediscovery of Two Major Monastic Buildings at Wherwell," *Proceedings of the Hampshire Field Club*

only conflicting descriptions of the provision made for Edward the Martyr's remains.[40] Wilton is known merely by a contemporary description of the timber church "in the form of a cross."[41] Substantial parts of a church underlie the present Romanesque and later abbey at Romsey, however, enough to show that it was a cruciform building; the north wall of its north porticus and the south wall of its south porticus are now visible as a result of excavations in the 1970s, and part of the north side of its apsidal chancel can be seen under a trap-door, discovered when the floors were lifted in 1899–1900 (Figure 9.3).[42]

Comparison with the chapel at Bradford at first glance suggests that Romsey Abbey was on a much larger scale. The length of its nave is however in doubt. The 1970s excavations found traces of foundations around the west end of the present church, but they were differently built from the apsidal Anglo-Saxon church, so that building must have terminated somewhere to the east. There is no archeological basis for the suggestion that its west wall lay between the two westernmost pillars of the present building. The Romanesque nave was built in two phases, with an interruption of about fifty years indicated by the differences between the masonry of the last three bays and the Norman work of the first four. It is unlikely that the Normans would have tolerated a nave shorter than that of their

---

and Archaeological Society 53 (1998): 137–54 at 152; and Yorke, *Nunneries*, p. 61.
40 John Chandler, *A Higher Reality: the History of Shaftesbury's Royal Nunnery* (East Knoyle: Hobnob Press, 2003), pp. 21–25.
41 Gem, "Towards an Iconography," 13–14.
42 The excavations are reported by Ian R. Scott, *Romsey Abbey. Report on the Excavations 1973–1991*, Hampshire Field Club and Archaeological Society Monograph 8 (Hampshire: Hampshire Field Club and Archaeological Society in co-operation with Test Valley Archaeological Trust, 1996), pp. 38–43 for dating, which depends upon the use of mortar colored pink by the use of crushed Roman brick and tile, on reused Roman stonework, and on radiocarbon dates clustering around the later tenth century which were obtained from graves thought contemporary with the structures.

predecessors, so they probably built the center part of their west end over the Saxon west wall foundations; they certainly used the south and north walls for the bases of the pillars in their first four bays. Their west crossing arch was just east of the east walls of the two Saxon porticuses, so most of the length of the first two Norman bays overlies their walls and their openings into the choir/crossing; the Anglo-Saxon nave would on that interpretation have only been the length of the next two bays, some ten meters rather than the seventeen meters proposed in the excavation report. In other words, it was much closer to the length of the Bradford chapel nave, though it was wider and the placing of the porticuses different. Nevertheless, it makes it more credible that the arrangement at Bradford allowed for the whole Shaftesbury community to have been envisaged as fitting inside.

If Holy Trinity church already existed at Bradford, the nuns would not have had to provide a church for parochial use when they acquired the estate. A small building was therefore all that they needed. Recent excavations at the Old Minster, Winchester, and St. Oswald's, Gloucester,[43] have shown how varied were major Anglo-Saxon buildings (Figure 9.6), so precise analogies for Bradford should perhaps not be expected. The lower chamber in the south porticus further emphasizes how exceptional the Bradford chapel is, demanding an exceptional explanation. If the charter of 1001 can be taken at face value, the provision of a lower chamber for some of the relics of the "other saints" at Shaftesbury is a permissible interpretation (Figure 9.7). Were it not for the charter, however, a direct association between Edward the Martyr and the surviving building would probably never have been suggested, and to say that the physical

---

43   Winchester: see Kjølbye-Biddle, "Winchester" and Biddle, "Archaeology"; Gloucester: see Carolyn Heighway and Richard Bryant, *The Golden Minster. The Anglo-Saxon Minster and Later Medieval Priory of St Oswald at Gloucester*, Council for British Archaeology Research Report 117 (York: Council for British Archaeology, 1999), p. 119.

evidence helps to confirm the documentary would foster a circular argument. Yet even if some doubt may linger over the precise authenticity of the phrases in the 1001 charter that associate Bradford directly with Edward, the structure still seems most appropriately identified as a "reliquary chapel" on architectural grounds.[44] The nuns created spaces into which could be made individual journeys of admiration and veneration, overseen in the principal chamber by the awe-inspiring rood.

---

44 This phrase was attributed to a lecture given by Dr. Harold M. Taylor by Jeremy Haslam, "The Towns of Wiltshire," *Anglo-Saxon Towns in Southern England*, ed. Jeremy Haslam (Chichester: Phillimore, 1984), pp. 87–148 at p. 93.

The Anglo-Saxon Chapel at Bradford-on-Avon, Wiltshire

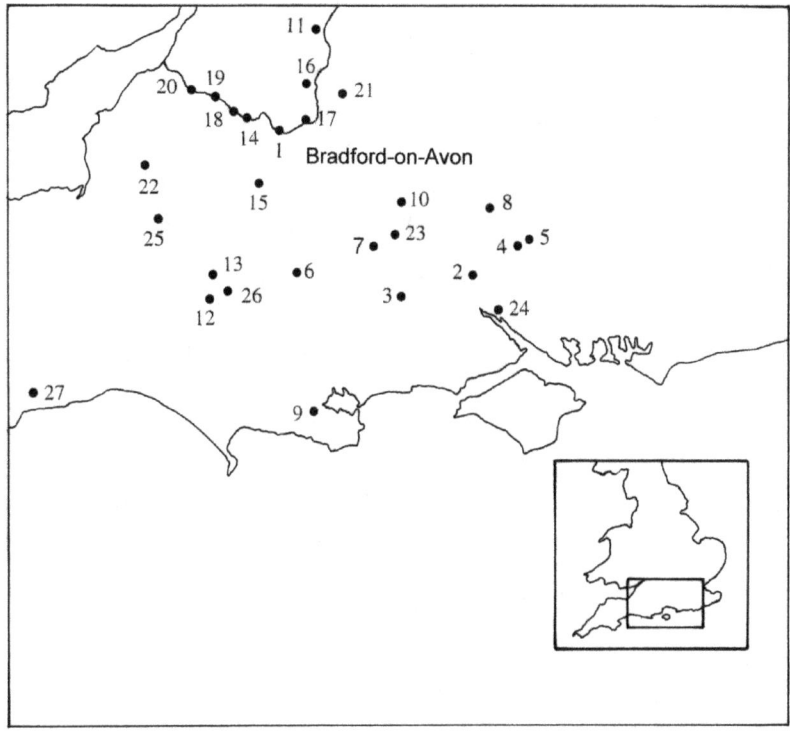

Fig. 9.1. Places in southern England mentioned in the text, or otherwise relevant. 1, Bradford-on-Avon; 2, Romsey; 3, Breamore; 4, Winchester; 5, Headbourne Worthy; 6, Shaftesbury; 7, Wilton; 8, Wherwell; 9, Wareham; 10, Amesbury; 11, Malmesbury; 12, Sherborne; 13, South Cadbury; 14, Bath; 15, Frome; 16, Chippenham; 17, Melksham; 18, Bitton; 19, Keynsham; 20, Bristol; 21, Calne; 22, Cheddar; 23, Old Sarum; 24, Southampton; 25, Glastonbury; 26, Milborne Port; 27, Sidbury.

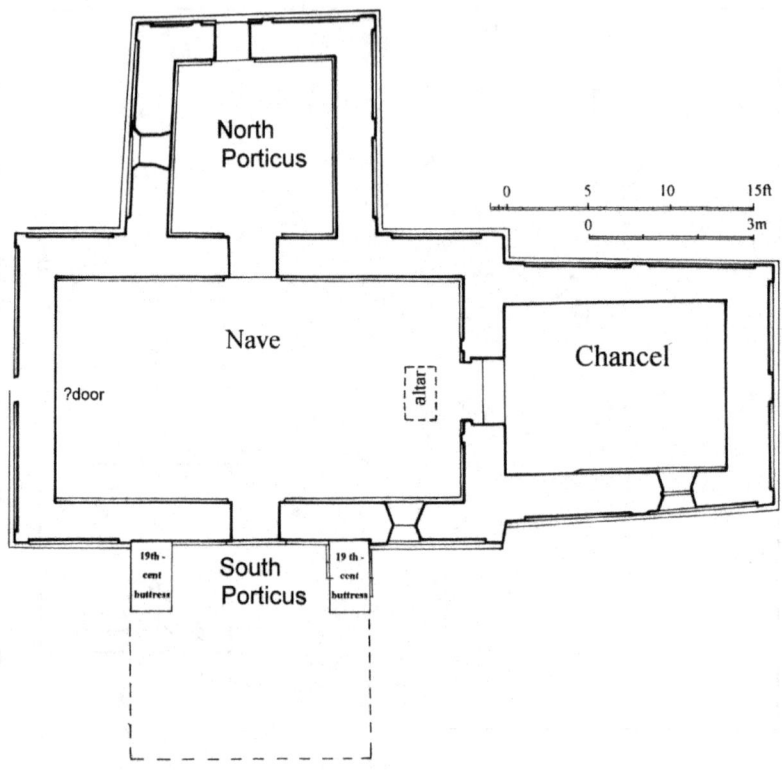

Fig. 9.2. Plan of Bradford-on-Avon chapel, adapted from Taylor, "Irvine's Work," (see n. 8, p. 321 above). A Victorian buttress replaced the east side of the Anglo-Saxon porticus, but its bottom courses were found to survive in 2000, and their outline is shown. Drawn by David A. Hinton.

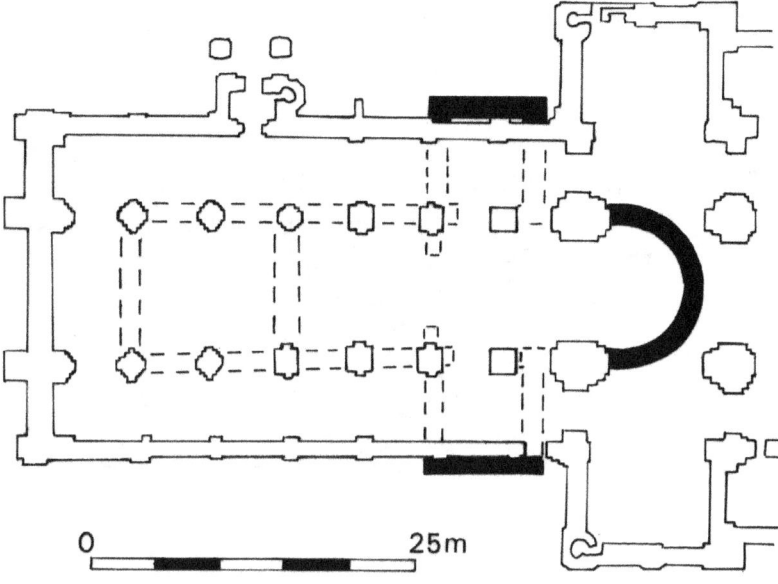

Fig. 9.3. Romsey Abbey church, adapted from Scott, *Romsey Abbey*, fig. 2 (see n. 42. p. 330 above), showing two possible lengths of the Anglo-Saxon nave.

Fig. 9.4. Scale drawing of the exposed area below the south porticus and parts of the nave; the differences between the west and east sides could be because the west end was underpinned in the early eighteenth century. Drawn by David A. Hinton.

The Anglo-Saxon Chapel at Bradford-on-Avon, Wiltshire

Fig. 9.5. Above: the south wall below the door into the nave, revealed in excavation in 2000. On the right, the wall is that of the Victorian east buttress, except for the three lowest courses, which are Anglo-Saxon. Below: the rubble footings of the south wall of the nave east of the east buttress, which is the wall on the left, again except for the bottom courses, here slightly stepped. Photo by David A. Hinton.

David Hinton

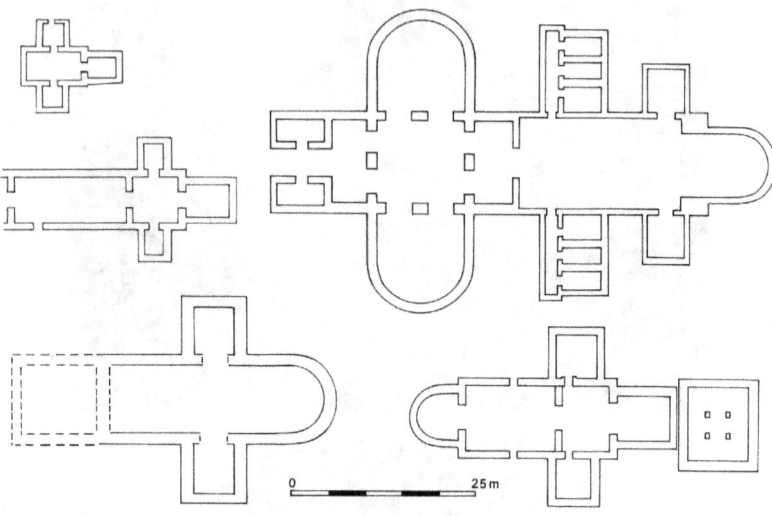

Fig. 9.6. Comparative outline plans of five Anglo-Saxon churches at the same scale: Top left – Bradford-on-Avon; Center left – Breamore; Lower left – Romsey; Lower right – St. Oswald's, Gloucester, as in Period 2; note that not only is the eastern crypt an addition to Period 1 but so also is the division of a choir area from the nave; Upper right – Old Minster, Winchester, c. 970.

The Anglo-Saxon Chapel at Bradford-on-Avon, Wiltshire

Fig. 9.7. Reconstruction of the east-facing section of Bradford-on-Avon, assuming the existence of a full-scale rood, a principal altar in front of the chancel arch, and subsidiary altars in the other chambers. An altar or shrine in the east arm beyond the chancel arch would, presumably deliberately, have been hidden from a visitor's first glance. Drawn by Barbara McNee.

New Media and the Nunburnholme Cross

Martin K. Foys

THIS ESSAY DIFFERS FROM ITS COMPANIONS in that it addresses the transitive, transeunt, trans-historical, transcultural and transdisciplinary qualities of the Anglo-Saxon cross through the application of New Media, the technological revolution of expression that shares such multivalent potential. The function and meaning of cross sculpture generally needs to be understood as more (as is tradition) than frozen historical moments of a primarily artistic nature. The focus of this essay, the relatively unknown Nunburnholme Cross, stands as a particularly clear proof of this need, and of the difficulty that earlier media forms (ironically, given Nunburnholme's current physical state, even the medium of stone sculpture itself) have in capturing the diachronic and synchronic matrices of meaning that must limn our understanding of such objects.[1]

---

1 Though it has been published after the fact, this essay predates a longer, expanded study of the Nunburnholme Cross in my 2007 book, *Virtually Anglo-Saxon: Old Media, New Media, and Early Medieval Studies in the Late Age of Print*. The later treatment does expand considerably upon ideas found in this essay, and shares some introductory and descriptive text. But these studies also differ in significant ways. *Virtually Anglo-Saxon* considers the cross with regards to shifting perceptions of medieval space and territory in light of new digital spaces such as cyberspace, and to the post-medieval Newtonian revolution that homogenized conceptions of "real" space as absolute and measurable. By comparison, this essay more specifically considers the sculpture from the New

New Media and the Nunburnholme Cross

In a talk a few years back on a more famous Anglo-Saxon stone sculpture, the Ruthwell Cross, Fred Orton commented that Ruthwell today stands as a sculpture remarkably "resistant to space."[2] Orton's phrase applies specifically to how Ruthwell, given its complicated reconstructive history and its eroded and fragmented condition, survives in a singular state that cannot accurately represent past physical iterations.[3] In other words, the current physical space Ruthwell occupies actually has the potential to mislead the viewer as to how it existed before. "Resistant to space" likewise describes a much more obscure monument from the period, the Anglo-Scandinavian Nunburnholme Cross. Nunburnholme, as we shall see shortly, resists space because its current physical state, the lack of its original spatial, cultural, and aesthetic contexts, as well as its incorrect reconstruction, all work in concert to deny any easy unpacking of its meaning. If anything, confronting the physical artifact *in situ* in Nunburnholme only serves to highlight such resistance, as this particular monument helps demonstrate how half a millennium of scholarship within the limitations of the printed medium has conditioned us to perceive surviving medieval monuments through modern lenses that render them resistant to fine interpretation.

The recent rise of New Media theory, though, gives us a useful vocabulary with which to begin to consider these micro- and

---

Media notions of remediation and transcoding, as might be practically applied to editing the object digitally.

2 Fred Orton, "Rethinking the Ruthwell Monument: Interpretation and Overinterpretation; Fragments and Critique; Tradition and History; Tongues and Sockets . . . Again," public talk given at the University of London, March, 2002.

3 Questions concerning the present physical condition of Ruthwell remain under debate, including whether the monument as restored is accurate to its original physical state, or whether even its sections might derive from two different monuments. See Fred Orton, "Rethinking the Ruthwell and Bewcastle Monuments: Some Strictures on Similarity; Some Questions of History," *Theorizing Anglo-Saxon Stone Sculpture*, ed. Catherine E. Karkov and Fred Orton (Morgantown: West Virginia University Press, 2003), pp. 65–92.

Martin Foys

macrocosmic resistances. New Media, simply put, are the new and pervasive digital technologies of representation that have developed in the past thirty years. New Media theory in part considers the ways in which digital media reformulate discourse and culture into models that are less linearly structured and therefore more able to accommodate the temporal and spatial eccentricities or disjunctions so emblematic of the Nunburnholme Cross in particular and many Anglo-Scandinavian and Anglo-Saxon crosses in general. Digital technology carries with it the potential to negotiate and document the particular ways in which pre-modern expressions today resist our conventional modes of studying them.

The Physical Nunburnholme Cross

Like so many other rarely studied objects of the surviving corpus of Anglo-Saxon stone sculpture, we still seem to know more about what we do not know about Nunburnholme than anything else.[4] In the late nineteenth century, sections of the Viking-era cross were rediscovered built into the walls of St. James Church in Nunburnholme, East Yorkshire.[5] The church at Nunburnholme was built in the late twelfth or early thirteenth century; during this time or later, the top and bottom fragments of the monument were integrated into the south porch of the building.[6] A head for the cross has never been found (though a mortise socket exists at the stone's top), and some questions remain as to whether there might originally have been a

---

4   James T. Lang, *York and Eastern Yorkshire*, Corpus of Anglo-Saxon Stone Sculpture III, 8 vols. (Oxford: Oxford University Press, 1991), pp. 38 and 189–193; I. R. Pattison, "The Nunburnholme Cross and Anglo-Danish Sculpture in York," *Archaeologia* 104 (1973): 209–34; and Lang, "The Sculptors of the Nunburnholme Cross," *Archaeological Journal* 133 (1976): 75–94.
5   Rev. M. C. F. Morris, *Nunburnholme: Its History and Antiquities* (London: Henry Frowde, 1907), p. 82; and J. Romilly Allen, "Pre-Norman Cross-Shaft at Nunburnholme, Yorkshire," *The Reliquary* VII (1901): 98–106, at 99.
6   Morris, *Nunburnholme*, pp. 69–88.

middle section of a third panel.[7] After their discovery, the sections of the monument were removed from the wall and "restored" incorrectly as a standing monument; the top section is now mounted on the bottom section, but turned 180 degrees around.[8]

The surviving sections of Nunburnholme reveal variations of the same design on all four faces.[9] Each side consists of two main panels, roughly equal in size, edged by molding, with a small figural design at top. The shaft is carved from ashlar, a limestone not typically found in the East Riding (Yorkshire) area. Most likely, the stone is recycled, quarried from Tadcaster by the Romans, and originally used in building at York.[10] The limestone was then presumably re-excavated at York during Scandinavian settlement in the late ninth or early tenth century, and transported to Nunburnholme for carving. Since James T. Lang, critics have generally agreed that two distinct sculptors worked on the stone during the Viking period. The so-called First Sculptor, distinguished by modern critics through a more sophisticated sense of modeling and inclined cutting, worked in late Anglian mode with "Carolingian echoes," and in a wholly Christian idiom.[11] However, the First Sculptor only completed somewhere in the vicinity of one and one-quarter sides. The Second Sculptor finished the piece, but worked in a style markedly different from that of the First Sculptor, using a technique generally characterized as less accomplished, and notably, introducing more explicitly secular and Scandinavian iconography to the work (see Figures. 10.1–10.2) for all sides of the sculpture.[12]

---

7 Pattison, *Nunburnholme Cross*, 210, and Lang, "The Sculptors," 92.
8 For the accepted argument that the two sections of Nunburnholme were assembled 180 degrees the wrong way around, see Pattison, passim.
9 Lang, "The Sculptors," provides a thorough stylistic analysis of each sculptor's work, and the face names here follow his designation.
10 Lang, *York and Eastern Yorkshire*, p. 189.
11 Lang, "The Sculptors," 86 and *York and Eastern Yorkshire*, p. 192.
12 Lang, "The Sculptors," provides a thorough stylistic analysis, passim, of each sculptor's work.

Martin Foys

The surviving sections of the cross reveal variations of the same design on all four faces. Each side consists of two main panels, roughly equal in size, edged by molding, with small figural design at top. In its "restored" state, the top and bottom sections of the monument have been reversed. The following description presents the cross in its earlier form before restoration; original sides have been aligned. Side D (Figure 10.1, top left and bottom right) reveals what the First Sculptor intended to be the design scheme for all of the sides. A frieze of two angels adorns the top, their heads centered on the corners, with arms reaching down to grasp an arch framing a beast in profile, with its head thrown back. Below the upper design, a pelleted arch and border frame the lower two panels, which each contain a figure dressed in ecclesiastical garments—a haloed saint above, and a figure holding a cup-like vessel below (likely indicating a mass celebration). Both figures wear square devices on their chests of indeterminate function, though the lower one might be a book satchel or *rational*.[13] The lower half of the bottom figure has been overcarved with a scene of two seated figures. The First Sculptor also likely carved the angel frieze at the top of Side B, and began the angels and borders of Side A.[14] The Second Sculptor, however, executed most, if not all of the rest of the original work, at times substantially altering the First Sculptor's scheme.

Side A (Figure 10.2, top left and bottom right) contains a "gripping angels" motif at the top, but, along with Side B, lacks the small beast figure that the First Sculptor included on Side D. The left border of the upper section also shows the outline of the First Sculptor's border design, but remains unexecuted, most obviously lacking the pelleting of the adjoining side. The upper right border does not as clearly follow the original design. The upper panel of Side A shows a secular figure, in half-profile, seated on a chair and holding a large,

---

13 Lang, "Sculptors," 85; Richard N. Bailey, *Viking Age Sculpture in Northern England* (London: Collins, 1980), p. 232.

14 Lang, *York and Eastern Yorkshire*, p. 192.

pommeled, Viking-type sword, wearing a hat or helm terminating in volutes. The lower figure lacks its head (perhaps obscured by the modern concrete join), but also consists of a seated figure in half-profile, holding a staff of some sort in the right hand, and grasping a rectangular object, possibly a book, in the left. Though the beginning of the feet of this figure remains, a later sculptor has overcarved the bottom of this scene with an intrusive depiction of a centaur and a smaller human figure.

Side B (Figure 10.1, bottom left and top right) possesses the same layout as Side A, preserving the gripping angels motif at top, but is entirely lacking the First Sculptor's border design. The upper panel contains a front-facing ecclesiastical figure, who wears a double cowl that transforms into a stole grasped in both hands. On top of the stole, the figure displays a large rectangular device; as with the lower figure on Side D, this could again represent a book satchel or *rational*. Some debate remains whether this figure is the work of the Second Sculptor, the First Sculptor, or even an additional sculptor.[15] In the lower panel, the Second Sculptor departs from the overall design by carving not a portrait but a beast chain instead.[16]

On Side C (Figure 10.2, bottom left and top right), the Second Sculptor abandons the gripping angels design entirely, replacing it with two small facing dragons, bound at their necks by a narrow band that loops around the body of the left-hand beast. The upper panel displays a Virgin Mary and Child, facing front. Mary has a deep, dished halo, and the Christ Child holds a rectangular object, possibly a book. As on Side A, the head of the lower-panel figure

---

15 Lang, "Sculptors," 80; see also Lang, "Pre-Conquest Sculpture in Eastern Yorkshire," in *Medieval Art and Architecture in the East Riding of Yorkshire, British Archaeological Association,* Conference Transactions IX for the Year 1983, ed. Christopher Wilson, (London: W. S. Maney and Son, 1989), pp. 1–8, at 2.

16 Since most beast chains occupy the entire side of a shaft, Lang (in *York and Eastern Yorkshire*, p. 192) acknowledges the "slim case" that the fragments represent two different monuments, but favors the stylistic unity promoted by the iconography of the other sides.

is missing; two large birds perch on the shoulders of a figure, who reaches down and places his hands on the heads of two lower figures, who in turn reach up and touch his lower torso. The scene is most probably a crucifixion, though some critics have read it as a scene of benediction.[17]

The Second Sculptor also saw fit to overcarve the bottom section of the First Sculptor's mass priest in the lower panel of side D, adding a scene of two figures seated, facing each other. Though a definitive claim cannot be made for the identity of this scene, Lang has presented a compelling argument that it represents part of the pagan Sigurd myth, where Sigurd cooks the heart of the dragon.[18] In a turn of plastic justice, a third sculptor, probably working more than one hundred and fifty years later, after the Conquest, then overcarved another pagan element onto a seated Second Sculptor figure, adding in a decidedly Romanesque figure of a centaur and child, an addition that has been described as a "Norman doodle."[19]

As it literally stands, the monument is fraught with interpretative difficulty. The production of its original meaning spans two centuries and three carving styles; other layers further pile on top and fill underneath this sculptural *historia*. Through time, the Nunburnholme cross has been a recycler of the Roman past, a recyclee later built into the thirteenth-century church, and finally a (botched) reconstruction in the nineteenth century. All of these diachronic moments of Nunburnholme's meaning serve to increase its modern-day resistance, since the differing configurations and purposes of this monument add temporal issues of interpretation to its more obvious spatial ones. The cultural syncretism of this Anglo-Scandinavian Christian cross

---

17 See Lang, *York and Eastern Yorkshire*, p. 193; and Bailey, *Viking Age Sculpture*, pp. 156–57.
18 Pattison, "Nunburnholme Cross," 230; and Lang, "Sigurd and Weland in Pre-Conquest Carving," *Yorkshire Archaeological Journal* 48 (1976): 83–94, at 89. For a full account of the Sigurd myth, see Bailey, *Viking Age Sculpture*, pp. 116–24.
19 Lang, "Pre-Conquest Sculpture," p. 2.

is confused, to say the least—first wholly Christian in its content, *then* twice with pagan and secular additions (in the Scandinavian content of the Second Sculptor and the Romanesque detail of the Third Sculptor), then demolished, and then Christian yet again, this time literally supporting the walls of an Anglo-Norman Church. To begin with, as an historical record of Christian conversion of pagan cultures, Nunburnholme also reminds us that the progression of early English faith from the Germanic and pagan to the English and Christian was neither chronologically linear nor ideologically smooth.[20]

Stone itself is hard, durable, and resistant to change. We tend not to think of carved sculpture as fluid and mutable, preferring to read the final physical form of monuments like Nunburnholme as the vestigial record of a singular object, designed and intended to be one way, and frozen in time. The surviving stone of Nunburnholme collapses its complicated *historia* into a "fixed" physical and temporal state. The usual scholarly mode of the reproduction of such monuments as a series of two-dimensional black and white photographs, frozen on the page, has the inevitable effect of further flattening them, and literally providing fixed perspectives for their study and interpretation.

The Remediated Nunburnholme Cross

Seeing the Nunburnholme Cross today—inside, in the 11' × 11' bell tower, and reconstructed the wrong way round—makes it difficult to have any real sense of the way the cross originally stood. One has trouble holding one side in the mind's eye while imagining the other (the room has a small mirror hung inside to aid, but its effectiveness is limited). The only way, currently, to come to grips with the reality

---

20 Nicholas Howe, *Migration and Mythmaking in Anglo-Saxon England* (New Haven: Yale University Press, 1989), pp. 108–42. For a fuller treatment of this argument, see *Virtually Anglo-Saxon,* pp. 170–79.

of Nunburnholme is through another medium of representation; to work with the physical monument, one needs printed reconstructions in hand while viewing it. Such reliance, in the terminology of New Media theorists Jay David Bolter and Michael Grusin, *remediates* the expression of the stone sculpture, as the logic of one medium, print, is then imposed upon another, sculpture, through reproduction and reception.[21] As Bolter and Grusin note, the logic of remediation inverts the "natural" progression of copy and source since the printed reproduction assumes the veracity of the original form that the physical object can no longer provide. This process inevitably refashions the represented subject twice: print reconfigures the monument on the page, and then the reader reconstructs an ideal form of the monument from a set of black and white line drawings or photographs and the accompanying printed words of scholarly interpretation.

As Walter Ong has pointed out, since "intelligence is relentlessly reflexive, so that even the external tools that it uses to implement its working become 'internalized,' that is, part of its own reflexive process," we eventually interiorize technologies of representation, thereby making them transparent and immediate.[22] Writing, printing, and photographic reproduction are technologies that have gradually become integrated in modern life to the point that they appear to function organically in their representational roles. The danger in such interiorization, though, is that we then become unable to grasp the limits of such media easily, or the degree to which they begin not to reproduce their subjects, but actively to *produce* and shape their meaning.

As readers and viewers, we therefore desire and expect transparency

---

21   The underlying theory behind Jay David Bolter and Richard Grusin, *Remediation: Understanding New Media* (Cambridge: MIT Press, 2000), passim.
22   Walter J. Ong, *Orality and Literacy: The Technologizing of the Word* (London: Routledge, 1982), p. 81.

as we use the media we have interiorized. But when the media fail to provide a transparent experience, we have an opportunity to better understand both the limits of the media we use *and* the material they represent. Going to Nunburnholme with paper reconstructions in hand (as I first did in 1997) to understand the "reality" of this monument, accentuates the lack of transparency in such interpretative moments, or what New Media theorists term "hypermediacy"—the explicit awareness of the representational mechanism and limits of a particular medium.[23] Hypermediacy, where in effect the apparatus of representation overwhelms the content represented, functions as a sort of *doppelgänger* to such desires of transparency. The remediated gap between our sense of what the Nunburnholme Cross is supposed to be and its current physical state produces a profound disjunction between the desire to lose one's self in the transparent reception of this artistic expression (to see the object as it should be) and the hypermediate need to filter this reception through the opacity of print. The result, the summation of standing in a cramped thirteenth-century bell tower staring at stone and then paper and then stone again, is more disorienting than orienting.

Digital media provide the opportunity to bridge such gaps, and remove some of the boundaries between representation and reality mandated by the limitations of print culture.[24] The most fundamental difference between digital and print media remains the fluidity that digital expression brings to its subject, in stark contrast to the static, fixed nature of printed reproductions. In virtual versions of the Nunburnholme Cross, one can construct models of the physical artifact from any point in its *historia*. Further, such versions could

---

23 Bolter and Grusin, *Remediation*, pp. 20–4.
24 See Edward Christie, "The Image of the Letter: From the Anglo-Saxons to the *Electronic Beowulf*," *Culture, Theory and Critique* 44.2 (2003): 129–50, who points out that such technology also creates its own interpretative gaps and limitations as it remediates prior forms, but such considerations are beyond the scope of this short, exploratory essay.

then be manipulated with respect to the spatial and cultural circumstances of the work, allowing one more fully to understand not simply its content, but its context as well, from recycled Roman pillar to modern-day reconstruction, and every stage in between.

My early efforts, detailed below, to use New Media in the study and reconstruction of the Nunburnholme Cross, only scratch the surface of such new modes of representation, while at the same time revealing the still considerable limitations in the ways we understand the revolutionary potential of New Media. The usual mode of websites, for instance, such as the one I used in conference presentations to introduce the details of Nunburnholme, remains overwhelmingly two-dimensional in format and content (see Figure 10.3). In this capacity, websites differ little from print photography in the static presentation of three-dimensional data—indeed, they more or less remediate the older technology, folding it into the new. But as Lev Manovich has theorized, digital forms also reformulate older media in distinct ways. Traditional media present textual and visual data in only one mode, as only one kind of audience, the human viewer, needs to process and understand it. Digital media, on the other hand, function by what Manovich has termed "transcoding." In transcoding, digital media break down discursive data into discrete numerical values of ones and zeros (binary code) that a machine can read, but simultaneously reformulate this binary code into cultural, human codes—the forms of signification readable by human users.[25] By breaking representations of physical data into pure numbers, transcoding provides ways

---

25 See Lev Manovich, *The Language of New Media* (Cambridge: MIT Press, 2001), pp. 45–48: "In new media lingo, to 'transcode' something is to translate it into another format. The computerization of culture gradually accomplishes similar transcoding in relation to all cultural categories and concepts. That is, cultural categories and concepts are substituted, on the level of meaning and/or language, by new ones that derive from the computer's ontology, epistemology, and pragmatics. New media thus acts as a forerunner of this more general process of cultural reconceptualization" (p. 47).

of viewing, arranging, and manipulating such data at several orders of magnitude greater than physical technologies. In the case of an object like Nunburnholme, transcoding could dramatically dissolve the finite physical boundaries of representation encouraged by print culture and the models of scholarship it engenders, and reconstruct this object over and over again as it is brought through space and time, and in ways more immediately accessible to student and scholar than currently exist, or can even be imagined.

Transcoding Nunburnholme: First Steps

I developed a prototype of a digital edition of Nunburnholme as an experiment, with an eye both to the current limitations of New Media praxis, and to the potential of a real revolution in the ways in which medieval stone sculpture, and indeed much of visual expression may be re-presented and studied. This prototype in turn is severely limited in its functionality, and merely gestures at what might be possible with a recalibration of how we can begin to "think digitally" about the study of medieval expression. In addition to including all the obvious features we have come to expect in electronic scholarship (color images, hyperlinked commentary, background essays, search feature, bibliography, and so forth), this prototype edition showcases functionality that, in its limited mode, critiques what digital treatments of medieval objects, for the most part, have *not* been doing.

For instance, we still tend to consider medieval stone sculpture not as three-dimensional objects (though we tacitly acknowledge such physicality), but on the scale of two dimensions, as most such monuments can conveniently be described in planar aspects—first face, second face, and so forth. Indeed, my description of Nunburnholme, above, presents the cross in exactly these terms, and thereby inscribes the object's contents within four individual flat spaces and instructs the reader to consider the object as such. But crosses such as Nunburnholme were designed to be viewed from a variety of angles and perspectives, and artists often designed figural linkages between the principal sides of a monument. On Nunburnholme, for example, the First Sculptor included the "gripping angels" motif (then abandoned by the Second Sculptor), visible only when one views the cross from one of its corners (see Figure 10.4).[26]

A fully realized digital version of Nunburnholme could further reclaim the work's dimensionality, both in iconography and in presented perspectives. In the past few years, the development of "stitching software" allows one to shoot an object at set increments around its circumference (for instance, thirty-six images at ten degree intervals) and then "stitch" these images into a virtual three-dimensional object. In such a rendering, the user can manipulate the object's presentation as if it were centered on a vertical axis, freely rotating the display from any desired perspective. In the Nunburnholme prototype, for instance, even a limited reproduction of eight perspective angles (four faces and four corners) allows for the ability to "spin" the monument, creating an impression of verisimilitude of the physical object (see Figure 10.5).

In the past, print media and their early digital counterparts could only imagine and present visual objects though a series of discrete and unconnected resolutions—flat planes of fixed size that the user either flipped through (in print) or jumped between (by digital links). In print, this occurred because of the physical imitations of the medium—only so much data could be presented on the page, and one was always forced to include a limited number of views, choosing exclusively between scale and detail, depending on particular interpretative needs. Most World Wide Web sites and other digital media (outside of the commercial videogame industry) likewise still remediate the constraints of their predecessors, offering only one or two options for magnification of an image (e.g., "click here for

---

26 This "gripping angels" motif may also be found on the Newgate cross-shaft fragment in the York City Museum: see Lang, *York and Eastern Yorkshire*, pp. 105–7.

a larger image"). But true realization of transcoding, coupled with the recent and considerable increase in computer processing speeds, renders such restrictions of display unnecessary, and makes possible a finely tuned control over the scale and detail of an object's display. The Nunburnholme prototype presents a rough articulation of this kind of fluid architecture of display, wherein the user can zoom from the large scale (all of the object displayed) to the level of individual detail, or stop at any point in between. Figure 10.6 shows the start and end points of such display, moving from large scale to fine detail (of course, the practical and fiscal realities of print publishing prohibits reproducing every one of the hundreds of scales views in between in this essay). Once magnified, the display then may also be positioned precisely in two dimensions by the user, who can scroll the image vertically and/or horizontally.

In the fixed environment of print scholarship, the linking of academic commentary to specific areas of visual discourse remains likewise restricted; commentary is either compromised in detail (only so much information may be placed in a caption close to an image), or in distance (the more information you include, the necessarily further away the linear nature of writing moves this information). Again, the depth, or virtual three-dimensionality of digital displays, can increase the immediacy of scholarly signifier to its signified. In the Nunburnholme prototype, for example, the "Commentary" mode provides for automatic tracking of scholarship, as the program cross-indexes the exact location of the user's mouse and area displayed, and then fills in the appropriate commentary in a text window (see Figure 10.7). The form and content of this scholarship window are likewise dynamic; the window "floats," allowing one to position it as desired, while the actual commentary provides appropriate links to other areas and information in the edition. Such scholarly content changes as one rolls the cursor over different areas of the cross.

The malleability of digital data also becomes particularly relevant when considering the compromised state of Nunburnholme's physical "restoration." The "Original" mode of the digital edition effectively recodes the earlier state of the carved monument, turning the bottom half of the sculpture 180 degrees to align it with the top, and still allowing the object to be "spun" in space (Figure 10.8). Such a repositioning makes interpretative connections easier, as all the design elements are returned to their original (albeit layered) physical proximities. More radically, the ease with which New Media may be copied and manipulated raises the possibility of reconstructing obscured or destroyed sections from the middle of the sculpture, by digitally recycling the existing work of the original sculptors in accordance with scholarly hypothesis. Figure 10.9 shows a "rebuilt" section from the middle of side A. The Second Sculptor was responsible for both the upper and lower figures on this face, so materials from the upper figure were appropriated to reconstruct the missing sections of the lower figure. The ease with which such manipulation can occur could make a range of conjectured reconstructions readily available, much in the way that an edition of an Old English literary text provides any of a number of editorial emendations for a single interpretative crux. Of course, to avoid confusion between the real and the reconstructed, such digital revisions would still need to be indicated as such in some way. At the same time, digital media also allow such indications to be easily removed, causing the lines of reconstruction briefly to be dissolved and restoring to fragmented works such as Nunbunholme a sense of the "whole" object, no matter how fabricated it might be.

The amorphous economies of scale that are possible in transcoded media also provide completely flexible and configurable architectures of analogue and source study. As Figure 10.10 shows, the Nunburnholme prototype also possesses the capability to display and arrange visually other analogues from the surviving body of Anglo-Saxon stone sculpture. As with the central display of Nunburnholme, users can magnify and position the selected analogue to present exactly the scale and detail desired, to the best comparative advantage. With such a flexibility of display, users are then able to orchestrate such study more closely. With this feature, the edition remediates the analogue of one of the Aycliffe Crosses back through print technology, as the image shown is a section of a black and white print photograph of the cross. However, electronic editions of such objects should not be considered stand-alone; on the contrary, wider implementation of the three-dimensional modeling of such monuments hinted at in this prototype should also eventually result in a network of such editions that could link dynamically to each other's needs. Examining the commentary for the detail on one face of Nunburnholme, one could then open a similar edition of a work such as the Aycliffe Cross to the exact place of analogy, and then compare both virtual models of these objects, bringing them into the same digital space, with the same powerful tools of presentation and manipulation.[27]

Because of their nature and state of survival, Anglo-Saxon stone crosses continue to resist easy study. This essay touches on only a few aspects of how digital media might transform the nature of stone-sculpture scholarship, and other aspects remain to be explored and developed: temporal context for instance, where the changing state of the stone may be assessed and displayed along a controllable timeline, moving from Roman pillar, through successive stages of sculpting (and valuably individuating the work of each sculptor), to destruction and then "restoration."[28] The spatial environment of

---

27 Such a network would in theory echo the intended functionality of the current *Corpus of Anglo-Saxon Stone Sculpture*, but, obviously, to much greater effect. The point was touched upon by Fred Orton, "Rethinking the Ruthwell and Bewcastle Monuments." Such a network of functional digital editions is the goal of my current project, Digital Mappaemundi, which seeks to create a resource for the study and editing of medieval maps of the world.

28 Brenda Laurel imagines such a "chronobar" in her discussion of the limitations of design software. See her *Computers as Theatre*, (Reading, Mass.: Addison Wesley, 1993), pp. 114–15; see also Lance Strate, "Hypermedia, Space, Dimensionality," *The Emerging Cyberculture: Literacy, Paradigm, and Paradox*, ed. Stephanie B. Gibson and Ollio O. Oviedo, (Cresskill: Hampton Press, 2000), pp. 267–86, esp. 274–77.

the monument also could be imagined and presented ranging from Anglo-Scandinavian countryside to Anglo-Norman church wall to Victorian antiquarian display, as could the aesthetic consideration of polychroming. And as Kevin Kiernan has shown in his *Electronic Beowulf*, even the lighting of the material manuscript should not remain fixed in editions, so the addition of dynamic brightness and contrast controls in digital editions of Anglo-Saxon sculpture could likewise provide new methods of analysis.[29]

The crude praxis of the Nunburnholme prototype showcased here also stresses the ways such early models remain beholden to the limitations of the earlier technologies they succeed. For instance, the Virtual Reality Centre at Teesside (VRC), in conjunction with the Northumbria Tourist Board, regional museums, and heritage groups, has begun to create virtual models of early medieval artifacts.[30] Along with virtual models of Anglo-Saxon monasteries and Roman forts, the VRC has digitized a small number of Anglo-Saxon crosses and cross fragments. These virtual models, though limited in detail, and graphic as opposed to photographic in the quality of their reproduction, are astonishingly manipulatable and highly transparent in presentation. Rotating one of the VRC models compares, virtually, to holding a small model of an object in one's hand, turning it any way one wishes, at any distance from one's eyes. Figure 10.11 shows six quick screen shots of the VRC model of one of the Anglo-Saxon Rothbury fragments, in degrees of rotation and magnification, taken as I manipulated the digital model online.[31] In such models, the potential of transcoding has become "reality"; cross-reference such

---

29 Andrew Prescott ("The Electronic Beowulf and Digital Restoration," in *Literary and Linguistic Computing: Journal of the Association for Literary and Linguistic Computing* 12.3 [1997]: 185–95) details Kiernan's use of ultra-violet light and forms of digital image processing in the edition.

30 "Virtual Reality Centre at Teesside Ltd—real time computer visualisation, simulation and motion capture," *http://vr.tees.ac.uk/* (September 28, 2008).

31 "All Saints Parish Church, Rothbury," *http://vr.tees.ac.uk/heritage/artefacts/rothbury/roth_cross.htm* (September 28, 2008).

polymorphic display with a congruent architecture for interpretation and commentary, and the scholarship of such early medieval art will enter a new and vital phase. In such virtual recursions, monuments like Nunburnholme will no longer resist space to the degree that they do now; instead, virtual space will accommodate such artifacts with greater critical ease than is currently possible within the fixed reality of physical space. The black and white remediated images of the digital Nunburnholme prototype and the digitized Rothbury fragments printed here cannot adequately convey the innovation they encode, but they do serve as fitting images both for how print technology continues to limit our study of medieval objects, and for what might well be the technological future of Anglo-Saxon stone sculpture scholarship.

Fig. 10.1: Nunburnholme Cross, side D (top left, bottom right) and side B (bottom left, top right). Program Source: Prototype of the Digital Edition of the Nunburnholme Cross, designed by Martin K. Foys.

Fig. 10.2: Nunburnholme Cross, side A (top left, bottom right] and side C (bottom left, top right). Program Source: Prototype of the Digital Edition of the Nunburnholme Cross, designed by Martin K. Foys.

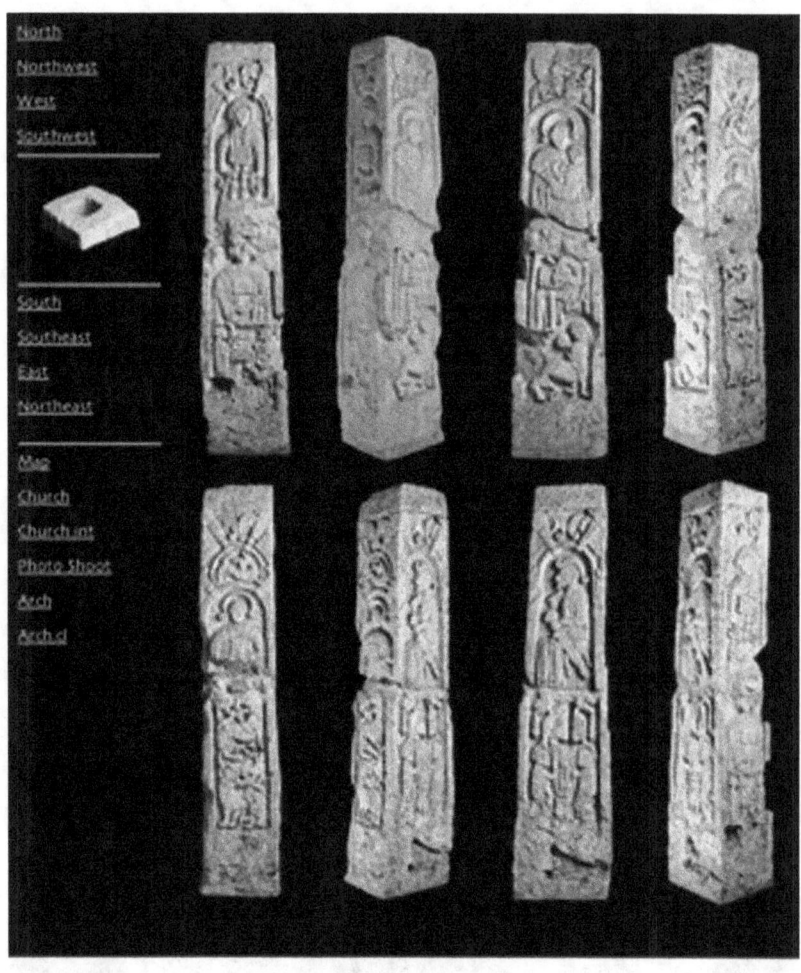

Fig. 10.3: "Flattened" images on a website presentation of the Nunburnholme Cross. Program Source: Prototype of the Digital Edition of the Nunburnholme Cross, designed by Martin K. Foys.

New Media and the Nunburnholme Cross

Fig. 10.4: Gripping angels motif on a corner of the Nunburnholme Cross. Program Source: Prototype of the Digital Edition of the Nunburnholme Cross, designed by Martin K. Foys.

Fig. 10.5: Early prototype of a digital edition of the Nunburnholme Cross, with rotation (note: lettering corresponds to a new eight-sided (A-H) scheme to account for corner faces). Program Source: Prototype of the Digital Edition of the Nunburnholme Cross, designed by Martin K. Foys.

New Media and the Nunburnholme Cross

Fig. 10.6: Levels of zoom within the digital prototype (note: lettering corresponds to a new eight-sided scheme to account for corner faces). Program Source: Prototype of the Digital Edition of the Nunburnholme Cross, designed by Martin K. Foys.

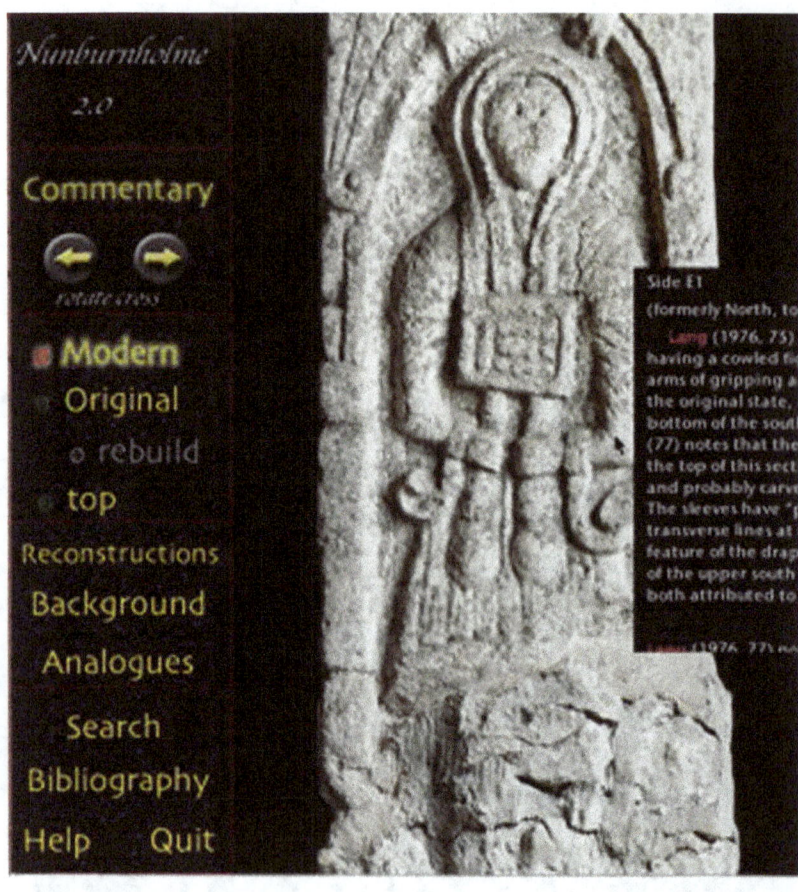

Fig. 10.7: Commentary mode for the digital prototype (note: lettering corresponds to a new eight-sided scheme to account for corner faces). Program Source: Prototype of the Digital Edition of the Nunburnholme Cross, designed by Martin K. Foys.

Fig. 10.8: "Original mode" for the digital prototype (note: lettering corresponds to a new eight-sided scheme to account for corner faces). Program Source: Prototype of the Digital Edition of the Nunburnholme Cross, designed by Martin K. Foys.

Fig. 10.9: Digital reassembly/reconstruction of Side A. Program Source: Prototype of the Digital Edition of the Nunburnholme Cross, designed by Martin K. Foys.

Fig. 10.10: "Analogue mode" for the digital prototype. Program Source: Prototype of the Digital Edition of the Nunburnholme Cross, designed by Martin K. Foys.

Fig. 10.11: Digital rendering of the Rothbury Cross fragment, by the Virtual Reality Centre at Teesside. "Virtual Reality Centre at Teesside Ltd – real time computer visualisation, simulation and motion capture," *http://vr.tees.ac.uk*.

The *Enkolpion* of Edward the Confessor: Byzantium and Anglo-Saxon Concepts of Rulership

Lynn Jones

IN 1685 WORKERS CLEARING THE SCAFFOLDING from Westminster Abbey after the coronation of James II discovered a hole in the tomb of Edward the Confessor.[1] An onlooker, a member of the choir named Henri Keepe, stuck his hand into the hole and pulled from beneath Edward's shoulder blade "a golden crucifix richly adorned and enameled." This quotation is from a pamphlet Keepe published in 1688 under the nom de plume Charles Taylour, titled *A True and Perfect Narrative of the Strange and Unexpected Finding of the Crucifix and Gold Chain of that Pious Prince, St. Edward, the King and Confessor*.[2] According to Keepe the cross was four inches high by three inches wide and held shut by two screws at the top, indicating

---

1 I would like to express my appreciation to the organizers of the Winchester conference, Sarah Larratt Keefer, Karen Louise Jolly, and Catherine E. Karkov, for their invitation and kind reception of a Byzantinist. My thanks go also to the Medieval Academy of America for providing a grant to cover travel expenses to England. Finally, I am grateful to the Winchester audience who were helpful in their comments and generous in their acceptance of an "other" in their midst.

2 Charles Taylour, *A True and Perfect Narrative of the Strange and Unexpected Finding of the Crucifix and Gold Chain of that Pious Prince, St Edward, the King and Confessor* (London, n.p., 1688), p. 6.

that it served as a reliquary. One side featured imagery described by Keepe as "the picture of our Saviour Jesus Christ in his passion and an eye from above casting a kind of beams upon him." The reverse featured "a Benedictine monk in his habit;" to either side of this "monk" were "capital roman letters" arranged in cruciform patterns.³ Keepe eventually presented the cross to James II, who wore and displayed it—Samuel Pepys is among those who saw it. The crucifix was lost when James, fleeing the country by boat, was robbed by fishermen.⁴

Although Keepe wrote his pamphlet three years after he had given the crucifix to the king, he assures us of the veracity of his description: "I procured an able Master in Drawing and Limning, to take an exact draught thereof, according to the full dimensions with the Reverse, Figures, and other adornments, the which I have now by my side."⁵ However, there is no drawing of the reliquary in Keepe's pamphlet, and to my knowledge there is no surviving depiction of it elsewhere. What *is* included is a diagram of the "capital roman letters" arranged on either side of the "monk."⁶

To the left:

$$\begin{matrix} & (A) & \\ Z & A & X \\ & A & \end{matrix}$$

To the right:

$$\begin{matrix} & P & \\ A & & C \end{matrix}$$

---

3   Taylour, *Narrative*, pp. 12–14.
4   For the presentation to James II see Taylour, *Narrative*, p. 10. For Pepys and the fate of Edward's *enkolpion* see Krijne Ciggaar, "England and Byzantium on the Eve of the Norman Conquest (the Reign of Edward the Confessor)," *Anglo-Norman Studies* 5 (1982): 79–95 at 93, with bibliography.
5   Taylour, *Narrative*, pp. 8–9.
6   Taylour, *Narrative*, p. 13.

The Enkolpion of Edward the Confessor

The Victoria and Albert Museum now houses a label describing this cross, written in a seventeenth-century hand. The label is generally agreed to have originated at James's court; the assumption is that when Edward's crucifix passed into the collection of James II, it was duly recorded by a court official.[7] The text of the label provides us with a slightly different reading of Edward's cross: "there was then found a gold cross hanging to a gold chain, soposed to have bin a boaut his neck, the cross was very neatly maid on one side a crusifax on the other a picture of the then pope."[8] These descriptions, and the object they described, attracted no further attention until the late nineteenth century. In 1883 John T. Micklethwaite, a member of the London Society of Antiquaries, examined Keepe's description of the object and noted that it did not match that of known English crucifixes dating from the sixth to eleventh centuries.[9] He suggested that the inscription was not Latin but Greek, that the letters spelled out the name of the prophet Zacharias, and that therefore the figure depicted on the reliquary was not a Benedictine monk but a Byzantine

---

7 There are three labels written by the same hand now in the Victoria and Albert Museum; one describes a textile fragment, a ribbon, and the reliquary and chain; the other two describe textile fragments. All three identify the contents they describe as being taken from the tomb in 1686, but as Buckton notes, the date was actually 1685: see *Byzantium: Treasures of Byzantine Art and Culture from British Collections*, ed. David Buckton (London: Published for the Trustees of the British Museum by the British Museum Press, 1994), pp. 151–53.

8 The text of the this label also mentions a silk fragment and ribbon which were kept with the reliquary: "part of ye cote wch was next to ye searcloath on ye boddy of King Edward ye Confessor taken from it in Aprill 1686 whe[n] ye tombe was found open, & ye little peese was a small part of a ribin tied a bout his head." The "ribin" has been lost, but the textile fragment matches fragments preserved at Westminster Cathedral, and have been dated by Buckton to the mid-eleventh century and given an eastern Mediterranean or western Asian provenance. See Buckton, *Byzantium*, p. 151.

9 John T. Micklethwaite, "Notes on the Cross Said to have been Taken Out of the Coffin of Edward the Confessor in 1685," *Proceedings of the Society of Antiquaries of London*, 2nd ser., 9 (1883): 227–30.

saint. Micklethwaite did not address the information provided by the anonymous seventeenth-century writer of the label; the Victoria and Albert Museum was not founded until 1899 and in the 1880s the label was still in the royal archives.[10]

In general, Micklethwaite's argument holds. The size of the cross, its materials, type of decoration and aspects of the iconography agree with surviving tenth- and eleventh-century Byzantine enameled cross reliquaries.[11] Such reliquaries, when worn on chains suspended around the neck, are known as *enkolpia*. All surviving eleventh-century Byzantine cruciform reliquaries originally held a fragment or fragments of the True Cross.[12] It thus appears that Edward was buried with a Byzantine *enkolpion*, a small reliquary worn on a chain around the neck that contained a fragment of the True Cross. That this object was important is apparent by its placement in Edward's tomb; *why* it was valued is the question that will be pursued here. I suggest that this reliquary, when viewed from the perspective of late eleventh-century Anglo-Saxon England, accommodated a multiplicity of messages. What these messages may have been is the subject of the following pages.

It should be noted that one element does not fit neatly into Micklethwaite's argument: Keepe's description of "the eye casting a kind of beams" down to the figure of Christ. There is no eye of God in the repertoire of Byzantine iconography, but I suggest this is not an insurmountable difficulty. Crucifixion scenes on Byzantine

---

10   Buckton, *Byzantium*, p. 151.
11   Anatole Frolow, *La Relique de la Vraie Croix* (Paris: Institut Français D'Études Byzantines, 1961), #96, p. 219; #111, pp. 223–24; #118, p. 225; #137, p. 237; #244, p. 282. See also David Buckton, "Byzantine Enamel and the West," *Byzantinische Forschungen* 13 (1988): 235–44.
12   For examples see Buckton, *Byzantium*, pp. 150–51; *Danmarks Middelalder*, ed. Thomas Christiansen, (Copenhagen: National Museum of Copenhagen, 1972), pp. 22–25, cat. nos. S–V; Helen Evans and William Wixom, ed., *The Glory of Byzantium. Art and Culture of the Middle Byzantine Era, AD 843–1261* (New York: Harry N. Abrams, 1997), pp. 169–74.

pectoral crosses and cross reliquaries frequently feature a sun and moon above the titulus.[13] It is evident from the descriptions that seventeenth-century viewers of the reliquary saw it relative to their contemporary frames of reference. In the same way that Keepe interpreted the image of Zacharias as a portrait of a "Benedictine monk," and the anonymous court official saw in the same image "a portrait of the then Pope," it is reasonable to suggest that in seeing a sun and moon as "the eye casting a kind of beams," Keepe again provided an unfamiliar iconography with a familiar interpretation.

It should be stressed that this reliquary, or more precisely its possession by Edward, should not be seen as an anomaly. As I have demonstrated elsewhere, the reliquary should rather be viewed in combination with coins and seals issued by Edward after 1053, following the deaths of his mother Emma and his father-in-law Godwin.[14] In these seals, and in other representations of kingship commissioned after 1053, Edward broke from the traditional Anglo-Saxon representations of rulership used by his predecessors. A silver penny, known as the "Sovereign/Martlets" type and issued in 1056 is illustrative of this break from tradition. It depicts Edward enthroned, with a profile head, holding a scepter in one hand and a sword in the other. While this is the first English coin to feature a portrait of an enthroned ruler, contemporary Byzantine and German courts both used this iconography.[15] Seals produced for Edward at approximately

---

13   For an *enkolpion* of approximately the same size and shape as Edward's, see Lesley von Matt, George Daltrop and Andrea Prandi, ed., *Art Treasures of the Vatican Library* (New York: Harry N. Abrams, 1974), cat. no. 131. For the same iconography on a pectoral cross, rather than an *enkolpion* see von Matt, *Art Treasures*, cat. no. 132. Other similar examples are illustrated and discussed in Evans and Wixom, *The Glory of Byzantium*, pp. 74–5, 78, 162–63 and 172; see also Buckton, *Byzantium*, p. 134.
14   Lynn Jones, "From Anglorum Basileus to Norman Saint: The Transformation of Edward the Confessor," *Haskins Society Journal* 12 (2002): 99–120.
15   Robert H. M. Dolley and Frederick E. Jones, "A New Suggestion Concerning the So-Called 'Martlets' in the 'Arms of St. Edward'," *Anglo-Saxon Coins. Studies*

the same time as this penny also appropriate current German and Byzantine imperial iconography.[16] They feature depictions of Edward enthroned and holding an orb, cross-topped staff or sword, and display the legend *Sigillum Adewardi Anglorum Basilei*. While several of these features are analogous to those found on foreign seals, it is important to note that the Anglo-Saxon borrowing was selective, and not slavish. German imperial seals feature an enthroned ruler, and orbs and scepters surmounted with birds and fleur-de-lis are also found on the seals of the eleventh-century emperors Conrad and Henry III.[17] The eastern title *basileus* had been used intermittently in England since the reign of Æthelstan, but never appeared on seals.[18] And while Edward's seals are two-sided, German and French seals are single-sided and do not include representations of swords. Only Byzantium offers contemporary parallels for double-sided seals and for the depiction of an armed ruler. The seals and coins of Isaac I Komnenos (r. 1057–1059) were the first to show the emperor with a sword. Byzantine *bullae* were double sided and were hung from, rather than affixed to, a document.[19]

The iconography on the Anglo-Saxon coins and seals suggests that Edward visually redefined his rule at the age of forty-eight, after the deaths of Emma and Godwin. No longer content to model the visual expression of his reign on earlier Anglo-Saxon traditions

---

Presented to F.M. Stenton, ed. Robert H. M. Dolley (London: Methuen, 1961), pp. 215–39, at p. 235.
16   Their analysis is complicated by the nature of the surviving evidence; here I follow the work of Brigitte Bedos-Rezak, "The King Enthroned: A New Theme in Anglo-Saxon Royal Econograpy [sic], The Seal of Edward the Confessor and its Political Implications," *Kings and Kingship*, ed. Joel Rosenthal, *Acta* 12 (Binghamton, NY: The Center for Medieval and Early Renaissance Studies, State University of New York at Binghamton, 1984), 53–87.
17   Reproduced in Bedos-Rezak, "The King Enthroned," figs. 8, 9.
18   Ciggaar, "England and Byzantium," pp. 85–86.
19   Georges Zacos and Andre Veglery, *Byzantine Lead Seals* (Basel: J. J. Augustin, 1972), pp. 76–77, nos. 85–86, pl. 23 nos. 85–86 *bis*.

of royal imagery, after C.E. 1053 Edward instead sought visually to equate his rule with those of his regal counterparts by emulating specific aspects of German and Byzantine imperial iconography.[20] In this it may be suggested that he was proclaiming his place in the wider, Christian family of rulers.

Individually, many of the seemingly foreign elements utilized by Edward after 1053 are not new, but had been previously incorporated into Anglo-Saxon royal imagery. Cnut is armed with a sword in a full-page illustration of a Liber Vitae produced in the New Minster; the inclusion of this sword in a service book suggests that it was a standard element of his royal imagery.[21] Emma's portrait in the *Encomium Emmae* incorporates non-Anglo-Saxon royal iconography, most notably that of the enthroned ruler.[22] What *is* new, I suggest, is

---

20 See Jones, "From Anglorum Basileus to Norman Saint," 99–120.

21 Cnut's image in the New Minster *Liber Vitae* (London, British Library MS Stowe 944, folio 6r) is similar to that of Edgar (r. 957/9–975) in the so-called "Charter of King Edgar" (London, British Library MS Cotton Tiberius A. iii, folio 2v) which was produced at New Minster in 966 and displayed there on special occasions. It is reasonable to assume that the artist of Cnut's *Liber Vitae* was familiar with and inspired by the earlier manuscript. For images and bibliography see Catherine E. Karkov, *The Ruler Portraits of Anglo-Saxon England* (Woodbridge: Boydell Press, 2004), pp. 133–42, and also her "Abbot Ælfwine and the Sign of the Cross" in this volume, pp. 117–122, above. Also see Francis Wormald, "Late Anglo-Saxon Art. Some Questions and Suggestions," *Studies in Western Art. Acts of the 20th Congress of the History of Art*, ed. Millard Meiss, 4 vols. (Princeton: Princeton University Press, 1963) I: 19–26; see also J. Gerchow, "Prayers for King Cnut: The Liturgical Commemoration of a Conqueror," *England in the Eleventh Century. Proceedings of the 1990 Harlaxton Symposium*, ed. Carola Hicks (Stamford: P. Watkins, Publishers, 1992), pp. 219–38.

22 For Emma's image in the New Minster *Liber Vitae* and in the *Encomium Emmae*, see Karkov, *Ruler Portraits*, pp. 123–33; see also Annemarie W. Carr, "Threads of Authority: The Virgin Mary's Veil in the Middle Ages," *Robes and Honor: The Medieval World of Investiture*, ed. Stewart Gordon (New York: Palgrave Press, 2001), pp. 59–94; and Pauline Stafford, "Emma: The Powers of the Queen in the Eleventh Century," *Queens and Queenship in Medieval Europe*, ed. Arthur J. Duggan (Woodbridge: Boydell Press, 1997), pp. 3–23.

Edward's consistent use after 1053 of these and other non-traditional forms of imagery in a comprehensive iconographic program that visually characterized Anglo-Saxon rule in imperial terms.

Edward's possession of a Byzantine *enkolpion* thus fits well into this new visual expression of rulership. In the eleventh century, the True Cross already had a long and well-known history. In order to understand Anglo-Saxon perceptions of cross relics, including their association with Byzantium, it is necessary to take a brief geographic and chronological detour. According to a legend formulated in the late fourth century, the True Cross was discovered in Jerusalem, then part of the eastern Roman Empire, by Helena, the mother of the emperor Constantine I.[23] According to this same legend, Helena divided the relic into two parts. One remained in Jerusalem and was eventually enshrined in the Church of the Holy Sepulcher; the other was sent to Constantine in Constantinople.[24] Late antique aristocratic women popularized ownership of relics of the True Cross as indications of status and piety, and these relics subsequently spread throughout the western Roman Empire.[25]

---

23 The most complete study, including a complete bibliography, of the legends surrounding Helena and the discovery of the cross is Jan W. Drijvers, *Helena Augusta. The Mother of Constantine the Great and the Legend of Her Finding of the True Cross* (Leiden: Brill, 1992). See too Peter W. L. Walker, *Holy City, Holy Places? Christian Attitudes to Jerusalem and the Holy Land in the Fourth Century* (Oxford: Clarendon Press, 1990), pp. 126–30.

24 Frolow, *La Relique*, #13, pp. 167–69. For the legend in the fifth century see Gregory of Tours, *Historiae Francorum*, ed. Wolfram Arndt and Bruno Krusch, MGH Scriptores rerum Merovincigarum 1 (Hanover: impensis bibliopolli Hahniani, 1885) 1.36; trans. Lewis Thorpe, *The History of the Franks* (London: Harmondsworth, 1974), pp. 90–91.

25 As first put forth by Peter Brown, "Relics and Social Status in the Age of Gregory of Tours," Stanton Lecture (1976), reprinted in Brown, *Society and the Holy in Late Antiquity* (Berkeley: University of California Press, 1982), pp. 222–50. For an analysis of the role of women in the development and acceptance of aristocratic Christianity, see Brown, "Aspects of the Christianization of the Roman Aristocracy," *Journal of Roman Studies* 51 (1961): 1–11.

The Enkolpion of Edward the Confessor

For the owners of these relics, one of their most appealing properties was their capacity for subdivision. This is illustrated by the cross relic obtained from the Byzantine Patriarch of Jerusalem in the late fourth century by Melania the Elder, a Roman noblewoman. Melania presented a portion of her relic to Therasia, the wife of Paulinus of Nola, who gave it, or a portion of it, to her husband. Paulinus subdivided the gift, wearing one splinter around his neck and enshrining another beneath the altar of St. Felix.[26] Therasia sent another splinter to Bassula, who gave it to her son-in-law, Sulpicius Severus in Gaul. Severus further divided his relic, wearing one fragment and depositing a splinter beneath the altar of his new foundation located near Toulouse.[27] In this example, the original fragment of the True Cross gifted by the Patriarch to Melania was divided eight times.

On a less positive note, cross relics are essentially splinters of wood and thus subject to counterfeit. I have argued elsewhere that the site, circumstance, and agent of the discovery of the cross established Byzantine control over cross relics and their distribution, and that a Jerusalem or Constantinopolitan provenance served to authenticate cross relics.[28] For much of the medieval period, other Christian cultures sought "authentic" fragments of the cross from Byzantium. This applied not only to non-Byzantine rulers and aristocracy, but also to the papacy and clergy. A letter dated C.E. 454 records Pope Leo I's reception of a cross relic from the Greek bishop of Jerusalem. In 514

---

26   Frolow, *La Relique*, #14 and 15, pp. 169–70.
27   Frolow, *La Relique*, #14 and 15, pp. 169–70. Sulpicius Severus's foundation was in Primalaculum and was dedicated to St. Claire. For this foundation see Severus, Epistle 31.6 (CSEL 29, 274), *Paulinus of Nola: letters, ancient Christian writers*, trans. Paul G. Walsh (Westminster, MD: Newmann Press, 1967).
28   An examination of issues of identity and Byzantine relics of the cross is forthcoming from the author; see too Lynn Jones, "Art and Ceremonial in Medieval Armenia: The Visual Expression of Bagratid Rulership," *Revue des Études Arméniennes* 28 (2001–02): 341–98. It should of course be noted that prior to C.E. 1099, the bishop and then Patriarch in Jerusalem was Byzantine, not Latin.

Avit, bishop and later saint of Vienne, asked Pope Symmachos to support his request for a relic of the True Cross from the current bishop of Jerusalem, Elias I.[29] In 568 Radegund, the former Merovingian queen and nun, successfully petitioned the Byzantine emperor Justin II (r. 565–78) for a relic of the cross; this same emperor also gave a fragment of the True Cross to John III, acknowledging his accession to the papacy.[30] Once outside of Byzantium, cross relics, whole or subdivided, were frequently amongst the gifts that circulated and re-circulated among the medieval royalty and aristocracy, including those in lands west of Byzantium, as we have seen with Melania the Elder; Radegund is believed to have subdivided her cross relic and given at least part of it to Gregory of Tours.[31]

Within Byzantium, the cross, regarded as the visible symbol of Christ's victory over death, became a symbol of the emperor's triumph over enemies, and relics of the cross were prominently

---

29   For Leo I, see Frolow, *La Relique*, #17, p. 171; for St. Avit, see Frolow, *La Relique*, #28, p. 177; Gregory himself, ever suspicious of relics, owned a silk that was said to have once wrapped the True Cross in Jerusalem: see Frolow, *La Relique*, #32, p. 178.

30   Baudonivia, *Vita Radegundis*, 2.16, *Sainted Women of the Dark Ages*, trans. Jo Ann McNamara and John E. Halborg (Durham, NC: Duke University Press, 1992), pp. 96–97. For the dating of the envoy's departure to Constantinople and his return with the relic, see Averil Cameron, "The Early Religious Policies of Justin II," *The Orthodox Churches and the West* (Studies in Church History 13), ed. David Baker (London: T. Nelson and Sons, Ltd, 1965), pp. 51–67; reprinted in Cameron, *Continuity and Change in Sixth-Century Byzantium* (London: Variorum Reprints, 1981), pp. 51–67. See also Frolow, *La Relique*, #34, pp. 180–81; and Cameron, "Early Religious Policies," p. 55.

31   If the relic of the cross said to be in the oratory of the monastery of St. Martin at Tours was indeed given to Gregory by Radegund, here she did emulate her female forebearers, giving the relic not to her male blood relative but to her spiritual brother in Christ. For this relic, which is dated to after the arrival of Radegund's relic in Poitiers, see Gregory of Tours, *De Gloria Martyrum*, ed. Bernard Krusch, MGH, Scriptores rerum Merovingicarum 1 (1885), 14; and Gregory of Tours, *Glory of the Martyrs*, trans. Raymond Van Dam (Liverpool: Liverpool University Press, 1988), p. 36; see also Frolow, *La Relique*, #31, p. 178.

The Enkolpion of Edward the Confessor

featured in imperial processionals and coronations.[32] The cross was also revered for its apotropaic and protective functions. Byzantine emperors, including Maurice (r. 582–602) and Heraklios (r. 610–41) began the enduring tradition of carrying fragments of the cross into battle to ensure victory, and hymns sung before military engagements invoked the cross as a weapon and source of protection.[33] During periods of siege a fragment of the cross was paraded along

---

32 For the evolution of the symbolism and veneration of the relic of the True Cross during the fourth to sixth centuries, see Sirarpie der Nersessian, "La fête de l'exaltation de la croix," *Annuaire de l'Institut de philologie et d'histoire orientales et slaves* 10 (1950): 193–98; see also Kenneth G. Holum, "Pulcheria's Crusade AD 421-22 and the Ideology of Imperial Victory," *Greek Roman and Byzantine Studies* 18 (1977): 153–72; Robert H. Storch, "The Trophy and the Cross: Pagan and Christian Symbolism in the Fourth and Fifth Century," *Byzantion* 40 (1970): 105–17; Drijvers, *Helena Augusta*, pp. 81–94; Hans J. W. Drijvers and J. W. Drijvers, *The Finding of the True Cross: The Judas Kyriakos Legend in Syriac* Corpus Scriptorum Christianorum Orientalium 565 subs. 93 (Louvain: Peeters, 1992), no pagination.

33 For the cross taken into battle by Maurice, see Charles de Boor and Paul Wirth, ed., *Theophylacti Simocattae Historiae* (Studgardt: B. G. Teubner, 1970), p. 220; for Heraclius, see *Georgii Pisidae Expeditio Persica, Bellum Avaricum, Heraclius*, ed. Isaac Bekkarus (Bonn: Weber, 1836), p. 107), and Anatole Frolow "La vraie croix et les expeditions d'Héraclius en Perse," *Revue des Études Byzantines* 11 (1953): 88–105, at 92. The continuation of this practice into the middle Byzantine period is documented in *Constantine VII Porphyrogenitus, De Ceremoniis*, ed. Alexander Vogt, 2 vols. (Paris: Les Belles Lettres, 1967), II: 485. Michael McCormack, (*Eternal Victory: Triumphal Rulership in Late Antiquity, Byzantium and the Early Medieval West* [Cambridge: Cambridge University Press, 1986], pp. 308–11, 314, 344, 375) discusses the adoption of this practice by non-Byzantine rulers. It was crusader practice for the Latin patriarch of Jerusalem, or occasionally the prior of the Holy Sepulcher, to carry the cross into battle. See also Frolow, *La Relique* #259, pp. 287–90; see also William, Archbishop of Tyre, *A History of Deeds Done Beyond the Sea*, trans. Ernst A. Babcock and Alexander C. Krey, 2 vols. (New York: Octagon Books, 1943), II. 388; see also Jonathan Riley-Smith, "The Latin Clergy and the Settlement in Palestine and Syria, 1098–1100," *Catholic Historical Review* 74 (1988): 36–54 at 52–54; and Jaroslav Folda, *The Art of the Crusaders in the Holy Land*, 1098–1187 (New York: Cambridge University Press, 1995), pp. 34–35, 49.

the walls of Constantinople.[34] It was also a Byzantine practice to distribute fragments of the cross, often enclosed in Byzantine-produced reliquaries, to foreign rulers, dignitaries, and religious officials to reward orthodoxy, confirm the political legitimacy of the recipient, or promote one individual or dynasty over another.[35]

The recipients of these fragments valued them for many reasons. Since it was the premier Christian relic, ownership of a fragment of the cross was an excellent way in which to display the owner's piety. Byzantine-granted cross relics also served to confirm and increase stature and authority by locating the recipient's rank in the wider Christian world. An example of the use of a cross relic to convey such a message is found in a tenth-century text which describes a fragment of the cross sent to the Armenian ruler Ashot Bagratuni by the Byzantine patriarch Photios.[36] The gift was intended to counter the caliph Moqtadir's elevation of Ashot to the status of King of Armenia; the Byzantine court had a vested interested in maintaining good relations with the rulers of Armenia, which served as a buffer state between itself and the caliphate. But in the eyes of the Byzantine church, Armenians were heretics, as they claimed an orthodox tradition divergent from that of Byzantine orthodoxy, and resisted domination and/or subsumation by the Greek Orthodox Church. While the cross relic presented to Ashot by Photios no longer exists, textual

---

34 Christopher Walter, "The Apotropaic Function of the Victorious Cross," *Revue des Études Byzantines* 55 (1997): 193–220.
35 Nicole Thierry, "Le Culte de la Croix dans l'Empire Byzantin du VIIe siècle au Xe," *Revista di studi bizantini slavi* 1 (1981): 205–18, passim; see also Hans-Gunther Thümmel, "Kreuze, Reliquien und Bilder im Zeremonienbuch des Constantinos Porphyrogennetos," *Byzantinische Forschungen* 18 (1992): 119–26.
36 There is no indication as to whether this relic came equipped with a Byzantine reliquary. See Frolow, *La Relique*, #109, p. 225; Alexander Vogt, *Basil Ier, empereur de Byzance (887–866) et la civilisation Byzantine à la fin du IXe siècle* (Paris: A. Picard, 1908), p. 316; Nesrop Aikinian, "Letter of Photius to Zak'aria katholikos of Armenia," *Handes Amsorya* (Yerevan, Armenia: n.p., 1968), pp. 57–61, 129–31.

The Enkolpion of Edward the Confessor

accounts confirm that Ashot displayed it, with the letter written by Photios, in his palace church.[37] Clearly this relic's secular associations with Byzantium were given primacy over its pious associations and its links with Eastern Orthodoxy.[38] I propose that this was also the case with the Byzantine relic owned by Edward the Confessor. Anglo-Saxon England, allied with the Latin Church, viewed the Byzantine church with suspicion. But, like Ashot in Armenia, it may be suggested that Edward saw in his relic of the cross something other than its link to Byzantine orthodoxy.

We shall return to what these associations might be below. First, is it possible to determine where or how Edward obtained his cross relic? There are two feasible answers to the "where" aspect of this question: England or Normandy. The argument for England is nearly impossible to prove. There are no surviving Anglo-Saxon or Byzantine texts that record any exchange between the two courts. However, circumstantial evidence does exist in the form of two Byzantine lead seals excavated on opposite sides of medieval Winchester. They date from the last years of Edward's life, and apparently indicate that official Byzantine documents were reaching the Anglo-Saxon court.[39]

Byzantine cross relics may also have entered England through Scandinavia or Hungary. As is well known, Harald Hardrada served in the Varangian guards before returning to Norway to assume the throne. He returned home with what the texts call "Byzantine gold and treasures."[40] The Byzantine historian Kekaumenos notes that after

---

37 Aikinian, "Letter of Photius," pp. 61–69.
38 For more on the True Cross, Byzantium and Armenia, see Lynn Jones, *Between Islam and Byzantium: Aght'amar and the Visual Construction of Medieval Armenian Rulership* (Aldershot, UK: Ashgate, 2007), pp. 85, 102, 104, 111–20.
39 Martin Biddle, ed., *Winchester in the Early Middle Ages* (Oxford: Clarendon Press, 1976), pp 43–54; Martin Biddle, "Excavations at Winchester 1962–1963: Second Interim report," *The Antiquaries Journal* 44 (1964): 21–32; Vincent Laurent, "Un Sceau Inédit du Patriarche de Jérusalem Sophrone II, trouvé à Winchester," *The Numismatic Circular* 72 (1964): 139–43.
40 For Harald, his treasure and a complete bibliography of source materials,

Harald became king in 1047 he remained "loyal to Constantinople," suggesting a continuation of diplomatic relations between Byzantium and Norway, and the continuing exchange of gifts that such relations required.[41] Edward the Confessor was famously childless, and in the later years of his life he used the prospect of naming his successor as a diplomatic tool, courting many possible applicants for the job. Harald was among those so courted, and he sent embassies with unspecified gifts to the English court; they may well have included the Byzantine *enkolpion*.[42] Edward the Exile, the son of Edmund Ironside and Edward's half-nephew, was also a candidate in the succession sweepstakes. When this Edward arrived in England from Hungary, according to tradition he brought with him great treasures and many holy relics. Given the intensive relations between Constantinople and Hungary at this time, it is certainly possible that some of the Exile's treasure consisted of Byzantine relics. When Edward the Exile died, his children, and his treasure, passed into King Edward's safekeeping.[43]

Similar evidence of indirect contact between Anglo-Saxon England and Byzantium offers Normandy as the place where Edward might more likely have received his *enkolpion*. Textual accounts preserve records of Norman-Byzantine interactions during the period of

---

see Krijne Ciggaar, *Western Travelers to Constantinople: the West and Byzantium* (Leiden: Brill, 1996), p. 117 and bibliography.

41 Kekaumenos, *Advice for an Emperor*, ed. Viktor G. Vasilevskii and Paul Jernstedt (St. Petersburg: n.p, 1896), pp. 7–24; see also Ciggaar, *Western Travelers to Constantinople*, p. 105, n. 109.

42 Frank Barlow, *Edward the Confessor* (Berkeley: University of California Press, 1970), p. 92.

43 For Byzantine-Hungarian relations, see Georges Moravesik, "Die Byzantinische Kultur und das Mittelalterliche Ungarn," *Sitzungsberichte der Deutschen Akademie der Wissenschaften zu Berlin, Klasse für Philosophie, Geschichte, Staats-, Rechts- un Wirtchafiswissenschafien* (Berlin: Academie Verlag, 1955), pp. 16–27; Ernst Marosi, "Die Rolle der byzantinischen Beziehungen fur die Kunst Ungarns im 11. Jahrhundert," *Byzantinischer Kunstexport*, ed. Herman L. Nickel (Halle: Martin-Luther-Universität Halle-Wittenberg, 1978), pp. 39–41.

Edward's Norman exile; one involves a Byzantine relic of the cross and brings us very close indeed to Edward. In 1026 a large group of pilgrims traveled from France to Jerusalem under the leadership of Richard of St. Vannes. Edward's uncle, Duke Richard II of Normandy, funded the enterprise. The earliest surviving account of this pilgrimage was included in the *Life* of Saint Richard, written ca. 1060 by Hugh de Flavigny. According to Hugh, the pilgrims stopped first in Constantinople, then continued to Jerusalem. There the Greek patriarch presented them with two relics of the cross along with the relics of some unspecified saints.[44]

While it is clear that without the emergence of further information we cannot pinpoint the method by which Edward obtained his Byzantine *enkolpion*, it is equally clear that there is no shortage of possible methods by which such a relic and reliquary could have made their way to Edward's court. There is no evidence that Edward's continental travels extended beyond Normandy and Flanders, but he was surrounded by people who did travel and who brought back with them objects acquired on their journeys. Texts also reveal that a staggering amount of luxury objects, including relics, were circulated and re-circulated between members of the ruling families in the lands that today constitute Europe.[45] Like many of his time, Edward was familiar with other cultures not only through travel but also through texts, pilgrimage tales, and objects.[46] It does not stretch the bounds of credulity to suggest that Edward possessed or was familiar with objects crafted in Scandinavia, Normandy, Germany, Russia, Hungary, Rome, Byzantium, and the Islamic world.

---

44 Jonathan Shepard, "Byzantine Diplomacy, 800–1204," *Byzantine Diplomacy*, ed. Jonathan Shepard and Stewart Franklin, (Aldershot: Ashgate, 1992), pp. 41–71 at 53–4.
45 Jones, "From Anglorum Basileus to Norman Saint," 108–9.
46 A point most recently underscored by Michael McCormick, *Origins of the European Economy. Communications and Commerce, A.D. 300–900* (Cambridge: Cambridge University Press, 2001), pp. 281–390.

We may now return to my initial question: how did Edward perceive his Byzantine *enkolpion*? The selective appropriation and emulation of Byzantine iconography in Edward's post-1053 issues of coins and seals document a sophisticated awareness of imperial iconography current in Constantinople and supports the assertion that he would have been aware of its Byzantine provenance. Of course, the political and/or pious associations intended by the bestower of such an object are not necessarily the same as those perceived by the recipient. I suggest that this is the case with Edward and his *enkolpion*. Just as his coins and seals issued after 1053 reflect appropriation from both Byzantine and non-Byzantine iconography, I suggest that Edward associated his Byzantine cross relic with a non-Byzantine imperial model.

In Germany and France in the eleventh century, the most famous owner of a Byzantine relic of the cross was not a living emperor but a dead one: Charlemagne. Tales of Charlemagne's acquisition of a cross relic can be traced to the opening of his tomb by Otto III in 1009. The earliest surviving account of this event, recorded by Theitmar of Merseburg, notes only that the body wore a cross suspended around his neck. It is not specifically referred to as a reliquary, and there is no mention of either a relic of the True Cross or Byzantium.[47] Nonetheless, by the mid-eleventh century, this cross had been identified by many writers as a relic of the cross granted to Charlemagne by the Byzantine Patriarch in Jerusalem. And this was not just any cross relic, but one which Charlemagne wore into battle and named "Warrior" for its apotropaic qualities. This tale spread throughout western Europe in general and France in particular: Anatole Frolow has untangled thirteen different textual versions of this legend written in France in the last half of the eleventh century.[48] These legends served as models for subsequent tales featuring members of the eleventh-century elite. One is the largely fantastic description of the

---

47 Frolow, *La Relique*, #75.7, pp. 207–8; #154, pp. 243–44; #158, pp. 245–46.
48 Frolow, *La Relique*, #75, pp. 198-202.

1035 pilgrimage to Jerusalem by Edward's cousin Duke Robert II of Normandy and his subsequent visit to Constantinople, bringing us once again very close to Edward via his Norman relations.[49]

Edward's Byzantine *enkolpion* leads to two conclusions. First, there is no evidence of a preference for Byzantine royal iconography or for Byzantine religious or secular art being a primary influence on Anglo-Saxon royal art in the last thirteen years of Edward's reign. The evidence presented above shows that Byzantine art was valued and appreciated in Edward's court; it also shows that such art was just one of many available resources appropriate for visually expressing imperial rank and piety. Second, the influence of paradigms of rulership closer to Anglo-Saxon England must be acknowledged. Charlemagne, both during his life and posthumously, was the premier model of a Christian king in Germany and France. As we have seen, it is through legends associated with Charlemagne, written during Edward's reign, that Byzantine relics of the cross are confirmed as authentic, apotropaic objects signifying the power and piety of their owners. The evidence therefore suggests that the Byzantine *enkolpion* was important to Edward precisely because it accommodated a multiplicity of associations: religious devotion, a claim to membership in the wider family of Christian rulers, Byzantine-boosted authenticity, and links with Charlemagne through an imperial fashion begun posthumously, two hundred years after his death.

---

49 This legend has been most recently examined by Elizabeth Van Houts, "Normandy and Byzantium in the Eleventh Century," *England in the Eleventh Century*, ed. Hicks, pp. 545–59.

Index

A

Aberlemno Churchyard, 23
Abisag, 71, 73, 74, 75, 76, 82, 86, 91, 94, 99
Abraham, 222
Acca, bishop of Hexham, 143, 152, 154
acrostic poetry, 53–102, 180
Adam, 136, 234
Adomnan, abbot of Iona, 43n, 152
Adoratio Crucis, 161
adventus, 149
Æcerbot, 282, 283, 284n, 286–89, 302, 314, 316
Ælfgar, bishop, 327
Ælfgifu, queen, 117, 118
Ælfgifu, kinswoman of king Edgar, 268n
Ælfric, abbot of Eynsham and homilist, 216, 220, 222, 230, 233, 234, 238, 240, 241, 248, 249, 252, 255, 258, 259, 263, 270, 295
  Colloquy, 282
  (Catholic) Homilies, 118n, 221, 239n, 248
  Genesis translation, 218
  De Temporibus Anni, 104, 124
Ælfric, archbishop of York, 258
Ælfsige, 104, 127
Ælfthryth, queen, 327
Ælfwine, abbot, 103–22,
Ælfwine's Prayerbook, 103–17
"aerated script," 85
Æthelberht, king of Kent, 209, 304
Æthelberht, king of Wessex, 258
Æthelflæd, 217
Æthelgar, 120
Æthelred, earl of Mercia, 217
Æthelred II, 126, 321, 326–28
Æthelstan, king of Wessex, 374
Æthelwold, bishop and abbot of Winchester, 104n, 115, 116, 118, 120, 329; *see also* Benedictional of St. Æthelwold
Æthelwold, abbot of Melrose, 151
Æthilwald, bishop, 38
agriculture, 280, 281, 283, 287, 290, 297, 302, 315
Ahenny, 23, 26
aius (Trisagion), 212
Alcuin of York, 76n, 173n, 180, 181
Aldfrith, king of Northumbria, 151
Aldhelm, abbot of Malmesbury and bishop of Sherborne, 54n, 58–60, 62, 63, 66, 69, 71, 78–80, 84, 86, 95–97, 100, 151, 180, 181, 322–23
  Carmen de uirginitate, 58, 60, 180
Alemanni, 208
Alfred(ian) culture, 226, 238, 255n, 299, 310, 327n
alliteration, 97, 99, 100, 168n, 173
alms bread, 308
ambo, 39
Ambrose of Milan, saint, 57, 222
  Intende qui Israel (*Veni redemptor gentium*), 163–64
Andrew, saint, 205
angel frieze, 344
angels, carved, 319, 325
angels, gripping, 344, 345, 352

387

Index

Anglo-Norman, 347, 356
Anglo-Saxon Chronicle, 252, 257, 266n, 269, 323
Anglo-Saxon poetry, 28
Anglo-Scandinavian, 6, 11, 341, 342, 346, 356
anguli, 81
ankh, 234n
Annunciation, 76n, 77n, 78, 138n, 142, 143, 144, 146, 150, 151, 155n
antiphon, 111, 141–42, 148
Antiphonary of Bangor, 163
Apollinaire, Guillaume, 175
Apollo, 177
apotropaic qualities, 11, 379, 384, 385
apparition, 254, 266
Arabic culture, 31, 80n
arable land, 281n, 284, 286
Ardagh chalice, 20, 23, 37
Arius, 105
Armenian (culture), 17, 39, 380–81, 381n
Ars grammatica, *see* Boniface
Ascension Day, 297
ashlar, 321, 324, 343
Ashot Bagratuni, ruler of Armenia, 380–81
Athlone crucifixion plaque, 45
Augustine of Hippo, saint, 57, 155n, 169, 170n, 183, 233n
Augustine of Kent, saint, 209, 266
Avit, bishop of Vienne, 378
axe poem, 183, 199
authenticity, 327, 332, 385
Aycliffe Crosses, 355

B

bakehouse, 304, 305
baking, 282, 302n, 304, 305, 309, 310
Bald's Leechbook, *see* Leechbook
baptism, 93n, 107, 142, 236, 263
barley, 281n, 318
barn, 300, 302
basileus, 374
basilica, 77, 140, 148, 149, 153, 158–60
Bavarians, 208
Bayeux Tapestry, 311–12
Be gesceadwisan gerefan (*Gerefa*), 282, 283n, 292n, 315n
beast, 23, 46, 74, 88, 344, 345

beast chain, 345, 345n
beat the bounds, 294
Bede, 22, 33, 43, 63, 70n, 143, 144, 151–53, 155, 159–60, 163, 181, 209, 210, 211, 240n, 266, 269, 272, 281, 285, 292
    De arte metrica. 181
    De temporum ratione, 63, 159, 160n, 285n, 292n
    Historia Ecclestiastica, 151, 210, 266, 269
beer, 304n
bell-tower, 347, 349
Benedict Biscop, 43
Benedictio seminis, 290
benediction, 39, 237, 290, 300, 302, 305, 314, 346
Benedictional of St. Æthelwold, 105n, 113, 325
Benedictine monk, 370, 373
Benedictine revival, 161
Beorhtwald, archbishop of Canterbury, 77, 78
Berechtuine, 38; *see also* Tullylease
Bertha, wife of Æthelberht, 209
Berhtwulf, king of Mercia, 267n
Bethlehem, 148
Bettystown Beach (brooch), 20, 23; *see also* Tara brooch
Bewcastle (Cross), 6, 13, 45, 341n, 355n
bible, *see* scripture
binary code, 350
birds, 23, 46, 292, 346, 374
bird-scaring, 292
blessing of the crops, 292
Bobbio, 32, 35
Boethius, 29
Bolter, Jay David, 348
Boniface, saint, 5, 13, 23, 53–102
    Ars grammatica, 53–102
    Nithardus vive Felix, 54n
    Vale Christo ueraciter, 54n, 76
Book of Life, 107, 117–19
border design, 344, 345
Bradford-on-Avon, 11, 319–39
bread, 10, 11, 23n, 254, 279–318
bread-making, 306–11
Breamore, 6, 13, 319, 320, 333, 338
Bredehoft, Thomas A., 167n, 168, 168n
Breton, 35
bridal chamber, 163, 164

388

Index

Brown, George Hardin, 4, 5
Brussels (reliquary cross), 46, 135
Brussels, Treasury of the Cathedral of St. Michel, 46
bullae, 374
Burchard Gospels, 41
Burghard, 65
burial, 157, 161, 162, 174
Buttermarket, Ipswich, 307
Byzantine (art), 4, 6, 11, 17, 22, 42, 119, 369–85
Byzantium, 11, 21, 369–85

C

Cairo, 39
calendar, 63, 104, 123, 290, 312, 313
caliphate, 380
calligramme, *see* Apollinaire, Guillaume
calligraphy, 19, 20
Calne, 324, 333
Calvary, 149
Canon Tables, 20, 24, 25, 30
Canterbury, 58, 59, 77, 83, 120n, 154, 156n, 179, 181, 211n, 258n, 290, 300, 313
cardinal points, 34n, 284
Carmen de uirginitate, *see* Aldhelm
carmen figuratum (carmina figurata), 10, 35, 45, 54n, 55–58, 61, 65, 67, 69, 72, 86, 89, 169, 175, 177–178, 180–181
Carndonagh, 38, 42, 43, 45
Carolingian (culture), xii, xiii, 6, 37, 44, 55n, 142, 158n, 172n, 181, 189, 343
carved angels, *see* angels
Cashel, 23
Cassiodorus, 36, 323
casts (Bewcastle and Ruthwell), 13
catacomb of Commodilla, 95n
cattle, 287n, 295
Ceadwalla, 245
Cedd, saint, 38
Céli Dé, 210
Celtic (culture), 17, 18, 23, 28, 34, 60, 209, 323; *see also* La Tène art
Cenred, king of Mercia, 151
centaur, 345, 346
Cenwealh, king of Gewisse, 323
Channel School, 26
Chapel of the Holy Cross, 42, 142

Charlemagne, 181, 384, 385
Charm 19, 210–13, 269, 272n, 273
charters, 63, 64, 83, 118n, 127, 217, 219, 256–58, 267, 268, 269, 322, 324, 325–29. 331, 332, 375
Charter, New Minster, 118, 119, 325, 375n
Chartres, 45, 57n–58n
Cheddar, 324, 333
CHI, letter, 67
CHI-RHO symbol, 6, 35, 55
CHI-shaped cross, 205
Christmas Day, 251, 262
Chronicon, 32
chronobar, 355n
Church of the Holy Sepulcher, 376, 379
circuitum (circulum) quadrangulum, 68, 79, 92n
Claudius Pontifical(s), 290, 300, 301n, 306n
climate, 290n
Clofesho, council of, 293, 297
cloisters, 142n
Clonmacnoise, 38
Cluny, 239n, 306–09
Cnut, king, 117, 118, 120, 131, 258n, 328, 375
Coatsworth, Elizabeth, 27, 325n
Codex Amiatinus, 96n
Codex Aureus, 35
coenobium, 324
collocation, 224, 226, 227n, 228, 251, 255, 256, 275
Columba, saint, 19, 25, 36, 38, 42n, 46, 152n
Columbanus, saint, 32
compass-work, 25, 26, 27,
computistical material, 63, 104, 312
Constantine, 6, 44n, 55, 152, 153, 159, 160, 177, 181, 188, 219, 235n, 376
Constantinian (basilica), 77, 159
Constantinople, 40, 43, 44, 76, 376, 378n, 380, 382–85
continent, xi, 4, 6, 7, 8, 9, 11, 12, 37, 64, 65, 85, 86, 161, 162, 209, 217, 225, 291, 294, 294n, 297, 307, 309n, 312, 313, 383
Cook, A.S., 185
Coptic (culture), 17, 21, 31, 34, 34n, 37, 39, 46, 234n

389

Corfe, 326n
Cork, County, 38
corn, 281n, 283, 298, 301, 303, 314, 318
corn-dollies, 298
Cornelius, martyr, 158
Cotton, Sir Robert, 103n
Cracow Pontifical, 307n
Cramp, Rosemary, 12, 25n, 27, 28n
Crashaw, Sir Richard, 175
Crediton, xiii, 53, 53n
Creed (*Credo*), 163, 213, 221; see also in liturgical incipits
crops, 292, 294, 296, 296n, 298–303, 318
cross
    altar cross, 117, 119, 120, 244n
    gesture (sign, marking) of the cross, 1, 5, 8, 10, 234–37, 240–43, 248, 249, 250n, 253–58, 266, 274, 307–8
    holy cross, 53, 72, 76, 79, 111, 112, 160, 181n, 234, 238–40, 249, 286, 317; see also Holy Cross, chapel of; Exaltation of the (Holy) Cross; Invention of the Holy Cross; Office of the Holy Cross
    legends (of the cross), 6, 157n, 159, 250n, 376, 376n, 384–85
    pectoral cross, 27, 237, 245n, 373
    processional, 20, 37–39, 41, 46, 120, 209, 244n, 254, 260, 266, 267, 294, 296, 379
    protection, 1, 5, 111, 211n, 241, 296, 379
    reliquary, see reliquary
    stone crosses, 20, 38, 245, 355
    True Cross, 40, 43, 77, 157n, 159, 372, 376–78, 379n, 381, 384; see also Helena, St.
cross-carpet pages, 9, 17–47
cross lexemes
    beam, 218n, 228–29, 230, 231
    bletsian, 237–41, 254, 275, 295, 296
    crouch, 214, 272, 273n
    cros, 209, 215, 230, 231, 272n
    cruc, 10, 204, 208–11, 213–15, 230, 231, 242, 244n, 253, 256n, 271–73, 275
    cristelmæl, 230n, 242, 262n, 263–67
    Cristes mæl, 10, 214, 242–43, 248n, 261, 262–71, 275, 285, 298
    eaxlgespann, 227, 228, 229, 231
    furca, 219, 223
    galga, 10, 207–09, 224–26
    galgtreow, 229
    kriuze, 208
    ksulon, 205
    mearcian, 236, 242n, 252, 254, 255, 258
    patibulum, 222–24, 226–28, 229n
    rod, 10, 211, 215–22, 228, 229, 230, 231, 237n, 238, 242, 243-48. 251, 252, 259, 262, 271, 272
    rodehengen, 220–22, 229, 230, 231
    rodetacen, 10, 221, 242–62, 265–70, 275, 295
    se(g)nian, 238–41, 254, 275
    signum crucis, 111, 239, 246, 249, 251, 259
    stauros, 205–07, 216
    treow, 211n, 228–29, 230, 231
    wearg-rod, 244
crucifix, 11, 44, 44n, 108, 109, 189, 245, 245n, 254, 261, 266–70, 275, 369–71
crucifixion, 33, 35, 86, 106, 111, 137, 143, 150, 155, 161, 162, 174, 206, 219, 220, 235n, 242, 244, 254n
crucifixion (in art), 21, 42–46, 105, 107–11, 113, 116, 117, 118, 119, 124, 128, 143, 325, 346, 372
cruciform design, 8–11, 67, 111, 113, 178–180, 184, 210, 319–20, 322, 330, 370, 372
crusade, 379n
crux gemmata, 20, 43
cryptography, 86
Curtius, Ernest R., 172n, 179
Cuthbert, bishop of Canterbury, 181
Cuthbert, saint, 19n, 27, 39n, 41, 81n
Cuthbert Gospel, 31
Cyprian, martyr, 158

D

dairy, 304n
Dalriada, 18
Damasus, pope, 23, 127
Danelaw, 215
daughter of Zion, 149
David, king, 74, 76, 108

Index

De Abbatibus, 319, 320
De Cruce (Hwætberht), 153
De Cruce Christi (Tatwine), 154
De Nuce), 185n; *see also* Ovid
De temporum ratione, see Bede
Deerhurst, 324
deposition, 174
Derrynaflan paten, 20, 37
descent into hell, 162, 163
Deshman, Robert, 105n, 113, 188, 189
Deusdedit, archbishop, 269
diacon, 264
Diatessaron, 31, 32
D(ictionary of) O(ld) E(nglish) C(orpus), viii, 210, 215, 217, 218, 220, 221, 226, 246, 262n, 269n
"difficult poetry," 82
digital edition, 351, 353, 362
Digital Mappaemundi, 355
digital technologies, 340n, 342, 349–57
display script, 23, 32, 66, 67, 81n,
dog-days, 299
Dokkum, 53n
Domesday Book, 304n
Donegal, County, 38, 42n, 45
Donore hoard, 25
doppelgänger, 349
Dorian nightingale, 184
Dorset, 258n, 326n, 327, 328
dove, 111
double cowl, 345
dragons, 274n, 345, 346
dreams, 125, 152, 187, 218
Dream of the Rood, The, 6, 7, 9, 10, 20, 35n, 39n, 46, 55n, 76n, 135–203, 223n, 227, 227n, 228, 229, 245n
dream-vision, 140–41, 143, 146, 151, 162
drinking-feast, 288
Dryhthelm, 151
Dud(d), 61–92
Dumfriesshire, 18n, 37
Dunadd, 18, 26, 36
Dunstan Pontifical, see Sherborne Pontifical
Durham Cassiodorus, 323
Durham Collectar, 300
Durham Gospels, 24, 45, 46
Durham Hymnal, 164n
Durham Ritual, 228, 229, 229n; *see also* Durham Collectar
Durrow, 34
Durrow, Book of, 17n, 24, 32–34, 37, 43, 46
Dutch (Middle Dutch), 204, 207n, 226n, 227

E

Eadburg, Abbess of Thanet, 54n
Eadfrith, bishop, 19, 30
Eadred, king of Wessex, 324
eall-reviser, 138–39
Eanulf, 268n
East Riding, Yorkshire, 343, 345n
Easter, 123, 124, 136, 142, 150, 151, 161, 164, 255n, 258n
Easter Tables, 123, 325n
ecclesiola, 322
Echternach, 34, 35
Echternach Gospels, 24
Edgar, king of Wessex, 118, 268n, 327, 375n
Edith, St., 327, 328n
Edmund Ironside, 329, 382
Edward the Confessor, king, 11, 369–85
Edward the Exile, 382
Edward the Martyr, 326–32
egg poem, 183, 184, 200
Egyptian cross, *see* TAU-shaped cross
Egyptian culture, 234
electronic scholarship, 351
elegiac couplets, 80, 85
elegy, 182
Electronic Beowulf, 349n, 356
Elene, 228
Elias I, bishop of Jerusalem, 378
elision, 87, 88, 95, 97
Emma, queen, 117, 131, 373, 374, 375, 375n; *see also* Ælfgifu
enamel-work, 11, 20, 369, 372
Encomium Emmae, 375
enkolpion, 11, 369–85
enigmata, 54, 58–60, 69, 80, 86, 153, 180
Enoch and Elias, 259–60
Épinal Glossary, 219
erce, 286, 317
Ernst, Ulrich, 54n, 69, 89, 92n, 93n,

Index

94n, 175, 177–79, 182
Eros, 183
eschatological visions, 151–52
escutcheons, 31n, 34, 323
Esquiline Hill, 148
estate management, 282
Ethiopia, 34
eucharist, 23, 41, 142, 161, 239n, 300n, 306, 310
Eusebian sections, 25
Eusebius, 153–54; *see also* Hwætberht
evangelists, 36, 206
evangelists (in art), 20, 22, 29, 30, 32, 108, 109, 179, 202
Exaltation of the (Holy) Cross, 41, 77, 157–61, 230n, 239n, 240
excavation, 321, 322, 325, 331, 337
exegesis, 20, 22, 29, 30, 31, 33, 47, 74, 75n, 171n, 179, 187, 205
Exodus, 216
exorcism, 213, 256n, 273
eye, 370, 372
Ezekiel, *see* scriptural references

F

Fahan, 38
farming, 280n, 281, 282n, 283n, 285, 287, 298, 315
Fates of the Apostles, 221
feasting, 279, 288, 293, 298, 311, 311n, 312, 313
fertility (of the earth), 283, 289
Fickermann, Norbert, 60n–61, 69, 75n, 88, 89, 91, 94n
field remedy, *see Æcerbot*
figura(e), 20, 22, 35, 35n, 47, 54n, 55–58, 61, 65, 67, 69n, 72, 86, 166–203
figured poetry, 166–203
First Sculptor (Nunburnholme), 343–46, 352
Flanders, 383
Fleming, John V., 185
Fletcher, Lord Eric, 322
fleur-de-lis, 374
"float," 353
Flotta, 39
flour, 10, 283, 303, 304, 308, 309, 318
food, 145, 279–83, 286, 291, 300, 304n, 308, 311–14, 318

food production, 279, 280, 282, 286, 291, 314
forehead, 107, 213, 235–37, 252, 255, 256n, 268, 271
Forthhere, 63
fortitudo Dei, 144, 150
Frankish (culture), 7, 208–09
Frankish (liturgy), 136
French (culture), 175, 374
French (language), 204, 214, 272
Frisia, 64
Frisian, Old, *see* Old Frisian
Frolow, Anatole, 372n, 379n, 384
Fulk, Robert D., 167–68

G

Gabriel, archangel, 143, 144, 150, 155n
gallows, 174, 186, 207, 223–29, 232, 244
Gaul, 56, 377
Gelasian rite, 153, 158n, 164
Genesis, book of, *see* scriptural references
Genesis, Old English poem, 168n,
genitive compound, 248–49, 262, 275
genuflection, 188n
geometr(ical) patterns), 20, 24n, 25, 27, 29–31 47, 80, 80n, 234
geometric philosophy, 34, 42, 80, 80n
German, Low, *see* Low German
German (Modern), xiii, xiv, 69, 204, 226n, 242, 243, 248n, 249, 252, 253, 255, 263
German, Old High, *see* Old High German
German(ic culture), 207, 373–75
germanus, 326n
Gewisse, 323
gibbet, 222–24, 244, 259
Glastonbury, 63, 182n, 333
globe, 113, 115n
Godwin, 312, 373, 374
Gog, 73–74, 81n
Golden Mean/Rule, 28
Golgotha, 140, 174
Good Friday, 21, 40, 41, 136, 140, 142, 152, 153, 156, 160, 161, 163, 258n
Gospel, St. John's, 34, 42, 86, 165n; *see also* scriptural references

Index

Gospel, St. Luke's, 33, 35, 149; *see also* scriptural references
Gospel, St. Mark's, *see* scriptural references
Gospel, St. Matthew's, 35, 42; *see also* scriptural references
Gospel of Nicodemus, 259
Gothic (culture), 45
Gothic (language), 206–08
grace (at meals), 311–14
graffiti, 95n, 177n
granary, 302
graves, 36, 330n
Greater Litany, 293, 297
Greek Anthology, 176, 182, 198, 199
Greek cross, 34, 42
Greek (or Hellenistic culture or language), 24, 34, 54, 59, 67, 78, 80, 80n, 176, 179, 183–83, 198, 199, 200, 203, 205–207, 212, 216, 218n, 371
Greek Orthodox Church, 377, 380, 383
green tree, 150–51, 156
Gregorian rite, 153
Gregory (the Great), pope, 44, 144, 145, 226, 227n, 246n, 248, 252, 310
  Dialogues, 238n, 246n, 248–49, 252, 310
  Regula Pastoralis, 226
Gregory II, pope, 64
Gregory of Nyssa, 155n, 233n
Gregory of Tours, 376n, 378, 378n
grid poem, 177–78, 181, 182
grinding, 10, 304, 304n
gripping angels, *see* angels
Grusin, Richard, 348

H

Habbakuk, *see* scriptural references
Hadrian, Abbot, 58–59, 179, 180n
Haemgisl, 151
Hagia Sophia, 76n
half-uncial (also semi-uncial), 26, 66
hapax legomenon, 216, 228, 244
Harald Hardrada, 381–82
Harold Godwineson, king of Wessex, 272n, 312
harrowing, 292
Harrowing of Hell, 106
Hartlepool, 38

harvest(ing), 10, 280, 282, 291, 292, 294, 297–300, 303
harvest home, 280
Hastings, 272n
Headbourne Worthy, 6, 319 333
healing, 145, 246n, 256, 270, 271
heathen, 236, 286
Heavenfield, 152
Hebrew, 23n, 31, 32n; *see also* Judaism, Jewish culture and Jews
Helena, St., 157n, 159, 376
Heliand, 168n, 285n
Hellenistic (culture), 59n, 175, 177, 182, 183, 185n, 186; *see also* Greek (culture)
Heraclius, emperor, 40, 379
Herbert, George, 175, 197
heresy, 143
heretics, 122, 143, 380
Hermes, 184, 207n, 223n
hexameter, 54, 57, 59, 61, 68, 80, 86, 173, 179n
Hexateuch, Old English, 218n, 224, 225n
Hexham, 143, 152, 154
hiatus, 87, 96
Hierusalem (basilica), 140, 153, 160
Hieatt, Constance, 172, 186n, 187, 187n
Hilkia, high priest, 159
Hippolyt, 233n
Historia Ecclesiastica, *see* Bede
Hollander, John, 169–70, 179, 182, 183, 184, 189
Holy Cross, chapel of, 42, 142
Holy Island, 19, 21, 38; *see also* Lindisfarne
Holy Sepulcher, 379n; Church of, *see* Church of the Holy Sepulcher
Holy Trinity, *see* Trinity, Holy
Holy Week, 41, 146–49, 150–51, 156
Hrabanus Maurus, 55, 86, 118, 172, 178, 180–82, 186–88, 196, 202
  Carmen 28, 172, 178, 187
  De Laudibus sanctae crucis, 172, 182, 182n, 186, 188, 196
Hugh de Flavigny, 383
Hungary, 381, 382, 383
Hunterston brooch, 26
Hwætberht, 153–54
Hyde Abbey, Winchester, 103–4, 117, 122n, 126–27

I

hypermedia, 349
hypermetric verse, 166–68, 172–74

iconoclasm, 19, 21, 43
iconography, 22, 44, 78n, 108n, 111, 142, 143, 145, 151, 189, 320n, 343, 345n, 352, 372, 373–76, 384–85
idolatry, 19, 21
imago poems, 178
impalement, 206
incarnation, 30, 35, 80, 143, 144, 146, 147, 150, 162, 164
incipit pages, 19, 20, 22, 23, 29, 32, 33, 36, 37, 47, 51
incipit(s), 108
Inishowen, 38; see also Donegal, County
insignia, 189
"Insular," 17, 23, 26–29, 32, 33, 35, 36, 37, 44, 46
insular, 8, 9, 11, 65, 66, 83, 84, 87, 163
intext, 177–78, 179
introit, 40n, 148
Invention of the Holy Cross, 250n
Iona, 23, 37n, 38, 43, 152
Ireland, 17, 18, 20, 23–26, 28–30, 32–35, 38, 39, 41, 42, 60, 66, 84, 85, 97, 100, 180, 209, 210, 215, 272, 307
Irene, empress, 21
Irish, Old, see Old Irish
Irish St. Gall Gospels, 34
Iron Age, 23, 28
Irvine, J.T., 321
Isaac, 222, 223n
Isaac I Komnenos, 374
Islamic (culture), 19, 21, 23n, 31, 41, 481, 381n, 383
Italian (culture), 36n, 176n
Italian (language), 204, 273n
Italy, 32, 33, 37, 176
Ixworth cross, 27

J

Jackson, E.D.C., 322
James II, king of England, 11, 369–70
Japheth, 73
Jarrow, 21, 36, 41, 66, 153; see also Monkwearmouth

Jehovah's Witnesses, 206n
Jerome, 18, 19, 23, 28, 30, 33, 37, 42, 74, 127; see also *Novum Opus* and Vulgate
Jerusalem, 40, 41, 149, 150, 159, 160, 236, 376–79, 381, 383, 384, 385
Jewish culture, 59, 220, 259n; see also Hebrew
Jews, 112
John the Archcantor, 151
John the Baptist, 44–45
John, saint and evangelist, 22, 107, 108, 118, 274n, 285, 316; see also scripture references
John III, pope, 378
Joseph, 218
Judaism, 21
Judas Iscariot, 112
Judas Kyriakos, 379n
Judgment Day, 114, 156
Justin II, emperor,. 42, 378, 378n

K

kalends, 293, 299
Keefer, Sarah Larratt, 161–62, 210n, 275n, 291n, 307n
Keepe, Henri, 369–73
Kells, Book of, 17n, 24, 34, 36n, 43, 81n
kenning, 186
Kent, 127, 209, 304
Kentish, 35, 83
key, 113–15, 118, 120
Khatchk'ar of Aputayli, 39
Kiernan, Kevin, 356
Kilpiö, Matti, 182, 186
Kyrie eleison, 110; see also liturgical incipits

L

La Tène art, 23, 25; see also Celtic art
label, 371–72
Labors of the Months, 290, 312–13
Lagore buckle, 25
lamb, 44, 88, 112, 202, 258n
Lambeth Psalter, 221, 222
Lammas Day, 299–301, 305, 314
landscape, 2, 6, 218
Lang, James T., 343, 345n, 346

Index

Last Judgment, 74, 107, 118, 120, 126, 132
Lastingham, 38
Lateran (baptistry, basilica), 142, 157, 159, 160–61
Lateran Council, 144n
law, Anglo-Saxon, 287n, 304n, 326
Law, Vivian, 54n, 62, 67n
lead seals, 381
lections, 18, 19, 25, 149, 157, 158
Leechbook, Bald's, 211, 213, 269, 271, 273, 299, 304n
Lehmann, Paul, 60, 62, 69, 92n, 207n
Leo I, pope, 377, 378n
Leo the Isaurian, 21
Leofric, earl of Mercia, 211–12, 272
Leofric Missal, 291n, 300, 301n, 306n, 313
Lesser Litany, 297
lexicology, 204
Liber Pontificalis, 77–78, 157n–60
Liber Vitae, 9, 103–5, 114n, 117–22, 126–27, 375, 375n
lichen, 270
Lichfield Gospels, 24, 27n, 33
limestone, 343
Lindisfarne, 19, 26, 27, 29, 37, 38, 41, 42; *see also* Holy Island
Lindisfarne Gospels, 17–52, 81
litany, 78, 104, 104n, 297n; *see also* Greater Litany
literary conceit, 186
litterae notabiliores, 25
liturgical incipits
  Ad crucem salutandum, 40
  Ave rex noster, fili David redemtor, 108n
  Benedic domine hanc creaturam nouam panis, 300
  Benedico te creatura panis, in nomine patris, 305
  Celi senator inclite, 115
  Credo in deum patrem, 163, 213, 221
  Cvm qve pervenero, Iesv benigne, 108n
  Deus de Libano veniet, 156
  Deus qui pro nobis filium tuum crucis patibulum, 229n
  Deus, qui uoliuisti pro redemptione mundi, 112
  Domine Iesv Christe, magister bone, svscipe, 108n
  Domine Iesu Christe qui hora nona in crucis patibulo, 229
  Domine sancte pater omnipotens aeterne deus, qui caelum et terram, 301
  Ecce lignum crucis, 110
  Flectamus omnes genua, 152, 153n
  In nomine Domini omne genu flectatur, 148
  Iustum deduxit Dominus per uias rectas, 114
  Kyrie eleison, 110
  Magnificat anima mea dominum, 317
  O beate Petre, 113n
  O crux splendidior cvnctis astris, 108n
  O crux viride ligno, qvia svper te, 108n
  O Iesv benigne, verbvm patris et eternum, 108n
  O Ieus clementissime, 114
  Obsecro te, Domine Iesu Christe filii Dei, 110
  Omnipotens et misericors deus qui benedixisti horrea ioseph, 302
  Omnipotens sempiterne deus creator generis humani, 290
  Pange lingua, 56, 136, 137
  Pater noster qui es in caelis, 110, 213, 273n, 316, 317, 318
  Prima causa est, qui in una die septem cruces adit, 110
  Salua nos, Christe saluator, 112n
  Tu es redemptor mevs, 108n
  Vidi aquam egredientem de templo, 141–42
liturgy, 3, 4, 6, 7, 18–19, 25, 39, 41, 136, 140, 142, 146, 148, 150–53, 158n, 160–63, 211n, 235, 243, 256, 280, 294n, 295n
Liudhard, bishop, 209
livestock, 281n, 282n, 287
loaf (of bread), 254, 282, 283, 302, 306–11, 314, 318
loan words, 204, 207n, 210n, 212, 214n, 215, 228, 230, 238, 244n, 246, 251, 267, 271, 273, 275
Logos, 19, 47, 86; *see also* Word

395

London Society of Antiquaries, 371
Lough Foyle, 38; see also Donegal, County
Low German, 204, 226n
Luxuria, 312
luxury objects, 383
Luke, saint and evangelist 22, 35, 274n, 285, 316; see also scriptural references
Lul(l), 54, 63n, 65, 181

M

Magog, 73–74, 81–82, 90, 93, 98
Magnificat, 317; see also liturgical incipits
Maihingen Gospels, 34
Mainz, 62, 65, 307n; see also Willibald of Mainz.
Malmesbury, 79, 84n, 333; see also Aldhelm, and William of Malmesbury
Manovich, Lev, 350
Manuscripts
  Alençon, Bibliothèque Municipale MS M 14, 115
  Cambridge, Corpus Christ College MS 41, 210n
  Cambridge, Corpus Christi College MS 144, 219n
  Cambridge, Corpus Christi College MS 162, 296
  Cambridge, Corpus Christi College MS 303, 246n
  Cambridge, Corpus Christi College MS 383, 315n
  Cambridge, Corpus Christi College MS 391, 210n
  Cambridge, Trinity College MS B. 16. 3, 182n
  Cambridge, University Library MS Gg. 3. 28, 221
  Cambridge, University Library MS Gg. 5. 35, 182n
  Cambridge University Library MS Ii. 4.6, 296n
  Durham Cathedral Library A. iv.19, see Durham Ritual or Durham Collectar
  Durham Cathedral Library MS B.ii.30, 323n
  Durham Cathedral Library MS B.iv.9, 181
  Florence, Biblioteca Medicea-Laurentiana MS Orient 81, 31
  Freiburg-im-Breisgau, Universitätsbibliothek Codex 702, 35
  Fulda, Hessisches Landesbibliothek, Codex Bonifatianus 3, 84n, 85n
  London, British Library MS Additional 49598, see Benedictional of St Æthelwold
  London, British Library MS Additional 61735, 315n
  London, British Library MS Cotton Augustus II.2, 83
  London, British Library MS Cotton Caligula A.vii, 285
  London, British Library MS Cotton Claudius A.iii, see Claudius Pontifical(s)
  London, British Library MS Cotton Claudius B.iv, 224, 225n
  London, British Library MS Cotton Cleopatra A.iii, 219n
  London, British Library MS Cotton Domitian A.viii, 252
  London, British Library MS Cotton Julius A.vi, 290n
  London, British Library MS Cotton Nero D. iv, see *Lindisfarne Gospels*
  London, British Library MS Cotton Tiberius A.iii, 375n
  London, British Library MS Cotton Tiberius A.xv, 83
  London, British Library MS Cotton Tiberius B.v, pt. 1, 182n, 290n
  London, British Library MS Cotton Tiberius C.vi, 29n, 312, 325
  London, British Library MS Cotton Titus D. xxvi, 9, 103, 105, 125, 130
  London, British Library MS Cotton Titus D. xxvii, 9, 103, 105, 123–24, 128, 129
  London, British Library MS Cotton Vespasian A.i, 156n, 164n
  London, British Library MS Cotton Vitellius E.xviii, 300
  London, British Library MS Harley

Index

3376, 219n
London, British Library MS Royal 1.B.vii, 36
London, British Library MS Royal 12.D.xvii, 211n
London, British Library MS Stowe 944, 9, 103, 131, 132, 375n
London, Lambeth Palace MS 427, 221–22
Marburg, Hessisches Staatsarchiv, Fragment 319 Pfarrarchiv Spangenberg (Depositum) Hr Nr. 1, 84n
Milan, Biblioteca Ambrosiana MS D.23.supra, *see* Milan *Orosius*
New York, Pierpont Morgan Library MS Glazier Codex 67, 31
Oxford, Bodleian Library MS Auct. F. 4. 32, 182n
Oxford, Bodleian Library MS Bodley 579, *see* Leofric Missal
Oxford, Bodleian Library MS Bruce 96, 32
Oxford, Bodleian Library MS Hatton 14, 295
Oxford, Bodleian Library MS Hatton 115, 304n
Oxford, Bodleian Library MS Laud Misc. 381, 218n
Oxford, Bodleian Library MS Tanner 10, 210n
Oxford, St. John's College MS 17 + London, British Library MS Cotton Nero C.vii, 268n
Paris, Bibliothèque Nationale de France MS lat. 17959, 62
Rouen, Bibliothèque Municipale MS 274, *see* Missal of Robert of Jumièges
St. Gallen, Stiftsbibliothek, Codex Sangallensis 196, 57
Trier, Stadtbibliothek MS 1104 (1321), 62
Würzburg, Universitätsbibliothek MS M.p.th.29, 62–63, 89, 100n, 101

March 25, 142, 146, 151
martyr, 53n, 64, 157, 189, 328; *see also* Edward the Martyr
Mark, saint and evangelist, 22, 274n, 285, 316; *see also* St. Mark's Day
Mary, mother of Christ, 75, 76, 78, 79n, 82, 86, 105, 106, 107, 108, 113, 114, 118, 124, 129, 142–44, 149–50, 155, 162, 230n, 285, 317, 345
Matthew, saint and evangelist, 22, 274n, 285, 316; *see also* scriptural references
Maurice, emperor, 379
meadowland, 286
media, 27, 28, 340, 342, 348–50, 352, 354, 355
Meigle, 23
Melania the Elder, 377–78
Merovingian, 37, 378
mesostich, 55, 56, 92n
metalwork, 18, 20, 23, 25, 27, 37, 38, 42, 46
metrics, 55n, 95, 97, 180
mice, 299, 302
Michael, archangel, 79n, 114
Middle English, 214, 271, 272
Middle High German, 226
Milan *Orosius*, 32
milling, 282, 303, 304
Milret of Worcester, 181
Milvian Bridge, 160, 188
minster, 269, 324
Missal of Robert of Jumièges, 290, 300, 302, 303
monastic sign language, 237, 239, 245, 263, 264, 264n, 267, 269, 306, 307, 309n
Monkwearmouth, 21, 36, 41, 66, 153; *see also* Jarrow
Monotheletism, 34, 143, 163
moon, 123, 124, 304n, 373
Moqtadir, caliph, 380
morphology, 243, 247, 248, 250, 251, 253, 257n, 261
Mote of Mark, 18
mother earth, 286, 287, 317
motif, 23, 27, 46, 162, 323, 344, 345, 352, 361
motif-pieces, 26, 28

N

New Media, 340–42, 348–51, 354
New Minster, Winchester, 9, 103, 113,

117–20, 126–27, 131, 325, 375
New Testament, *see* Testament, New
Newgate cross-shaft fragment, 352n
Nicaea, Council of, 21
Night Office, 265n
Ninian, saint, 23
Nithardus vive Felix, *see* Boniface
Noraduz Cemetary, 39
Norman-Byzantine interactions, 382
Norman Conquest, 214, 294, 300, 308, 311, 370n
Norman doodle, 346
Normandy, 381–83, 385
Northumbria, 23, 26, 41, 46, 66, 164, 209, 356
Northumbria Tourist Board, 356
Norway, 381–82
Novum Opus, 19, 42 *see also* Jerome
Nubia, 34
numerical symbolism, 24, 29, 30, 57, 80n, 110, 173n, 284
Nunburnholme Cross, 11, 340–57
Nunnaminster, 324, 329
nunnery, 324, 329
Nursling, 62

O

Odda, earl, 324
Odysseus, 184
Offa, king of Mercia, 257n
Office of the Holy Cross, 104–5, 111, 112, 124
Office of the Trinity, 104, 105, 124
Office of the Virgin Mary, 104, 105, 113, 124
Ogilvy, J.D.A., 181
Old Frisian, 207n, 208, 214, 218, 228, 238, 244, 265
Old Gelasian sacramentary, 164; *see also* Gelasian rite
Old High German, 207n, 208n, 209, 214, 218, 225, 226, 238, 244
Old Hymnal, 163
Old Irish, 209, 215, 272n
Old Minster, Winchester, 115, 126, 320, 331, 338
Old Norse, 238
Old Saxon, 168n, 189n, 208n, 209, 214, 218, 238, 244
Old Testament, *see* Testament, Old

Olicrosse, 272n
Ong, Walter, 348
Oracula Sibyllina, 59
oral poetry, 170
oral-formulaic theory, 141n
oratorio, 39, 41; *see also* prayer mat
orb, 374
Orkney, 39
Orosius, 299; *see also* Alfredian
orthodox Christian practice, 21, 33, 43, 162, 234, 280–81, 285, 287, 296, 380, 381
orthography, 247
Orton, Fred, 77, 341, 355
Oswald, king and saint, 152, 153, 245, 246
Oswy, king of Northumbria, 269
Otfrid, 225
Otto III, emperor, 384
Ottonian (art), xii, 119
Oðinn, *see* Woden
outline poem, 177, 182–84, 186
ovens, 305, 310
overcarving, 344, 345, 346
Ovid, 71, 71n, 185n

P

pagan (culture), 12, 55, 282n, 286, 346, 347
palatalization, 204, 208, 273n
Palatine Anthology, 176n, 182
palindrome, 172, 178, 188
palma poetica, 177
Pan, 184
Pange lingua, *see* Venantius Fortunatus
papal liturgy, 140, 148, 158, 160, 161
paradox, 1, 86, 153, 154, 155, 235n
Paris, 184
parousia, 146, 162
Passion narratives, 41, 108, 109, 124, 136, 143, 146–51, 255, 256, 259
pasture, 284, 286
Patch, Howard, 185
Pater noster, 110, 213, 273n, 316, 317, 318; *see also* liturgical incipits
Paton, W.R., 183
patriarch, 377, 379n, 380, 383, 384
patronage, 10, 118, 323
Patten, Faith H., 185, 186n
pectoral cross, *see* cross, pectoral

Index

pectorale, 237
Pehthelm, bishop of Whithorn, 151–52, 155
Penelope, 184
pentameter, 61, 80, 85
Pepys, Samuel, 370
performance, 2, 3, 5, 122, 235, 237, 241, 255–58, 273
pericopes, 25
perpetual virginity, 155, 155n
Persian 31, 32, 40, 175
Peter, saint, 77, 105, 106, 112, 113–16, 118–20, 122, 125, 130
petroleum, 271
pistolboc, 263, 263n, 264
Pharaoh, 218, 224
phonology, 247, 263, 263n, 265, 275
Photios, patriarch of Byzantium, 380–81
Pictish (culture), 17, 23, 26, 28
piety, 22, 92, 93, 311, 376, 380, 381, 384, 385
Pilate, 112, 222
pilgrimage, 41, 42n, 140, 383, 385
pipe, 184
place-names, 5, 215, 272n
Planudean Anthology, 176n
plowing, 10, 282–83, 286, 288–90, 292, 317, 318
Plow Monday, 280, 287n, 288
Plow Sunday, 288
Poitiers, 136, 378n
pope, 23, 42, 44, 64, 77, 78n, 118n, 140, 142, 148, 158–60, 371, 373, 377, 378
Pope, John C., 167, 168, 248n
Porphyrius, Publilius Optatianus, 55, 57, 177, 178, 180–82, 201
porticus, 320–31, 334, 336
prayer mat, 21, 39, 41, 47
presbyteral liturgy, 158n
Present Day English, 96, 204, 214, 224, 231, 237, 243, 245n, 265, 272, 273n
procession, 20, 39, 120, 142, 209, 260, 266, 294, 296; *see* processional cross
prognostics, 104, 125
proskynesis, 188
prosopopoeia, 185, 185n
prostration, 188n
Prudentius, 312
psalms, 31, 47, 106n, 109, 110, 121, 125, 144, 148, 164; *see also* scriptural references
pseudo-Augustine, 223
Psychomachia, *see* Prudentius
punctuation, 87, 94n, 146n, 171
Puttenham, George, 176, 176n
 The Arte of English Poesie, 176

Q

quern-stone, 36, 304n
Quinity, 106n; *see also* Trinity with Mary
quoin scars, 320
Qur'an, 31

R

Rabbula Gospels, 46
Radegund, queen, 378
radiocarbon dating, 330
rainbow-arc, 113
Ramsey Abbey, 320
rational, 344, 345
Ravenna, 43
Rectitudines singularum personarum, 282, 288, 292n, 298, 315n
regiam aulam, 324
Regula Sancti Benedicti, 257n
Regularis Concordia, 161–62
relic(s), 1, 19n, 20, 38, 39n, 40, 42, 46, 77, 127, 148, 159, 160, 241, 244, 260, 261, 279, 293–97, 326, 328, 329, 331, 376–85
reliquary, 11, 42, 46, 152, 153, 159, 332, 370–73, 380n, 383, 384
remediation, 341n, 347–50, 352, 355, 357
repetition, 97, 110, 187
representation, 21, 43, 44, 67, 75n, 172, 205, 245n, 282, 342, 348–51
"resistance to space," 341
resurrection, 1, 30, 41, 58, 106, 113, 165, 174, 229n, 264, 305
Reuter, Timothy, xi–xiv, 6, 14, 53
Revelation (of St. John), 73, 74, 81, 82, 107; *see also* scriptural references
Rheged, 18
rhetoric, 138, 185
ribin (ribbon), 371n
Richard of St.Vannes, 383

Richard II, duke of Normandy, 383
rick cup, 298
rick top, 298
riddles, 153, 154, 155, 185
Roberts, Jane, 139n, 242n
Rogationtide, 123, 260, 280, 292, 294, 296–97, 314
Romainmoutiers, 39
Roman culture, 17, 18, 22, 24, 25, 26n, 56, 57, 85, 159, 223, 235n, 286n, 330n, 343, 346, 350, 355, 356, 376, 377
Roman rite, 33, 41, 140, 142, 148, 150, 152, 156, 157, 160, 161, 162, 164, 244n, 293
Romanesque, 26, 330, 346, 347
Roman-German Pontifical, 307n
Romsey Abbey, 6, 127, 319, 320, 330, 333, 335, 338
Rothbury, 356–57, 368
royal estate, 324
rubrication, 57
rulership, 373, 376, 385
runes, 10, 24, 36n, 140, 144, 162, 207n
Rupertus Cross, 37, 42
Russia, 383
Ruthwell Cross, 10, 13, 45, 46, 135–45, 151–52, 156, 162, 189, 190n, 341

S

Sacramentary of Padua, 40
Sacramentary of Fulda, 296n
sacrifice, 20, 23, 30, 81, 93, 106, 107, 110, 111, 188, 222, 233, 235n, 238n, 242, 283
St. Anthony's cross, *see* TAU-shaped cross
St. Gall, 34, 35, 57n, 142n
St. Gatien Gospels, 35
St. James's Church, Nunburnholme, 342
St. Laurence's (chapel), 11, 319, 322, 328; *see also* Bradford-on-Avon
St. Mark's Day, 297
St. Martin at Tours (monastery), 378n
St, Martin's (church), Wareham, 328
St. Oswald's (church), Gloucester, 331, 338
St. Patrick's Cross, 38; *see also* Carndonagh
Salmasius, 176n
salvation, 1, 3, 77, 105, 113, 116, 117, 119–22, 149, 152, 159, 172, 233, 242, 252, 254, 259n, 260n, 261, 275
San Vincenzo al Volturno, 36n, 37, 38
Sancta Crux/Halig Rod project, 2, 3, 7, 8, 13, 204
  Durham seminar, 4, 5, 7, 12–14
  Manchester seminar, 4–6, 13
  Winchester seminar, xi, 4, 6–8, 13, 14, 315, 369
Sancta Maria (papal station), 148–50
Satan, 36, 73, 106, 168n, 224
satchel, 344, 345
Saxon Old, *see* Old Saxon
Saxulf, abbot, 269
Scandinavian (culture) 208, 287n, 343, 347, 381, 383; *see also* Anglo-Scandinavian
Scandinavian (languages), 204, 215, 228, 230
scansion, 10, 95, 95n, 97, 100, 167n
scepter, 373
schism, 19
Schlauch, Margaret, 185
scribal errors, 88, 96
scriptura continua, 56, 57, 85
scriptural references
  1 Corinthians 1:23–28, 235n
  2 Corinthians 10:7–10, 235n
  2 Corinthians 12:9, 235n
  Ephesians 2:13, 140
  Ezekiel 9:4, 236
  Ezekiel 38, 73, 82
  Ezekiel 39, 73, 82
  Ezekiel 47:1–2, 141n
  Genesis 10, 82
  Genesis 10:3, 73
  Genesis 40:19, 218
  Genesis 40:22, 224
  Habbakuk, canticle of, 156, 156n
  Isaiah 62:11–63:7, 149
  John 3:1–15, 158n
  John 3:13, 106n
  John 3:14, 41
  John 8:28, 41
  John 15:1, 46
  John 15:1–5; 6:56, 145
  John 18:1, 41

Index

John 18–19, 108
John 19:34–35, 109
2 Kings 22:8–13, 159
3 Kings 1:1–4, 74
Luke 11:47–54, 158
Luke 22:1–23:53, 149
Luke 23:31, 156
Matthew 13:44, 157n, 159
Philippians 2:5–11, 147–48, 150
Psalm 3, 109
Psalm 3:5, 109
Psalm 18, 164
Psalm 23:8, 144
Psalm 53:4, 109
Psalm 53, 109
Psalm 66, 109
Psalm 69, 109
Psalm 85, 109
Psalm 101, 148, 148n
Psalm 104:16, 47
Psalm 109, 106n
Psalm 140, 109
Revelation 7:1, 81n
Revelation 7:2–3, 107n
Revelation 20:7, 73, 81, 81n
Revelation 20, 82
Revelation 20:9-10, 74
Wisdom 10:10, 114n
sculpture (stone), 20, 25, 27, 38, 45, 46, 321, 328, 340–42, 343, 347, 348, 351, 354, 355. 356, 357
seal [of Christ], 111, 256
seals, 373, 374, 381, 384
seasons (of the year), 124, 285
Second Coming, 20, 47, 162
Second Sculptor (Nunburnholme), 343–47, 352, 354
secular (culture), 5, 12, 275, 304, 343, 347, 381, 385
Sedulius, 60
seed, 288, 289–92, 303, 317
self-reflexivity, 187
Selsey, 120n
semantics, 8, 206n, 207, 216, 247, 253, 261
semi-uncial, see half-uncial
sententia, 138, 139n
Septuaginta, 218
sepulcher, 156
Serenus, bishop of Marseilles, 44

Sergius, pope, 77–78, 158–60
Sessorian Palace, 160
Seven Sleepers, 104, 123, 249n
Sewan, 39;
  see also Noraduz Cemetary
Shaftesbury Abbey, 321, 322, 326–29, 331, 333
sheep, 281n
Sherborne, 58, 63, 258n, 322, 333
Sherborne Pontifical, 325
shoulder-clasps, 323
shoulder, 236–37, 260, 346, 369
shoulder-span, 227
Sibbi, king, 269
sibilant, 204
Sigeberht, Letter to, 60–79
Sighere, king, 269
Sigurd, 346
silver casket, 158
silver penny, 373–74
Simeon, saint, 78
Sim[m]ias of Rhodes, 175–77, 183, 184, 199, 200
Sisam, Kenneth, 136, 221
Six Ages of the World, 104, 125, 127
slayer of God, 137, 174n
Sovereign/Martlets, 373
sowing (seed), 282, 288–92
Spanish (language), 204
"spin," 352, 354
staccato (verses), 167–68
stational (crosses, mass), 41, 140, 148–50, 169n, 153
stauracis, 159
Stevick, Robert, 25n, 26n, 27, 28, 30, 42n, 167n, 168n, 171n, 189n
stigmata, 263
"stitching software," 352
Stockholm, 35
stole, 345
stone sculpture, see sculpture (stone)
storage (of harvest), 302, 303
sun, 107n, 164, 216, 317, 373
supernatural (beliefs or explanations), 280, 283, 286–89, 305
Sutton Hoo, 20, 23, 323
Swanton, Michael, 167, 227, 228
swastika, 234n
sword, 211, 345, 373, 374, 375
Syagrius of Autun, 57, 72

Index

Symmachus, pope, 42 as Symmachos, 378
syntax/syntactic groups, 67, 70, 139n, 164, 168n, 171n, 173, 221n, 242, 247–51, 253, 257n, 261, 266, 275
Syria, 379n
Syriac/Syrian (culture), 17, 46, 77, 379n
Syrinx, 184

T

tabula ansata, 31n, 42
Tadcaster, 343
Tara brooch, 20, 23, 25, 26n, 38n; *see also* Bettystown Beach brooch
tattooing, 177n
Tatwine, 154
TAU-shaped cross, 34, 42, 205, 234n, 258n, 259n
Taylor, H.M., 76n, 320, 322, 332, 334
Taylour, Charles, 369–70
technologies, 342, 348, 351, 356
technopaignia, 179
telestich, 55, 56, 60, 68, 74, 80n, 81, 92n
Testament, New, 79, 82, 86, 205, 218n, 233
Testament, Old, 59n, 73, 79, 80, 82, 86, 149, 218n, 233, 258n
Thanet, 54n, 209
Theitmar of Merseburg, 384
Theocritus of Syracuse, 175, 183–84, 203
Theodore of Tarsus, archbishop of Canterbury, 58–59, 66, 77, 179, 180n
threshing, 298, 303
Tiberius Psalter, 29n, 325
titulus, 138n, 139, 140, 143–45, 162, 373
torta, 308, 309
Traherne, Thomas, 175
transcoding, 341n, 350–51, 353, 354, 356
"transeptal" design, 320
transparency, 239, 240n, 247, 262, 265, 348, 349, 356
Tree of Life, 41, 145, 233
Trinity, Holy, 105–8, 111–13, 114, 124, 129, 239n, 241, 296, 324, 331; *see also* Office of the Holy Trinity
Trinity, Office of, *see* Office

Trinity with Mary, 105, 106, 107, 108, 111–13, 114, 124, 129
Trisagion, *see* aius
True Cross, *see* cross, True
Trullo, council of, 44
Tullylease, 23, 26, 38, 42
turas, 41; *see also* pilgrimage
Turin Gospels, 35

U

uncial, 66, 83
underworld, 162, 165

V

Vale Christo ueraciter, *see* Boniface
Varangian guards, 381
Venantius Fortunatus, 56, 57, 59, 72, 136–37, 180–181, 223
  Vexilla Regis, 56, 111, 223
  Pange lingua, 56, 136, 137
Veneration of the Cross, 39, 40, 159, 161
Vercelli, 76n, 171, 171n, 191
Vercelli Book, 10, 135–41, 295
Vercelli Homilies, 260–61, 266, 267, 269, 295
Vergil, 56, 80, 84n
vernacular, 85, 97, 100, 127, 152, 161, 162, 182, 183, 185, 210, 211
versus intextus, 55, 57–58, 66–68
Versus Sibyllae de die iudicii, 59
vexillum, 174
Victoria and Albert Museum, 371, 371n, 372
Victorian period, 321, 334, 337, 356
Viking age, 342–45
Vikings, 326
vine, 23, 46
vine-scroll motif, 23, 37, 46, 138n, 139n, 140, 145
Virgin and Child, 21, 345
Virtual Reality Centre at Teeside, 356, 368
Virtually Anglo-Saxon, 340n, 347n
vision and resonance, 179, 183
Vision of Leofric, 210, 211n, 272n
Vita Sancti Oswaldi, 320
volutes, 345
Vulgate, 18, 33, 81, 106n, 159, 218; *see also* Jerome

Index

W

Wærferth, bishop of Worcester, 310
Wales, 60
Waltham, Holy Rood of, 272n
"Warrior," 384
Wealdhere's letter, 83n
Wearmouth-Jarrow, 66, 153
weeding, 292
Wessex, 258n, 323, 324, 329
Westminster Abbey, 369
Westminster Cathedral, 371n
wheat, 281n, 309, 318
Wherwell, 329, 333
white bread, 308
Whithorn, 151–52, 155
Wilfrid, bishop, 79
William, duke of Normandy and king of England 127, 311
William of Malmesbury, 79, 322, 329
Willibald of Mainz, 53n
wills, 246n, 256, 257
Wilton, 327, 330, 333
Wilton Cross, 27
Winchester, 103, 115, 116, 117, 119, 121, 126, 161–62, 222, 320n, 324, 329, 331, 333, 338, 381; *see also* New Minster, Winchester; Hyde Abbey, Winchester; and Old Minster, Winchester
wine, 301
wisdom, 29, 74, 75, 94, 173n, 299
Woden, 207, 219
wool, 281n
Woolf, Rosemary, 185, 223
Word, 19–21, 30, 39, 47, 86, 93n, 108; *see also* Logos
Wormald, Patrick, xi, xii, xiv, 8, 287n, 326 327n
worship, 3, 5, 21, 77, 154, 159, 188n, 189, 221, 233, 234, 246n, 324n, 329
Wulfere, king, 268–69
Wulfila, bishop, 206–07
Wulfstan of Winchester, 115
Wulfstan, homilist, 295, 315n, 327n
Wulfstan, archbishop of York, 326
Würzburg, 61, 62, 63, 64, 65, 68, 100
Wynfreth, 54n, 62–64, 68, 69, 81, 92

Y

yeast, 307, 310
York, 38n, 76n, 290, 320n, 342n, 343, 345n, 352n

Z

Zacharias, 371, 373
zoom, 353, 363
zoomorphic ornament, 24, 25, 29, 31n, 34, 41

www.ingramcontent.com/pod-product-compliance
Lightning Source LLC
Chambersburg PA
CBHW071436300426
44114CB00013B/1463